THE STUFFED COUGAR

TOO

Published by
**The Patrons Association of
The Collegiate School
Richmond, Virginia**

DEDICATION

To everyone whose enthusiasm and interest in THE STUFFED COUGAR
have made possible THE STUFFED COUGAR, TOO.

Printed by
Cadmus Communications
Richmond, Virginia

FOREWORD

As members of the Collegiate family, we can scarcely believe that it has been nearly twenty years since the original publication of THE STUFFED COUGAR. Many of us have made the transition from Collegiate student to Collegiate parent, and a number of those who contributed to THE STUFFED COUGAR in 1973 now attend Collegiate functions as doting grandparents. We feel it is only fitting that the chairman of THE STUFFED COUGAR, TOO is the daughter of the chairman of THE STUFFED COUGAR.

One thing has not changed since 1973: we still love good food! Never fear. We continue to treasure our food-stained and tattered copies of THE STUFFED COUGAR as trusted companions that have seen us through years in the kitchen. Yes, on occasion, we still indulge, and sometimes bulge!

On the other hand, we of the 90's are now a faster-paced generation. We chop, grind, roast and bake with fancy machines in record time. We are a generation very concerned about good health and strive to maintain this by emphasizing good nutrition in combination with increased physical activity.

With all of this in mind, we have sought to provide in THE STUFFED COUGAR, TOO a cookbook for a new generation. Hopefully, it will become another trusted favorite in the kitchen, taking its place alongside its predecessor on the bookshelves of food lovers from coast to coast.

WHO PUT THE COUGAR IN YOUR KITCHEN?

Chairman

Ann Beauchamp

Co-Chairmen

Katie Belk
Allyn Crosby
Gay Jewett
Sandy King
Gail Smith

Art

Susan Gordon

Index

Lynn Felton

Committee Members

Nancy Breeden
Cindy Chewning
Virginia Chewning
Debbie Cunningham
Dianne Gibson
Robin Gregson
Leigh Hulcher

Donna Jacobs
Cathy Lee
Sharon Phillips
Sherrill Smith
Mary E. Vetrovec
Jan Winston

A special "thank you" to the many hundreds of Collegiate parents, grandparents, alumni, and friends who submitted recipes, and the two hundred recipe testers whose generous efforts helped to make this book possible.

We are also truly grateful for the encouragement and support from Expert/Brown.

TABLE OF CONTENTS

Page

APPETIZERS AND SNACKS   7

BEVERAGES. 31

SOUPS AND STEWS 39

SALADS AND SALAD DRESSINGS 57

GRILLED FOODS 91

MEATS AND GAME 109

POULTRY 135

SEAFOOD 165

EGGS AND CHEESE. 185

PASTA AND RICE 193

VEGETABLES AND SIDE DISHES. 211

BREADS. 241

CAKES. 261

PIES 279

DESSERTS. 293

COOKIES AND CANDIES. 313

HINTS FOR HEALTHIER EATING 333

TABLES. 344

INDEX 347

KEY TO ABBREVIATIONS USED

c. . . . . cup(s)

t. teaspoon(s)

T. Tablespoon(s)

pt(s). . . . . pint(s)

qt(s). . . . . quart(s)

gal. . . . . gallon(s)

oz. ounce(s)

lb(s). . . . . pound(s)

pkg(s).. . . . . package(s)

min.. . . . . minute(s)

hr. hour(s)

Wherever flour is indicated as an ingredient, it is all-purpose, pre-sifted, unless otherwise specified.

All measurements are level.

Many recipes have been designated "Quick" (**Q**) or "Light" (**L**). "Quick" (**Q**) refers to dishes that can be completely prepared, cooked and served in approximately 30 minutes or less. You will discover, though, that many other recipes become "quick" if one ingredient, such as a meat, is cooked ahead of time. There are also numerous recipes for which the preparation is simple, but which have extended cooking, chilling or freezing time.

"Light" (**L**) is a more subjective term. Recipes selected as "Light" are reasonably low in cholesterol, fat and sodium, or a sincere effort has been made to make a recipe lighter. Our nutrition information is borrowed largely from the American Heart Association's guidelines, but "Light" designations are solely the opinions of the cookbook committee. Consult the Cougar's Hints for Healthier Eating for more information.

APPETIZERS

& SNACKS

Appetizers and Snacks

Peanut butter on crackers isn't enough for dinner. It's just an advertisement!

Kelly Way, '01

Cold Appetizers:

Fruit Kabobs with Coconut Dressing **L**	10
Veggie Pizzas	10
Sesame Broccoli Stems	10
Marinated Carrot Sticks **L**	11
Hidden Valley Ranch Pinwheels	11
Cheese Straws	11
Cheese Wafers	12
Pickled Shrimp	12
Pickle Delights **Q**	12
Tortilla Roll-Ups **Q**	13
Pam's Pork Tenderloin	13

Cold Dips:

Simply Scrumptious Fruit Dip **Q**	13
Dill Weed Dip **L**	14
Low-Fat High-Taste Vegetable Dip **L**	14
Hummus **L**	14
Honey Curry Dip	15
Priscilla's Taco Dip **Q**	15
Tostito Olé **Q**	15

Cold Spreads:

Delicious Apple Spread **Q**	16
Caviar Mold	16
Caviar Pie	16
Cashew Spread	17
Chutney Cheese Appetizer	17
Strawberry Preserves Cheese Ball	17
Liptauer Cheese Balls	18
Lulu Paste	18
Thelma Phillips' Crab Spread	18
Cold Salmon Mousse	19
Shrimp Butter	19
Shrimp Mold	20

Hot Appetizers:

Artichoke Puffs **Q L**	20
Avocados Stuffed with Crabmeat au Gratin **Q**	20
Stuffed Mushroom Caps	21
Spinach Cheese Squares	21
Sarah's Hot Cheese Appetizers **Q**	21
Stonewall Court Cheese Puffs	22
Horse Point Crab Appetizers **Q**	22
Bristol Bacon Roll-Ups	22
Cheese and Bacon Puffs **Q**	23
Taco Tartlets	23
Pepperoni Quiche	24

Hot Dips:

Broccoli Cheese Dip **Q**	24
Cheese Dip **Q**	24
Chili Con Queso	24
Hot Crab Dip **Q**	25
Crabmeat Dip	25
Creamy Crabmeat Dip **Q**	25
Nacho Dip Supreme	26

Hot Spreads:

Spicy Artichoke Spread	26
Brie en Croûte	26

Snacks:

Caramel Corn	27
Granola **Q**	27
Homemade Granola **Q**	27
Outrageous Granola **Q**	28
Backpackers' Mix **Q**	28
Chex After-School Mix **Q**	28
Glazed Peanuts **Q**	29
Orange Pecans **Q**	29
Toasted Pecans **Q**	29
Pita Chips **Q L**	30

L FRUIT KABOBS WITH COCONUT DRESSING

1 red apple, unpeeled
1 pear, unpeeled
1 T. lemon juice
21 unsweetened pineapple
chunks

21 seedless grapes
21 fresh strawberries, capped
21 wooden skewers

Cut apple and pear into 21 bite-sized pieces and toss in lemon juice. Place 1 piece of each fruit on skewer and drizzle dressing over all. Yield: 21 skewers.

DRESSING

1½ c. vanilla low-fat yogurt
1½ T. coconut

1½ T. reduced-calorie orange
marmalade

Combine all ingredients and mix well.

CATHY LEE

VEGGIE PIZZAS

2 (8 oz.) cans crescent rolls
2 (8 oz.) pkgs. cream cheese,
softened
1 c. mayonnaise

1 pkg. Hidden Valley Ranch
Dressing Mix
Assorted fresh vegetables, finely
chopped

Pat dough into jelly roll pan and roll to edges so dough is not too thick. Bake according to package directions until browned and let cool. Combine cream cheese, mayonnaise, and dressing mix and spread on top of crust. Using an assortment of colors, top with your favorite vegetables. Cut into squares and serve cold. (Best when made same day to serve.) Serves 10 to 12.

SUGGESTION: Some vegetables, such as broccoli and cauliflower can be blanched very briefly (1 to 2 minutes) in boiling water, if desired.

SUSAN STANEWICK

SESAME BROCCOLI STEMS

4 T. white vinegar
4 T. sugar
2 t. salt

2 lbs. fresh broccoli stems, cut into
1/8" diagonal strips
4 T. sesame oil
Sesame seeds, toasted

Combine vinegar, sugar and salt in jar. Add broccoli and shake jar to coat well. Refrigerate overnight, shaking occasionally. Drain and place broccoli on serving dish and drizzle with sesame oil. Top with sesame seeds. Serve with toothpicks. Serves 6 to 8.

JANE FAIN

MARINATED CARROT STICKS   *L*

8 carrots, peeled and cut into 3"
  sticks
3 T. vinegar
3 T. vegetable oil

1 clove garlic, crushed
¾ t. seasoned salt
¼ t. salt (optional)
Fresh parsley, minced

Place carrots in shallow baking dish. Combine vinegar, oil, garlic and salts. Stir well. Pour over carrots and toss until well coated. Cover tightly and refrigerate overnight. To serve, drain well, arrange attractively on serving dish, and sprinkle with parsley. Serves 10 to 12.

BONNIE MOREAU

HIDDEN VALLEY RANCH PINWHEELS

2 (8 oz) pkgs. cream cheese,
  softened
1 pkg. Hidden Valley Ranch
  Dressing Mix
2 green onions, chopped

4 (12") flour tortillas
½ c. red pepper, diced
½ c. celery, diced
1 (2.25 oz) can sliced black olives,
  drained

Mix together cream cheese, dressing mix, and onions. Spread mixture on tortillas and sprinkle with red pepper, celery and olives. Roll each tortilla and wrap tightly in foil. Chill for 2 hours. Cut off ends and slice rolls into pinwheels. Yield: approximately 36.

DIANNE GIBSON

CHEESE STRAWS

1 (5 oz) jar Old English Cheese
½ c. margarine, softened
1½ c. flour

¾ t. salt
¼ t. red pepper

Cream together cheese and margarine. Mix together flour, salt and pepper. Add to cheese mixture, a small amount at a time. Spoon into cookie press and squeeze out as 2" strips on a lightly greased cookie sheet. Bake at 400° for 8 to 10 minutes. Yield: 3 dozen.

DERENDA REYNOLDS

CHEESE WAFERS

9 oz. sharp cheese, cut into
   chunks
½ c. butter
1½ c. flour

1 t. salt
1 t. red pepper
Pecan halves

In food processor mix cheese and butter. Add flour, salt and pepper. Process to form ball. Pat into half dollar size and top with pecan half. Bake on ungreased cookie sheet at 475° for 10 minutes. Yield: 24 to 36.

VARIATION: For cheese straws, add 1 t. baking powder. Roll out, cut into straws, and bake as above.

NANCY KENNON

PICKLED SHRIMP

2-3 lbs. raw shrimp
Celery tops
4 t. salt
¼ c. pickling spice
6-8 bay leaves
1 T. white vinegar
Dash red pepper

1 medium purple onion, thinly
   sliced
1¼ c. vegetable oil
1 c. white vinegar
2 t. salt
2½ t. celery seed
1 (2 oz) bottle capers and juice
Dash Tabasco

Clean and devein shrimp. Place shrimp in large pot, cover with water, and boil 3 to 5 minutes with celery tops and next 5 ingredients. Do not overcook. Drain and rinse. In shallow pan alternate layers of shrimp and onions. Mix together oil, vinegar, salt, celery seed, capers, and Tabasco and pour over shrimp and onions. Chill for at least 24 hours. Keeps for several days in refrigerator. Yield: 2 to 3 pounds.

KATHY WATSON

Q   PICKLE DELIGHTS

Bet you can't eat just one!

2 (8 oz.) pkgs. cream cheese,
   softened
3 (4 oz.) pkgs. chipped beef

1 (46 oz.) jar whole Vlasic Crunchy
   Dill Pickles

Spread cream cheese on double layer of chipped beef. Wrap beef around whole pickle and slice into ¼-inch rounds. Arrange on serving plate and place toothpick into each. Yield: approximately 50.

PEGGY CONWAY

TORTILLA ROLL-UPS   **Q**

Endless options—be creative!

Flour tortillas
Cream cheese, softened
Ripe avocado, peeled and
  mashed

Turkey breast slices
Bacon, cooked and crumbled
Swiss cheese, thinly sliced

Spread cream cheese on tortillas and layer avocados, turkey, bacon and cheese. Roll up and slice into 1" to 1½" widths. May be served as hors d'oeuvre or larger slices as luncheon dish. Yield: as many as desired.

VARIATION: Many ingredients, such as salsa, black olives and grated cheeses may be used.

SUSAN STANEWICK

PAM'S PORK TENDERLOIN

Wonderful flavor and very tender. Can be served as main dish.

¼ c. soy sauce
¼ c. bourbon

2 T. brown sugar
2½-3½ lbs. pork tenderloin

Combine soy sauce, bourbon and brown sugar in bowl and marinate tenderloin for at least 8 hours. Place tenderloin and marinade in baking dish. Bake at 325° for 1 hour, basting several times. Cool and slice thinly. Serve with party bread and sour cream sauce. Serves 8 to 10.

SOUR CREAM SAUCE

⅓ c. sour cream
⅓ c. mayonnaise

1 T. dry mustard
2-3 green onions, finely chopped

Combine all ingredients and mix well.

DIANNE GIBSON

SIMPLY SCRUMPTIOUS FRUIT DIP   **Q**

1 (8 oz.) pkg. cream cheese,
  softened
1 (16 oz.) jar marshmallow cream
½ t. cinnamon
½ t. nutmeg

Apples, sliced and tossed with
  lemon juice
Pineapple spears
Mandarin oranges

Combine cream cheese, marshmallow cream, cinnamon and nutmeg and mix well. Chill and serve with fruit. Yield: 3 cups.

KATHY WHITE

13

APPETIZERS AND SNACKS

L   DILL WEED DIP

Serve with fresh vegetables or chips.

⅔ c. fat-free mayonnaise
⅔ c. light sour cream
1 t. dill weed

1 T. parsley flakes
1 T. onion, minced
Dash of salt

Combine all ingredients, mix well, and chill at least 1 hour. Yield: 1⅓ cups.

FRANCEE SWIFT

L   LOW-FAT HIGH-TASTE VEGETABLE DIP

1 c. cottage cheese, low-fat
1 c. plain yogurt
3 green onions, chopped
1 (10 oz) pkg. chopped spinach,
    thawed and drained
1 pkg. Knorr Vegetable Soup Mix

1 (8 oz) can sliced water
    chestnuts, drained and
    chopped
1 c. Cheddar cheese, regular or
    low-fat, shredded (optional)

Combine cottage cheese, yogurt and onions in blender and mix well. Pour into large bowl and add remaining ingredients. Stir well. Refrigerate 2 hours. Serve with assorted vegetables, crackers or chips. Yield: 4½ cups.

CAROL HESS

L   HUMMUS

Serve with pita bread for flavorful dip.

2 (20 oz) cans chick peas
    (garbanzo beans), drained,
    reserving juice
4-5 cloves garlic
1-2 t. cumin
½ c. lemon juice

¼ t. cayenne pepper
½ reserved juice from chick peas
1 T. tahini seasoning
1-2 t. salt
Olive oil

Place all ingredients except olive oil in food processor. Process and slowly add olive oil until consistency is no longer grainy. Chill. When ready to serve, pour onto flat dish and pour small amount of olive oil on top. Sprinkle with cumin and cayenne pepper for garnish. Yield: approximately 2½ cups.

NOTE: Best when Spanish brands of chick peas are not used.

BARBARA VRANIAN

HONEY CURRY DIP

Certain to evoke compliments!

1½ c. light mayonnaise
3 T. onion, grated
3 T. ketchup
3 T. honey

1 T. lemon juice
1 t. curry powder
Assorted fresh vegetables, cut

Combine all ingredients in given order and stir well. Refrigerate at least 2 to 3 hours. (Best when chilled overnight.) Serve with raw vegetables. Yield: 1¾ cups.

TEMPLE SHANKLIN

PRISCILLA'S TACO DIP Q

Always a big hit!

3 avocados, mashed
2 T. lemon juice
½ t. salt
¼ t. pepper
1 c. sour cream
½ c. mayonnaise
1 pkg. taco seasoning mix

2 (10.5 oz) cans jalapeño bean
    dip
8 oz. Cheddar cheese, grated
2 c. tomatoes, chopped
6 oz. black olives, chopped
1 c. green onions, chopped
2 bags assorted taco chips (blue
    or white corn, tostados, etc.)

In small bowl combine avocados, lemon juice, salt and pepper and set aside. In another bowl combine sour cream, mayonnaise and taco seasoning mix and set aside. On large serving platter leaving room around edges, layer bean dip, avocado mixture, sour cream mixture, cheese, tomatoes, olives and onions. Surround with chips. Serves 8 to 10.

PRISCILLA BURBANK

TOSTITO OLÉ Q

So colorful and tasty!

2-3 large avocados, chopped
Juice of ½ lemon
8 oz. picante sauce (mild, medium
    or hot)

6-8 oz. Mozzarella cheese,
    shredded
½ bunch green onions including
    tops, chopped
Unflavored Tostito chips

In pie plate or ceramic quiche dish place avocados and sprinkle with lemon juice. Top with picante sauce, cheese and onions. Serve with chips. Serves 6 to 8.

DEB POVLISHOCK

Q   DELICIOUS APPLE SPREAD

A nice Christmas gift.

1 (8 oz.) pkg. cream cheese,
    softened
¼-½ c. brown sugar
½ t. vanilla

½ t. maple extract
Tart apples (such as Granny
    Smith), sliced
Lemon juice

Combine cream cheese, brown sugar, vanilla and maple extract and mix well. Chill. In small bowl toss apples with lemon juice to prevent browning. Serve cheese mixture in mound on serving plate surrounded by apples. Yield: 1½ cups.

MARIE LOWDEN

CAVIAR MOLD

4 eggs, hard-boiled and reserving
    1 yolk, chopped
1 envelope unflavored gelatin
3-4 T. hot water
2 T. onion, grated
½ c. mayonnaise
1 T. Worcestershire

White pepper to taste
1 (3½ oz) jar black caviar
1 (8 oz) container sour cream
1 (3½ oz) jar red caviar
Bremner wafers or assorted
    crackers

Prepare eggs and set aside. In small bowl dissolve gelatin in water for 10 minutes. In blender or food processor mix onion, mayonnaise, Worcestershire, pepper and eggs. Simmer gelatin over water for 5 minutes and add to blended mixture. Fold in black caviar. Spray 2-cup mold with no-stick cooking spray and pour in mixture. Refrigerate until firm. Unmold and frost with sour cream. Sprinkle with chopped egg yolk and red caviar. Serve with crackers. Yield: 2 cups.

ANDY BENNETT

CAVIAR PIE

9 eggs, hard-boiled
4 T. butter, melted
4 T. mayonnaise
2 T. onion, chopped

1 c. sour cream
1 (3½ oz) jar red caviar
1 (3½ oz) jar black caviar
Assorted crackers

Set aside 3 egg yolks. Dice and chop remaining eggs. Add butter and mayonnaise and mix until smooth. Add onion. Spread mixture into pie plate and frost with sour cream. Spoon rings of red and black caviar and reserved egg yolks around top of pie. Serve with crackers. Yield: 2½ cups.

PAGE MARCHETTI

CASHEW SPREAD

A delicious holiday treat.

1 (8 oz.) pkg. cream cheese,
   softened
1 c. chutney
1 c. cashew pieces
⅔ c. sour cream

½-1 t. curry
4 slices bacon, cooked and
   crumbled
3-4 green onions, chopped
Melba crackers

Combine first 5 ingredients and mix well. Place into serving dish and sprinkle bacon and onions around edges. Chill. Serve with melba crackers. Yield: 3 cups.

SANDY KING

CHUTNEY CHEESE APPETIZER

1 (8 oz.) pkg. cream cheese,
   softened
1 c. Cheddar cheese, grated
4 T. sherry

1 (9 oz.) jar Major Grey's Chutney
Green onions including tops,
   chopped
Wheat Thins

Cream cheeses with sherry and spread on serving platter ½ inch deep. Top with chutney and refrigerate. Before serving, top with onions. Serve with Wheat Thins. Serves 6 to 8.

TYLER KILPATRICK

STRAWBERRY PRESERVES CHEESE BALL

1 lb. sharp Cheddar cheese,
   grated
1 c. mayonnaise
1 small onion, grated

Few drops of Tabasco
Black pepper to taste.
Dash of cayenne pepper
Strawberry preserves

Combine first six ingredients and mound on serving plate or put in a mold. Chill. When ready to serve spread strawberry preserves on top and serve with crackers. Yield: 4 cups.

BRENDA WILKINS

VARIATION: Use ¾ cup of fat-free mayonnaise, add 1 cup chopped pecans and 1 teaspoon garlic salt. Serve in ring mold with strawberry preserves in the center.

SUE NASCHOLD

LIPTAUER CHEESE BALLS

A Viennese recipe.

1 (8 oz.) pkg. cream cheese, softened
1 c. margarine, softened
4 oz. Roquefort or other bleu cheese
2 t. paprika

1 t. Pickapeppa or Worcestershire
1½ T. capers, drained
2 t. anchovy paste
Chives or parsley, minced or freeze-dried

Process or mash cream cheese and gradually beat in remaining ingredients (except chives or parsley). Chill until firm. Take ¼ to ½ mixture out of refrigerator at a time and shape into ball. (Wet fingers helps process). Roll each ball into chives or parsley and wrap in plastic wrap and 2 thicknesses foil. Freeze until ready to serve. Thaw 1 hour before serving. Serve with assorted crackers. Yield: 2 large or 4 small balls.

NOTE: If prepared in food processor, mixture will be smoother and may be too soft to form into balls. If so, serve in crock and top with chives or parsley.

MIMI BIGELOW

LULU PASTE

1 lb. sharp cheese
1 (4 oz.) jar pimientos with juice
1 t. dry mustard
1 c. mayonnaise

¼ c. ketchup
Salt, red pepper, and Worcestershire to taste

Put cheese, pimientos and their juice through a meat grinder. Combine with remaining ingredients and mix well. Serve with crackers or bread rounds.

NANCY KENNON

THELMA PHILLIPS' CRAB SPREAD

A hit at every party!

1 (8 oz.) pkg. light cream cheese, softened
1 small onion, grated
1 T. light mayonnaise
2-3 t. horseradish

1 T. Worcestershire
4 T. prepared seafood sauce or ½ c. chili sauce plus 1 t. horseradish
¼-½ lb. fresh crabmeat

Mix together first 5 ingredients. Spread mixture onto serving platter and top with seafood sauce. Sprinkle crabmeat over sauce, chill, and serve with crackers. Yield: 2½ cups.

JOANNE RAMSEY

COLD SALMON MOUSSE

2 c. canned salmon, boned,
skinned, drained and flaked
1 envelope gelatin
1/4 c. cold water
1/2 c. boiling water
1/2 c. mayonnaise
1 T. lemon juice
1 t. onion, grated

1 t. Tabasco
1/4 t. paprika
1 t. light salt
1 1/2 c. cottage cheese (cream-style
is best)
Greens for garnish
Cucumbers, sliced

Place salmon in medium bowl and set aside. Soften gelatin in cold water. Add boiling water and stir until dissolved. Cool. Mix gelatin with mayonnaise, lemon juice, onion, Tabasco, paprika, and salt. Chill mixture until consistency of beaten egg whites. Fold into salmon. In blender or food processor whip cottage cheese until smooth and creamy. Fold into salmon mixture. Pour into 1 1/2 c. mold that has been greased with mayonnaise. (Use fish mold, if possible.) Chill until set. Unmold on greens and serve with cucumbers. Serves 8.

CARTER FILER

SHRIMP BUTTER

1/2 c. butter, softened
1 small onion, minced
4 T. mayonnaise
Juice of 1 lemon

1 (8 oz.) pkg. cream cheese,
softened
1 1/2 lbs. shrimp, cooked and
chopped

In mixing bowl combine all ingredients except shrimp and beat until smooth. Fold in shrimp and chill. Serve with crackers. Serves 8 to 10.

ISABEL FINE

SHRIMP MOLD

¼ c. ketchup
Dash lemon juice
Dash Worcestershire
Horseradish to taste
½ envelope unflavored gelatin
¼ c. water
2 (8 oz.) pkgs. cream cheese,
   softened

Juice of 1 lemon
2 T. ketchup
½ t. seasoned salt
1 lb. cooked shrimp, cut in half if
   large
Bremner Wafers

Make hot sauce combining first 4 ingredients. In small saucepan sprinkle gelatin over water and dissolve over low heat, stirring constantly. Add to hot sauce and pour mixture into 4-quart mold sprayed with no-stick cooking spray. Refrigerate until jelled. Mix together cream cheese, lemon juice, ketchup, salt, and shrimp and carefully spread over jelled hot sauce. Chill. To serve, unmold and serve with crackers. Yield: approximately 4 cups.

GAY JEWETT

Q L   ARTICHOKE PUFFS

6-8 Holland Rusk rounds
½ c. plus 1 T. fat-free mayonnaise
6-8 slices tomato
8 t. onions, minced

1 (8½ oz) can artichoke hearts,
   drained and halved
1½ c. low-fat Cheddar cheese,
   grated

Spread each round with mayonnaise and top with tomato slice. Top each with onions and 2 to 3 artichoke heart halves. Combine remaining mayonnaise with cheese and spread on each round. Bake on ungreased cookie sheet at 350° for 15 minutes. Serves 6 to 8.

JOAN WILKINS

Q   AVOCADOS STUFFED WITH CRABMEAT AU GRATIN

1 c. Hollandaise sauce, prepared
1 lb. backfin crabmeat, picked
1 t. cayenne pepper
1 t. lemon peel

4 avocados, unpeeled and cut in
   half
1 c. Monterey Jack cheese, grated

Combine Hollandaise, crabmeat, pepper and lemon peel and toss. Fill avocado halves with crabmeat mixture and top with cheese. Bake at 450° for 15 minutes or until cheese is melted and slightly browned. Serves 8.

PATSY ARNETT

STUFFED MUSHROOM CAPS

12 large mushrooms
3 T. margarine or oil
1 small onion, chopped
¾ c. bread crumbs

2 T. red wine
Salt, pepper, garlic powder,
  Tabasco, Worcestershire and
  paprika to taste

Remove mushroom stems from caps, chop and reserve. Dip caps in margarine or oil, place on cookie sheet and brown in 375° oven. Drain and set aside to cool. Sauté remaining ingredients including stems. Stuff cooled mushroom caps. Heat in 350° oven about 15 minutes. Yield: 12.

LINDA FERGUSON

SPINACH CHEESE SQUARES

3 eggs
1 c. milk
1 c. flour
1 t. baking powder
1 t. seasoned salt
1 T. onion, chopped

2 (10 oz.) pkgs. chopped spinach,
  thawed and drained
1 lb. Monterey Jack cheese with
  jalapeños, grated
1-1½ jalapeño peppers, chopped
  (optional)
4 T. butter

Beat eggs. Add milk, flour, baking powder and seasoned salt and beat again. Add onion, spinach and cheese and mix well. Add peppers, if desired. Place butter in 9" x 13" baking dish and heat in 350° oven to melt. When melted, pour in mixture, smoothing top with spoon. Bake for 35 minutes. Let cool 40 minutes before cutting. Freezes well. Yield: 90 squares.

McALISTER MARSHALL

SARAH'S HOT CHEESE APPETIZERS 　Q

Children love them, too!

Firm white bread (such as
  Pepperidge Farm)
Margarine, softened
Onion, sliced very thinly or slivered
  (Vidalia is best)

Sharp Cheddar cheese, grated
Mayonnaise
Cayenne pepper

Cut bread into rounds and leave out overnight. When ready to bake, spread each round with margarine and top with a tiny bit of onion. Mix cheese with enough mayonnaise to hold together. Add pepper to taste. Spread mixture on top of rounds and broil until cheese is melted. Serve hot. Yield: As many as desired. Make lots!

ALLYN CROSBY

STONEWALL COURT CHEESE PUFFS

1 egg
½ c. milk
1 loaf Pepperidge Farm white
  bread

½-1 c. butter or margarine, melted
8 oz. Parmesan cheese, grated

Beat together egg and milk. Remove crusts from bread. Dip 1 piece of bread in egg mixture and place between 2 pieces of dry bread. Repeat for remaining slices. Wrap each 3-slice stack in foil and refrigerate overnight. Cut into thirds (strips) or fourths (triangles). Roll in butter, then Parmesan cheese. Freeze if desired. Bake in oven at 375° for 10 minutes or, if frozen, for 15 minutes. Yield: 27 strips or 36 puffs.

VARIATION: Substitute cinnamon sugar for Parmesan cheese to make cinnamon puffs.

ALLYN CROSBY

Q HORSE POINT CRAB APPETIZERS

Nice to have in the freezer for unexpected company.

½ c. butter or margarine, softened
1 (5 oz.) jar Old English Cheese
  spread
1½ t. fat-free mayonnaise
½ t. garlic powder

½ t. seasoned salt
7 oz. crabmeat
6 English muffins, split
Paprika to garnish

Blend butter and cheese spread. Add mayonnaise, garlic powder, seasoned salt, and crabmeat and mix well. Spread on 12 muffin halves and sprinkle with paprika. Cut each half into 8 wedges. May be wrapped well and frozen. Place on cookie sheet and broil until bubbly and golden. Yield: 96 wedges.

ISABEL FINE
DEB POVLISHOCK

INGER RICE
SUSAN STANEWICK

BRISTOL BACON ROLL-UPS

Always the first to disappear!

1½ lb. loaf soft, thin-sliced white
  sandwich bread
1 (8 oz.) pkg. cream cheese,
  softened

1-2 T. chives, chopped
1 lb. regular or low-salt thin-sliced
  bacon

Remove crusts from bread. With rolling pin flatten each piece and spread with cream cheese and chives mixture. Roll each as tightly as possible and slice in half. Wrap each roll spirally with half slice of bacon, securing with toothpick. Place roll-ups, folded side down, on drip-through rack of broiler pan and bake at 325° for 30 to 45 minutes or until browned and crisp. Yield: 36 to 48.

LYNN FELTON

CHEESE AND BACON PUFFS   Q

12 slices bread or pastry shells
1½ c. Cheddar cheese, grated
1 t. dry sherry

2 t. horseradish
½ c. bacon, cooked and
   crumbled

Cut bread into rounds and toast on one side. Combine remaining ingredients and mix well. Spread mixture on rounds and broil until bubbly. Yield: approximately 30.

DOROTHY MEYER

TACO TARTLETS

Teenagers love this!

MEAT SHELLS

1 lb. lean ground beef
2 T. taco seasoning mix

2 T. ice water

Combine meat ingredients and press (uncooked) into bottom and sides of miniature tart pans.

FILLING

1 c. sour cream
2 T. red salsa
2 oz. black olives, chopped

1 c. tortilla chips, coarsely crushed
   and divided
½ c. Cheddar cheese, shredded
Taco sauce

Combine sour cream, salsa, olives, and ¾ cup tortilla chips and spoon into shells, mounding slightly. Combine remaining tortilla chips and cheese and sprinkle over each tart. Bake at 375° for 10 minutes. Garnish with taco sauce. Serve hot. Yield: 32.

SUSAN STANEWICK

PEPPERONI QUICHE

A spicy dish that men will love!

2 c. hot pepperoni, diced
1 c. Mozzarella cheese, shredded
1 c. Muenster cheese, shredded

2 eggs
2 c. milk
1½ c. flour

Mix all ingredients together and turn into well greased 9" x 13" baking dish. Bake at 400° for 20 to 25 minutes. Cool for 20 minutes. Cut into 2" x 2" squares. May be reheated in microwave on medium high. Serves 8 to 10.

DEB POVLISHOCK

Q   BROCCOLI CHEESE DIP

½ c. onions, chopped
1 (8 oz.) can sliced mushrooms, drained
3 T. butter
2 (10 oz.) pkgs. frozen chopped broccoli, cooked and drained

2 (10¾ oz.) cans cream of mushroom soup
1 pkg. slivered almonds
1 (6 oz.) roll garlic cheese or sharp Cheddar, grated, plus garlic powder
1 king-size pkg. corn chips

Sauté onions and mushrooms in butter and mix with remaining ingredients. Stir over low heat until cheese melts. Keep warm to serve. Serve with corn chips. Yield: 6 cups.

NANCY KENNON

Q   CHEESE DIP

Divinely simple and simply divine!

1 c. sharp Cheddar cheese, shredded

1 c. mayonnaise
½-¾ c. onion, minced

Combine all ingredients and mix well. Heat at 350° until brown and bubbly. Serve with wheat thins. Yield: 2½ cups.

NANCY GEORGE

CHILI CON QUESO

1 c. onion, chopped
1 clove garlic, chopped
1 T. butter
1½ c. tomatoes, chopped and drained

1 (14 oz.) can green chilies
1 t. salt
½ t. pepper
1 lb. Velveeta Cheese, cut in chunks

24

Sauté onion and garlic in butter until tender. In double boiler combine onion, garlic, and remaining ingredients and cook over medium heat for 30 minutes. Serve warm with corn chips. Serves 24.

VARIATION: One (10 oz.) can of chopped Ro-Tel tomatoes with chilies can be substituted for tomatoes and green chilies. For more zing, add additional chili peppers to taste.

MARY MADELYN TUCKER

HOT CRAB DIP   Q

½ lb. backfin crabmeat, picked   1 (8 oz.) pkg. cream cheese,
3 T. sherry   softened
2 T. horseradish   Crackers or melba rounds

Combine crab, sherry, horseradish and cream cheese. Heat on low until warm. Serve in chafing dish with crackers or melba rounds. (Triple recipe for 50 people.) Serves 10 to 15.

ISABEL FINE

CRABMEAT DIP

1 lb. crabmeat, picked   2 c. milk
2¼ t. dry mustard   ½ t. salt
1½ T. mayonnaise   Pepper to taste
2 T. Worcestershire   ¼ t. paprika
¼ c. butter   Tabasco to taste
¼ c. flour

Combine crabmeat, mustard, mayonnaise and Worcestershire. Make a cream sauce with butter, flour, milk, salt, pepper, paprika and Tabasco. Pour sauce over crabmeat mixture and serve hot in chafing dish. Serve with toasted slivers of bread. Yield: 4 cups.

NANCY KENNON

CREAMY CRABMEAT DIP   Q

Impresses the crowd but doesn't do in the cook!

½ c. butter or margarine   1 lb. crabmeat, picked
3 (8 oz.) pkgs. cream cheese with   1 t. Worcestershire
   chives, softened   Dash Tabasco

Melt butter in large skillet over low heat. Gradually add cream cheese, stirring constantly until melted. Add crabmeat, Worcestershire and Tabasco. Serve in chafing dish with crackers. Yield: 4 cups.

SUE NASCHOLD

NACHO DIP SUPREME

Hearty enough to be a meal!

1 lb. ground beef
1 pkg. taco seasoning
1 large onion, diced
1 (16 oz.) can re-fried beans or
    bean dip

1 (4½ oz.) can green chilies or 2-3
    hot peppers, diced
1 (6 oz.) jar taco sauce (mild,
    medium or hot)
2-3 c. sharp cheese, grated
Tortilla chips or corn chips

Brown beef and drain. Add taco seasoning, onion and water as directed on package. Simmer until onions are tender. In baking dish layer beans, beef mixture, chilies or hot peppers, taco sauce and cheese. Bake, uncovered, at 350° for 30 minutes. Serve with chips. Serves 10.

VARIATION: Lean ground sirloin and low-fat cheese may be used.

GRACE PARKER
KAREN PICKETT

SPICY ARTICHOKE SPREAD

1 (8½ oz.) can artichoke hearts,
    chopped
1 (4½ oz.) can green chile
    peppers, chopped

1 c. mayonnaise
1 c. Parmesan cheese, finely
    grated

Combine all ingredients and stir. Spoon into oven-proof baking dish and bake at 350° for 30 minutes. Serve with crackers or bagel chips. Yield: 2½ cups.

SHARON PHILLIPS

BRIE EN CROÛTE

1 sheet frozen puff pastry
1 (8 oz.) round of Brie
½ c. brown sugar

¼ c. butter
½ c. pecans, chopped
2 egg whites, beaten

Thaw puff pastry for 20 minutes and place Brie in center. Combine brown sugar, butter and pecans in small saucepan and heat until sugar dissolves. Spread brown sugar topping on cheese. (Use amount according to preference.) Wrap pastry around cheese, seal seams, and brush with egg whites. Top may be decorated with pastry cut-outs (attach with egg white mixture). Bake at 350° for 25 to 30 minutes. Let cool about 15 minutes before serving. (Baked cheese needs to firm slightly.) Serve with crackers.

MARGARET BARGATZE

CARAMEL CORN

1 c. unpopped popcorn
1 c. butter

1 c. sugar
⅓ c. water

Pop popcorn and put into large roasting pan. Mix together other ingredients and bring to boil over medium high heat. Stirring frequently, cook until candy thermometer reaches 290° (about 12 minutes). Carefully pour over popcorn, stirring once to coat. Place in oven and bake at 300° for 15 minutes. Stir again and bake an additional 5 minutes. Transfer to foil to cool. Break into clumps. Yield: 20 cups.

CELIE GEHRING

GRANOLA   Q

A healthy and delicious way to start the day.

1 (18.2 oz.) can old-fashioned oats
1 t. cinnamon
½ t. nutmeg
1 T. sesame seeds
¼ c. wheat germ
¼ c. sunflower seeds

½ c. slivered almonds or pecans
¼ c. oat bran
⅓ c. canola oil
⅓ c. honey
½ c. raisins

Mix together first 8 ingredients. Combine oil and honey and add to dry ingredients, pressing out any lumps. Pour into large flat pan and bake at 325° for 30 minutes, stirring every 10 minutes. Remove from pan and add raisins. Store in airtight container. Yield: 4 to 5 cups.

ANN CUTCHINS

HOMEMADE GRANOLA   Q

A great way to add fiber to the diet!

3 c. uncooked oatmeal
1 c. wheat germ
1 c. unsweetened coconut
2 T. cinnamon
2 T. brown sugar

¼ c. powdered milk
⅓ c. honey
⅓ c. oil
1 t. vanilla
Raisins or dates (optional)

Mix together first 6 ingredients. Combine honey, oil and vanilla in microwave-safe bowl and heat on high for 1 minute. Drizzle honey mixture over dry ingredients. Using hands, toss thoroughly to coat. Microwave at half power for 15 minutes, being careful not to burn. Let cook completely before removing from dish. Add raisins or dates, if desired. Store in airtight container. Yield: 5 to 6 cups.

KATHY WHITE

APPETIZERS AND SNACKS

Q   OUTRAGEOUS GRANOLA

5 c. uncooked oats	1 c. wheat germ
1 c. sliced almonds	1 c. raisins
1 c. walnut pieces	1 c. currants
1 c. pecan pieces	Dried fruit (optional)
1 c. sesame seeds	1 c. honey
1 c. unsalted sunflower seeds	1 c. canola oil

Preheat oven to 300°. Combine all dry ingredients except fruit in very large bowl and toss well. Heat honey and oil just enough to melt. Pour over dry ingredients and mix well. Spread into 2 jelly roll pans. Bake for 30 minutes or until lightly browned, turning every 10 to 15 minutes. Watch carefully towards end of baking time to prevent burning. Remove from oven and cool. Stir in raisins, currants and dried fruit, if desired. Yield: 15 cups.

ALICIA ALFORD

Q   BACKPACKERS' MIX

3 qts. popped popcorn, cooled	1 c. fresh coconut, shredded
1 c. peanuts	1 c. sunflower seeds
1 c. raisins	¼ t. salt (optional)

Combine all ingredients in large bowl and toss. Pack loosely in empty coffee cans with plastic covers. Yield: 4 quarts.

CAROL FLIPPEN

Q   CHEX AFTER-SCHOOL MIX

Great snack!

9 cups Chex cereal	¼ c. butter or margarine
1 c. semi-sweet chocolate chips	¼ t. vanilla
½ c. peanut butter	1½ c. confectioners' sugar

Place cereal in bowl and set aside. In small pan melt chocolate, peanut butter and butter over low heat or in microwave. Stir until smooth and remove from heat. Add vanilla and pour mixture over cereal. Stir. Pour sugar and cereal into bag and shake to coat. Spread on wax paper to cool. Store in plastic bag.

BETTIE HALLBERG

GLAZED PEANUTS   **Q**

A delicious gift!

2 c. raw peanuts   1 c. water
½ c. sugar

Combine all ingredients in saucepan and cook over medium-high heat until water disappears and sugar crystalizes. Do not let mixture get dry or flaky. Spread nuts on cookie sheet and bake at 300° for 30 minutes, stirring every 5 minutes. Cool and store in airtight container. Yield: 2½ cups.

SHARON PHILLIPS

ORANGE PECANS   **Q**

1 T. orange rind, grated   1 c. sugar
¼ c. orange juice   4 c. pecan halves

Combine orange rind, juice and sugar in large saucepan and cook over medium heat until it comes to full boil. Stir in pecans and cook until pecans are coated and syrup is absorbed. Remove from heat and stir just until pecans are separated. Spread on wax paper to cool. Store in airtight container. Yield: 4 to 5 cups.

SHARON PHILLIPS

TOASTED PECANS   **Q**

A great gift!

½ c. butter   1 t. paprika
1 T. salt   1 lb. pecans

Preheat oven to 325°. In shallow baking pan melt butter and stir in salt and paprika. Add pecans and toss to coat well. Bake for 20 to 25 minutes, stirring often. Do not let them get too brown. Yield: 1 pound.

EILEEN SMITH

VARIATION

1 lb. pecans   Butter
1 T. mayonnaise   Salt to taste

Toss pecans with mayonnaise until moistened. Dot with butter and bake at 350° for 20 to 25 minutes, stirring often. Sprinkle with salt and cool. Yield: 1 pound.

CATHY LEE

Q L **PITA CHIPS**

Great with salsa or spaghetti sauce.

Pita bread rounds

Any combination of garlic powder, chili powder, cayenne pepper, salt and parsley

Split pita rounds into 2 flat halves. Cut each into 6 to 8 triangles. Arrange on baking sheet and sprinkle with any combination of above seasonings. Bake at 325° for 8 to 10 minutes until lightly browned. Cool on racks and store in airtight container. Yield: 72 to 96 chips.

LINDA MAY

VARIATION: Sprinkle rounds with Molly McButter and a little water before baking.

STUART TROPE

BEVERAGES

Beverages

I love to eat dinner with Grandma because after dinner we crush ice so she can pour Baileys and Cream over hers and I can pour Kool-Aid over mine.

Johnny Archer, '04

Non-Alcoholic:
Beach Weekend
  Fizzies *L* 34
Lassi *L* 34
Shelley's Orange Julius *L* 34
Virgin Mary Mix 34
Golden Banana Slush
  Punch 36
Party Punch 36
Mint Tea *L* 37
Hot Spiced Cider 38
Wassail *L* 38

Alcoholic:
Beach Weekend Fizzies *L* ... 34
Augusta Bloody Mary Mix 35
Kahlua 35
Bourbon Slush 35
Scotch or Whiskey Sour Mix .. 35
Swamp Water 36
Hartley's Eggnog 37
No-Yolk Eggnog 37
Kahlua Coffee 38
Hot Spiced Cider 38
Wassail *L* 38

33

L   ## BEACH WEEKEND FIZZIES

These look snazzy on a brunch table.

2 c. fresh orange juice
2 c. pineapple juice

1 pt. peach frozen yogurt or
   sherbet of your choice

Blend all ingredients in blender. Serve in wine glasses and garnish with mint leaves, cherries, colorful straws, etc. Serves 8.

VARIATION: Add 1 c. club soda after you blend, if you like "fizzy" drinks; add a touch of rum or vodka if you like them "dizzy".

TIP: You can make these ahead and put blender container in freezer. Defrost slightly and blend again before serving.

ALLYN CROSBY

L   ## LASSI

A delicious low-fat nutritious drink.

1 c. plain yogurt
1 fruit of choice (banana, peach,
   mango, etc)
1 c. water

2 t. sugar or artificial sweetener to
   taste
1 t. vanilla

Blend all ingredients until puréed. Pour over ice. Serves 2 to 3.

VIRGINIA CHEWNING

L   ## SHELLEY'S ORANGE JULIUS

Wonderful for a brunch! Tastes like a dreamsicle.

1 (6 oz) can frozen orange juice
1 c. milk
1 c. water

½ c. sugar
1 t. vanilla
8-10 ice cubes

Combine all ingredients in blender and blend on high for 30 seconds. Serve immediately. Serves 4 to 6.

KATHY WHITE

VIRGIN MARY MIX

1 (46 oz) can V-8 juice
1 (32 oz) can clamato juice
1 (10½ oz) can beef bouillon
2 dashes lime juice

2 t. celery salt
Pepper, Tabasco, and
   Worcestershire to taste

Combine all ingredients. Yield: 2 quarts.

JUDI NEWCOMB

AUGUSTA BLOODY MARY MIX

1 t. seasoned salt
½ t. Tabasco
⅓ c. lime juice
1 T. Worcestershire

½ (46 oz) can V-8 juice
2 (10½ oz) cans beef bouillon
1 T. horseradish
1 c. vodka (optional)

Combine all ingredients and mix well. May be served cold or hot. Serves 8 to 10.

MIMI RHOADS

KAHLUA

3¼ c. sugar
Water
1 (2") vanilla bean

4 T. instant coffee
1 fifth 100 proof vodka

Dissolve sugar in 1 pint water, add vanilla beans and boil gently for 30 minutes. Set aside. Dissolve coffee in ¼ c. boiling water. Pour into a ½ gallon dark-colored bottle along with the Vodka. Add vanilla bean mixture. Let age 2 weeks in a dark place. Do not let sit after boiling or it will crystallize. If you do not have a ½ gallon dark-colored bottle, use any ½ gallon bottle and place in a brown paper bag to age. Yield: ½ gallon.

SANDY LACY

BOURBON SLUSH

Tasty and refreshing!

2 tea bags
1 c. hot water
1 c. sugar

1 (6 oz) can orange juice, thawed
½ (6 oz) can lemonade, thawed
½-¾ c. bourbon

Steep tea bags in water for 3 minutes. Remove bags. Add remaining ingredients, mix well and freeze. Remove from freezer 1 hour before serving. Pour slush in individual glasses. Yield: 10 (4 oz.) drinks.

ROBIN SLATER

SCOTCH OR WHISKEY SOUR MIX

1 c. orange juice
1 (6 oz) can frozen lemonade
½ c. water

12 oz Scotch or bourbon
(optional)

Mix all ingredients together and serve over ice. Yield: about 1 quart.

DEB POVLISHOCK

SWAMP WATER

This recipe is always requested!

2 (12 oz.) cans frozen limeade
1 (6 oz.) can frozen lemonade
2 big handfuls mint leaves

1 (12 oz.) can water
Rum, bourbon or gin
Club soda

Purée first 4 ingredients in blender. To make an individual drink, use ratio of ⅓ swamp mix, ⅓ your choice of liquor, and ⅓ club soda. Serves 20.

ROBIN SLATER

GOLDEN BANANA SLUSH PUNCH

Never fails to inspire raves and requests for the recipe.

2 c. sugar
6 c. water
10 mashed ripe bananas
1 (12 oz.) can frozen lemonade
1 (12 oz.) can frozen orange juice

1½-2 (46 oz.) cans pineapple
  juice
3-6 qts. chilled ginger ale
Strawberries to garnish
  (optional)

Bring sugar and water to boil in large saucepan until sugar is fully dissolved. Cool. Mash bananas in food processor or blender. Add mashed bananas, lemonade, orange juice and pineapple juice to sugar syrup, blending well. Freeze mixture until firm in 3 plastic containers. This punch base *must* be made ahead and will keep for several weeks in freezer. Remove punch base from freezer and place in refrigerator to thaw 3 hours before time of intended use. Mix each container with 1 or 2 quarts chilled ginger ale until punch is of the desired consistency (slushy or thinned). Garnish with strawberries if desired. Serves 50 punch-cup servings.

LYNN FELTON

PARTY PUNCH

Keep in freezer and serve as needed.

3 (3 oz.) pkgs. jello (any flavor)
4 c. sugar
9 c. boiling water
4 c. cold water

2 (6 oz.) cans frozen lemonade
2 (46 oz.) cans unsweetened
  pineapple juice
16 liters ginger ale

Mix jello and sugar with boiling water to dissolve. Add cold water, lemonade, and pineapple juice. Freeze in quart containers (about 8). When ready to serve put 1 frozen container of punch in bowl, pour 2 liters ginger ale over frozen ring.

HINT: Freeze punch mixture in aluminum cake pans. Serves 100.

SANDY KING

MINT TEA   *L*

7 tea bags
7 mint sprigs
1 c. sugar
1 qt. boiling water
3¼ c. water

2¼ c. pineapple juice
1 (6 oz.) can frozen lemonade, thawed
Mint sprigs for garnish

Combine first 3 ingredients. Pour boiling water over tea mixture, cover and let stand 30 minutes. Remove tea bags and mint sprigs; discard. Transfer tea to large pitcher and add water, pineapple juice, and lemonade concentrate; stir well. Serve over ice and garnish with mint sprigs. Yield: 2½ quarts.

ANNE NELSON MORCK

HARTLEY'S EGGNOG

Well worth the calories!

1 dozen eggs
1½ c. sugar
1 c. bourbon
1 c. brandy
½ c. rum
1 pt. coffee cream

1 pt. whole milk
1 pt. whipping cream
½ t. cinnamon
½ t. ground ginger
½ t. cloves
½ t. nutmeg

Separate eggs; beat yolks with wire wisk and add sugar until thickened and light colored. Add bourbon, brandy, and rum slowly (this cooks the egg yolks). Continue mixing and add spices and milk. Beat egg whites until stiff and whip cream; add to egg yolk mixture. Yield: 1 gallon.

CABELL LONGAN

NO-YOLK EGGNOG

For those who enjoy the real eggnog—this is a delicious low cholesterol alternative.

1 (10 oz.) pkg. egg substitute, thawed
2 c. bourbon
½ c. brandy
¾ c. sugar

2 (12 oz.) cans evaporated skim milk
2 c. dairy cream substitute
1 c. half and half
1 dozen egg whites

Beat egg substitute 5 minutes on high speed of electric mixer. Reduce speed and very slowly pour in bourbon and brandy. Add sugar, evaporated skim milk, dairy cream substitute and half and half. At this point, mixture can be stored in refrigerator. Best when made at least one day ahead. When ready to serve, beat egg whites and fold into refrigerated mixture. Yield: 2 liters.

LAURA LEE CHANDLER

KAHLUA COFFEE

Perfect when sitting by a warm fire on a cold winter evening!

6 c. hot coffee
1 c. chocolate syrup
¼ c. kahlua

⅛ t. cinnamon
Whipped cream

Mix first 4 ingredients together in saucepan over low to medium heat until thoroughly mixed. Pour in coffee mug and top with whipped cream. Serves 6 to 8.

KATHY WHITE

HOT SPICED CIDER

Everyone loves the not-too-sweet flavor.

1 gal. apple juice or cider
1 c. orange juice
1 (6 oz) can frozen lemonade

2 t. cinnamon
¼ t. cloves
¼ t. allspice

Combine ingredients and heat until very hot. Serves 25.

VARIATION: Add a pint of Applejack Brandy.

SUE THOMPSON

L
WASSAIL

Recommended by the High Museum in Atlanta.

1 gal. apple cider
1 (6 oz) can frozen orange juice
1 (6 oz) can frozen lemonade
6 sticks cinnamon
1 t. nutmeg

1 t. pumpkin pie spice
Sliced oranges and lemons for
    garnish
Rum or sherry, to taste (optional)

Bring first 6 ingredients to a boil and simmer 20 to 30 minutes. Add sliced fruit for last 5 minutes, to heat through. Add rum or sherry, if desired.

SUE NASCHOLD

Soups & Stews

Soups and Stews

When I'm hungry I feel like an empty bag inside.

Lauren Minor, '03

Cold Soups:

Chilled Cucumber Soup 42
Great Gazpacho **L** 42
Ruthie's Parsley Soup **Q** 46

Vegetable Soups:

New Year's Day Good Luck
Bean Soup 42
Black Bean Soup 43
Gourmet's Black Bean Soup... 43
Creamy Cabbage
Soup **Q** 44
Cream of Carrot Soup 44
Golden Carrot Soup 45
Cauliflower Soup 45
Cheddar Cheese Soup 45
Ruthie's Parsley Soup **Q** 46
Split Pea Soup 46
Potato Soup **Q** 46
Halleluia Soup 47
Country Spinach Soup **Q** ... 47
Tortellini and Spinach Soup .. 48
Winter Squash and Apple
Soup 48

Gypsy Soup 49
Vegetable Soup 49

Meat or Poultry Soups and Stews:

Easy Beef Stew 50
Easy Ground Beef
Vegetable Soup 50
Hearty Beef and Barley
Soup 51
Homemade Chili 51
Andy's Gourmet Chili 52
White Chili Casserole 52
Dixie's Chicken Chili **L** 53

Seafood Soups and Stews:

Clam Chowder I 53
Clam Chowder II 54
Manhattan Clam Chowder .. 54
Sailing Stew **Q** 55
Frogmore Stew **Q** 55
Oyster Bisque 55
Oyster Stew—Chick's
Beach Style **Q** 56
Oyster and Spinach Bisque .. 56

SOUPS & STEWS

CHILLED CUCUMBER SOUP

2 medium cucumbers, peeled and sliced
1 c. buttermilk, divided
½ c. light cream
1 small green onion, including 3" of top

Few sprigs of parsley
½ t. salt
¼ t. garlic salt
Dash of white pepper
½ t. white wine tarragon vinegar
½ c. sour cream

Purée cucumbers in a blender with ½ c. buttermilk, cream, green onion, and parsley. Add garlic salt, salt, pepper, ½ c. buttermilk and vinegar. Blend a few seconds. Add sour cream and blend only long enough to mix. Refrigerate several hours or overnight to develop the flavor. Serve thoroughly chilled, and garnish with a thin slice of cucumber or chopped parsley. Serves 2.

MIM SCHUTE

L GREAT GAZPACHO

1 (10 oz) can V-8 juice
½ medium cucumber, chopped
1 medium tomato, chopped
1 T. sugar
¼ c. red wine vinegar
¼ c. salad oil
2½ c. V-8 juice

1 medium tomato, finely chopped
½ medium cucumber, finely chopped
1 small onion, finely chopped
1 garlic clove, crushed (optional)
Croutons (optional)

Blend first six ingredients in blender. Add mixture to next four ingredients. Chill. Serve very cold. May add 1 garlic clove, or top with croutons, if desired. Serves 4 to 6.

MISSY BUCKINGHAM

NEW YEAR'S DAY GOOD LUCK BEAN SOUP

2 c. mixed beans (your choice)
Ham hock
1 (16 oz.) can tomatoes
1 red pepper or ½ to 1 t. chili pepper

1 garlic clove
1 large onion, chopped
2 bay leaves
Salt, pepper to taste

Wash beans and place in 3 to 5 quart kettle. Cover with water and soak overnight. Rinse beans and drain. Add 2 quarts water and ham hock. Simmer 2 hours. Add all other ingredients. Cook 1½ hours, or more if

42

needed. Add water if necessary. Serve with homemade corn bread. Serves 6 to 10.

SHARON PHILLIPS

BLACK BEAN SOUP

1 lb. black beans
8 c. water
½ c. olive oil
2 c. onion, chopped
2 garlic cloves, crushed

2 green peppers, finely chopped
1 t. salt
1 t. cumin
Parmesan cheese, for garnish
Sour cream, for garnish

Rinse beans and soak overnight in cold water. Put beans and 8 c. water (using soak water) in large pot. Turn on low. In skillet, heat olive oil and sauté onion, garlic, and green peppers until tender. Add to beans. Add salt and cumin. Simmer over low heat until beans are cooked and liquid is thickened, about 2½ to 3 hours. Serve with Parmesan cheese or sour cream, if desired. Serves 6.

BRYCE JEWETT

GOURMET'S BLACK BEAN SOUP

2 c. dried black beans
2 c. onion, chopped
1 c. celery, chopped
3 t. dried parsley
2 fresh thyme sprigs, or ¼ t. dried
1 bay leaf
3 T. butter
1¼ lb. ham hock

6 c. beef broth
¼ c. dark rum (or to taste)
Lemon juice to taste
Salt and pepper to taste
Garnishes: chopped hard-boiled
   eggs, parsley, sour cream,
   lemon slices

Soak beans in water to cover overnight, and drain. In heavy kettle cook onion, celery, parsley, thyme and bay leaf in butter over low heat for 10 minutes. Add ham hock, beans, broth, 4 c. water, salt and pepper to taste. Bring mixture to boil, reduce heat and simmer for 3 hours. Add water if necessary for desired consistency. Discard ham hock and bay leaf; put soup through food processor in small batches, then return to pot. Stir in rum and lemon juice, salt and pepper to taste. Garnish with hard boiled egg slices, parsley, lemon slices, sour cream or whatever you please. This soup is more flavorful when refrigerated overnight and served hot the next day. Serves 6.

DEBBIE CUNNINGHAM

Q CREAMY CABBAGE SOUP

A quick evening meal with bread and fruit.

3 T. butter or margarine
1 onion, chopped coarsely
1 T. caraway seeds
2 T. flour
2 (10¾ oz) cans chicken broth

½ head of green cabbage,
chopped coarsely
4 oz. white Cheddar cheese,
grated
¼ c. cream (optional)

Sauté onion in butter until translucent. Add caraway seeds and stir for a minute or two. Add flour, mix well. Whisk in chicken broth, stirring well until mixture thickens slightly. Add chopped cabbage, cover, and heat over medium heat for 7 to 10 min. Several minutes before serving, add Cheddar cheese and stir well. Cream can be added for extra rich flavor. Good served with pumpernickel bread. Recipe can easily be doubled. Serves 4.

RANDEE HUMPHREY

CREAM OF CARROT SOUP

2 T. butter or margarine
¾ c. onion, chopped
8-10 sweet carrots, peeled and
chopped
3-5 potatoes, peeled and
chopped
6 c. chicken broth
½ t. dried thyme

1 small bay leaf
1 clove garlic, halved
⅛ t. Tabasco
½ t. sugar
½ t. salt
1 c. milk
1 T. butter or margarine

Heat 2 T. butter in soup kettle, add onion, and cook 5 minutes, stirring constantly. Add the carrots and potatoes and stir for 2 to 3 minutes. Add chicken broth and remaining ingredients except milk and 1 T. butter. Bring to a boil, reduce heat, and simmer for 50 minutes. Put the soup through a blender and process until smooth. Return to heat and bring to a boil. Add milk and heat thoroughly. Correct seasonings as needed. Remove from heat, and stir in 1 T. butter. Serve hot. Serves 8.

ESTHER KELLY

GOLDEN CARROT SOUP

Even children who don't like carrots will like this soup!

¼ c. plus 2 T. butter
1 lb. carrots, scraped and sliced
1 large onion, chopped
1 qt. boiling water
¼ c. uncooked rice

1 t. salt
1 T. flour
2 c. beef bouillon
1 c. toasted bread cubes

Melt ¼ c. butter in a heavy kettle or Dutch oven. Sauté carrots and onions for 20 minutes. Add water, rice and salt. Cook 25 minutes. Purée mixture in blender until smooth. Melt 2 T. butter and stir in flour until smooth. Add bouillon and carrot mixture. Heat well and serve garnished with toasted bread cubes. Serves 6.

ANN BEAUCHAMP

CAULIFLOWER SOUP

Exceptional taste, especially on a winter day!

WHITE SAUCE

3 T. flour
3 T. butter

1½ c. milk
¼ lb. Cheddar cheese, grated

Combine flour, butter and milk over low heat to make sauce. Add cheese, stir and set aside.

1 celery stalk, chopped
1 carrot, chopped
½ small onion, chopped

3-4 c. cauliflower, chopped
3 c. water
3 chicken bouillon cubes

Cook vegetables in water with bouillon cubes added for 30 minutes. Mash vegetables in liquid and add white sauce. Heat and serve. Serves 3 to 4.

KIM BAIN

CHEDDAR CHEESE SOUP

1 c. potatoes, diced
½ c. celery, chopped
½ c. carrots, chopped
½ c. onion, chopped
½ c. green pepper, chopped
4 T. butter

1 (10¾ oz) can chicken broth plus
   water to equal 3 cups
Dash white pepper
2 c. milk
½ c. flour
3 c. Cheddar cheese, grated
1 T. parsley

Sauté vegetables in butter. Add broth, water and pepper. Cover and simmer 30 minutes. Blend milk and flour. Stir into broth. Add cheese, then cook and stir over low heat until thick. Add parsley. Serves 4.

NANCY CHEELY

Q   RUTHIE'S PARSLEY SOUP

Delicious hot or cold!

4 c. potatoes, diced	2 c. parsley (no stems)
1 c. onions, diced	3 c. chicken stock, divided
¼ c. butter	1½ c. milk
¼ t. curry	1 t. salt
1 t. Worcestershire sauce	1 c. heavy cream
1¼ c. water	¼ t. pepper

Combine potatoes, onion, butter, curry, Worcestershire and water in saucepan. Bring to boil and simmer until potatoes are tender. Put parsley and 1½ c. stock in blender and process until smooth. Blend potato mixture with some milk until smooth. Combine parsley and potato mixtures in soup pot and add remaining ingredients. Heat to serve or chill and serve very cold. Serves 6 to 8.

KATHY HERSHEY

SPLIT PEA SOUP

Without the ham hock!

1 lb. dried green split peas	1 large onion, chopped
6 c. water	2½ c. potatoes, diced
4 c. broth or water	2 carrots, chopped
¾ c. chopped celery with some leaves	1 clove garlic, minced
	1 t. cumin
2 leeks (white parts only), chopped	2 T. soy sauce
	Salt and pepper to taste

Wash and clean the dried peas. Put them in a large soup pot with the broth, water, celery, leeks, onion and garlic. Bring to a boil and simmer about 1½ hours. Add potatoes, carrots, cumin, soy sauce and salt, if desired. Bring back to a boil and simmer about 20 minutes. (Can be made in crock pot. To do so, put all ingredients in at once and simmer. Vegetables will be softer.) Serves 8 to 10.

ALEX THOMPSON

Q   POTATO SOUP

2 c. milk	2 c. potatoes, cooked and diced
4 T. flour	1 T. pimiento, chopped
3 T. butter or margarine	1 c. sharp Cheddar cheese, shredded
¼ t. salt	

Heat milk, flour, margarine and salt. Add potatoes, pimiento and cheese. Simmer until cheese is melted. Bacon bits, frozen peas or ham can be added if desired. Serves 4 to 6.

DERENDA REYNOLDS

HALLELUIA SOUP

A hit at family get-togethers.

⅓ lb. slab bacon or salt pork
4 large onions, peeled and sliced
4 large potatoes, peeled and
  sliced
5 c. chicken broth
2 T. flour
⅓ c. cold water

1 t. salt
⅛ t. coarsely ground black
  pepper
½ t. sugar
¼ t. powdered sage
Butter (for topping)

Slice and dice bacon. Brown it in a large heavy soup pot. Add chicken broth, potatoes and onions. Bring to a boil, lower heat, and cook gently for 30 minutes or until potatoes are tender. Blend together flour, water, salt, pepper and sugar. Add ½ c. of soup stock to the flour mixture, stir until smooth, and mix into soup. Bring to a boil, stirring constantly. Serve hot dotted with butter and sprinkled with sage. Serves 4.

DOROTHY MEYER

COUNTRY SPINACH SOUP   Q

2 T. butter or margarine
1 small onion, finely chopped
1 T. cornstarch
2 c. chicken stock

Pinch of nutmeg
Freshly ground black pepper
1 (10 oz) pkg. frozen spinach
4 oz. half and half

Melt butter in large saucepan, add onion and cook gently for 5 minutes. Add cornstarch, stirring constantly for 1 minute. Gradually stir in stock, pepper and nutmeg and bring to a boil. Add frozen spinach and simmer for 15 minutes, stirring occasionally. Purée soup in food mill or blender and adjust seasoning to taste. (May be frozen at this point.) To serve, add half and half and heat to gentle boiling point. Adjust seasoning, if necessary. Serves 4.

BARBARA COOKE

TORTELLINI AND SPINACH SOUP

2 T. olive oil
2 uncooked slices bacon, diced
3 garlic cloves, minced
1 medium onion, chopped
4-5 (10¾ oz.) cans chicken broth
2 t. dried Italian herb blend

9 oz. tortellini, spinach or cheese
1 (28 oz.) can crushed tomatoes
8 oz. fresh spinach, chopped
1 c. Parmesan, fresh, grated
Salt and pepper to taste

Heat olive oil in pot over medium-high heat. Add bacon, garlic, and onion. Cook until lightly browned, about 10 to 15 minutes. Add broth and herbs. Bring to a boil. Stir in tortellini and simmer uncovered until tortellini is cooked, 10 to 12 minutes. Stir in crushed tomatoes and simmer another 5 minutes. Add spinach and cook until wilted, about 3 minutes. Season with salt and pepper. Serve with Parmesan on top. Serves 6.

ALICIA ALFORD

WINTER SQUASH AND APPLE SOUP

3 c. winter squash, butternut or hubbard
3 green apples, Greening or Granny Smith
3 (10¾ oz.) cans chicken broth, fat removed
½ c. water

3 slices white or whole wheat bread, crusts removed and cubed
¾ c. onion, chopped
1 t. salt
¼ t. rosemary
½ t. marjoram
Parsley for garnish

Peel and halve squash. Remove seeds and cut into large cubes. Peel, core and roughly chop apples. In 4-quart kettle combine squash, apples, chicken broth, water, bread cubes, onion, salt, rosemary and marjoram. Slowly bring to a boil, reduce heat and simmer uncovered for about 30 minutes. Cool. Purée in small batches in food processor or blender. Reheat slowly. Garnish with chopped parsley. Serves 6.

KATHIE MARKEL

GYPSY SOUP

Interesting flavor and color.

2 T. olive oil
2 large onions, chopped
2 large garlic cloves, crushed
1 stalk celery, chopped
1 large sweet potato, peeled and cubed
1 large regular potato, peeled and cubed
1 green pepper, seeded and chopped
3 c. chicken broth or water
1 bay leaf

2 t. paprika
1 t. turmeric
1 t. dried basil
Dash cinnamon
Dash cayenne pepper
Salt to taste
1 c. tomato, chopped (fresh or canned)
1½ c. chickpeas, cooked (if canned, rinse well)
1 T. tamari or soy sauce

In a large stock pot, sauté the onion, garlic, celery, sweet potato, white potato and green pepper in oil for 5 minutes. Add the next 8 ingredients. Bring the soup to a boil, reduce heat, cover and simmer for 15 minutes. Add tomatoes and chickpeas and simmer soup for about 10 minutes longer. Stir in the tamari and serve. Serves 8 to 10.

ALEX THOMPSON

VEGETABLE SOUP

A hearty but low-cal soup that's great on a winter's evening!

1 soup bone with meat
2 stalks celery with leaves
1 medium onion, chopped
1½ T. Worcestershire
3 medium potatoes, chopped
1 (15 oz) can green beans

3 carrots, peeled, sliced
2 T. parsley
1 (28 oz) can crushed tomatoes
1 (15 oz) can creamed corn
½ (10 oz) box frozen tiny peas

Place bone in pot with 1½ quarts water, Worcestershire, celery and onion. Cook covered until meat is tender. Let cool, remove all fat from bone and meat, chop meat and save. Skim all fat from top of liquid. Place chopped meat and bone, onion and celery back in liquid. Add all ingredients but peas and corn. Simmer until potatoes are tender. Add corn and peas. Cook 30 more minutes. Adjust seasonings to taste. Serves 10.

SUE THOMPSON

EASY BEEF STEW

Makes its own gravy!

2 lbs. stewing beef
4 carrots, cut in 2" pieces
1 onion, chopped
2 stalks celery, chopped
1 (10-15 oz.) can stewed tomatoes
  (cut in small pieces)
1 slice bread, crumbled
3 T. tapioca

Salt and pepper to taste
1 green pepper, chopped
  (optional)
2 large potatoes, cubed and
  boiled slightly (optional)
1 (6-8 oz.) can green peas,
  drained (optional)

Mix all in heavy casserole and cook covered at 250° or over low heat on the stove top for at least 5 hours. (Cook all day in a crockpot.) Add peas last. Stir once if you're home. Serves 6.

ALLYN CROSBY

EASY GROUND BEEF VEGETABLE SOUP

1½ lbs. ground beef
2 onions, chopped
1 (10 oz.) pkg. frozen okra
1 (12 oz.) can shoe peg corn
1 (10 oz.) pkg. frozen baby limas
1 (14½ oz.) can tomatoes

2 (10¾ oz.) cans tomato soup
1½ cans water (more if needed)
½ t. chili powder
¼ t. oregano
Salt and pepper to taste
Garlic salt to taste

Brown meat and pour off fat. Place browned meat in a large pot and add all other ingredients. Bring to a boil, lower heat, and simmer 1½ hours, stirring occasionally. Can be frozen. Serves 4 to 6.

RICHIE HILBERT

VARIATION: Substitute 1 (15 oz.) can French-style string beans for okra.

HEARTY BEEF AND BARLEY SOUP

Great for chilly autumn evenings or football weekends!

2 lbs. lean stewing beef, cubed
1 t. salt
1 large bay leaf
½ t. dried thyme leaves
½ t. dried savory leaves
¼ t. crushed red pepper
6 c. water
⅓ c. pearl barley

1 (16 oz) can stewed tomatoes
1 (10½ oz) can condensed beef
  broth
1 c. carrots, sliced
1 c. celery, sliced
3 medium onions, coarsely
  chopped
¼ c. fresh parsley, chopped

Combine beef, salt, bay leaf, thyme, savory, red pepper and water in a 4-quart soup pot. Cover and cook until mixture boils. Reduce heat to medium and simmer one hour. Skim any fat from soup. Add barley and simmer, covered, another 45 minutes until beef is tender. Add tomatoes, beef broth, and remaining vegetables, except parsley. Bring soup back to a boil before reducing heat again. Simmer about 45 minutes more, until barley and vegetables are tender. Stir in parsley. Serve with green salad and crusty French bread. Serves 8.

LYNN FELTON

HOMEMADE CHILI

1 lb. extra lean ground beef
1 large onion, chopped
1 clove garlic, minced
½ c. green pepper, chopped
1½ t. oregano
2-3 t. chili powder
⅛-¼ t. ground red pepper
½ t. dried cilantro

¼ t. coriander
1½ t. cumin
Ground pepper to taste
1 (29-32 oz) can tomato purée
2 (15½ oz) cans Campbell Chili
  Beans in Zesty Sauce
3-4 dashes Tabasco (optional)

Brown the ground beef, onion, garlic and green pepper in 4-quart Dutch oven. Pour off fat. Add tomato purée, beans and remaining spices. Heat to boiling. Reduce heat to low and simmer 30 to 60 minutes, stirring occasionally. Adjust seasonings as desired. Serves 6 to 8.

MELANIE JONES

ANDY'S GOURMET CHILI

¼ c. vegetable oil
4 medium onions, coarsely chopped
2 garlic cloves, pressed (or ½ t. garlic powder)
4 lbs. chopped sirloin
3 (14½ oz) cans whole plum tomatoes, drained and chopped
1 (8 oz) can tomato sauce
3 (4 oz) cans chile peppers, chopped

1 beef bouillon cube
½ c. black olives, pitted and sliced
2 oz Tabasco or hot sauce
6 T. chili powder
1 t. oregano
2 t. cumin
2 t. cayenne pepper
2 t. paprika
1 t. crushed red pepper
1 (15 oz) can pinto beans, drained and rinsed

Sauté onion and garlic in oil over medium heat in a skillet until translucent and soft, and transfer to a large pot. Sauté ground beef in the unrinsed skillet until no longer pink and pour into strainer. Drain well and add to onions in pot. It helps to add a little water to the pot when starting. Add the remaining ingredients, except the beans, and cook over low heat for 30 minutes. Add beans before serving, allowing enough warming time for beans to be hot. If refrigerating or freezing, leave beans out until ready to reheat for serving. Serves 10 to 12.

CONNIE GARRETT

WHITE CHILI CASSEROLE

1 T. salad oil
1 medium onion, chopped
1 garlic clove, minced
1 t. ground cumin
2 large chicken breasts, skinned, boned, cut into 1" chunks
2 (4 oz) cans green chilies, peeled and chopped
2 chicken bouillon cubes

1 (15-19 oz) can white kidney beans (cannellini), drained
1 (15-19 oz) can garbanzo beans, drained
1 (12 oz) can white corn
Hot pepper sauce
1 c. Monterey Jack cheese, shredded
Parsley for garnish

Preheat oven to 350°. In a small pan, add oil and cook next 3 ingredients until onion is tender. In 2½ quart casserole combine onion mixture with chicken, the next 5 ingredients and 1½ cups water. Cover and bake 50 to 60 minutes until chicken is tender. To serve, stir hot pepper sauce into chili to taste, and top with shredded cheese. Garnish with parsley, if desired. Serves 8.

MARY SUE DONAHUE
GRACE PARKER

DIXIE'S CHICKEN CHILI   *L*

1 (28 oz.) can Italian plum tomatoes
3 chicken breasts, skinned and
   boned
½ c. defatted chicken broth
1 large onion, chopped
2 T. garlic, chopped
2 medium zucchini, cut in 1" cubes
2 red bell peppers, cored,
   seeded, cut into 1" squares
2 T. chili powder
2 t. ground cumin
2 t. curry powder
1 t. dried oregano
⅛ t. ground allspice
1 c. dark red kidney beans, drained
1 T. fresh lemon juice
4 T. parsley, chopped
Freshly ground pepper
1 c. plain yogurt (for garnish)
4 scallions, thinly sliced (for garnish)

Preheat oven to 375°. Cut tomatoes in 1-inch pieces and reserve liquid. Cut chicken breasts in half lengthwise and place in shallow roasting pan. Pour ½ c. tomato liquid over chicken and cover well with foil. Bake 20 minutes. Remove chicken from liquid and cool slightly. Cut into 1-inch pieces, cover and reserve. Discard cooking liquid. Place broth in heavy pot. Add onion and garlic and cook 3 minutes over low heat, stirring occasionally. Add zucchini and red peppers. Cook covered for 8 minutes. Add reserved tomatoes and remaining liquid, chili powder, cumin, curry powder, oregano and allspice. Simmer uncovered over low heat for 3 minutes, stirring once. Add reserved chicken, kidney beans, lemon juice, 2 T. parsley and black pepper. Simmer over low heat uncovered 10 to 12 minutes, stirring occasionally. Season to taste and stir in remaining parsley. Serve hot over brown or white rice. Garnish with yogurt and scallions. Serves 10.

DIXON KENDRICK

CLAM CHOWDER I

8 c. potatoes, diced
2 c. yellow onions, minced
1 (1.8 oz.) box of Knorr Leek Soup
   and Recipe Mix
2 T. bacon grease
3 (6½ oz.) cans minced clams
2 (11 oz.) cans golden sweet corn
½ c. butter
2 c. half and half
2 c. whole milk
Salt and pepper to taste

In Dutch oven place potatoes and onions and cover with water. Simmer covered until potatoes are cooked and onions are clear in color, stirring frequently. Add the envelope of leek soup mix, bacon grease, and 1 can of minced clams and its liquid. Stir well and simmer uncovered for 15 minutes. Drain the remaining cans of clams and the cans of corn. Add to Dutch oven. Stir well and add butter. Allow it to melt, then add the half and half and milk. Add seasonings and heat thoroughly. Serves 12.

SANDY LACY

CLAM CHOWDER II

4 (6½ oz.) cans minced clams, drained, reserving juice
2 c. potatoes, diced
1 c. onion, diced
1 c. celery, diced
¾ c. butter or margarine, melted
¾ c. flour
4 c. half and half
1½ t. salt
½ t. sugar
Pepper
Lawry's seasoning salt
Parsley, chopped, for garnish
Dried thyme for garnish

In large saucepan pour reserved claim juice over vegetables; add enough water to cover vegetables. Cover and simmer 20 minutes. While vegetables are cooking make sauce. In another saucepan blend flour into butter until smooth. Gradually add half and half, blending well. Cook over moderate heat, stirring constantly until mixture is bubbly hot and thickened. Add vegetables, liquid and clams. Heat thoroughly but do not boil. Add salt, sugar, pepper and seasoned salt to taste. Use chopped parsley and dried thyme for garnish. Serves 8.

MARGARET ROBBINS

MANHATTAN CLAM CHOWDER

2 (16 oz.) cans Del Monte Stewed Tomatoes, Italian style
1 large onion, chopped
3 stalks celery, chopped
1-2 handfuls celery leaves, chopped
¼-½ t. salt
3 (6½ oz.) cans chopped clams with liquid
½ t. coarsely cracked pepper
⅛ t. Tabasco
1 bay leaf
3 medium potatoes, scrubbed
2 carrots, scrubbed

Chop potatoes and carrots as for soup. Put all ingredients into a large pot and stir together well. Bring mixture to a boil, then immediately reduce heat and simmer, covered, for 2 hours. This is even better if prepared ahead, allowed to stand a little while, and briefly reheated just before serving. Serves 6.

SUE WHITTAKER

SAILING STEW   **Q**

Easy but elegant.

½ c. butter
2 lbs. shrimp
2 (8 oz.) cans minced clams in juice
1 (10½ oz.) can Harris she-crab soup

2 (19 oz.) cans chunky clam chowder
Garlic salt to taste
Pepper to taste
Fresh parsley, 3 T. or to taste
Vermouth to taste

Melt butter, add cleaned raw shrimp, and stir in remaining ingredients. Simmer and serve. Serves 10 to 12.

BRENDA WILKINS

FROGMORE STEW   **Q**

Great fun for a crowd!

¼ c. Old Bay seasoning
12 links Smithfield sausage, hot
8 ears yellow corn, broken in half

4 lbs. medium shrimp, raw, unshelled

Bring Old Bay and 6 quarts water to a boil. Add sausage and boil 5 minutes. Add corn and boil 5 minutes more. Add shrimp and cook until pink, about 2 minutes. Drain immediately. Dump on newspapers spread on table. Serve with French bread and dirty rice and enjoy! Serves 8.

TERRELL WILLIAMS

OYSTER BISQUE

1 pt.-1 qt. oysters
4 T. butter
4 T. onion, finely chopped
4 T. celery, finely chopped
4 T. flour
3 c. warm milk

1 c. warm chicken stock
1 t. Worcestershire sauce
1 t. salt
1 t. pepper
Parsley (optional)

Drain oysters. Reserve liquor. Heat oysters in heavy stock pot stirring for 2 minutes or until edges curl. Remove oysters and liquor. Heat butter in stockpot. Sauté onion and celery until tender. Add flour and cook 5 minutes, stirring constantly. Slowly stir in stock, milk, and oyster liquor. Cook slowly for 10 minutes, stirring frequently. Add oysters and seasonings. Keep hot in top of double boiler or simmer on low in stockpot for 1 hour before serving. Add parsley when serving if desired. Oysterette crackers are a great accompaniment. Serves 8.

DEB POVLISHOCK

Q OYSTER STEW—CHICK'S BEACH STYLE

8 strips bacon
2 T. butter (not margarine)
1 small onion, chopped
2 stalks celery, chopped

1 pt. oysters
1 qt. half and half
Salt and pepper to taste

Microwave bacon between paper towels until done. Drain and set aside. Lightly cook onion and celery in butter; cut oysters in half and sauté until oysters curl, about 5 minutes. Pour off half of watery mixture. Add crumbled bacon and half and half and heat thoroughly. Season with salt and pepper to taste and serve. Serves 4.

LOUISE ARBUCKLE

OYSTER AND SPINACH BISQUE

½ c. butter
1 medium or large onion, puréed
2 cloves garlic, puréed
1 pt. oysters
⅓ c. flour
2 c. half and half

2 c. heavy cream
1 (10 oz.) pkg. frozen chopped
  spinach, or fresh, chopped
2 bouillon cubes dissolved in ¼ c.
  water
Salt and white pepper to taste

Melt ¼ cup butter in large pot. Sauté the puréed onion and garlic in butter. Add oysters and sauté until edges curl. While cooking melt remaining butter in a pan and stir in flour to make a roux. Stir constantly until smooth. Add roux to onion and oysters. When mixture begins to boil, add half and half, cream, spinach and chicken base. Cook until spinach is done, but don't let boil. Stir constantly. Add salt and white pepper to taste. Serves 2 to 4.

NANCY McCANDLISH

SALADS &
SALAD DRESSINGS

Salads and Salad Dressings

I think I was a dinosaur that was an herbivore millions of years ago because I like salad and broccoli and asparagus that most kids think are yuk.

Bennett Sooy, '05

Vegetable Salads:
Artichoke Rice Salad 60
Bean Relish Salad 60
Chick Pea Salad. 60
Marinated Bean Salad 61
Green Bean and Celery Salad....... 61
Happy New Year Good Luck Salad.... 61
Broccoli Salad. 62
Aunt Ollie's Broccoli Cauliflower
 Salad 62
Broccoli Cauliflower Salad **Q** 62
Holiday Vegetable Salad **L** 63
Fumi Salad **Q** 63
Chinese Cole Slaw 64
Fruited Cole Slaw **L** 64
Healthy Cole Slaw **L** 64
Low-Cal Cole Slaw **L** 65
Marinated Slaw **L** 65
Country Herb Potato Salad 65
French-Style Potato Salad **L** 66
Italian-Style Potato Salad **L** 66
Refrigerator Potato Salad............ 66
Marinated Summer Garden **L** 67
Sunday-Best Aspic 67
Tomato Aspic I 67
Tomato Aspic II 68
Festive Vegetable Salad. 68
Vegetable Marinade 68
Carroll Cottrell's Romaine Salad **Q** ... 69
Chef Salad by Committee. 69
Leisy's Favorite Salad **Q** 70
Mandarin Orange Tossed Salad...... 70
Walnut Salad **Q** 71
Fruit Salads:
Sweet and Sour Cantaloupe **Q** 71
Fresh Cranberry Relish Salad......... 72
Cranberry Freeze 72
Frozen Cranberry Salad 72
Thanksgiving Cranberry Salad........ 72
Filled Fruit Halves **Q** 73
Fruit Salad **Q** 73
Island Fruit Salad **L** 74
Minty Fruit Salad **L** 74
Mandarin Orange Tossed Salad...... 70
Spiced Orange Salad.............. 74
Pineapple Buttermilk Salad 75
Pineapple Strawberry Ring........... 75
Holiday Raspberry Salad Mold 76
Meat and Poultry Salads:
Harvey Gamage Salad............. 76

Taco Salad **Q** 76
Barbara's Famous Chicken Salad..... 77
Blackened Chicken Salad **Q** 77
Carolina Plantation Salad **Q**. 77
Cuban Chicken Salad **L** 78
Curried Chicken Salad 78
Tarragon Chicken and Rice Salad.... 78
Turkey Salad 79
Seafood Salads:
Carolina Plantation Salad **Q**. 77
Crab Louis **Q** 79
Yellow Peppers Stuffed with Crab
 and Dill **Q L** 80
Shrimp Salad Supreme **Q** 80
Shrimp and Macaroni Salad......... 80
Shrimp and Shells. 81
Curried Shrimp Salad 81
Curried Rice and Shrimp Salad 81
Waterfront Tuna Salad 82
Pasta Salads:
Shrimp and Macaroni Salad......... 80
Shrimp and Shells. 81
Antipasto Sea Shell Salad. 82
Cold Pasta New Orleans 83
Easy Pasta Salad 83
Fat-Free Pasta Salad **L** 83
Italian-Style Pasta Salad 84
Mediterranean Pasta Salad.......... 84
Party Pasta Salad 84
Tortellini Salad. 85
Salad Dressings:
Miss Molly's Aspic Dressing **L** 85
Bleu Cheese Walnut Dressing 86
Creamy Bleu Cheese Dressing **Q** ... 86
Mom's Cole Slaw Dressing **Q** 86
Blender French Dressing **Q** 86
Mom's French Dressing **Q** 87
White French Dressing.............. 87
Honey Mustard Dressing **Q** 87
Italian Dressing **Q** 87
Creamy Pepper Dressing **Q L** 88
Ranch Dressing **Q L** 88
Jebbie's Spinach Salad Dressing 88
Spinach Salad Dressing **Q**. 88
Norwood Dressing **Q L**. 89
Tomato Dressing **Q** 89
Tomato Marinade I 89
Tomato Marinade II **Q L** 89
French Vinaigrette 90
New Orleans Vinaigrette 90

ARTICHOKE RICE SALAD

1 (6.9 oz.) box Rice-A-Roni, chicken flavored
4 green onions, chopped
12 stuffed green olives, chopped
1 (6 oz.) jar marinated artichoke hearts, drain and reserve liquid
⅓ c. mayonnaise

Cut artichoke hearts into bite-sized pieces. Cook Rice-A-Roni according to package directions and cool. Add onions, olives, and artichoke pieces. Combine artichoke marinade and mayonnaise. Add to rice mixture and mix well. Chill several hours before serving. Serves 6 to 8.

VARIATIONS: Add 1 t. curry powder. Add shrimp for a main course. Add black olives instead of green. Add 1 (8 oz.) can water chestnuts, drained and sliced.

STEWART ALBERTSON
MARTHA BAUMGARTEN

BEAN RELISH SALAD

1 (16 oz.) can French-style green beans, drained
1 (16 oz.) can white shoe peg corn, drained
1 (10 oz.) pkg. frozen green peas, thawed
1 medium onion, chopped
4 stalks celery, chopped
1 medium green pepper, chopped
½ c. pimientos, chopped
½-¾ c. sugar
½ c. cider vinegar

Combine all ingredients in a 1-quart bowl and mix. Cover and chill in refrigerator overnight. Drain before serving. Yield: 6 to 8 cups.

SHARON PHILLIPS

CHICK PEA SALAD

Great for picnics!

1 (16 oz.) can chick peas, drained
1 (16 oz.) can cut wax beans, drained
1 (16 oz.) can cut green beans, drained
1 (15 oz.) can kidney beans, drained
1 ripe tomato, diced
½ c. scallions, chopped
½ c. fresh parsley, chopped
2 cloves garlic, minced
4 T. wine vinegar
½ c. olive oil
Salt to taste
Pepper to taste

Combine all ingredients in large salad bowl, toss lightly, and chill at least several hours before serving. Best if made a day ahead. Serves 10 to 12.

NANCYE WINTER

MARINATED BEAN SALAD

No oil!

1 (16 oz.) can garbanzo beans
1 (16 oz.) can cut green beans
1 (15 oz.) can red kidney beans
1 (16 oz.) can cut wax beans
1 (16 oz.) can corn
1 c. celery, chopped
½ c. onions, chopped

1 medium green pepper, chopped
1 medium red pepper, chopped
1½ c. water
1½ c. cider vinegar
1½ c. sugar

Drain beans and corn and pour into large bowl. Add celery, onions and peppers and mix. Combine water, vinegar and sugar and stir well. Pour over vegetables and refrigerate at least 24 hours before serving. (May be kept in refrigerator for 1 week.) Stir well with slotted spoon before serving. Serves 8 to 10.

SANDY ROBINS

GREEN BEAN AND CELERY SALAD

1 lb. fresh green beans, steamed until crisp-tender

1 c. celery, chopped
Lettuce

In large bowl combine beans and celery. Pour marinade over all and toss well. Chill several hours before serving. Arrange on lettuce leaves. Serves 4.

MARINADE

6 T. canola oil
2 T. white vinegar
1 t. prepared mustard
½ t. MSG

¼ t. salt
¼ t. tarragon, crushed
2 T. onion, finely chopped
⅛ t. pepper

Combine all ingredients and mix well.

KATHIE MARKEL

HAPPY NEW YEAR GOOD LUCK SALAD

1 (15 oz.) can black-eyed peas, rinsed and drained
1 tomato, chopped
1 cucumber, peeled, seeded and cut into small pieces
½ c. green pepper, chopped

½ c. onion, sliced
1 thick slice Smithfield ham, chopped
1 (.7 oz.) pkg. Good Seasons Italian Dressing

Combine peas, tomato, cucumber, pepper, onion and ham in salad bowl and toss. Mix dressing according to package directions and pour approximately half of dressing over salad. Chill for several hours before serving. (Corned beef may be substituted for ham.) Serves 4.

PAT COMESS

SALADS AND SALAD DRESSINGS

BROCCOLI SALAD

1 bunch broccoli, cut into florets
1 small onion, thinly sliced
½ c. pecans or almonds

5 slices bacon, cooked and
 crumbled
¼ c. raisins, dark or white,
 (optional)

Combine broccoli, onion, and nuts in salad bowl. Pour dressing over salad and toss well. Refrigerate overnight. Before serving, add bacon and raisins. Serves 6 to 8.

DRESSING

1 c. mayonnaise
¼-½ c. sugar

2 T. vinegar

Combine mayonnaise, sugar and vinegar and mix well.

VARIATIONS: Add 1 red Delicious apple, chopped. Add 1 c. sharp Cheddar cheese, grated.

JANNY CASLER
LINDA HYSLOP
JANE JONES

DEB POVLISHOCK
MARGARET ROBBINS

AUNT OLLIE'S BROCCOLI CAULIFLOWER SALAD

1 cauliflower, cut into small florets
1 bunch broccoli, cut into small
 florets
1 green pepper, cut into 1" pieces

3 stalks celery, sliced
1 small purple onion, cut into rings
2-3 carrots, sliced

Combine vegetables in 2-quart covered bowl and toss. Pour dressing over salad, mix well and chill covered at least 4 hours. Serves 10 to 12.

DRESSING

¾-1 c. sugar
½ c. cider vinegar
1 c. canola oil

2 T. dry mustard
1 t. salt
2 T. poppy seeds

Combine all ingredients and mix well.

SHARON PHILLIPS

Q BROCCOLI CAULIFLOWER SALAD

1 bunch broccoli, cut into florets
1 cauliflower, cut into florets
1 small onion, chopped
1 (16 oz.) pkg. frozen peas

Ranch Dressing (enough to cover
 vegetables)
1 (3 oz.) can chow mein noodles

62

Combine broccoli, cauliflower and onion in bowl and toss. Cover and refrigerate until ready to serve. Stir in peas and cover vegetables with dressing. Sprinkle noodles evenly over all. Serve at once. Serves 8 to 10.

SUGGESTION: Broccoli and cauliflower may be blanched first to bring out color.

MIA NORTON

HOLIDAY VEGETABLE SALAD   *L*

Good anytime!

2 c. cauliflower, thinly sliced
½ medium purple onion, thinly sliced
⅓ c. stuffed green olives, sliced
⅓ c. bleu cheese, crumbled
¼ c. green pepper, cut in strips

5 T. vegetable oil
3 T. white wine vinegar
¼ t. dry mustard
½ t. basil
¼ t. salt
⅛ t. pepper

In large bowl combine cauliflower, onion, olives, cheese and green pepper. In small bowl stir together oil, vinegar, mustard, basil, salt and pepper. Pour over vegetables and toss lightly to coat all. Cover and refrigerate at least 2 hours. Best when chilled overnight. Stir well before serving. Serves 6 to 8.

CAROL RANELLI

FUMI SALAD   *Q*

8 T. slivered almonds
8 T. sesame seeds
1 small cabbage, shredded

4 green onions, chopped
2 (3 oz.) pkgs. Ramen noodles, without seasoning mix, broken

Brown almonds and sesame seeds, separately, in hot skillet (no oil or butter). Combine cabbage and onions in bowl. Just before serving, stir in almonds, sesame seeds and uncooked noodles. Toss dressing over all. Serves 12.

DRESSING

4 T. sugar
2 t. Accent
2 t. salt

1 c. vegetable oil
6 T. rice vinegar

Combine all ingredients in blender and mix until smooth.

KATHY ELLIS

CHINESE COLE SLAW

1 (16 oz) can French-style green beans, drained
1 (14 oz) can Chinese vegetables, drained
1 (8½ oz) can tiny English peas, drained
1 (8 oz) can water chestnuts drained
1½ c. celery, chopped
1 medium onion, thinly sliced

Combine all vegetables in large bowl and pour marinade over all to coat well. Chill well before serving. Store in refrigerator. Yield: 5 cups.

MARINADE

1 c. sugar
¾ c. vinegar
1 T. mustard seed
Salt to taste
Pepper to taste

Combine all ingredients in small saucepan and heat until sugar is melted.

KATHY SPAHN

L   FRUITED COLE SLAW

2 ripe pears, peeled and diced
1 apple, peeled and diced
1 T. lemon juice
1½ c. cabbage, shredded
¼ c. raisins

Toss pears and apples with lemon juice. Add cabbage and raisins. Pour dressing over slaw and toss well. Chill before serving. Serves 4.

DRESSING

½ c. plain low-fat yogurt
½ t. lemon juice
1 t. honey

Combine yogurt, lemon juice and honey and mix well.

CAROL SHAPIRO

L   HEALTHY COLE SLAW

1 lb. cabbage, shredded
1-2 carrots, shredded
¼ c. green pepper, julienned
¼ c. red pepper, julienned

Combine cabbage, carrots and peppers in large bowl, pour dressing over slaw and refrigerate at least 2 hours before serving. Best when chilled overnight. Serves 4 to 6.

DRESSING

2 t. sugar
½ t. Beau Monde seasoning
¼ t. freshly ground black pepper

2 T. white wine vinegar
2-3 dashes hot pepper sauce
½ c. light mayonnaise

Combine all ingredients and whisk until smooth.

LINDA MAY

LOW-CAL COLE SLAW   *L*

Good with grilled fish.

2 c. cabbage, shredded
½ green pepper, chopped
½ red pepper, chopped
1 carrot, shredded
3 T. light mayonnaise
1 T. minced onion (optional)

2 packets sugar substitute
Dash red wine vinegar
Dash celery seed
Dash mustard seed (optional)
Salt to taste (optional)
Pepper to taste (optional)

In large bowl combine all ingredients and stir well. Refrigerate overnight. Serves 4 to 6.

ALLYN CROSBY

MARINATED SLAW   *L*

½ head green or purple
  cabbage, shredded
½ small purple onion, sliced

½ medium red or green pepper,
  sliced
2 carrots, grated

In large bowl combine cabbage, onion, pepper and carrots. Pour dressing over slaw and toss well. Marinate and refrigerate at least 30 minutes. To keep crispness in slaw, drain marinade after chilling. Serves 5 to 6.

DRESSING

⅔ c. vinegar
⅓ c. safflower oil

¼ t. celery seed

In small bowl combine all ingredients and mix well.

AMY RAMKO

COUNTRY HERB POTATO SALAD

1 c. prepared ranch salad
  dressing
4 t. Dijon mustard
¼ t. dill weed

¼ c. fresh parsley, chopped
¼ c. green onions, sliced
2 lbs. small red potatoes, cooked,
  cooled, and sliced into rounds

In mixing bowl combine dressing, mustard, dill weed, parsley and onions. Add potatoes and toss lightly to mix. Serve at once or chill. Serves 4 to 6.

NANCY LIPSCOMB

SALADS AND SALAD DRESSINGS

L   FRENCH-STYLE POTATO SALAD

1¼ lb. small red potatoes, cooked
   and cut into ¼" slices
3 T. dry white wine
¼ c. light olive oil
2 T. white wine vinegar

1½ T. Dijon mustard
½ t. freshly ground pepper
Salt to taste
¼ c. parsley, finely chopped
2 green onions, thinly sliced

In large bowl combine potatoes and wine and toss gently. In small bowl whisk together oil, vinegar, mustard, pepper and salt. Stir in parsley and onions. Pour dressing over potatoes and toss gently to coat. Serve at room temperature. Serves 4.

LINDA HYSLOP

L   ITALIAN-STYLE POTATO SALAD

This salad has a little bite to it!

8 medium red potatoes, cooked,
   peeled and sliced
½ c. celery, finely sliced
⅓ c. green onions, sliced
¼ c. wine vinegar
½ t. pepper

2 T. Dijon mustard
2 T. parsley
¼ c. chicken stock
Low calorie Italian salad dressing,
   enough to hold ingredients
   together

Combine potatoes, celery and green onions in large bowl. Mix together remaining ingredients and toss with vegetables. Chill and serve. Yield: 5 cups.

PAT MARTIN

REFRIGERATOR POTATO SALAD

Best when made with unpeeled red potatoes!

8 medium potatoes, cooked and
   sliced into ⅛" pieces
Salt to taste
1½ c. mayonnaise
1 c. sour cream
1½ t. horseradish

1 t. celery seed
½ t. salt
1 c. parsley, chopped
2 medium onions, finely chopped,
   or 1 carton frozen chives

In large serving bowl arrange layer of half of potato slices and salt lightly. Combine mayonnaise, sour cream, horseradish, celery seed and salt. In another bowl combine parsley and onion. Spread half of mayonnaise mixture over potatoes and layer half of the parsley and onions on top. Repeat layer. Do not stir! Cover and store in refrigerator for at least 8 hours. Best when made day ahead. Serves 8 to 10.

MIM SCHUTE

66

MARINATED SUMMER GARDEN   L

3 tomatoes, chopped
1 cucumber, sliced

1 small onion, thinly sliced

Combine vegetables, pour marinade over, and refrigerate at least one hour. May marinate overnight if desired.

MARINADE

¼ c. red wine vinegar
2 T. sugar
Salt to taste

3 T. water
Dash of olive oil
Freshly ground pepper to taste

Mix thoroughly.

BARBARA JONES

SUNDAY-BEST ASPIC

FIRST LAYER

1 (3 oz.) pkg. lemon jello
1 c. boiling water
½ c. mayonnaise
2 c. small curd cottage cheese,
    blended until smooth

½ t. salt
1 t. onion, grated
¾ green pepper, finely chopped

Dissolve jello in boiling water. Add next five ingredients. Pour into bottom half of greased mold and refrigerate until set, about 1 hour.

SECOND LAYER

1 (3 oz.) pkg. lemon jello
1 c. hot tomato juice
⅔ c. cold tomato juice
1 t. salt

1 c. celery, diced
1-2 (6 oz.) jars marinated artichoke
    hearts, drained

Dissolve jello in hot tomato juice. Add next three ingredients and pour on top of congealed first layer. Arrange artichokes in mold and refrigerate until set. Serves 12 to 15.

ANDY BENNETT

TOMATO ASPIC I

2 c. V-8 juice
4 onion slices
8 whole cloves
1 (3 oz.) pkg. lemon jello

1 t. Worcestershire
Salt and pepper to taste
Juice of ½ lemon

Simmer V-8 juice, onion, and cloves for 10 minutes. Strain into bowl and add lemon jello, Worcestershire, salt, pepper and lemon juice. Pour into 4 individual molds and refrigerate until firm. Serves 4.

MARGARET TRAYNHAM

TOMATO ASPIC II

1 (3 oz.) pkg. lemon jello
1¼ c. hot water
1 (8 oz.) can tomato sauce

1½ T. apple cider vinegar
2 T. horseradish

Dissolve jello in water. Add remaining ingredients and chill in mold until set. Serves 4.

STUART TROPE

VARIATIONS: Add 1 c. chopped celery, 2 c. cooked shrimp, or green olives.

FESTIVE VEGETABLE SALAD

3 c. broccoli florets
3 c. fresh asparagus, cut into 1½"-2" pieces

¼ lb. snow peas
2 tomatoes, chopped
Ranch dressing

The day before serving microwave broccoli florets for 2 minutes. Dip in cold water and drain. Repeat for asparagus pieces. Remove ends from snow peas and microwave for 1 minute. Dip in cold water and drain. Mix vegetables together and refrigerate overnight. On serving day add tomatoes to cold vegetables. Toss with ranch dressing and refrigerate for several additional hours. Serves 6 to 8.

GAY JEWETT

VEGETABLE MARINADE

A delicious alternative to a tossed salad!

¾ c. vegetable oil
½ c. vinegar
1 t. salt
2 T. poppy seeds
1 t. dry mustard
1 c. sugar
1 small purple onion, sliced in half circles

4 stalks broccoli
1 small cauliflower
3 stalks celery
1 medium green pepper
8 large mushrooms
1 (1 lb.) pkg. zigzag frozen or fancy cut carrots

Combine oil, vinegar, salt, poppy seeds, mustard and sugar and mix well. Cut vegetables into bite-sized pieces, slicing celery and mushrooms. Pour marinade over vegetables and refrigerate for 24 hours. Serves 4 to 6.

KATHY WHITE

SALADS AND SALAD DRESSINGS

CARROLL COTTRELL'S ROMAINE SALAD Q

1 head Romaine lettuce
¾ c. vegetable oil
1 T. olive oil
1 T. vinegar
1 T. lemon juice

1 clove garlic, minced
1 T. sugar
¼ plus ½ c. Parmesan cheese
Croutons (homemade are best)
Pepper to taste

Separate Romaine lettuce leaves. Whirl oils, vinegar, lemon juice, garlic, sugar and ¼ c. Parmesan in blender. Just before serving, toss lettuce with dressing. Sprinkle remaining Parmesan cheese and croutons on top. Pepper to taste, if desired. Serves 4 to 6.

JANA THOMAS

CHEF SALAD BY COMMITTEE

Wonderful for a crowd. Everyone brings something!

2 (6 oz.) jars marinated artichoke
   hearts, drained, chopped and
   reserving liquid
½ lb. fresh mushrooms, sliced
1 c. vegetable oil
⅓ c. red wine vinegar
½ t. garlic powder
½ t. dry mustard
½ t. salt
½ t. pepper
1 t. sugar
3 medium heads iceberg lettuce,
   torn
1 lb. chicken, cooked and sliced
1 lb. roast beef, cooked and
   sliced

1 lb. ham, cooked and sliced
1 pt. cherry tomatoes
1 c. radishes, sliced
1 c. cucumber, unpeeled and
   sliced
2 c. cauliflower florets
½ c. black olives, sliced
1 small purple onion, sliced into
   rings
2 avocados, chopped
3 eggs, hard-boiled and
   quartered
1 lb. bacon, cooked and
   crumbled

Combine artichoke hearts and mushrooms and set aside. In small bowl combine reserved artichoke marinade with oil, vinegar, garlic powder, mustard, salt, pepper and sugar. Mix well. Pour dressing over artichoke hearts and mushrooms and toss. Cover and chill 4 hours. In large salad bowl combine lettuce, chicken, beef, ham, tomatoes, radishes, cucumber, cauliflower, olives, onion, and avocados. Toss gently. Pour dressing over salad and toss. Arrange eggs around salad edges and sprinkle bacon over top. Serves 18.

KATIE BELK
CATHY TULLIDGE

SALADS AND SALAD DRESSINGS

Q LEISY'S FAVORITE SALAD

A family favorite from a Hawaiian restaurant.

1-2 T. olive oil
Salt to taste
1 clove garlic, cut
1-2 heads Romaine lettuce,
    broken into bite-sized pieces

3-4 green onions, sliced
10-12 slices bacon, cooked and
    crumbled
Romano cheese, grated, to taste
Croutons to taste

Prepare wooden salad bowl by pouring in oil, sprinkling with salt and rubbing with garlic. Remove garlic. Add lettuce, onions, bacon and cheese to salad bowl. Pour dressing over salad, sprinkle with croutons, and toss. Serves 4.

DRESSING

3 T. olive oil
2 T. red wine vinegar
Freshly ground black pepper to
    taste

Generous pinch oregano
1 coddled egg

In small bowl combine oil, vinegar, pepper and oregano and mix well. Coddle egg by placing cold egg in enough water to cover egg in saucepan and heat to boiling. Remove pan from heat, cover and let stand 30 seconds. Immediately cool egg in cold water. Peel egg and whip into dressing.

RUTH LEISY

MANDARIN ORANGE TOSSED SALAD

½ head lettuce, torn into bite-
    sized pieces
½ head Romaine lettuce, torn into
    bite-sized pieces
1 c. celery, chopped

2 green onions, sliced
1 (11 oz.) can mandarin oranges,
    drained
½ c. sliced almonds, toasted

In salad bowl combine all ingredients, pour dressing over all and toss. Serves 4 to 6.

VARIATION: Warm ¼ c. sliced almonds over low heat with 1 T. plus 1 t. sugar. Stir constantly until sugar is melted and almonds are coated. Cool and break apart. Add to salad.

SALADS AND SALAD DRESSINGS

DRESSING

½ t. salt
Dash of pepper
¼ c. vegetable oil
1 T. parsley, chopped

2 T. sugar
2 T. vinegar
Dash of Tabasco

Combine all ingredients and mix well.

DRESSING VARIATION: Add 1 t. Dijon mustard and 1 T. poppy seeds.

KATHY ELLIS
LEIGH FARMER
KAKI NELSON

WALNUT SALAD   **Q**

1 bunch fresh spinach or Romaine
  lettuce, torn in bite-sized pieces
1 small avocado, peeled and
  sliced

½ medium red onion, sliced
½ c. feta cheese, crumbled
½ c. walnuts, chopped

DRESSING

½ c. olive oil
⅓ c. red wine vinegar
1 T. dried basil
2 T. sugar

2 large cloves garlic, minced
½ t. salt
1½ t. freshly ground pepper

Combine dressing ingredients in a blender and pour over salad ingredients. Serves 4.

KATHY ELLIS

SWEET AND SOUR CANTALOUPE   **Q**

Tasty and unusual combination!

1 bunch green leaf lettuce
2 medium cantaloupes, scooped
  into balls

1 small purple onion, sliced
6 slices bacon, cooked and
  crumbled

On 4 individual salad plates layer lettuce, melon balls, onion and bacon. Pour dressing over each. Serves 4.

SWEET AND SOUR DRESSING

1 egg
½ c. sugar

¼ c. water
¼ c. vinegar

Break egg into small saucepan and stir over medium heat. Stir in sugar, water and vinegar and mix well.

SANDY KING

71

SALADS AND SALAD DRESSINGS

FRESH CRANBERRY RELISH SALAD

1 lb. fresh cranberries, chopped
1 red apple, chopped
2 oranges, chopped

1 (15 oz) can crushed pineapple, undrained
1 c. sugar
Grated rind of 1 orange

Combine all ingredients and mix well. Store in covered container in refrigerator until ready to use. Serves 6 to 10.

SHARON PHILLIPS

CRANBERRY FREEZE

1 (3 oz) pkg. cream cheese, softened
2 T. mayonnaise
1 (16 oz) can whole berry cranberry sauce

1 (8¼ oz) can crushed pineapple, drained
½ c. walnuts, chopped
1 c. whipped topping
Lettuce leaves

In mixing bowl beat cream cheese with mayonnaise until light and fluffy. Add cranberry sauce, pineapple and walnuts. Fold in whipped topping. Line 9" x 5" loaf pan with plastic wrap, pour in mixture and cover with plastic wrap. Freeze overnight. To serve lift salad from pan, slice, and arrange on lettuce leaves. Serves 10.

GAIL SMITH

FROZEN CRANBERRY SALAD

2 (16 oz) cans whole berry cranberry sauce
1 (20 oz) can crushed pineapple, drained

2 c. sour cream
½ c. confectioners' sugar

Combine all ingredients and pour into mold or muffin tins lined with paper cups. Freeze. Yield: 24 salads.

SHIRLEY WALKER

THANKSGIVING CRANBERRY SALAD

1 (15¼ oz) can crushed pineapple
1 (6 oz) pkg. cherry jello
7 oz ginger ale
1 (16 oz) can whole cranberry sauce

1 (8 oz) container whipped topping
1 (8 oz) pkg. cream cheese, softened
Pecans, toasted
2-3 T. butter

Add enough water to drained pineapple juice to make 1 cup. Bring juice to boil and dissolve jello. Stir in ginger ale and cool. Refrigerate until partially set and add pineapple and cranberry sauce. Pour into mold and allow to set. In small bowl beat whipped topping and cream cheese until smooth. Spread on top of jello mixture. When ready to serve top with buttered pecans. Serves 8 to 10.

MIM SCHUTE

FILLED FRUIT HALVES Q

Colorful and light accompaniment to a heavy meal.

1 (8 oz.) pkg. cream cheese, softened
2 T. honey
1 T. mayonnaise
¼ t. ground cardamon

1 (16 oz.) can peach, pear or apricot halves
Lettuce leaves
Raisins, nuts or sunflower seeds

Combine cream cheese, honey, mayonnaise and cardamon and mix until smooth. Fill center of fruit with cheese mixture and arrange on lettuce leaves. Garnish with raisins, nuts or sunflower seeds. Serves 5 to 6.

SUGGESTION: For buffet serve several fruits and vary garnishes.

SUSAN THOMPSON

FRUIT SALAD Q

1 lb. fresh spinach or any combination of greens
1 (11 oz.) can mandarin oranges, drained

1 (6 oz.) can pineapple tidbits, drained
2 kiwis, peeled and sliced
½ c. strawberries, sliced

In salad bowl combine all ingredients and toss. Pour dressing over salad and mix well. Serves: 8 to 10.

DRESSING

1 T. honey
2 T. mint apple jelly
2 T. lemon juice

2 T. lime juice
¼ t. lime rind

Combine all ingredients and stir well.

MARY SUMNER

SALADS AND SALAD DRESSINGS

L ISLAND FRUIT SALAD

1 small fresh pineapple, peeled
  and cut into chunks
2 c. melon balls
2 c. peaches, peeled and sliced
1 c. strawberries, sliced

1 c. seedless grapes
1 pear, peeled and sliced
2 bananas, sliced
2 oranges, peeled and sectioned
Lemon juice

In large salad bowl combine all fruits, sprinkling each with lemon juice as prepared. Cover and chill. Pour dressing over fruit and toss gently. Serves 6 to 8.

DRESSING

¾ c. orange juice
¼ c. vegetable oil
1 T. sugar
½ t. salt

½ t. paprika
¼ t. celery seed
½ clove garlic, crushed

Combine all ingredients and mix well.

JACKIE THOMAS

L MINTY FRUIT SALAD

Excellent for brunches and summer evenings.

2 (11 oz.) cans mandarin oranges,
  drained
1-2 (16 oz.) cans pineapple tidbits,
  drained
1 cantaloupe, sliced

1 honeydew melon, sliced
3 kiwis, peeled and sliced
1-2 pts. strawberries, sliced
1 pt. blueberries
Any other seasonal fruit (optional)

In large bowl combine all fruits. Pour marinade over all and toss gently. Chill thoroughly. (Best when refrigerated overnight.) Serves 20.

MARINADE

1 c. honey
1 c. orange juice

½ c. lemon juice
½ c. fresh mint leaves

Combine all ingredients and mix well.

TRICIA GREGORY

SPICED ORANGE SALAD

Delicious with pork or chicken.

1 (11 oz.) can mandarin oranges
½ c. water
¼ c. sugar
8 whole cloves

1 cinnamon stick
1 (3 oz.) pkg. lemon jello
¾ c. orange juice
3 T. lemon juice

74

Mix undrained oranges with water, sugar, cinnamon and cloves in small saucepan. Heat to boiling, reduce heat and simmer for 5 minutes. Remove from heat and discard cinnamon and cloves. Pour hot mixture over jello in bowl, stirring until jello is dissolved. Stir in orange and lemon juices. Pour into four individual molds or one large mold. Refrigerate until firm. Serves 4.

CAROL RANELLI

PINEAPPLE BUTTERMILK SALAD

1 (20 oz.) can crushed pineapple, drained
2 T. sugar
1 (6 oz.) pkg. orange flavored gelatin
2 c. buttermilk
1 (8 oz.) container frozen whipped topping, thawed
1 c. pecans, chopped

Combine pineapple and sugar in small saucepan and bring to boil, stirring occasionally. Remove from heat, add gelatin, stirring until dissolved. Cool. Add buttermilk and stir. Fold in whipped topping and pecans. Spoon into 8" x 12" pan and chill until firm. Cut into 8 squares. Serves 8.

MARGARET ROBBINS

PINEAPPLE STRAWBERRY RING

1 (6 oz.) pkg. strawberry jello
1½ c. boiling water
2 (10 oz.) pkgs. frozen sliced strawberries
1 (13½ oz.) can crushed pineapple, drained
¼ t. salt
1 (8 oz.) pkg. cream cheese at room temperature
½ c. sour cream

Dissolve jello in water and stir in partially thawed strawberries, pineapple and salt. Pour half of mixture into 8 cup mold. Refrigerate until firm. Keep remaining half at room temperature. Beat cream cheese and sour cream until smooth. Spread even layer over chilled firm jello. When remaining jello begins to congeal, spoon over cream cheese layer. Chill overnight. Serves 8.

JANET DOUGLAS

HOLIDAY RASPBERRY SALAD MOLD

Good served with turkey!

1 (10 oz) pkg. frozen raspberries, thawed
2 c. water, divided
½ c. currant jelly
2 (3 oz.) pkgs. red raspberry jello

½ c. sherry
¼ c. lemon juice
2 c. pitted dark, sweet cherries, drained

Drain raspberries, reserving liquid. Combine jelly and ½ c. water. Heat and stir until jelly melts. Add remaining 1½ c. water and the jello. Heat and stir until the jello dissolves. Remove from heat. Add sherry, lemon juice, and reserved raspberry liquid. Chill until partially set. Fold in raspberries and cherries. Pour in lightly greased 6-cup mold and chill until firm. Serves 10 to 12.

JANET DAUGHDRILLE

HARVEY GAMAGE SALAD

Easy main dish summer salad.

London Broil or sirloin, broiled and cut into strips
3-4 tomatoes, cut into wedges
1 purple onion, thinly sliced

Lettuce
Good Seasons Italian Dressing, made with olive oil and red wine vinegar

Combine beef, tomatoes and onion in bowl, pour in dressing and toss well. Arrange on beds of lettuce. Serves 2 to 4.

CAROL SHAPIRO

Q   TACO SALAD

1 lb. hamburger, cooked and drained
1 head lettuce, torn
1 (16 oz) can light red kidney beans, drained

1 (8 oz) pkg. taco chips, crushed
1 c. Cheddar cheese, grated
2 medium tomatoes, diced
½ onion, diced
1 (8 oz.) bottle Catalina dressing

Combine all ingredients, toss and serve. Serves 6 to 8.

DEB POVLISHOCK

VARIATION: Add 1 large sliced avocado for garnish. Try Thousand Island dressing instead of Catalina.

JONI TRUSCOTT

BARBARA'S FAMOUS CHICKEN SALAD

Tasty light entrée for covered dish dinners!

4 chicken breasts with bones
1 small cabbage, shredded
4-5 green onions, chopped
1 (3 oz.) pkg. chicken flavored
    Ramen noodles, uncooked and
    crushed
2 (2¼ oz.) pkgs. sliced almonds
4 T. sesame seeds

1 c. vegetable oil
8 T. wine vinegar
2 t. salt
1 t. pepper
2 T. sugar
Chicken flavor packet from
    Ramen noodles

Place chicken in microwave-safe dish and microwave on high 4 minutes per breast. Let cool. In large salad bowl combine cabbage, onions, noodles, almonds and sesame seeds. Bone chicken and slice into bite-sized pieces; add to cabbage mixture. Combine oil, vinegar, salt, pepper, sugar and seasoning packet and mix well. Pour over salad and serve. Serves 4 to 6.

BARBARA VRANIAN

BLACKENED CHICKEN SALAD   Q

2 chicken breasts, cooked, boned,
    and cut into bite-sized pieces
2-3 T. olive oil
Chef Prudhomme's Blackened
    Chicken Magic
Leaf lettuce

¼ purple onion, thinly sliced
1 (11 oz.) can mandarin oranges,
    drained
2-3 slices bacon, cooked and
    crumbled
Light Italian dressing

Sauté chicken in oil in skillet and sprinkle with Chicken Magic. In salad bowl combine lettuce, onion, oranges and bacon. Top with blackened chicken and toss with dressing. Serves 2 to 4.

CAROL SHAPIRO

CAROLINA PLANTATION SALAD   Q

1 c. shrimp, cooked and deveined
1 T. lemon juice
3 c. chicken, cooked and cut into
    bite-sized pieces

1 c. celery, diced
⅔ c. mayonnaise
Salt to taste
Pepper to taste

Sprinkle shrimp with lemon juice and set aside. Combine chicken, celery, mayonnaise, salt and pepper. Stir in shrimp. Serves 8.

JUSTIN FRACKELTON

SALADS AND SALAD DRESSINGS

L   CUBAN CHICKEN SALAD

1 fryer chicken
1 carrot, sliced
1 stalk celery, sliced
10 peppercorns
Salt to taste

Fresh parsley to taste, chopped
½-¾ c. light mayonnaise
2-3 Granny Smith apples,
   chopped
15-20 green stuffed olives

In Dutch oven combine chicken, carrot, celery, peppercorns, salt and parsley and bring to boil. Continue cooking for 30 minutes or until done. Remove chicken and shred. In salad bowl combine chicken with mayonnaise, apples and olives. Serves 4 to 6.

VARIATIONS: Add cold, cooked pasta, peas, asparagus and pimiento and serve on bed of lettuce.

JOY HEINER

CURRIED CHICKEN SALAD

3 c. chicken or turkey, cooked
   and cubed
1 c. seeded grapes, halved
1 c. celery, chopped
4 T. almonds, toasted

1 c. mayonnaise
1 c. sour cream or plain yogurt
2 t. soy sauce
1 t. curry powder
½ t. salt

In large salad bowl combine chicken or turkey, grapes, celery and almonds. In small bowl combine mayonnaise, sour cream or yogurt, soy sauce, curry powder and salt and mix well. Pour sauce over chicken mixture, stir well and refrigerate. Serves 6.

SUGGESTION: Serve on lettuce, sandwich buns or over cantaloupe slices.

GAIL SMITH

TARRAGON CHICKEN AND RICE SALAD

1 c. mayonnaise
¼ c. parsley, chopped
½ t. dried tarragon
½ t. salt
⅛ t. pepper
2 c. cooked rice

1½ c. chicken, cooked and cubed
½ c. green pepper, chopped
½ c. red pepper, chopped
½ c. carrots, thinly sliced
¼ c. green onions, sliced

In large bowl stir together mayonnaise, parsley, tarragon, salt and pepper. Add rice, chicken, peppers, carrots and onions and toss to coat well. Cover and refrigerate until well chilled. Yield: 5 cups.

ESTHER KELLY

TURKEY SALAD

2 c. turkey breast, cooked and
   cubed
1 c. celery, chopped
2 T. mayonnaise

1 T. sour cream
Lemon juice to taste
Seasoned salt to taste

VINAIGRETTE DRESSING

½ t. salt
⅛ t. freshly ground pepper
¼-½ t. prepared mustard

¼ c. vinegar or lemon juice
¾ c. vegetable oil

Combine ingredients for vinaigrette dressing and mix well. Marinate turkey in dressing overnight. Drain. Mix well with celery, mayonnaise, sour cream, lemon juice, and seasoned salt. Serves 2 generously.

NANCY KENNON

CRAB LOUIS   **Q**

A great summer salad!

1 head lettuce
1 lb. fresh crabmeat
2 eggs, hard-boiled and cut in
   wedges

1-2 large tomatoes, cut in wedges
Salt to taste
Paprika for garnish

Line 4 salad plates with lettuce leaves. Shred remaining lettuce and arrange on leaves. Place ¼ pound crabmeat in center of each plate and circle with egg and tomato wedges. Sprinkle with salt. Pour Louis Dressing over each salad and garnish with paprika. Pass remaining dressing. Serves 4.

LOUIS DRESSING

1 c. mayonnaise
¼ c. sour cream
¼ c. chili sauce

¼ c. onion, chopped
1 t. fresh lemon juice
Salt to taste

Combine all ingredients and mix well. Chill.

CARPIE COULBOURN

SALADS AND SALAD DRESSINGS

Q L YELLOW PEPPERS STUFFED WITH CRAB AND DILL

8 yellow peppers
4 papayas or mangoes, puréed
1½ c. plain low-fat yogurt
2 lbs. lump crabmeat, drained
2 T. yellow pepper, diced
2 T. green pepper, diced
2 T. red pepper, diced
3 T. onion, diced

2 T. celery, diced
½ t. garlic, minced
1 t. black pepper
1 t. fresh dill, minced
5 unsalted soda crackers, crushed
½ t. garlic powder
½ t. onion powder
¼ c. low-fat mayonnaise

Cut tops off yellow peppers and core. Poach peppers in boiling water for 1½ minutes, remove from water, and drain. Blend papaya purée with yogurt and set aside. Combine crab with remaining ingredients. Stuff peppers with crab mixture and place atop papaya and yogurt sauce. Serves 8.

JEAN JONES

Q SHRIMP SALAD SUPREME

¾-1 c. mayonnaise
1 t. salt
¼ t. pepper
6 green onions, chopped
3 T. green olives, sliced

1 (4 oz) jar chopped pimiento
1 green pepper, chopped
2½-3 c. cooked rice
2½-3 c. cauliflower florets
1½-2 lbs. medium cooked shrimp

In a large bowl, combine mayonnaise, salt, pepper, onions, olives, pimiento, and green pepper. Add rice and cauliflower and mix well. Add shrimp and toss. Serves 8 to 10.

SHERRILL SMITH

SHRIMP AND MACARONI SALAD

Delicious as a main course or as a side dish!

1 (8 oz.) pkg. small elbow
  macaroni
¾ jar pimiento, chopped
1 small onion, minced
½ c. celery, chopped

1 c. mayonnaise
3 T. French dressing
2 lbs. cooked shrimp (cut up if
  desired)

One day before serving, cook macaroni 10 to 12 minutes. Drain and cool. Add pimiento, onion, celery, mayonnaise, and French dressing. Refrigerate. On serving day add shrimp. If needed, add additional mayonnaise and French dressing. Serves 12 to 15.

STACY FONVILLE

SHRIMP AND SHELLS

SALAD

1 (12 oz.) box small pasta shells
1 (10 oz.) pkg. frozen peas
1 c. sweet red pepper, diced
½ c. celery, diced

¼ c. red onion, diced
1 lb. shrimp (cooked and
  deveined)

Cook pasta according to instructions on box. Rinse under cold water and drain. Cook peas in ½ c. water until done, but still crisp. Drain and cool. In large bowl combine pasta, peas, pepper, celery and onion. Refrigerate.

DRESSING

1 c. plain low-fat yogurt
3-4 T. mayonnaise
3 T. dried dill weed
2 T. horseradish

2 T. lemon juice
2 t. Dijon mustard
Salt and white pepper to taste

Combine ingredients for dressing and chill. Just before serving, fold dressing into salad, adding shrimp last. Serves 4 to 6.

ELINOR HART

CURRIED SHRIMP SALAD

1 lb. cooked shrimp, chilled
½ green pepper, chopped
1 c. celery, chopped
4 green onions, chopped
½ c. mayonnaise

½ c. sour cream
Juice of one lemon
1½ t. curry powder
½ t. salt
"Chut-Nut" by Raffetto

Mix shrimp, green pepper, celery, and green onions. Combine remaining ingredients except Chut-Nut and add to shrimp mixture. Refrigerate at least 4 hours. Curry flavor intensifies and lemon flavor subsides with time. Top with Chut-Nut just before serving. Serves 4.

VARIATION: Lump crab may be substituted for the shrimp.

MARY MADELYN TUCKER

CURRIED RICE AND SHRIMP SALAD

2 c. white rice, cooked
½ c. stuffed green olives, sliced
1 c. green pepper, chopped

¼ c. green onions, thinly sliced
¼ c. capers
1 lb. small cooked shrimp

DRESSING

2 c. mayonnaise
2 T. curry powder

Juice of ½ lemon
Salt and pepper to taste

Toss salad ingredients. Combine dressing ingredients and blend. Add dressing to salad and mix well. Refrigerate. Serves 8.

KATHY WATSON

SALADS AND SALAD DRESSINGS

WATERFRONT TUNA SALAD

7 medium plums
2 (7 oz.) cans tuna, drained and
   flaked
1 c. low-fat sour cream
2 T. lemon juice
1 lb. fresh green beans
1 head Romaine lettuce

2 hard-boiled eggs, sliced
2 medium red potatoes, cooked,
   peeled, and sliced
Fresh tomatoes, sliced or cut into
   wedges
Lemon slices for garnish
Parsley for garnish

Cut plums into wedges. Combine about half the wedges with the tuna, sour cream, and lemon juice. Steam green beans in a small amount of water for 8 to 10 minutes or until crisp-tender. Drain. Line 4 large individual salad bowls with Romaine lettuce. Shred remaining lettuce and heap into bowls. Scoop tuna mixture into center of each bowl and surround with green beans, eggs, potatoes, tomatoes, and remaining plum wedges. Garnish with lemon slices and parsley, if desired.

DRESSING

⅓ c. white vinegar
¼ c. sugar
1 T. Dijon mustard

1 clove garlic, minced
¼ t. salt
½ c. vegetable oil

Combine dressing ingredients and blend until smooth. Pour over salads. Serves 4.

VARIATION: Grapes may be substituted for plums.

KATHY ELLIS

ANTIPASTO SEA SHELL SALAD

1 lb. shell macaroni, cooked and
   drained
4 oz. Provolone cheese, cut in ¾"
   cubes
4 oz. hard salami, cut in ¾" cubes
4 oz. pepperoni, thinly sliced

3 tomatoes, coarsely chopped
3 ribs celery, chopped
2 medium green peppers, seeded
   and chopped
3 t. onion, chopped

In large salad bowl combine all ingredients. Add dressing, tossing lightly to mix well. Cover with plastic wrap and chill thoroughly in refrigerator. Serves 8 to 10.

DRESSING

¾ c. olive or salad oil
½ c. white or red wine vinegar
2 t. oregano

1½ t. salt
1 t. pepper

Combine all ingredients in blender and mix well.

82

COLD PASTA NEW ORLEANS

½ lb. vermicelli, broken and
    cooked for 4 minutes
1 (3-lb.) chicken, cooked and cubed

1 c. mayonnaise
Fresh parsley, chopped
Cherry tomatoes (optional)

Combine vermicelli with dressing, cover and refrigerate overnight. Add chicken and mayonnaise and refrigerate several hours. Garnish with parsley and cherry tomatoes. Serves 4 to 6.

DRESSING

¼ c. wine vinegar
2 t. Dijon mustard
½ t. chopped garlic

½ c. olive oil
Salt to taste
Pepper to taste

Mix all ingredients well.

ELLEN LeCOMPTE

EASY PASTA SALAD

1 lb. pasta, cooked and drained
1 (16 oz.) bottle Italian dressing
3 tomatoes, diced
2 cucumbers, diced
1 bunch green onions, chopped

1 (8 oz.) jar black olives
8 oz. Parmesan or Romano
    cheese, grated
½-¾ (2.75 oz.) bottle McCormicks
    Salad Supreme

In large bowl combine pasta and dressing, mix well and refrigerate at least 12 hours. Add remaining ingredients and toss. Serves 8 to 10.

MARGARET BARGATZE

FAT-FREE PASTA SALAD   *L*

Good summer salad for cook-outs.

1 (8 oz.) pkg. seashell pasta,
    cooked and drained
½ c. celery, chopped
½ c. onion, chopped

1 large ripe tomato, chopped
½ c. cucumber, chopped
½ c. green pepper, chopped

Combine pasta and vegetables, pour on dressing and chill for several hours. Stir to mix well before serving. Serves 10 to 12.

DRESSING

½ c. fat-free Catalina dressing
½ c. fat-free mayonnaise

Salt to taste
Pepper to taste

Combine dressing ingredients and mix well.

DEB POVLISHOCK

ITALIAN-STYLE PASTA SALAD

4 oz. angel hair pasta or vermicelli
1 (6 oz) jar marinated artichoke
hearts
½ small zucchini, sliced
1 carrot, shredded

2 oz. Genoa sliced salami, cut into
strips
1 c. Mozzarella cheese, grated
2 T. Parmesan cheese, grated

Break pasta in half, cook as directed, drain, and set aside. Drain artichoke hearts and reserve marinade for dressing. Coarsely chop artichoke hearts and halve zucchini slices. Combine all ingredients in a bowl and toss. Pour dressing over top and toss to coat. Store in refrigerator in a covered dish for several hours before serving. Serves 8 to 10.

DRESSING

Marinade from artichoke hearts
2 T. salad oil
2 T. white wine vinegar
½ t. dried oregano

½ t. dried basil
¾ t. dry mustard
1 clove garlic, crushed

Combine in jar and shake thoroughly.

CAROL RANELLI

MEDITERRANEAN PASTA SALAD

1 lb. rotini spirals, cooked and
drained
1 bunch broccoli florets, blanched
and refreshed in cold water
1 (7 oz) can white tuna in spring
water, drained
1½ red peppers, diced
4 T. capers

4 T. red wine vinegar
1 clove garlic
½ T. oregano
½ T. salt
¾ t. coarsely ground black
pepper
¾ c. olive oil

In large bowl combine pasta, broccoli, tuna and peppers and toss. In blender or food processor purée remaining ingredients, except oil. Slowly pour in oil, continuing to blend. Cover vegetables with dressing and toss. Chill. Serves 5 to 6.

KATHY WATSON

PARTY PASTA SALAD

A tasty sweet and sour pasta.

1 lb. shell or corkscrew pasta,
cooked
2 cucumbers, chopped
1 green pepper, chopped
1 large purple onion, chopped

2 (16 oz) cans whole tomatoes,
drained and chopped
Salt to taste
Pepper to taste

84

In large bowl combine pasta and vegetables and pour marinade over all. Season with salt and pepper. Refrigerate several hours. Best if chilled overnight. Serves 10 to 12.

MARINADE

¾ c. vinegar
1¼ c. sugar

Water

In measuring cup, combine vinegar and sugar. Stir, then add enough water to make a total of 2 cups liquid. Put in saucepan and bring to boil until sugar dissolves.

MARGARET BARGATZE

TORTELLINI SALAD

⅓ c. tarragon vinegar
1 t. salt
1 t. dry mustard
1 t. paprika
¼ t. pepper
⅔ c. olive oil
1 clove garlic, crushed

2 t. capers, drained
½ t. oregano
½ t. parsley, chopped
2 T. pine nuts
1 lb. spinach tortellini, cooked and drained

Combine first five ingredients and mix well. Add remaining ingredients except tortellini and mix again. Remove garlic. Pour mixture over tortellini and let stand 2 to 3 hours. Serve cold or at room temperature. (For a more colorful combination, combine spinach tortellini with any colored plain or corkscrew pasta or tomato fettucini.) Serves 2 to 4.

NANCY McCANDLISH

MISS MOLLY'S ASPIC DRESSING   L

1 (24 oz.) container light cottage
     cheese
½ c. Hellman's light mayonnaise
1 medium cucumber, chopped

1 medium onion, chopped
1 t. lemon juice
Salt to taste
Pepper to taste

Combine all ingredients in blender and blend until smooth. Spoon over tomato aspic. Yield: 4 cups.

BERTIE FISHBURNE

BLEU CHEESE WALNUT DRESSING

1 ½ c. walnuts, roasted
2 T. red wine vinegar
2 T. Dijon mustard
⅛ t. salt
⅛ t. pepper

½ c. light cooking oil, (olive,
  canola or peanut)
1 T. fresh parsley, chopped
⅔ c. Roquefort or bleu cheese,
  crumbled

Preheat oven to 275°. Spread walnuts in shallow pan and roast for 30 minutes or until golden. (Watch very carefully as walnuts burn easily.) Remove walnuts from oven and cool. In small bowl combine vinegar, mustard, salt and pepper. Whisk in cooking oil, parsley and cheese. Stir in walnuts. Yield: 3 cups.

MELINDA WAY

Q   CREAMY BLEU CHEESE DRESSING

A great dip for fresh vegetables.

8 oz. bleu cheese
2 c. mayonnaise
1 c. sour cream

3 T. lemon juice
3 oz. cream cheese
1 small onion, finely chopped

Combine all ingredients in blender and blend until well mixed and creamy. Keeps well in refrigerator for 1 month. Yield: 4 cups.

SANDY KING

Q   MOM'S COLE SLAW DRESSING

2 T. sugar
¼ t. salt
1 T. canola oil
1 T. mayonnaise

2 T. cider vinegar
½ T. dry minced onion
½ t. dry mustard

Combine all ingredients and mix well. Pour over cabbage. Chill. Yield: ½ cup.

SHARON PHILLIPS

Q   BLENDER FRENCH DRESSING

1 t. sugar
½ t. paprika
½ t. dry mustard

½ t. salt
⅓ c. vinegar
⅔ c. vegetable oil

Combine all ingredients in blender and mix at high speed until smooth. Yield: 1 cup.

NANCY KENNON

MOM'S FRENCH DRESSING   **Q**

Very good over tossed or fruit salad.

¼ c. canola oil
½ c. cider vinegar
2 cloves garlic, minced

½ c. sugar
½ c. ketchup

Combine all ingredients and mix well. Store in refrigerator. Yield: 1¾ cups.

SHARON PHILLIPS

WHITE FRENCH DRESSING

Everyone will ask for this recipe!

1 t. salt
1 t. white pepper
½ t. sugar
1 t. Dijon mustard
5 T. tarragon vinegar

¼ c. olive oil
½ c. vegetable oil
1 clove garlic, pressed
1 egg, beaten
½ c. table cream

Combine all ingredients and mix well. Refrigerate. Keeps well for 1 week. Yield: 1½ cups.

MARIE CARTER

HONEY MUSTARD DRESSING   **Q**

½ c. olive or vegetable oil
4 T. red wine or raspberry vinegar
2 T. Dijon mustard
2 T. honey

Dash of salt
Dash of pepper
Dash of nutmeg

Combine all ingredients, mix well and chill. Yield: ¾ cup.

SANDY KING

ITALIAN DRESSING   **Q**

¼ c. olive oil
2 T. vinegar
1 t. salt

¼ t. MSG or Accent
¼ t. pepper

Combine all ingredients and mix well. Especially good with mixed lettuce, black olives, tomatoes, mushrooms and feta cheese. Yield: ½ cup.

MARGARET BARGATZE

SALADS AND SALAD DRESSINGS

Q L   CREAMY PEPPER DRESSING

2 c. light mayonnaise
1 c. skim milk
2 T. Parmesan cheese, grated
1 T. freshly ground pepper
1 T. cider vinegar

1 t. fresh lemon juice
1 t. garlic salt
Dash of Tabasco
1 t. Worcestershire

Whisk together all ingredients and chill. Yield: 3¼ cups.

MIMI RHOADS

Q L   RANCH DRESSING

1 c. low-fat buttermilk
½ c. non-fat plain yogurt
1 T. non-fat mayonnaise
1 T. fresh parsley, finely chopped,
   or 1 t. dried flakes
2 medium cloves garlic, crushed

¾ t. onion powder
½ t. dried basil, crushed
¼ t. celery seed
¼ t. salt
¼ t. freshly ground pepper
¼ t. white wine vinegar

Blend buttermilk, yogurt and mayonnaise until smooth. Stir in remaining ingredients until well mixed, cover and refrigerate. Yield: 1¾ cups.

JOAN WILKINS

JEBBIE'S SPINACH SALAD DRESSING

½ c. sugar
¼ c. vinegar
½ c. ketchup

½ c. vegetable oil
¼ t. garlic powder
1 t. salt

Combine all ingredients and mix well. Refrigerate. Serve over fresh spinach, crisp bacon, sesame seeds, shredded mozzarella and chopped spring onions. Yield: 1¾ cups.

ALLYN CROSBY

Q   SPINACH SALAD DRESSING

½ c. sugar
½ c. white vinegar
½ t. salt
½ t. dry mustard

½ t. dry minced onion
1 egg, slightly beaten
½ c. vegetable oil

Combine sugar, vinegar, salt, mustard, onion and egg and mix well. Gradually stir in oil. Chill. Yield: 1½ cups.

LIVY RANDOLPH

NORWOOD DRESSING *Q L*

Great over tomatoes and onions.

1 t. sugar
1 t. salt

½ t. dry mustard
½ c. vinegar

Combine all ingredients and mix well. Yield: ½ cup.

NANCY KENNON

TOMATO DRESSING *Q*

Oil free! Great with summer tomatoes.

1 large plum tomato, seeded and
   coarsely chopped
1 medium clove garlic, minced
1 medium green onion, finely
   chopped
1 t. Dijon mustard
3 T. red wine vinegar

¼ t. dried oregano
¼ t. salt
¼ t. sugar
⅛ t. freshly ground pepper
⅛ t. cayenne pepper
¾ c. V-8 juice
1 T. parsley, minced

In food processor purée tomato, garlic and onion. Add mustard, vinegar, oregano, salt, sugar and peppers and blend. Slowly add V-8 juice and mix well. Pour into jar, add parsley, cover and refrigerate. Yield: 1 cup.

JOAN WILKINS

TOMATO MARINADE I

⅓ c. olive oil
¼ c. red wine vinegar
1 t. salt (optional)
¼ t. pepper
½ clove garlic, minced

2 T. onion, chopped
1 T. fresh parsley, chopped
1 T. fresh basil, chopped, or
   1 t. dried basil

Combine ingredients in a jar, cover tightly, and shake well. Pour over tomatoes, cover, and refrigerate for several hours before serving.

JO ANN CHARLESWORTH

TOMATO MARINADE II *Q L*

1 T. olive oil
3 T. apple cider vinegar
¼ c. brown sugar
1 t. salt

2 T. onion, chopped
1 t. parsley, chopped
1 t. tarragon
1 t. pepper

Combine ingredients and mix well. Pour over tomatoes just before serving.

STUART TROPE

89

SALADS AND SALAD DRESSINGS

FRENCH VINAIGRETTE

A good marinade for fresh vegetables.

¼ c. tarragon vinegar
¾ c. vegetable oil
1 t. sugar
½ t. salt

½ t. dry mustard
½ t. black pepper
1 t. dried parsley
1 t. dried chervil

Combine all ingredients and mix well. Refrigerate. Yield: 1 cup.

KATHY WATSON

NEW ORLEANS VINAIGRETTE

¾ c. olive oil
¼ c. vinegar
1 t. salt
¼ t. pepper
½ t. sugar

½ t. dry mustard
½ t. Worcestershire
½ t. Accent
Bleu cheese to taste, crumbled
(optional)

Combine all ingredients and mix well. Refrigerate several hours before using. Yield: 1 cup.

MARGARET BARGATZE

Grilled Foods

What does my tummy feel like when it's full? I don't know because my tummy's hardly ever full.
Harrison Jones, '03

Beef:
Beef Saté Indonesia **Q** 94
Grilled Flank Steak 94
Marinated Shish Kabobs 94
Poultry:
Barbecue Chicken I **L** 95
Barbecue Chicken II 95
Cajun-Style Chicken **L** 96
Southside Curried
    Marmalade Chicken 96
Grilled Fruited Chicken **L** ... 96
Kenzie's Chicken 97
Chicken Kossuth.............. 97
Grilled Lemon Chicken **L** ... 98
Lemon Mustard Chicken **L** .. 98
Marinated Chicken Breasts... 99
Chicken Teriyaki.............. 99
Vegi-Chicken Grill **L** 100
Raspberry Grilled Cornish
    Hens **L** 100
No-Salt Fajitas 101
Pork:
Grilled Pork Tenderloin........ 101
Garlic Grilled Pork
    Tenderloin **L** 102

Teriyaki Pork Chops **Q** 102
Barbecued Spareribs 102
Seafood:
Ellen's Seafood Kabobs **Q** .. 103
Grilled Shrimp 103
Easy Grilled Shrimp **Q** 104
Cajun Grilled Shrimp **L** 104
Marinated Thai Shrimp 104
Grilled Rockfish Coriander ... 105
Barbecued Swordfish 105
Grilled Tuna
    Mediterranean **L** 105
Marinated Swordfish
    or Tuna 106
Marinated Tuna Steaks 106
Sauces and Marinades:
Barbecue Sauce 107
Carolina-Style Barbecue
    Sauce **L** 107
Beef Marinade 107
Francie's Marinade 108
Low-Calorie Marinade for
    Beef or Chicken **L** 108
Fish Marinade 108

GRILLED FOODS

Q   BEEF SATÉ INDONESIA

2 lbs. flank steak, sliced crosswise
    into ½" thick strips

MARINADE

¼ c. olive oil
1 c. onion, chopped
4 cloves garlic, pressed
1 t. fresh ginger, grated
¾ c. water

3 T. soy sauce
4 t. chili powder
1 T. peanut butter
1 T. turmeric
¼ c. brown sugar

Heat oil in skillet over medium-high heat. Add onion, garlic, and ginger and
sauté until soft. Add remaining marinade ingredients and stir to make a
paste. Simmer on low for 2 minutes. Remove from heat, add meat, and stir
to coat well. Thread meat onto skewers when cool enough to handle. Grill
as usual. Serves 6 to 10.

ELIZABETH STOYKO

GRILLED FLANK STEAK

1½ lbs. flank steak

MARINADE

¼ c. soy sauce (light or regular)
¾ c. vegetable oil
¼ c. honey
2 T. vinegar

2 T. green onion, finely chopped
1 clove garlic, minced
1½ t. ground ginger

Cut shallow diagonal slashes in each side of steak. Mix together marinade
ingredients. Pour marinade over steak in a sealable plastic bag or close-
fitting baking dish. Cover and marinate 4 to 6 hours, turning meat occasionally. Place steak about 4 inches above hot coals. Cook until nicely
browned, about 5 to 6 minutes. Turn and baste with marinade. Cook 4 to 6
additional minutes for medium rare, or longer to desired doneness. To
serve, cut thin slanting slices diagonally across the grain of the steak. Serves
3 to 4.

LYNN FELTON

MARINATED SHISH KABOBS

2 lbs. lean beef, cut in 1" cubes
1 large onion, cut in 1" sections

1 green pepper, cut in 1" sections
8-12 large mushrooms

MARINADE

1 clove garlic	2 T. brown sugar
¼ c. olive oil	½-1 t. ginger
¼ c. fresh lemon juice	1 t. lemon peel, grated
⅛-¼ c. soy sauce	

Crush garlic clove and add to olive oil to release flavor. Add remaining marinade ingredients. Marinate beef overnight for maximum flavor. Turn once in the morning. Steam the cut vegetables for a few minutes to soften slightly. Place vegetables and beef cubes onto skewers and baste kabobs with marinade. Cook on grill for 10 to 15 minutes, depending on your taste. Serve over rice. Serves 4 to 6.

JOANNE RAMSEY

BARBECUE CHICKEN I   *L*

2 chickens, cut up

SAUCE

¼ c. cooking oil, or butter or margarine, melted	2 T. salt
1 c. cider vinegar	½ t. pepper
¼ c. water	1 t. poultry seasoning

Combine sauce ingredients. Grill chicken as usual, basting every 5 minutes with sauce, or as often as needed to prevent burning. Cook until meat is very tender.

CAROL RANELLI

BARBECUE CHICKEN II

The children's favorite chicken!

8 chicken breast halves, boned and skinned

MARINADE

2 T. Dijon mustard	1 t. Worcestershire
4 T. vinegar	2 cloves garlic, minced
4 T. molasses	Dash of Tabasco
½ c. ketchup	

Combine marinade ingredients. Marinate chicken in half of the marinade for at least one hour, or as long as overnight. Grill or broil for 10 minutes. Turn and coat chicken with reserved marinade and continue to cook for 5 minutes longer. There will be extra marinade, which can be used as a sauce for serving, or refrigerated for later use. Serves 4 to 8.

LEE MERRICK

95

L   CAJUN-STYLE CHICKEN

4-6 chicken breast halves, skinned

MARINADE

½ t. fresh garlic, minced
1 t. onion, minced
1 t. parsley, chopped
1 t. celery flakes

1 T. stone ground or Dijon mustard
1 T. balsamic vinegar
⅛ t. cayenne pepper
¼ c. extra light olive oil

Mix marinade ingredients in a bowl, add chicken, and stir well. Seal bowl and place in the refrigerator for 1 hour. Place chicken on grill over low coals and cook until well done, about 30 minutes. Turn only once during cooking time. Place on warm platter and serve immediately. Serves 4 to 6.

BILL FLOWERS

SOUTHSIDE CURRIED MARMALADE CHICKEN

2 (3½ lb.) chickens, quartered or
   8-10 chicken breast halves,
   boned

GLAZE

1 c. orange marmalade
1 c. Dijon mustard
¼ c. honey

1 T. curry powder
1 T. lemon juice

Simmer glaze ingredients in heavy saucepan over low heat for 5 minutes, stirring constantly. Cool. (Glaze can be prepared up to 3 days ahead, covered and refrigerated. Bring to room temperature before using.) Brush chicken pieces on all sides with glaze and let stand at room temperature for 1 hour. Grill chicken over medium heat, basting with remaining glaze until done. Serves 6 to 8.

ANNE NELSON MORCK

L   GRILLED FRUITED CHICKEN

6-8 chicken breast halves, boned

MARINADE

¼ c. orange marmalade (light or
   reduced sugar, if desired)
¼ c. Dijon mustard

2 T. lime or lemon juice
½ t. fresh ginger, grated

Combine marinade ingredients. Brush on both sides of chicken breasts. Marinate for 30 minutes at room temperature or cover and marinate for 2 hours in the refrigerator. Grill over medium coals for 5 to 6 minutes or until done. Serves 6 to 8.

SUSAN OTTENI

KENZIE'S CHICKEN

Tasty and different. Good served with orzo.

12 (4-5 oz) chicken breast halves,
    boned and skinned

MARINADE

¾ c. fresh lemon juice	1½ t. light salt
¾ c. vegetable oil	¼ t. thyme
¼ c. onion, minced	1½ T. dry mustard

Mix marinade ingredients together. With a sharp knife, score both sides of each breast in a cross-hatch pattern, about ⅛" deep. Pour ⅓ of the marinade into a shallow glass bowl. Add half the chicken in a single layer and cover with another ⅓ of the marinade. Put the remaining breasts in a layer on top and pour on the remaining marinade. Cover and refrigerate for 3 hours or overnight, turning occasionally. Remove from refrigerator for 30 minutes and bring to room temperature. Preheat broiler or grill. If broiling, place on rack about 4 inches from heat for 3 minutes on each side. Juices from chicken should run clear when chicken is pierced with a fork. Serve warm. Serves 10 to 12.

CARTER FILER

CHICKEN KOSSUTH

Chicken pieces of your choice,
    to serve 8

MARINADE AND BASTING SAUCE

1 pt. vinegar	3 T. ketchup
1 T. salt (or less)	Juice of 2 lemons
1 T. brown mustard	Lots of black pepper

Combine marinade and basting sauce ingredients and mix well. Pierce meaty parts of chicken with fork and marinate for at least 2 hours or all day in the refrigerator.

GRILLED FOODS

BROWNING SAUCE

2 T. sugar
1 T. salt
½ c. margarine or butter
6 T. ketchup

2 T. mustard
2 T. Worcestershire
1 t. black pepper

When ready to grill, prepare browning sauce by combining all ingredients in a saucepan and heating just enough to blend. If sauce is too thick to spread, add a bit of vinegar. Baste chicken with marinade and basting sauce as you grill over a low fire for 40 to 60 minutes. About 15 minutes before chicken is done, start basting with browning sauce. Serves 8.

ALLYN CROSBY

L   GRILLED LEMON CHICKEN

8 pieces of chicken, skinned
Fresh parsley for garnish

1 lemon, sliced, for garnish

MARINADE

¼ c. fresh lemon juice
¼ c. honey
⅛ t. paprika

⅛ t. cayenne pepper
⅛ t. dry mustard

Combine marinade ingredients and mix well. Place chicken in an 8" square glass baking dish. Cover with marinade and keep at room temperature for 30 minutes, turning several times. When ready to cook, this can be broiled or grilled. For oven broiler: broil on top rack for 15 minutes on each side. For grill: cook over medium coals for 30 to 40 minutes, brushing with marinade several times. Garnish with parsley and lemon slices. Serves 8.

TORREY SHUFORD

L   LEMON MUSTARD CHICKEN

8 chicken breast halves, boned
and skinned

MARINADE

½ c. lemon juice
1 T. lemon zest, finely chopped
¼ c. Dijon mustard
¼ c. finely chopped herbs
(combination of thyme, basil,

oregano, rosemary, and/or
parsley)
¾ t. salt
¼ t. coarsely ground pepper

Combine marinade ingredients and mix well. (If fresh herbs are not available, use 4 tablespoons of dried herbs.) In a large non-metallic dish arrange chicken pieces and cover with marinade. Refrigerate 2 to 4 hours. Prepare grill for medium heat. Grill chicken 3 inches from coals for 7 to 10 minutes on each side. Serves 6 to 8.

NANCY LIPSCOMB

MARINATED CHICKEN BREASTS

12 chicken breast halves, boned
   and skinned

MARINADE

1 c. soy sauce
½ c. pineapple juice
¼ c. sherry

¼ c. brown sugar
¾ t. garlic, minced

Combine marinade ingredients. Place chicken in a large shallow pan and pour marinade over chicken. Marinate for 30 minutes. Grill chicken, basting with marinade every 5 minutes. Cooking time is about 15 minutes. For a larger crowd, increase accordingly. Serves 10 to 12.

SALLIE CROSS

CHICKEN TERIYAKI

Easy and terrific!

10-12 chicken breast halves,
   boned

MARINADE

1 c. soy sauce
1 c. olive oil
½ c. fresh lime juice
1 T. honey

2 slices fresh ginger
2 gloves garlic, crushed
Salt, black and red pepper, to
   taste

Combine marinade ingredients. Marinate chicken in mixture for several hours in the refrigerator. Grill 3 to 4 minutes per side. Serves 8 to 10.

NANCY McCANDLISH

GRILLED FOODS

L   VEGI-CHICKEN GRILL

4 chicken breast halves, boned
   and skinned
2 (12″ x 18″) sheets heavy duty
   aluminum foil
1 small onion, sliced
1 t. Dijon mustard
1 t. mayonnaise
2 carrots, pared, cut in strips

1 small zucchini, unpared, cut in
   ¼″ slices
1 (2-3 oz.) can sliced mushrooms,
   drained
⅛ t. cracked pepper
⅛ t. dried basil
¼ t. garlic salt
1 T. butter
2 t. Parmesan cheese, or to taste

Pound chicken breasts to ¼″ thickness between wax paper sheets. Tear foil into 4 pieces. Place one slice of onion on each piece of foil, then layer with the chicken, one fourth of the mustard-mayonnaise mixture, the vegetables, spices, and a dab of butter. Seal packets by folding the edges together, and cook over medium-hot coals for 20 to 30 minutes, or until tender. Cut an X in the foil, sprinkle each packet with ½ teaspoon of Parmesan cheese and heat until cheese is melted. (This can also be cooked in a 450° oven for 18 to 20 minutes.) Serves 4.

KATHY WHITE

L   RASPBERRY GRILLED CORNISH HENS

4 (1½ lb.) cornish hens

MARINADE

⅔ c. low sugar red raspberry
   spread
⅓ c. crème de cassis

1 T. packed brown sugar
½ t. ground ginger

Remove giblets from hens. Rinse with cold water and pat dry. Split hens lengthwise, using a sharp knife. Combine marinade ingredients in a small saucepan and cook over medium heat until thoroughly heated, but do not allow to boil. Coat grill with cooking spray. Grill hens 6 inches over medium-hot coals for 20 to 30 minutes, turning and basting with marinade mixture every 5 minutes. Serves 8.

SUGGESTION: The skin may easily be removed from the hens before cooking. After splitting hen down the middle, pull skin to each side and then over each leg. Remove skin from leg. Snip skin around wings. Pull skin over each wing and remove. Reduce cooking time by a few minutes to prevent drying out.

PAT MARTIN

100

GRILLED FOODS

NO-SALT FAJITAS

FAJITA SEASONING

2 t. black pepper
2 t. garlic powder
½ t. oregano

½ t. onion powder
⅛ t. each of basil, cardamon,
 cumin, fenugreek, thyme

Mix all ingredients and store in jar.

4 chicken breast halves, boned
 and skinned
2 onions, thinly sliced
2 green or red peppers, thinly
 sliced

8 flour tortillas
1 (8 oz.) container sour cream
Guacamole

Place chicken breasts in ovenproof dish and sprinkle fajita seasoning generously on both sides. Marinate for 1 to 2 hours or overnight in the refrigerator. Grill chicken until done. Sauté onions and peppers in a small amount of oil until slightly cooked. Slice chicken and add to vegetable mixture. Serve with tortillas (softened in microwave for 15 seconds each). Spread each tortilla with sour cream, guacamole, pico de gallo (if desired), chicken, onions, and peppers. Roll up and enjoy. Serves 4.

PICO DE GALLO (OPTIONAL)

1 onion, diced
1 tomato, diced

3-4 jalapeño peppers, diced

Mix all ingredients and chill.

BARBARA VRANIAN

GRILLED PORK TENDERLOIN

2 (¾-1 lb.) pork tenderloins

MARINADE

½ c. peanut oil
⅓ c. soy sauce
¼ c. red wine vinegar
3 T. lemon juice

2 T. Worcestershire
1 T. fresh parsley, chopped
1 T. dry mustard
1½ t. cracked pepper

Combine marinade ingredients. Place in a shallow container or heavy-duty zip-top plastic bag. Add tenderloins, turning to coat. Cover or seal and chill for 4 hours or overnight. Remove tenderloins from marinade. Grill, covered, 6 inches from medium coals (300° to 400°) for 12 to 14 minutes, or until done. Turn and baste once during cooking time. Serves 6.

TORREY SHUFORD

L GARLIC GRILLED PORK TENDERLOIN

2 (¾-1 lb.) pork tenderloins or thick
  center-cut pork chops

MARINADE

3 T. olive oil	½ t. salt
1 T. white wine vinegar	¼ t. pepper
2 t. fresh rosemary, chopped	2 cloves garlic, crushed

Combine marinade ingredients and stir well. Place meat in a dish and brush on marinade to coat. Cover and chill for 3 hours. Grill meat covered over hot coals for 12 to 15 minutes, or until meat thermometer registers 160°, turning once. Cut into slices and serve. When grilling thick cuts, cook 7 minutes on first side, then 6 minutes on second side. Serves 6.

CAROL SMITH

Q TERIYAKI PORK CHOPS

A family favorite!

8 (½") lean pork chops

MARINADE

½ c. teriyaki sauce	½ c. Italian dressing

Combine marinade ingredients and marinate chops for 20 minutes, turning frequently. Grill or broil for 5 minutes on each side. Brush with marinade while cooking. (This marinade is also great with chicken.) Serves 6 to 8.

SALLIE CROSS

BARBECUED SPARERIBS

Great for summer cookouts!

2 racks baby back spareribs	1½ T. salt
⅓ c. vinegar	1 onion

Have your butcher roll each rack of ribs and tie it. Simmer rolled ribs with vinegar, salt, onion, and enough water to cover for 45 minutes. This can be done in advance.

SAUCE

1 c. ketchup	1 t. dry mustard
12 drops Tabasco	Garlic salt
5 T. vinegar	Salt
2 T. A-1 or Worcestershire	

Combine sauce ingredients and mix well. Untie ribs and place flat on the grill. Cook for 20 to 30 minutes about 8 to 10 inches above the fire, turning and basting ribs with sauce every 5 minutes. Do not let fire flame, as sauce burns. Cut ribs between the bones and serve with extra sauce. Serves 4.

RUTH LEISY

ELLEN'S SEAFOOD KABOBS   **Q**

Quick, easy, and delicious for a crowd!

1 lb. large shrimp

1 lb. sea scallops (or any combination you prefer)

MARINADE

Juice of 1 lemon
2 T. olive oil
2 cloves garlic, minced
1 t. coarse salt

½ t. freshly ground pepper
Any fresh vegetables (mushrooms, peppers, tomatoes, etc.)

Mix marinade ingredients together and toss with seafood for 5 to 10 minutes. Skewer seafood and vegetables. Preheat grill until very hot. Grill skewers near heat just until browned, then turn and lightly brown again. This can also be broiled in the oven for about 5 minutes on one side, then 3 minutes on the other. Serves 4 to 6.

DEBBIE CUNNINGHAM

GRILLED SHRIMP

2 lbs. jumbo shrimp

MARINADE

3 cloves garlic, finely chopped
1 medium onion, finely chopped
¼ c. parsley, chopped
1 t. basil

1 t. dry mustard
1 t. salt
½ c. olive or peanut oil
Juice of 1 lime

Devein shrimp using sharp knife, but leave shells intact. Combine marinade ingredients and add shrimp. Let marinate for 4 to 5 hours. Grill shrimp on wire mesh grill topper over hot coals for 5 minutes, or until done. Serves 4 to 6.

SARA BAIRD

Q EASY GRILLED SHRIMP

2 lbs. shrimp, shelled and
 deveined

MARINADE

4 cloves garlic, minced
½ c. butter or margarine
¼ c. fresh lime juice

2 T. fresh parsley, chopped
Freshly ground pepper to taste
Dash of paprika

Sauté garlic in butter and remove from heat. Stir in lime juice, parsley, pepper and paprika. Arrange shrimp in a hinged grilling basket (or thread on skewers) and baste liberally with the marinade. Grill over medium-hot coals for 3 to 5 minutes, basting and turning often. Serves 4.

TYLER KILPATRICK

L CAJUN GRILLED SHRIMP

This dish is fat-free, salt-free, and delicious!

16-20 shrimp
No-oil Italian dressing
Chef Prudhomme's Cajun Magic
 Seasoning (or other Cajun
 seasoning)

Cocktail sauce

Peel and devein shrimp. Place in flat dish and pour on Italian dressing. Marinate for 2 hours or overnight. Remove shrimp from marinade and put on skewers. Sprinkle a little Cajun seasoning on each shrimp and grill 1 to 2 minutes on each side. Serve with cocktail sauce. Serves 4.

BARBARA VRANIAN

MARINATED THAI SHRIMP

1½ lbs. jumbo shrimp

MARINADE

½ c. soy sauce
½ c. light vegetable oil
2 T. lemon juice

1 t. ginger
3 cloves garlic, finely minced

Peel, devein, and wash shrimp. Place in bowl. Mix marinade ingredients and pour over shrimp. Cover and marinate at least 3 hours. Skewer shrimp and cook over hot coals for 4 to 5 minutes on each side. Serve immediately. Serves 6.

CELIE GEHRING

GRILLED ROCKFISH CORIANDER

2 lbs. rockfish, filleted and skinned

MARINADE

½ t. ground coriander
1 T. freshly squeezed lemon juice
1 T. balsamic vinegar

1 T. stone ground or Dijon mustard
¼ c. extra light olive oil

Pat fillets dry and set aside. Mix marinade ingredients, add fish, and stir well. Seal bowl and place in refrigerator for 1 hour. Place fish on grill over low coals, turning once and cooking until done, about 15 to 20 minutes. Place on warm platter and serve immediately. (This marinade also works well with tuna, dolphin, and Spanish mackerel.) Serves 4.

BILL FLOWERS

BARBECUED SWORDFISH

6 (6 oz) swordfish or tuna steaks, 1"
thick

2 T. unsalted butter
Pepper to taste

MARINADE

2 c. fresh orange juice
½ c. low-salt soy sauce
1 c. red wine vinegar
½ c. olive oil
1 onion, finely chopped
1 t. dried red pepper flakes

1 t. ground cumin
1 t. or more freshly ground pepper
1½ T. whole mixed pickling spice
1 (6 oz) can tomato paste
½ c. sugar

Mix marinade ingredients together. Arrange steaks in dish large enough to hold them all in a single layer. Pour the marinade over them and marinate for 24 hours, or overnight. Drain the steaks, reserving the marinade. Grill steaks on oiled rack 3 to 4 inches above glowing coals for 5 to 7 minutes on each side, basting with reserved marinade. Top each steak with a dab of butter and fresh pepper. Serves 6.

MIA NORTON

GRILLED TUNA MEDITERRANEAN ***L***

1 lb. fresh tuna steaks, ½-¾" thick
1 t. olive oil

Lemon wedges
Fresh cilantro or parsley sprigs

MARINADE

1 T. capers, rinsed and drained	½ t. dried rosemary, crushed
1 T. olive oil	¼ t. salt
3 T. white wine	Freshly ground black pepper to
2 T. lemon juice	taste
1 clove garlic, crushed	

Combine all marinade ingredients. Arrange tuna steaks in dish and cover with marinade. Let marinate for 20 minutes, turning after 10 minutes. Grill as usual. If broiling, brush foil-lined baking sheet with oil and arrange the steaks on the sheet. Pour half of marinade over steaks. Broil for 4 minutes until top is slightly seared. Turn the steaks over with a spatula and pour remaining marinade over them. Broil another 4 minutes, or until fish flakes easily with a fork. Garnish with lemon and fresh cilantro or parsley. Serves 4.

DEANE MOUNTCASTLE

MARINATED SWORDFISH OR TUNA

This tastes even better on a Jenn-Aire.
The fish seems to retain its moisture better.

6 swordfish or tuna steaks, at least
   ½" thick

MARINADE

½ c. soy sauce	¼ c. vegetable oil
½ c. dry sherry	1 clove garlic, crushed
1 T. lemon juice	

Mix marinade ingredients in shallow container or heavy plastic food bag and add fish. Refrigerate no longer than 3 hours. Grill until just cooked through, about 5 to 8 minutes per side. This may vary depending upon heat of the coals. Serves 6.

CAROL SMITH

MARINATED TUNA STEAKS

1½-2 lbs. fresh tuna steaks

MARINADE

¼ c. sesame oil	1 T. brown sugar
½ c. vegetable oil	¼ c. soy sauce
¼ c. rice wine vinegar	2 T. chopped ginger
2 T. vermouth	3 cloves garlic, minced

Combine marinade ingredients and mix well. Marinate tuna steaks in mixture for 4 hours. Remove from marinade and grill or broil. Serves 3 to 4.

BRUCE BASKERVILLE

BARBECUE SAUCE

Easy and everyone loves it!

1½ c. ketchup
1 (6 oz.) can frozen lemonade
¾ c. water
¼ c. Worcestershire
¼ c. prepared mustard
¼ c. corn oil

2 T. onion, minced
1 t. MSG
Lemon pepper to taste
Paprika to taste
Garlic salt to taste

In saucepan, mix all ingredients. Heat to boil, reduce heat, and simmer for 5 minutes. Delicious on chicken, pork chops, or ribs.

LIBBY ROBERTSON

CAROLINA-STYLE BARBECUE SAUCE   *L*

1 large onion, finely chopped
2 T. oregano
2 T. garlic powder
4 T. Texas Pete
1 (6 oz.) can tomato paste
2 T. black pepper
2 T. No-Salt

1 T. cayenne pepper
2½ c. vinegar
1½ c. brown mustard
1½ c. ketchup
1 c. liquid brown sugar
8 T. sugar substitute
2 T. celery seed

Brown onion in saucepan. Combine rest of ingredients and bring to a boil. Reduce heat and simmer for 1 hour. Sauce is then ready to serve on sliced blade roast, or to be mixed into chopped beef or pork barbecue. Serves 40.

JAMES COCHRANE

BEEF MARINADE

Excellent for London Broil!

½ c. lemon juice
½ c. soy sauce
2-3 cloves garlic, chopped or
   pressed

¾ c. vegetable oil
¼ c. Worcestershire

Mix all ingredients in 9" x 13" pan. Put beef in pan and pierce with a fork on both sides. Let marinate in refrigerator overnight, turning occasionally, or at room temperature for several hours, turning often. Drain marinade and grill beef to desired doneness. Serves 6 to 10.

BARBARA PARKER

FRANCIE'S MARINADE

For chicken, swordfish, or tuna.

⅓ c. soy sauce
2 t. lime peel, grated
¼ c. lime juice
2 cloves garlic, minced

1 T. Dijon mustard
¼ c. peanut or vegetable oil
¼ c. scallions, chopped
½ t. ground pepper

Mix all ingredients. Marinate chicken or fish 2 to 4 hours. Baste occasionally as you broil or grill.

ALLYN CROSBY

L   LOW-CALORIE MARINADE FOR BEEF OR CHICKEN

½ c. brewed coffee
½ c. light soy sauce
1 T. vinegar

1 T. Worcestershire
1 medium onion, chopped

Mix all ingredients together. Place meat in a zip-top plastic bag with marinade for 12 to 24 hours. Grill or broil meat as usual.

MIMI RHOADS

FISH MARINADE

1½ lbs. fish (swordfish works well)

MARINADE

¼ c. soy sauce
¼ c. sherry
¼ c. onion, minced
2 T. vegetable oil
½ t. fresh ginger or ¼ t. powdered
   ginger

2 T. wine vinegar
1 T. sugar
1 t. garlic, minced
½ t. dry mustard

Combine marinade ingredients and pour over fish in a glass dish. Cover and refrigerate for 3 to 6 hours, turning frequently. Grill fish for 8 to 10 minutes per inch of thickness. Baste with marinade while cooking. Serves 3 to 4.

LEIGH FARMER

MEATS & GAME

Meats and Game

Daddy scares me when he's in the kitchen.
Will Cosby, '05

Beef:
Boeuf Bourguignon 112
Lazy Beef Casserole 112
Beef Broccoli Stir-Fry **Q L**.... 113
Beef Stroganoff Without
  Panic 113
Lean and Light
  Stroganoff **L** 114
Flank Steak Teriyaki 114
Marinated Broiled Flank
  Steak **L**.................... 114
Boeuf Au Gingembre......... 115
Rosy Eye of Round Roast 115
Easy Barbecued Brisket....... 115
Finland Brisket 116
Rocky Mountain Brisket
  With Barbecue Sauce...... 116

Ground Beef:
Chuck Wagon Skillet.......... 116
Five Spice Beef and Rice..... 117
Meatloaf with Potato and
  Mozzarella 117
Moist and Easy Meatloaf..... 118
Gumbo Sloppy Joes **Q** 118
Sloppy Joes **Q**.............. 118
Spaghetti Pie 118
Taco Casserole **Q**.......... 119
Upside Down Pizza........... 119
Quick and Easy Beef 'N
  Cheese Pie 120

Veal:
Veal Cutlets with Garlic
  Mint Sauce **Q L** 120
Veal à la Normande **Q**..... 120
Veal à L'Orange **L** 121
Zurich Geschnitzeltes **Q**..... 121

Lamb:
Armenian Meatballs 122
Rack of Lamb with
  Raspberry Mint Sauce...... 122

Lamb Roast................... 123
Stuffed Leg of Lamb.......... 123

Pork:
Easy Ham in the Crock Pot... 124
Zucchini Sausage Boats 124
Braised Pork with Pickles...... 124
Pork Chops with Black
  Currant Preserves.......... 125
Creole-Style Pork
  Chops **L** 125
Lemon Barbecued Pork
  Chops 126
Roast Pork with Sweet and
  Sour Sauce................. 126
Breaded Pork Tenderloin
  Royale...................... 126
Mushroom Pork **Q L**........ 127
Pork Strips with Oyster
  Sauce **Q**.................. 127
Pork Tenderloin with Raisin
  Sauce **Q**.................. 128
Pork Burritos or Chalupas..... 128
Bourbon Pork Tenderloin
  with Mustard Sauce 129
Orange Pork Tenderloin **L**.. 129
Pork Tenderloin with
  Rosemary and Thyme **L**... 130

Meat Seasoning:
Demi-Glacé 130

Game:
Doves Cacciatore 131
Island Farm Doves 131
Peter's Favorite Doves 132
Cypress Banks Barbecued
  Duck....................... 132
Grilled Wood Ducks **L**....... 133
Grilled Quail **L**.............. 133
Tuckahoe Vermouth
  Venison..................... 133
Schnucki's Spiedies **L**....... 134

111

MEATS AND GAME

BOEUF BOURGUIGNON

Better if prepared one day ahead.

4 lbs. London Broil, cut into 1½"
   cubes
¼ c. olive oil
¼ c. sherry
¼ c. butter
1 slice ham, ¼" thick, diced
1 lb. small fresh mushrooms,
   quartered
3 cloves garlic, minced
2 T. tomato paste

¼ c. soy sauce
6 T. flour
2 (10½ oz) cans beef broth
4 c. red Burgundy wine, divided
1 (14 oz) jar whole small white
   onions
½ t. thyme
3-4 T. fresh parsley, minced
Salt and pepper to taste

Heat oil and brown beef in oven-proof casserole on top of the stove. Transfer beef to a large bowl using a slotted spoon and pour sherry over top. Melt butter in casserole and sauté ham, garlic, and mushrooms until mushrooms are soft, then transfer to the bowl with the beef using a slotted spoon. Remove casserole from heat and add tomato paste, soy sauce, and flour. Whisk to make a smooth paste. Add beef broth and 1 c. wine. Return to burner and bring to a boil over low heat. Add beef, ham, garlic, mushrooms, onions, thyme, parsley, salt, and pepper. Bake at 350° for 4 hours, adding 1 c. remaining wine every 45 minutes. If prepared a day ahead, reheat at 325° for 1 hour. Serves 6.

MARIE CARTER

LAZY BEEF CASSEROLE

2 lbs. beef chuck or stew beef, cut
   into 2" chunks
1 c. Burgundy, Claret, or other red
   wine
1 (10½ oz.) can undiluted
   consommé

¾ t. salt
Cracked pepper
½ t. rosemary
1 medium onion, sliced
¼ c. sifted flour
¼ c. bread crumbs

Combine beef, wine, consommé, salt, pepper, rosemary, and onion in a casserole. Mix flour with bread crumbs and stir into beef mixture. Cover and bake at 300° for about 3 hours, or until beef is tender. Serves 4.

TORREY SHUFORD

BEEF BROCCOLI STIR-FRY   *Q L*

2 T. reduced-salt soy sauce
1 T. cornstarch
1 T. white vinegar
1 T. fresh ginger, minced
1 t. clove garlic, minced
1 t. red pepper flakes
¾ lb. round steak

2 t. vegetable oil, divided
1 small bunch broccoli, cut in florets
2 carrots, sliced diagonally
1 bunch green onions, sliced
¾ c. low-sodium beef broth or water

Combine first 6 ingredients in a bowl. Slice steak across the grain 1/8" deep and toss with soy sauce mixture. Marinate for 10 minutes. Stir-fry beef in a wok with 1 t. oil. Remove meat from wok. Add the remaining 1 t. oil, broccoli, carrots, and onion. Stir-fry for 1 minute. Add broth, and cook vegetables until tender, about 5 to 7 minutes. Return meat to wok and heat thoroughly. Serves 4.

JEAN JONES

BEEF STROGANOFF WITHOUT PANIC

2 lbs. top round, cut in ½" strips
3 onions, thinly sliced
¾ c. butter, divided
1 T. dry mustard
1 t. salt

¼ t. pepper
1 c. sour cream, divided
2 bay leaves
1 T. flour
Fresh parsley, chopped

The day before serving, sauté onions slowly in ½ c. butter until light golden in color, about 20 minutes. Remove from heat. Sauté beef strips in ¼ c. butter, just long enough for them to turn gray and release their juices. Strain this juice over the onions. Stir mustard, salt, pepper, and 1 T. sour cream into the onion mixture. Bury the bay leaves in this and add the meat. Mix well, place on low heat, and simmer covered gently for 45 minutes, stirring occasionally. Remove from heat, cool, and refrigerate overnight. (The dish can be frozen at this point.) Fifteen minutes before serving, simmer again on a low flame until done. Cooking time will depend on the quality of the meat. Sprinkle with flour, stir well, and add remaining sour cream and continue cooking on very low heat, stirring constantly until well-blended. Do not boil. Garnish with chopped parsley and serve over cooked broad or fine noodles.

MIM SCHUTE

MEATS AND GAME

L LEAN AND LIGHT STROGANOFF

1¼-1½ lbs. lean flank steak
Plain meat tenderizer
1 large onion, thinly sliced
1 t. beef bouillon
1 c. water
2 T. parsley

2 T. ketchup
1 t. Dijon mustard
½ c. light sour cream
2 T. flour
2 T. dry wine (red or white)
Cooked noodles

Score steak in a diamond pattern, sprinkle with tenderizer, and let stand for 20 minutes. Sear or grill both sides of meat over high heat. (This can be done up to a day ahead. Refrigerate meat after it has cooled to room temperature.) Spray a large skillet with no-stick cooking spray. Sauté onion in skillet. Add bouillon, water, parsley, ketchup, and mustard. Cook uncovered, stirring occasionally. Slice meat thinly against the grain. Blend sour cream with flour. Stir into skillet, then add wine and meat. Heat gently, stirring until thoroughly heated. Serve over noodles. Serves 4.

NANCY EMERSON

VARIATION: Add sautéed mushrooms.

FLANK STEAK TERIYAKI

1-1¼ lb. flank steak
⅔ c. olive or canola oil
2 T. soy sauce

1 T. honey
½ t. ginger
¼ c. Teriyaki marinade sauce

Mix oil, soy sauce, honey, ginger, and Teriyaki sauce. Place flank steak in shallow baking dish. Pour marinade over steak. Marinate for at least 4 hours or overnight, turning once. Bake uncovered in marinade at 325° for 45 to 50 minutes. Slice thinly and serve over noodles or rice. Spoon reserved sauce over meat. Serves 8.

SUZANNE COWLEY

L MARINATED BROILED FLANK STEAK

1¼ lb. flank steak
1 T. prepared mustard
2 T. dry wine or sherry

2 T. lemon juice
2 T. soy sauce
2 T. Worcestershire

Score meat in a diamond pattern on both sides. Brush mustard over all surfaces of meat and place in a shallow pan. Combine remaining ingredients and pour over meat. Cover and marinate 8 hours in the refrigerator. Remove meat from the marinade. Broil or grill to desired doneness, basting with remaining marinade. To serve, slice thinly diagonally across the grain. Serves 4 to 5.

SHIRLEY WALKER

BOEUF AU GINGEMBRE

4-5 lbs. eye of round roast
4 slices ginger root
1 clove garlic, sliced

3 T. salad oil
¾ c. soy sauce
½ c. dry white wine

Make slashes in roast and tuck into each a sliver of either garlic or ginger root. Combine oil, soy sauce, and wine. Place roast and sauce together in a resealable plastic bag overnight in the refrigerator. Remove roast from bag and place in a greased shallow roasting pan. Cook at 450° for 30 minutes (45 minutes for a larger roast). Turn heat off, leaving roast in oven for an additional 20 minutes. Remove from oven and let stand for 10 minutes before slicing. Serves 6 to 8.

CAROLINE LaMOTTE

ROSY EYE OF ROUND ROAST

Eye of round roast
1 T. safflower oil
½ t. garlic powder
1 t. light salt

½ t. paprika
½ t. pepper
1 t. ground oregano

Rub oil over entire surface of meat. Combine the seasonings in a bowl and rub over roast. Place meat on a rack with the fat side up. Bake at 350° for 20 minutes per pound. The result will be a roast with a brown outer surface with an even rareness in the middle.

BEVERLY BATES
ANGELA MOORE

EASY BARBECUED BRISKET

3-4 lb. brisket, fat trimmed
1 c. ketchup
1 (1 oz) pkg. onion soup mix

12 oz ginger ale
Carrots and onions, sliced
(optional)

Combine ketchup, onion soup mix, and ginger ale and pour over brisket. (Add carrots and onions, if desired.) Cover and cook at 375° for 2 hours. Uncover and cook for 1 hour longer. Serves 6 to 8.

SALLIE THALHIMER

FINLAND BRISKET

1 (3 lb.) brisket
Salt to taste
1 (12 oz.) bottle chili sauce

1 (6 oz.) bottle horseradish
1 large green pepper, cut up

Sear meat on top of stove to seal in juices. Place in roasting pan and salt lightly. Place on top of brisket in order: chili sauce, horseradish, and green pepper. Add enough water to cover the bottom of the pan. Cook at 300° to 325° for 1½ to 2 hours, until done. To serve, slice brisket thinly and pour juices on top for added flavor. Serves 8 to 10.

WENDY JAFFE

ROCKY MOUNTAIN BRISKET WITH BARBECUE SAUCE

Good by itself or on onion rolls!

1 (4 lb.) beef brisket
2 T. liquid smoke
1½ t. salt

1½ t. pepper
2 T. chili power
1 t. crushed bay leaves

Rub meat completely with liquid smoke. Place meat, fat side up, in a large roasting pan. Combine salt, pepper, chili powder, and bay leaves. Sprinkle on top of meat. Cover tightly and bake at 325° for 4 hours. Scrape seasoning off meat and cut in very thin slices across the grain. Serve with barbecue sauce. Serves 6 to 8.

BARBECUE SAUCE

3 T. brown sugar
1 (14 oz.) bottle ketchup
½ c. water
2 T. liquid smoke
Salt and pepper to taste

4 T. Worcestershire
3 t. dry mustard
2 t. celery seed
6 T. butter
¼ t. cayenne pepper

Combine all ingredients and bring to a boil, stirring occasionally. Cook for 10 minutes.

KAKI NELSON

CHUCK WAGON SKILLET

A one-dish meal!

2 T. butter or margarine
¼ c. onion, chopped
1 lb. ground beef
1 t. salt
⅛ t. pepper
2 c. medium noodles, uncooked

1 c. celery, chopped
½ c. ripe olives, sliced
1 (1 lb.) can stewed tomatoes
¼ c. water
2 c. Cheddar cheese, cubed

Combine butter and onions in a large skillet and sauté onions until tender. Add meat, sprinkle with salt and pepper, and brown slowly. Layer noodles, celery, and olives over meat. Pour tomatoes and water on top, then sprinkle with cheese. Cover, reduce heat, and simmer 30 to 35 minutes. Serves 6.

VARIATION: Cook meat with a packet of taco seasoning mix.

GORDON KELLETT

FIVE SPICE BEEF AND RICE

A one-pan casserole my whole family will eat!

1 lb. lean ground beef
¾ c. onion, chopped
½ t. salt (or less)
Dash of pepper
½ bay leaf
⅛ t. chili powder
⅛ t. thyme

⅛ t. oregano
1 (10¾ oz.) can cream of
  mushroom soup
1 (16 oz.) can tomatoes, undrained
  and mashed
1 c. instant brown or white rice,
  uncooked

Brown beef with onions in a frypan. Remove meat from pan and drain off fat. Return meat to frypan and add remaining ingredients. Simmer uncovered, stirring occasionally, until liquid from tomatoes is absorbed and rice is tender, about 20 to 25 minutes. Serve with a green salad or fruit for a quick supper. Serves 4.

VARIATION: Add 1 (4 oz.) can mushrooms, sliced.

LYNN FELTON

MEATLOAF WITH POTATO AND MOZZARELLA

1½ lbs. lean ground beef
¾ c. bread crumbs
½ c. Parmesan cheese, grated
¼ c. dried parsley
1 onion, chopped
2 eggs

½ c. milk
½ t. pepper
1 t. salt
2 T. olive oil, divided
2 c. mashed potatoes
8 oz. Mozzarella cheese, sliced

Combine all ingredients except oil, potatoes, and Mozzarella. Mix well. Place half of the meat mixture in the bottom of a 10" square or 8" square baking dish, which has been rubbed with 1 T. olive oil. Next layer the potatoes and Mozzarella. Top with remaining meat mixture. Brush top with remaining oil. Bake at 350° for 1 hour, or until top is browned. Let stand for a few minutes before slicing. Serves 6.

BARBARA PARKER

MOIST AND EASY MEATLOAF

Children love this!

1 c. tomato juice
¾ c. Quaker oats (regular or
    quick)
1 egg

1 medium onion, chopped
½ t. salt
¼ t. pepper
1½ lbs. lean ground beef

Mix together first six ingredients. Add ground beef to the mixture. Press in loaf pan and bake at 350° for 1 hour. Serves 4 to 6.

VARIATION: Put a thin layer of ketchup on top of meatloaf before baking.

Q   GUMBO SLOPPY JOES

1 lb. extra lean ground beef
1 small onion, diced
1 (10¾ oz.) can chicken gumbo
    soup

2-3 T. ketchup
1 T. mustard
1 T. Worcestershire

Brown ground beef and onion. Drain well. Return to pan, add remaining ingredients, and simmer until well-blended. Serve on whole wheat buns or open-face over whole wheat bread. Serves 6 to 8.

BONNIE MOREAU

Q   SLOPPY JOES

A quick, easy sandwich.

1 lb. lean ground beef
1 T. vinegar
1 T. prepared mustard

1 T. Worcestershire
¾ c. ketchup
1 t. celery salt

Brown meat, pour off grease, and remove from pan. Mix vinegar, mustard, Worcestershire, and ketchup in pan and bring to a boil over low heat. Add meat and celery salt. Simmer for about 15 minutes. Serve on hamburger buns. Serves 4 to 6.

JULIA KIMBRELL

SPAGHETTI PIE

6 oz. spaghetti
2 T. margarine
⅓ c. Parmesan cheese, grated
2 eggs, beaten, or egg substitute
1 lb. extra lean ground beef
½ c. onion, chopped
¼ c. green pepper, chopped

½ (14½ oz.) can tomatoes,
    undrained and cut up
1 (6 oz.) can tomato paste
1 t. sugar
1 t. dried oregano
½ t. garlic salt
1 c. cottage cheese
½ c. Mozzarella cheese, shredded

Cook spaghetti according to package directions and drain well. Stir margarine into hot spaghetti; add Parmesan and eggs. Form spaghetti mixture into a "crust" in a buttered 10" deep-dish pie plate. In a skillet cook beef, onion, and green pepper until vegetables are tender and meat is browned. Drain off fat. Stir in tomatoes, tomato paste, sugar, oregano, and garlic salt. Heat thoroughly. Spread cottage cheese over bottom of spaghetti. Fill pie with tomato mixture and bake uncovered at 350° for 20 minutes. Sprinkle Mozzarella on top and bake 5 minutes longer. Freezes well. Serves 6.

VARIATION: Use prepared spaghetti sauce to reduce preparation time.

LINDA SMITH

TACO CASSEROLE   Q

1 lb. ground beef or turkey
1 (1¾ oz.) envelope taco
  seasoning
1 (15 oz.) can tomato sauce or 1
  (11 oz.) jar chunky salsa

1 (16 oz.) can refried beans
¼ c. black or green olives, sliced
2 c. corn chips, crushed
½-1 c. Cheddar cheese, shredded

Cook meat until no longer pink. Add remaining ingredients, except cheese and chips. Layer meat mixture over half of corn chips in the bottom of a 1½-quart casserole. Cook in microwave on full power for 5 minutes, or until hot. Cover meat with remaining chips and top with cheese. Heat again in microwave until cheese is melted. Serves 6.

KATE LEWIS

UPSIDE DOWN PIZZA

Children love this!

2 lbs. ground beef
1 c. onion, chopped
2 (8 oz.) cans tomato sauce
1 (1¼ oz.) pkg. spaghetti sauce mix

1 (8 oz.) container sour cream
2 c. Mozzarella cheese, shredded
1 (8 oz.) pkg. refrigerated crescent
  rolls

Cook meat and onions together until meat is browned. Drain well. Stir in tomato sauce and spaghetti sauce mix. Cook over low heat for 10 minutes, stirring frequently. Spoon meat into a lightly greased 9" x 13" baking dish. Top with sour cream, then cheese. Unroll crescent rolls and place on top of cheese. Bake uncovered at 350° for 20 minutes. Serves 6.

VARIATION: To lighten this recipe, substitute 8 oz. plain, non-fat yogurt for the sour cream.

CABELL LONGAN

QUICK AND EASY BEEF 'N CHEESE PIE

1 egg, slightly beaten
1 lb. lean ground beef
½ t. oregano leaves
¼ t. salt
Dash of pepper
1 (8 oz) can tomato sauce

1 (1½ oz.) pkg. Italian-style
    spaghetti sauce mix with
    mushrooms
2 c. Cheddar cheese, shredded
1 (8 oz) pkg. refrigerated crescent
    rolls

Reserve 1 T. beaten egg. Combine meat, remaining egg, oregano, salt, and pepper in bowl. Mix together tomato sauce and spaghetti sauce mix. Add ½ c. of this mixture to meat mixture. Pat into a 9" pie plate and top with cheese. Unroll the crescent dough and divide into triangles. Form a loose circle with points of triangles overlapping in the middle of the pan. Crimp edges. Brush dough with 1 T. egg and bake at 350° for 30 to 35 minutes. Let stand for 10 minutes before serving. Add enough water to the remaining spaghetti sauce mixture to make 1 cup, or the thickness you prefer. Heat thoroughly. Cut pie into wedges and serve with the hot sauce. Serves 6 to 8.

MARGARET WALTON

Q L   VEAL CUTLETS WITH GARLIC MINT SAUCE

4 (3 oz.) veal cutlets
½ c. fresh mint leaves
2 oz. pine nuts, toasted and
    divided
2 cloves garlic, minced
2 T. flour

¼ t. salt
Pinch ground red pepper
2 t. olive oil
½ c. low-sodium beef broth
2 c. mushrooms, thinly sliced
2 t. lemon juice

In a food processor, combine mint, 1 oz. pine nuts, and garlic. Process until finely chopped and set aside. Combine flour, salt, and pepper. Dredge cutlets in this mixture. Brown cutlets in olive oil in large non-stick skillet for 3 to 4 minutes on each side. Remove veal to serving plate and keep warm. Add broth to skillet, stirring to loosen any brown bits. Stir in mushrooms and lemon juice and cook for 2 minutes, stirring constantly. Stir in mint mixture and cook for 2 minutes, or until thoroughly heated. To serve, spoon sauce over meat and top with pine nuts. Serves 4.

BARBARA LINGO

Q   VEAL À LA NORMANDE

⅓-½ lb. veal scallopini per person
1 egg, beaten
Bread crumbs
Butter

Sunflower or peanut oil
Salt and pepper
8 oz sour cream

120

Dip veal in egg, then coat with bread crumbs. Sauté veal quickly over medium-high heat in skillet in an equal amount of butter and oil. Add salt and pepper. Remove veal while still tender and keep warm. Turn off heat under skillet, add sour cream to juices in pan, and stir to combine thoroughly. Pour sauce over veal and serve.

NANCY McCANDLISH

VEAL À L'ORANGE   *L*

4 lean veal chops, well-trimmed
  and cut ½" thick
1 T. oil
½ c. orange juice

1½ t. cornstarch
½ c. water
1 t. sugar
1 orange, cut in thin slices

Brown veal chops in oil in a large skillet and pour off excess fat. Pour orange juice over chops, cover and reduce heat. Cook slowly for 30 minutes. Remove chops and keep warm. Dissolve cornstarch in water and add to orange juice in skillet. Add sugar and cook until thickened, stirring constantly. Return chops to skillet and heat thoroughly. Add orange slices. May be served over rice. Serves 4.

CAROL FLIPPEN

ZURICH GESCHNITZELTES   *Q*

One of the most popular dishes in Switzerland!

1½ lbs. veal, boneless and thinly
  sliced
2 T. butter
Salt and Pepper
1 onion, chopped

1 c. mushrooms, sliced
¾ c. dry white wine
¾ c. light cream
Few drops lemon juice
1 T. fresh parsley, chopped

Sauté the veal in butter on both sides until browned. Remove from pan, sprinkle with salt and pepper, and keep warm. Reduce heat under pan, add onion and mushrooms, sauté a few minutes, and pour in wine. Simmer until liquid is reduced by half. Add the cream and bring to a boil. Reduce heat and add the veal, its juices, and lemon juice. Season with salt and pepper and serve topped with parsley. This is traditionally served with potatoes (rösti), but also goes well with pasta or rice. Serves 4 to 6.

MARGARET LAMPE

MEATS AND GAME

ARMENIAN MEATBALLS

Kids love it!

1 lb. ground lamb
¼ lb. mild sausage (optional)
1 egg, beaten
½ t. salt
⅛ t. pepper
¼ t. garlic salt

1 c. Cheddar cheese, shredded
1 c. soft bread crumbs
1 c. dried parsley flakes
⅓ c. onion, finely minced
1 (8 oz.) can tomato sauce
¼ c. Parmesan cheese, grated

Lightly mix lamb, sausage, and egg. Blend in salt, pepper, and garlic salt. Add Cheddar cheese, bread crumbs, parsley, and onion. Shape into balls and brown in non-stick frying pan. Spray shallow 1-quart baking dish with no-stick cooking spray. Place browned meatballs in dish. Pour tomato sauce over meatballs. Sprinkle tops with Parmesan cheese. Bake covered at 350° for 20 minutes. Remove cover and bake another 10 minutes. Serve with rice and corn. Serves 4.

ELLEN LeCOMPTE

RACK OF LAMB WITH RASPBERRY MINT SAUCE

This is my most requested dinner party entrée!

RASPBERRY MINT SAUCE

1 (12½ oz.) bottle raspberry
    vinegar (use one of good
    quality)
½ to 1 c. sugar

1 T. lemon juice
2 T. cornstarch
2 T. fresh mint, minced

Bring raspberry vinegar to a boil in a medium saucepan. Lower heat and add sugar to sweeten. Add lemon juice to cut the tartness. In a separate small bowl, mix the cornstarch with a little water to form a watery paste. Pour cornstarch mixture into vinegar mixture to thicken. Cook over low heat until sauce thickens. Let sauce cool, then add mint leaves. Sauce can be reheated, but do not allow it to boil. Water can be added for desired consistency, if needed.

2 racks of lamb (with racks
    removed)
1 (8 oz.) jar Dijon mustard

Salt and pepper
Flour
Oil

Rub lamb with mustard, salt, and pepper, then roll in flour. Lamb can be marinated overnight at this point, but it is not necessary. Pour enough oil in a hot skillet to cover the bottom. Sear lamb on all sides until just browned and remove from skillet. Place lamb in baking dish and bake at 500° for 20 to 25 minutes. Slice lamb into round medallions and serve on a puddle of raspberry mint sauce. Serves 6 to 8.

PATSY ARNETT

122

LAMB ROAST

Half lamb shank or sirloin
Accent
Ground Oregano
Rosemary

¼ c. safflower oil
2 bay leaves
½ c. water

Shake Accent, oregano, and rosemary over all of lamb. Heat oil in Dutch oven and braise all exposed sides of lamb over medium-high heat. Remove from heat, add bay leaves and water. Cover and bake at 325° for 25 minutes per pound. Allow ½ lb. minimum per person.

ANGELA MOORE

STUFFED LEG OF LAMB

8 lb. leg of lamb, boned,
  butterflied, and well-trimmed
  (4-5 lbs. boneless)
1 lb. spinach or Swiss chard, stems
  removed and coarsely chopped
6 large cloves garlic, sliced
3 T. olive oil, divided
¼ lb. feta cheese, crumbled

Salt and pepper
1½ t. dried rosemary, divided
1 onion, sliced
1 c. dry red wine
1½ c. beef broth
½ c. water
1 T. cornstarch, dissolved in 2 T.
  cold water

Wash spinach well and drain. Place in covered saucepan and steam in water remaining on the leaves for 3 to 5 minutes, or until wilted. Drain, run under cold water, drain again, and pat dry with kitchen towel. Cook garlic in skillet with 2 T. oil over moderate heat, stirring until golden brown. Transfer to bowl wth slotted spoon. Cook spinach in skillet, stirring for 1 minute, or until excess liquid is gone. Let cool and stir feta into spinach gently. Pat lamb dry, spread out with boned side up, and season with salt and pepper. Spread the lamb evenly with spinach and feta mixture, leaving a 1" border around the edges. Beginning with the short side, roll lamb up jelly roll fashion and tie tightly with kitchen string. Place in roasting pan and rub with remaining 1 T. oil, 1 t. rosemary, salt, and pepper. Roast lamb at 325° for 30 minutes. Scatter onion around lamb and roast for an additional 1 to 1¼ hours, or 20 minutes per pound.

When lamb is done, transfer to cutting board and place roasting pan over moderately high heat. Add wine, deglaze pan, scraping up brown bits, and boil mixture until reduced by half. Strain mixture through a fine sieve into a saucepan, add broth, remaining rosemary, water, and any juices from the cutting board. Boil mixture until reduced to 2 cups. Add the cornstarch mixture to the wine mixture. Simmer for 2 minutes, stirring constantly. Add salt and pepper and keep warm. Remove strings from lamb and serve with sauce. Serves 6.

SUSAN HAMILL

EASY HAM IN THE CROCKPOT

3-4 lb. precooked 98% fat-free
   ham
½ c. brown sugar

1 t. dry mustard
1 t. prepared horseradish
¼ c. diet cola, divided

Combine brown sugar, mustard, and horseradish. Moisten with just enough cola to make a smooth paste. Rub ham with mixture. Place in crockpot and add remaining cola. Cook on low for 6 to 8 hours or on high for 2 to 3 hours. Serves 8 to 10.

VARIATION: Add peeled sweet potatoes to crockpot while cooking.

KIM NEWLEN

ZUCCHINI SAUSAGE BOATS

4 medium zucchini
¼-½ lb. bulk pork sausage
¼ c. onion, chopped
6 T. plus 2 T. Parmesan cheese,
   grated and divided
½ c. cracker crumbs, finely
   crushed

1 egg, slightly beaten
¼ t. salt
¼ t. thyme
Dash of garlic salt
Dash of black pepper
Dash of paprika

Cook whole zucchini in boiling salted water until barely tender, about 7 to 10 minutes. Cut zucchini in half lengthwise and scoop out pulp, keeping shells intact. Place pulp in bowl and mash. Cook sausage with onion; drain off excess fat. Stir in mashed pulp. Add 6 T. Parmesan and remaining ingredients except paprika. Spoon mixture into zucchini shells and place in shallow 9" x 13" baking dish. Sprinkle with 2 T. Parmesan and paprika. Bake at 350° for 25 to 30 minutes. Serves 4.

SHARON PHILLIPS

BRAISED PORK WITH PICKLES

A favorite with men!

6 loin pork chops
1 large onion, chopped
1 t. flour
1-2 t. salt (optional)
2 t. brown or Dijon mustard

1 c. beef stock or broth
2 T. pickle, chopped (preferably
   dill)
Freshly ground pepper to taste

Remove bone and fat from chops, cut into strips. Brown strips in skillet sprayed with no-stick cooking spray. Remove pork from pan, add onion, and simmer 3 minutes. Add flour, salt, mustard, and pepper. Stir until well-blended. Gradually add stock and pickle and simmer 5 minutes. Return pork to skillet and spoon sauce over all. Cover and simmer until tender, about 15 minutes. Serve over rice. Serves 6.

CLARE NEWBRAND

PORK CHOPS WITH BLACK CURRANT PRESERVES

6 center cut pork chops (1-1½" thick)
1½ T. Dijon mustard

¼ c. black currant preserves
Salt and pepper to taste
⅓ c. white wine vinegar

Mix mustard with preserves in a bowl. Brown both sides of pork chops in a large skillet. Season with salt and pepper and spoon currant mixture over chops. Cover, reduce heat, and cook for 20 minutes. Transfer to platter and keep warm in oven. Remove excess fat from skillet, add vinegar, and bring to a boil while scraping up brown bits from bottom. When sauce is reduced by one-third, pour over chops and serve. Serves 6.

KATHY WATSON

CREOLE-STYLE PORK CHOPS   *L*

4 (4 oz.) thick lean top loin pork chops, boneless
½ c. onions, chopped
½ c. celery, chopped
½ c. green pepper, chopped
½ c. sweet red pepper, chopped
3 cloves garlic, crushed

1 (8½ oz.) can whole tomatoes, undrained and chopped
½ t. hot sauce
½ t. pepper
2 c. hot cooked white rice (cooked without butter or salt)
1 t. cornstarch
¼ c. no-salt chicken broth

Trim fat from chops. Coat skillet with no-stick cooking spray and brown chops on all sides over medium-high heat. Remove from heat. Spray skillet again and sauté next 5 ingredients until tender. Remove ½ c. of this mixture and set aside. Add tomatoes, hot sauce, pepper, and chops to skillet. Cover and cook for 15 minutes, turning once. Stir reserved ½ c. vegetables into rice. Spoon onto serving plate and arrange chops on top of rice. Combine cornstarch and chicken broth and add to vegetables in skillet. Cook over medium heat stirring constantly, until mixture begins to boil. Continue boiling for 1 minute or until thickened. Spoon over chops. Serves 4.

LYNN HAW

LEMON BARBECUED PORK CHOPS

6 loin pork chops
1-2 T. oil
6 lemon slices
½ c. ketchup

¼ c. cider vinegar
¼ c. water
2 heaping T. dark brown sugar

Brown pork chops in hot oil and drain. Place chops in baking dish and top with lemon slices. Combine ketchup, vinegar, water, and sugar and pour over chops. Cover tightly and bake at 350° for 45 minutes. Serves 3 to 6.

TYLER KILPATRICK

ROAST PORK WITH SWEET AND SOUR SAUCE

A dish that has never failed to get rave reviews!

1" or thicker rib pork chops
   (1 per person)
Flour
2 c. sugar
1 c. distilled vinegar

2 T. green pepper, chopped
1 t. salt
1 c. plus 2 T. water, divided
4 t. cornstarch
2 t. paprika

Dredge chops in flour and place in pan, bone side down. Brown at 450° for 30 minutes. Remove from pan and transfer to baking dish bone side up (or lay down if they won't stand). Combine sugar, vinegar, green pepper, salt, and 1 c. water. Simmer for 5 minutes. Combine cornstarch and 2 T. water. Add to sugar mixture. Add paprika and cook until sauce thickens. Pour sauce over chops and bake at 300° for 2½ hours, basting occasionally. Serve sauce over meat.

CHERYL BOSWELL

BREADED PORK TENDERLOIN ROYALE

A wonderful company dish!

2 lbs. pork tenderloin (in cutlets)
Salt and pepper
3 T. flour
2 eggs
2 T. water
1 c. plain bread crumbs
5 T. butter, divided

½ green pepper, diced
½ lb. fresh mushrooms, sliced
1 medium onion, diced
1 (10¾ oz) can cream of
   mushroom soup
3 T. milk
2 T. chili sauce

Pound pork cutlets with flat mallet until ½" thick. Sprinkle with salt and pepper. Coat cutlets lightly with flour, shaking off excess. Beat eggs with water. Dip floured cutlets in egg mixture, covering completely. Allow excess egg mixture to drip off. Dredge cutlets in bread crumbs and allow to dry on rack. Heat 3 T. butter in skillet and brown cutlets until golden. Place in greased 8" x 12" baking dish. Place 2 T. butter, onions, peppers and mushrooms in skillet. Sauté vegetables until limp and drain. Mix soup, milk and chili sauce. Add to onion mixture and spread over meat. Cover with foil and refrigerate 1 hour. Bake covered at 300° for 2 hours. Serves 6 to 8.

PEGGY CONWAY

MUSHROOM PORK   *Q L*

¾ lb. pork tenderloin, cut in 4 slices
½ t. lemon pepper
⅓ c. plain yogurt
¼ c. dry white wine
¼ c. water
1 T. cornstarch
1 t. beef bouillon
1 (4 oz.) can mushrooms, drained
2 T. green onions, chopped

Pound pork slices between sheets of plastic wrap until ¼" thick and sprinkle with lemon pepper. Spray a cold skillet with no-stick cooking spray and brown pork for 4 minutes on each side. Add the remaining ingredients, stirring until thickened. Cook for 2 additional minutes. Serves 4.

JEAN JONES

PORK STRIPS WITH OYSTER SAUCE   *Q*

1 lb. pork tenderloin, cut in ½" strips
2 T. peanut oil
2 cloves garlic, crushed
4-6 slices ginger root
1 medium onion, cut in wedges
4-6 T. oyster or Hoisin sauce
1 T. Chinese cooking wine
1 T. sugar
¼ t. Chinese five-spices powder
1 T. dark soy sauce
½ c. water, divided
1 T. tapioca starch
Sesame oil
2 T. green onion, chopped (for garnish)

Sauté garlic, ginger root, and onion in peanut oil in hot wok for a few seconds. Add pork strips and stir-fry a few seconds longer. Add oyster sauce, cooking wine, sugar, five-spices, soy sauce, and ¼ c. water. Cover and cook over medium-high heat for 10 minutes. Dissolve tapioca in ¼ c. water and a few drops of sesame oil. Add to the pork and bring to a boil. Serve with plain white rice and garnish with green onion. Serves 4 to 6.

MARILYN CORBETT

MEATS AND GAME

Q PORK TENDERLOIN WITH RAISIN SAUCE

Sauce is also wonderful with duck and goose.

2 lbs. pork tenderloin, cut in ¼"
   slices
1½ c. port wine, divided
1½ c. raisins

2 t. butter
¼ c. olive oil
¼ c. balsamic vinegar

In a small saucepan combine 1 c. port wine and raisins. Simmer for 15 minutes. Sauté tenderloin slices in butter and olive oil until browned. When tenderloin is done, add raisin sauce, vinegar, and remaining wine. Simmer for 5 to 10 minutes and serve immediately. Serves 6.

CINDY BROOKS

PORK BURRITOS OR CHALUPAS

A fairly authentic Mexican dish that is easy to make.

2 pork tenderloins
1 lb. dried pinto beans
1 large onion, chopped
2 cloves garlic, minced
2 fresh jalapeño peppers, minced
   (use gloves)

Salt and pepper to taste
3 T. chili powder, divided
1 T. comino
8 c. water
Corn tortillas, fried crisp or flour
   tortillas, steamed

Wash beans well. Mix with onion, garlic, jalapeños, salt, 1 T. chili powder, and comino. Pour in bottom of large roasting pan. Season meat with additional salt and pepper, if desired, and 2 T. chili powder. Place meat on top of beans and pour in water. Cover and roast at 325° for about 5 hours. When done, pull meat apart in strips and partially mash beans. Serve on crisp corn tortillas for chalupas. Serve on soft flour tortillas for burritos. Serve with any of the following: grated Monterey Jack or Vermont Cheddar cheese, chopped avocado or guacamole, chopped tomatoes and onions with cilantro, picante sauce, or cream. Serves 8 to 12.

JANA THOMAS

MEATS AND GAME

BOURBON PORK TENDERLOIN WITH MUSTARD SAUCE

An easy and elegant main dish.

2 pork tenderloins, 1½ lb. each ½ c. bourbon
½ c. soy sauce 4 T. brown sugar

Prepare marinade 2 to 3 hours before cooking tenderloins. Mix together soy sauce, bourbon, and brown sugar. Place pork in shallow non-metal dish and cover with the marinade. Marinate at room temperature for 2 to 3 hours, turning tenderloins 2 to 3 times during this period. Remove meat from marinade and bake in roasting pan for 1 to 1½ hours at 325°. Juice should run clear when meat is pierced. Carve in thin diagonal slices and serve with mustard sauce. Serves 6.

MUSTARD SAUCE

1 T. dry mustard 2 T. vinegar
4 T. Dijon mustard 4 egg yolks, beaten
2 T. sugar 1 c. heavy cream
½ t. salt

Place all ingredients except cream in top of double boiler. Cook while stirring constantly until thickened, about 10 minutes. Cool slightly, then whisk in cream. Serve sauce at room temperature. (Sauce may be prepared 3 days before serving.)

MARIE CARTER

ORANGE PORK TENDERLOIN *L*

1 lb. pork tenderloin ¾ c. water
1½ T. Dijon mustard ¼ c. orange marmalade, divided
1 clove garlic, minced ¼ c. chicken stock or bouillon
¼ t. dried thyme

Make a cut in the tenderloin lengthwise down the center about halfway through. (If using two pieces, cut each this way.) In a small bowl mix mustard, garlic, and thyme. Spread this mixture along the cut. Reshape and tie the tenderloin(s), if desired. Place on roasting rack. Add water to pan, brush pork with 2 T. marmalade and bake at 400° for 40 to 45 minutes. Mix remaining marmalade with chicken stock. Simmer for 2 to 3 minutes, or until thickened. Spoon sauce over sliced pork. Serves 4.

SHIRLEY WALKER

MEATS AND GAME

L   PORK TENDERLOIN WITH ROSEMARY AND THYME

Leftovers make great fried rice!

MARINADE

½ t. dried thyme (leaf)
Several sprigs fresh rosemary or ½
   t. dried rosemary
¾ t. dry mustard
¼ c. lower-salt tamari or soy
   sauce

3-4 T. dry sherry
Dash of Worcestershire
Freshly ground black pepper to
   taste
⅛ t. dried red pepper flakes
1-2 T. parsley, chopped or dried

Combine marinade ingredients in a 11½" x 12½" plastic bag and mix well.

1½ lbs. pork tenderloin, fat
   removed

Olive oil no-stick cooking spray

Add tenderloin to marinade in plastic bag and marinate for several hours in the refrigerator, turning occasionally. Remove from refrigerator 30 to 45 minutes before cooking. Drain tenderloin, reserving marinade. Spray tenderloin with cooking spray and place on rack in small roasting pan. Add ¼" water to the pan and roast at 350° for 40 to 50 minutes, until no longer pink. Boil marinade and use it to baste the tenderloin several times during roasting period. Once tenderloin is done, remaining marinade can be added to the roasting pan juices. Chicken bouillon granules, a dash of oyster sauce, and more sherry or tamari can also be added. Simmer mixture several minutes before serving. This natural juice sauce can also be thickened for gravy, if desired. Serves 4.

LINDA MAY

DEMI-GLACÉ

This adds rich flavor to gravies, sauces, or any beef-based meal.

½ c. butter
1 carrot, sliced
1 large yellow onion, cut in chunks
1 celery stalk with leaves,
   chopped
½ c. flour

3 (10¾ oz) cans beef consommé
2 cloves garlic, minced
½ c. parsley, chopped
2 scallions, chopped
Pinch of thyme
Salt and pepper to taste

In a heavy pan melt butter and sauté carrots, onions, and celery until tender. Stirring constantly, add flour and mix well. Add consommé, garlic, parsley, scallions, and thyme. Season with salt and pepper. Bring mixture to boil, reduce heat, and simmer for 45 minutes. Drain through a sieve. Freeze in ice cube trays. Cubes may be stored in sealed containers or plastic bags for up to 6 months.

KATHY ELLIS

MEATS AND GAME

DOVES CACCIATORE

16-24 doves
3-4 T. olive oil
4 cloves garlic, chopped
1 c. fresh mushrooms, sliced
1 (2¼ oz.) can pitted black olives

2-3 t. parsley
Salt to taste
Pepper to taste
1 c. white wine
2 (12 oz.) cans tomato sauce

Braise doves in hot oil. Turn doves over and add garlic and mushrooms. Add olives, parsley, salt, pepper and wine. Cover and steam for 5 minutes. Pour in tomato sauce and cook until doves are tender, about 15 minutes. Serves 6 to 8.

NOTE: Chicken may be substituted for doves.

LINDA STEPANIAN

ISLAND FARM DOVES

12 doves
Salt to taste
Pepper to taste
3-4 T. vegetable oil
2 medium onions, chopped
6 strips of bacon
1 (10¾ oz.) can cream of celery
soup

1 (10¾ oz.) can cream of
mushroom soup
2 c. beer
1 (3 oz.) can sliced mushrooms, or
fresh mushrooms
2 T. dried parsley
½ lemon, sliced

Remove dove breasts from bones by cutting meat closely to breast bones. Sprinkle with salt and pepper. Brown lightly in skillet in hot oil. Remove meat from skillet and set aside. Sauté onions and bacon in skillet until onions are transparent. Drain. Place meat, onions and bacon into large baking dish. Combine soups and beer and spread over meat mixture. Top with mushrooms, parsley and lemon slices. Bake at 325° for 2 hours, or until doves are tender. Serve over rice. Serves 4 to 6.

SCOTT RUTH

PETER'S FAVORITE DOVES

16 doves
Salt to taste
Pepper to taste
Flour
12 slices bacon
4 T. Worcestershire

⅔-1 c. beef consommé or red
  wine
¾ lb. fresh mushrooms
2 T. butter
1 t. freshly squeezed lemon juice
Fresh parsley, chopped (optional)

Wash doves well after cleaning and pat dry. Salt and pepper inside and out and roll lightly in flour; set aside. Cook bacon in large dutch oven until crisp; remove from grease and drain. Brown doves on all sides in hot grease. Turn doves breast side down and add Worcestershire sauce and consommé or wine. Cover and cook over low heat for 20 minutes. Sauté mushrooms in butter and lemon juice in separate pan. Add mushrooms to doves. Turn breasts up and continue cooking for additional 20 minutes. (Additional consommé or wine may be added.) Crumble bacon; sprinkle bacon and parsley over doves before serving. Serves 6 to 8.

NOTE: 8 small ducks may be substituted for doves.

LUCY HOLBROOK

CYPRESS BANKS BARBECUED DUCK

2 large or 4 small ducks
Salt to taste
Pepper to taste
Paprika to taste
2½ T. prepared mustard

2 T. ketchup
½ c. water
2 T. Worcestershire
4 T. port wine
2 T. butter

Remove breast from bone by cutting meat closely to bone with sharp knife. Sprinkle with salt, pepper and paprika. Blend mustard and ketchup. Add water, Worcestershire, wine and butter. In small saucepan warm ingredients over low heat. Line broiler pan with heavy duty aluminum wrap and place meat on top. Broil for 10 minutes. Remove from heat and baste with sauce. Broil additional 5 minutes. Move basted meat to outdoor grill and cook until hot and browned. (Do not overcook.) Serve with wild rice. Serves 4.

RAY RUTH

GRILLED WOOD DUCKS   *L*

2 small ducks
2 T. A-1 Sauce

6 T. frozen orange juice
    concentrate or honey

Split ducks up back and cut out backbone with game shears. Crack breastbone and lay ducks flat on grill. Combine A-1 Sauce and orange juice or honey and baste both sides of ducks. Cook breast side up over hot coals until underside is done (approximately 10 minutes). Turn and cook on breast side for 5 minutes or until skin is crisp. Be careful to not burn sauce. Allow ½ duck per person. Serve with wild rice. Serves 4.

MARILYNN WARE

GRILLED QUAIL   *L*

Good-bye dry game!

4 quail
Honey mustard to taste

2 slices bacon

Soak quail in water for 30 minutes. Dry on paper towels. Coat all sides with honey mustard and wrap ½ slice bacon around each. Secure with toothpicks. Grill approximately 20 minutes, turning every 5 minutes. Do not overcook! Serves 2.

MIMI RHOADS

TUCKAHOE VERMOUTH VENISON

2 lb. venison
2-3 T. vegetable oil
2 (10¾ oz.) cans cream of
    mushroom soup

1 (1 oz.) pkg. Lipton Dried Onion
    soup mix
½ c. dry Vermouth or white wine
1 lb. fresh mushrooms, sliced
3 T. butter

Cube venison and remove all white membrane. Brown meat in oil in large skillet. Combine soup, soup mix and Vermouth or wine. Place meat in 2½-quart casserole and pour soup mixture over top. Cover and bake at 350° for 2½ hours. Sauté mushrooms in butter and pour over meat. Continue baking for 30 minutes. Serve over rice. Serves 4 to 6.

SCOTT RUTH

L

SCHNUCKI'S SPIEDIES

Venison family favorite.

5 lb. venison
⅓ c. vegetable oil
½ c. vinegar
2 cloves garlic
1 t. basil
1 t. rosemary
¼ t. Worcestershire
2 T. parsley

1 t. oregano
1 t. salt (optional)
½ t. pepper
1 t. celery salt or seed
1 t. garlic salt or powder
Lo-Cal Italian dressing
Lo-Cal Italian bread, sliced

Prepare meat by removing all white membranes on venison. Cube meat into 2" to 3" pieces. Place in large shallow pan. Combine remaining ingredients except Italian dressing and bread in small mixing bowl and stir well. Pour mixture over meat and mix well. Cover meat tightly and marinate in refrigerator for 3 days. Place cubes on skewers and grill, basting with marinade, and turning frequently. Serve as open-face sandwich, folding up sides of bread. Pour small amount of Italian dressing over meat. Serve with cucumber salad, potato salad or cole slaw. Serves 10.

ANNETTE McCABE

Poultry

I think my Daddy needs to go on a diet because his big toe is getting too fat.
William Hedgepeth, '05

Chicken:

Chicken Antonio **Q** 138
Arabian Schwarma Bassett 138
Apricot and Currant
   Chicken 138
Bok Choy Chicken **Q** 139
Chicken Cacciatore 139
Caribbean Chicken 140
Chicken and Cashew
   Stir-Fry **Q** 140
Cheese Glazed Chicken 140
Chicken Breasts with
   Cheeses 141
Company Chicken 141
Light Chicken Cordon
   Bleu **Q L** 142
Crispy Chicken 142
Curried Chicken I 142
Curried Chicken II **L** 143
Curried Chicken III 143
Chicken Curry Casserole 144
Curry Glazed Chicken **L** 144
Chicken Dijon 144
Light Chicken Divan **L** 145
Chicken and Dressing
   Casserole 145
Chicken Enchiladas **L** 145
Chicken Fiesta 146
Flat Chicken **Q** 146
Herb Baked Chicken Breasts ... 146
Chicken Breasts with Herbs
   and Wine **Q L** 147
Herbed Roast Chicken 147
Harriet's Italian Chicken 148
Chicken Italiano 148
Easy Jambalaya **L** 148
Oven Jambalaya 149
Chicken Jerusalem I 149
Chicken Jerusalem II 150
Lemon Chicken I **L** 150
Lemon Chicken II **L** 150
Twenty-Minute Lemon Garlic
   Chicken **Q L** 151

Lemon Chicken and
   Thyme **Q L** 151
Creamed Chicken
   Macaroni Casserole 152
Chicken Mandalay 152
Sautéed Chicken with
   Mandarin Oranges **Q L** 152
Marg Lee Chicken 153
Monterey Chicken 153
Pauline Morris's Chicken **L** 154
Sautéed Chicken in
   Mushroom Sauce **Q L** 154
Orange Glazed Chicken **L** ... 154
Oriental Sunshine
   Chicken **L** 155
Parmesan Baked Chicken 155
Chicken Parmigiana **Q** 156
Parsley and Parmesan
   Baked Chicken **L** 156
Chicken Piccata **Q L** 156
Poppy Chicken Casserole 157
Chicken Pot Pie 157
Chicken Breasts Romano 158
Gourmet Hot Chicken Salad ... 158
Chicken Scallopini **Q** 159
Slow-Cook Chicken 159
Spicy Chicken with Red and
   Green Peppers **Q** 159
Curried Chicken Spaghetti
   Casserole 160
Chicken and Squash
   Casserole 160
Chicken Tarragon (or
   Paprika) 160
Chicken in a Basket **L** 161
Chicken Yum Yum 161
Wine Baked Chicken Breasts ... 162
Chicken Livers Delicious 162

Cornish Hens:
   Baked Cornish Hens 162

Turkey:
   Taco Pie **Q** 163
Microwave Turkey
   Vegetable Lasagna **L** 163
Turkey Tetrazzini 164

Q   CHICKEN ANTONIO

1 lb. chicken thighs or breasts, cut
   into bite-sized pieces (thighs
   recommended for moistness
   and tenderness)
2 T. olive or vegetable oil

4 cloves garlic, minced
2 c. fresh mushrooms, sliced
½ c. black olives, sliced
½ c. cooking sherry
½ c. beef broth

Toss chicken in pan with oil to coat thoroughly. Sauté chicken, garlic, mushrooms and black olives. Cook until garlic is tan, stirring constantly. Add sherry and broth and cook until juice has almost evaporated. Serve with plain cooked spaghetti and Italian bread. Serves 4 to 6.

PATSY ARNETT

ARABIAN SCHWARMA BASSETT

2 lbs. chicken breasts, cut into 1"
   pieces
¼ t. black pepper
¼ t. cinnamon
¼ t. cayenne pepper
¼ t. allspice
¼ t. cloves

1 t. cardamon
¾ t. plus pinch of salt
2 T. plus 2 t. lemon juice
5-6 cloves garlic, crushed
¾ c. plus 1 T. olive oil
6 (8") pita shells

In a large bowl combine chicken, spices, ¾ t. salt, and 2 T. lemon juice. Turn chicken and coat well. Cover and marinate for 4 hours or overnight. To make sauce crush garlic and mix with a pinch of salt. Add 2 t. lemon juice. Add ¾ c. oil in a slow stream, beating until the consistency of mayonnaise. Heat 1 T. oil in skillet and sauté chicken. Drain on paper towels. Brown pita shells in skillet for 1 minute on each side. Fill shells with chicken and top with garlic sauce for sandwiches. Serves 6.

HENRY STERN

APRICOT AND CURRANT CHICKEN

6-8 chicken breast halves
Salt and pepper to taste
1 t. ground ginger
1½ c. bitter orange marmalade
⅓ c. apple juice

⅓ c. fresh orange juice
8 oz. dried apricots
8 oz. dried currants
¼ c. brown sugar

Place chicken pieces, skin side up, in a shallow roasting pan. Sprinkle with salt, pepper, and ginger. Spread marmalade over chicken. Pour apple and orange juices into pan and bake at 375° for 20 minutes. Remove from oven and add apricots and currants. Sprinkle with brown sugar. Bake for an additional 40 to 45 minutes, basting chicken frequently, until chicken is shiny golden brown. Remove chicken, apricots, and currants to a warmed serving platter and pour pan juices over top. Extra juice can be served in a sauceboat. Serves 6 to 8.

BETTY HOFFER

BOK CHOY CHICKEN Q

½ lb. chicken, boned, skinned and
    cut into small pieces
6 T. peanut oil, divided
4 t. cornstarch, divided
1 t. sugar
1½ lb. bok choy, diagonally sliced

½ c. chicken stock
½ t. salt
Broccoli, snow peas, and/or green
    onion, sliced into 1½" lengths
    (optional substitutes for bok
    choy)

Heat 3 T. peanut oil in wok until oil barely begins to smoke. Toss chicken with 2 t. cornstarch and sugar. Stir-fry chicken until just cooked. Remove from wok and set aside. Heat remaining oil, add bok choy, and stir-fry 30 seconds. Add chicken stock and salt and bring to a boil. Cover and steam 1 minute. Dissolve remaining cornstarch in 1 T. water. Return chicken to wok and mix with greens. Add cornstarch solution and toss to coat. Turn on to warm platter and serve immediately. Serves 2 to 3.

LAURA SHUFORD

CHICKEN CACCIATORE

For everyday or entertaining.

4 chicken breast halves, skinned
    and boned (whole or in pieces)
1 c. onion, sliced
½ t. fresh garlic, minced
2 T. olive oil
1 (16 oz.) can tomatoes, chopped
    and undrained
1 (8 oz.) can tomato sauce

1 t. salt
¼ t. pepper
½ t. celery seed
1 T. lemon juice
1 t. oregano
1 bay leaf
¼ c. white wine
2 c. cooked noodles

Sauté onions and garlic in oil until tender, about 10 minutes. Add all other ingredients except chicken, wine and noodles. Stir until thoroughly combined. Add chicken; cover and simmer for 1 hour, stirring occasionally. Add wine and cook uncovered on medium heat for 15 minutes. Remove bay leaf and serve over noodles. Serves 4.

CAROLYN MEACHAM

CARIBBEAN CHICKEN

½ lb. chicken pieces
2 T. lime juice
1 qt. cold water
3 T. olive oil
2 t. salt

½ t. pepper
2 cloves garlic, minced
1 T. vinegar
1 t. oregano

Preheat broiler. Rinse chicken in lime juice and water. Drain and pat dry. Combine remaining ingredients and brush on chicken. Broil 20 to 25 minutes on each side. This can also be grilled. Serves 2.

RONNIE THORNTON

Q CHICKEN AND CASHEW STIR-FRY

3 c. uncooked chicken breasts, skinned, boned, and cubed
2 T. peanut oil
1 c. green pepper, sliced
1 bunch green onions, with tops, chopped
1 c. celery, diagonally sliced
1 c. fresh mushroom caps, sliced

1⅓ c. cashews
3 T. dry sherry
3 T. soy sauce
5 t. cornstarch
1 clove garlic, minced
½ c. water
1 t. pepper

Heat oil in skillet over medium high heat. Add green pepper, green onion, celery and chicken. Stir-fry for 5 minutes. Add mushroom caps and cashews; stir-fry for 2 additional minutes. Combine sherry, soy sauce, cornstarch, garlic, water and pepper. Add to skillet; cook and stir until sauce thickens. Serve with rice. Serves 4.

ANN CRENSHAW

CHEESE GLAZED CHICKEN

A quick family favorite that is suitable for company.

6 chicken breast halves, skinned
2 T. flour
1 t. paprika
1 t. salt, divided
2 T. butter or margarine
1 T. oil
¼ c. dry sherry

1 T. cornstarch
¾ c. light cream
½ c. white wine
1 T. fresh lemon juice
½ c. Swiss or Cheddar cheese, grated

Place chicken in a plastic bag with flour, paprika, and ½ t. salt. Shake until chicken is coated. Brown chicken in butter and oil. Add sherry; cover and simmer for 25 minutes. Blend cornstarch, cream, and ½ t. salt. Stir into pan

140

drippings and continue cooking until sauce thickens slightly. Add wine and lemon juice and heat a few minutes longer. Sprinkle cheese over top. Cover and let stand 5 minutes or until cheese melts. Serves 6.

JANET DAUGHDRILLE

CHICKEN BREASTS WITH CHEESES

6 chicken breast halves, boned, with skin left on
1 c. Ricotta cheese
1 c. cheese, grated (½ c. Gruyère, ½ c. Parmesan recommended. Other options: Cheddar,

Provolone, Mozzarella, Jarlsburg)
1 egg, beaten
¼ c. walnuts, finely chopped
¼ t. nutmeg
⅛ t. pepper
2 T. butter, melted

Combine cheeses, egg, walnuts, nutmeg, and pepper. Stuff filling between skin and meat of each breast half. Tuck skin under to seal. Secure with toothpick. Place breasts skin side up in baking dish. Brush with butter and bake uncovered at 350° for 40 to 45 minutes.

APRICOT SAUCE

⅓ c. chicken broth
⅓ c. apricot nectar

2 t. cornstarch
6 whole dried apricots

Mix chicken broth, apricot nectar and cornstarch and boil for 2 minutes. Place cooked breasts on serving platter and put apricot on each one. Top with prepared sauce. Serves 6.

BRUCE BASKERVILLE

COMPANY CHICKEN

2 small broiler chickens (cut-up) or equivalent number of breasts
6 T. butter, melted
8 oz. bacon, finely diced
1 large onion, chopped
2 T. flour

1 T. curry
1 c. beef bouillon
¼ c. orange marmalade
2 T. chili sauce
2 T. lemon juice

Roll chicken in butter and place in baking dish. Brown bacon and onion in skillet. Gradually add flour, stirring until smooth. Add remaining ingredients and simmer 15 minutes. Cover chicken with half the sauce. Bake at 400° for 20 minutes. Add remaining sauce and bake for 20 additional minutes. (Sauce can be made ahead of time and refrigerated.) Serves 6.

MIM SCHUTE

Q L   LIGHT CHICKEN CORDON BLEU

4 chicken breast halves, skinned
  and boned
4 thin slices lean ham or turkey
  ham
4 thin slices low-fat Swiss cheese

Salt and pepper
3 T. parsley, chopped and divided
2 T. light mayonnaise, divided
¼ c. bread crumbs

Pound chicken until thin between two pieces of wax paper. Place 1 slice of ham, 1 slice of cheese, salt, pepper and ¼ of the parsley on each breast half. Roll up and secure ends with toothpicks. Spread 1½ t. mayonnaise on each piece of chicken. Roll in bread crumbs and place in an 8" square baking pan, which has been sprayed with no-stick cooking spray. Put on middle rack of oven and bake at 450° for 20 minutes, or until golden and done. Serves 4.

NANCY EMERSON

CRISPY CHICKEN

Good family fare.

8 chicken breast halves, boned
1 large egg
3 T. milk
1-1½ c. instant potato flakes

1 t. garlic powder
⅓ c. Parmesan cheese, grated
⅓-½ c. butter or margarine,
  melted

Beat egg and milk together. Mix potato flakes, garlic powder, and Parmesan cheese. Roll chicken in egg mixture, then in potato flake mixture. Place in a lightly greased baking dish. Pour butter over breasts and bake at 400° for 50 minutes. Serves 8.

VARIATION: An assortment of chicken pieces (with bones left in) can be used, and the result is a fried chicken substitute for a picnic dinner!

CONNIE GARRETT
BONNIE MOREAU

CURRIED CHICKEN I

2 chickens, cooked, boned and
  chopped
½ c. butter or margarine
1 clove garlic, crushed
1 onion, chopped
3-4 celery sticks, chopped
Fresh mushrooms, sliced
⅓ c. flour

1 t. salt
3-4 t. curry
4 c. chicken broth (reserve from
  cooking chickens)
1 c. Major Grey's Chutney
¼ almonds, chopped
1 t. Dijon mustard

Brown meat in butter, add garlic, onions, celery, and mushrooms, cooking over medium heat until celery and onions are clear. Add flour, salt, and curry. Cook about 5 minutes; add chicken broth, then chutney, almonds, and mustard. Simmer approximately 45 minutes until tender. Serve over hot rice. Serves 8.

CYNTHIA CECIL

CURRIED CHICKEN II   *L*

2 c. cooked chicken (or any cooked meat)
½ c. onion, chopped
3 T. oil
3 T. flour (more if needed)
½ t. ginger
2 t. cumin
¼ t. red pepper
1 t. salt

1½ t. coriander
½ t. turmeric
1 t. pepper
¼ t. ground cloves
½ t. cinnamon
2 t. curry
1 lemon (grated rind and juice)
4-6 c. liquid (stock or water with chicken cubes)

Sauté onion in oil. Mix all dry spices and add to onion, cooking and stirring 3 minutes over low heat. Add lemon and 4 cups liquid; simmer until sauce thickens slightly. Add meat and more liquid, if needed. Prepare ahead of time; freezes well. Serves 6.

KATHY WATSON

CURRIED CHICKEN III

2 c. chicken, cooked and chopped
1 large onion, chopped
1 large cooking apple, chopped
1-2 T. butter or margarine
1 T. flour
1 T. sugar

2-4 t. curry
Salt and pepper
1 T. coconut, moistened with a little boiling water
Juice of 1 lemon
8 oz. chicken stock
2 T. golden raisins

Sauté onion and apple in butter until softened. Mix flour, sugar, curry, salt and pepper; add to onion mixture. Stir in coconut and lemon juice, then add as much stock as needed to produce a thick sauce. Sprinkle in golden raisins and simmer. Add chicken. Serves 6 to 8.

ENID TRUSCOTT

SUGGESTED TOPPINGS FOR CURRIED CHICKEN I, II, AND III: bananas, hard-boiled eggs, raisins, apples, chutney, peanuts, bacon, sunflower seeds, currants, toasted coconut, sweet chow-chow, pineapple, onions.

CHICKEN CURRY CASSEROLE

3 lb. chicken fryer, skinned and
    cut-up (or 6 large pieces)
2 T. margarine
1 onion, finely chopped
1 apple, finely chopped
1 T. curry

1 (10¾ oz) can cream of
    mushroom soup
1 c. cream
Salt
Paprika

Melt butter in saucepan and sauté onion, apple, and curry until onion is
transparent. Add the soup and cream. Spread chicken in buttered casserole dish and season with salt and paprika. Pour sauce over chicken and
bake, uncovered at 350° for 1½ hours. Serve with rice. Serves 6.

JOANNE RAMSEY

L CURRY GLAZED CHICKEN

Incredibly easy and good!

1 (2-2½ lb.) broiler-fryer, cut up (or
    equivalent number of breasts)
2 T. margarine or butter
¼ c. honey

3 T. Dijon mustard
2 t. curry
½ t. salt

Put margarine in 9" x 13" baking pan, then place in oven to melt while oven
is heating to 375°. Remove pan from oven; stir in honey, mustard, curry and
salt. Add chicken pieces, turning to coat thoroughly. Bake uncovered for 45
minutes, turning and basting several times. Serves 4. (This makes a generous
amount of sauce and would also be good on the grill.)

ELIZABETH STOYKO

CHICKEN DIJON

16 pieces of chicken, boned
1 t. salt
1 c. milk
1½ c. sour cream
1 c. Dijon mustard
3 t. paprika

2 t. celery salt
2 T. Worcestershire
3 t. lemon juice
3 cloves garlic, pressed
Pepper
1 c. cracker crumbs, finely crushed

Combine salt and milk. Soak chicken in mixture for 1 hour. In a separate
bowl, mix next 7 ingredients. Let stand for 1 hour. Dry chicken and sprinkle
with pepper. Heavily coat chicken pieces with sour cream mixture. Sprinkle
with cracker crumbs and place on a greased rack in a shallow baking pan.
Bake at 400° for 15 minutes, then lower temperature to 325° and continue
baking for 20 minutes. Serves 8 to 10.

MIM SCHUTE

LIGHT CHICKEN DIVAN   *L*

4 chicken breast halves, skinned,
  boned, and cooked
2 T. light soft margarine
3 T. flour

1 (10¾ oz.) can chicken broth, fat
  removed
3 T. dry sherry
½-1 c. skim milk, warmed
1 bunch broccoli, steamed

Melt margarine and add flour to make a roux. Gradually add chicken broth, stirring constantly to make a smooth, thick sauce. Cook 5 minutes. Add sherry and stir. Add milk and cook until thickened. Arrange broccoli and chicken on serving platter. Cover with sauce. Serve with steamed rice. Serves 4.

KATHY DeLOYHT

CHICKEN AND DRESSING CASSEROLE

"This is my family's #1 most requested recipe!"

1 chicken, cooked and cubed
1 (10¾ oz.) can cream of chicken
  soup
½ c. mayonnaise
1 c. celery, diced

1 t. onion, minced
½ c. Pepperidge Farm herb
  dressing
Dash each salt and pepper
½ c. slivered almonds (optional)

Place chicken in bowl and add all other ingredients. Pour into greased baking dish and bake at 350° for about 25 minutes. Serves 8.

PATSY ARNETT

CHICKEN ENCHILADAS   *L*

8 oz. chicken breasts, skinned,
  boned, cooked, and chopped
½ c. onion, chopped
2 cloves garlic, minced
1½ c. Mexican-style stewed
  tomatoes, chopped and
  undrained

½ c. fresh mushrooms, sliced
Salt and pepper to taste
4 (6") flour or corn tortillas
4 oz. reduced-fat Cheddar
  cheese, shredded and divided
½ c. plain low-fat yogurt
Black olives, sliced (optional)

Spray 1 10" non-stick skillet with no-stick cooking spray. Sauté onion and garlic, stirring constantly for about 1 minute. Add tomatoes and their liquid, mushrooms, salt and pepper. Cook, stirring occasionally, until sauce is thickened, about 6 to 8 minutes. Transfer half the sauce to a small bowl and combine with chicken. Set remaining sauce aside. Microwave tortillas 10 seconds until flexible. Spread with ½ oz. cheese and ¼ chicken mixture. Roll to enclose and place seam side down in 8" square pan. Repeat with remaining tortillas. Top with remaining sauce and cheese. Bake at 350° for 15 to 20 minutes. Garnish with yogurt and olives. Serves 4.

SUSAN WRENN

POULTRY

CHICKEN FIESTA

This is even better the second day.

1 roasting chicken breast, cooked
and cut into bite-sized pieces
1 (10¾ oz.) can cream of chicken
soup
1 (10¾ oz.) can cream of
mushroom soup

1 can Ro-Tel whole tomatoes,
drained
1 c. Cheddar cheese, grated
1 (10-count) pkg. flour tortillas

Mix chicken, soups, tomatoes, and cheese. Shred tortillas and use to cover bottom of a 9" x 13" pan. Top with half of the chicken mixture. Repeat. (This may be done in 3 layers in a small round casserole.) You will not need all the tortillas. Bake at 350° for 30 minutes. Serves 6.

CRISTY JARVIS

VARIATION: Try Monterey Jack or a combination of cheeses. Sprinkle extra cheese on top.

Q   FLAT CHICKEN

6-8 chicken breast halves, boned
and skinned
Flour for dredging
3-4 eggs, beaten

1 c. Parmesan cheese, grated
Olive oil
¼ c. butter
½-1 c. white wine

Flatten chicken and cut into pieces. Dredge in flour, then in mixture of eggs and cheese. Fry in hot oil until brown. Remove from pan, but do not drain. Remove excess oil from pan and add butter. Lay chicken in pan and add wine. Cover and simmer 10 minutes. Serve with rice. Serves 6 to 8.

LINDA STEPANIAN

HERB BAKED CHICKEN BREASTS

6 chicken breast halves (boneless
if desired)
2 t. salt
¼ t. pepper
¼ c. butter or margarine, melted,
or corn oil

2 T. lemon juice
2 t. rosemary or herb of choice
(possibly ginger or oregano)
Thin lemon slices for garnish

Sprinkle chicken with salt and pepper. Place in a shallow baking pan. Combine butter, lemon juice, and herb. Spoon over chicken. Bake at 375° for 40 to 45 minutes, basting occasionally with pan juices. Garnish with lemon slices. Serves 6.

BRENDA JOHNSON

146

CHICKEN BREASTS WITH HERBS AND WINE   *Q L*

4 chicken breast halves, skinned
   and boned
2 T. margarine
¼ t. marjoram

¼ t. thyme
1 t. parsley
¼ c. white wine

Melt margarine in baking dish in microwave. Add herbs to margarine. Dip chicken in margarine, coating both sides. Place chicken in baking dish and cover with plastic wrap. Microwave for 4 minutes. Add wine, cover, and continue cooking for 3 minutes. Check for doneness and cook longer if necessary. (Remember that chicken will cook a little longer as it sits.) Pour juices over chicken before serving. Serves 4.

BARBARA PARKER

HERBED ROAST CHICKEN

A delicious French method of roasting.

1 (3-4 lb.) whole chicken
1 carrot, thinly sliced
1 small onion, chopped
3 T. margarine, divided
1 t. plus additional thyme or dill

2 slices bacon
Paprika
1 beef bouillon cube
¾ c. hot water
Juice of 1 lemon

Place carrot, onion, 1 T. margarine and 1 t. thyme in chicken. Lay bacon on chicken and dot with 2 T. margarine. Dust generously with thyme and paprika. Roast chicken at 450° for 15 minutes. Reduce heat to 350°, and roast for 1½ to 1¾ hours more. Combine bouillon and hot water and baste chicken every 15 minutes after heat is lowered. Put chicken on serving platter. Separate pan juices from fat. Return juices to roasting pan, add lemon juice and heat while scraping pan bottom. Serve sauce over chicken. This is wonderful with rice. Serves 4 to 6.

JOANNE RAMSEY

HARRIET'S ITALIAN CHICKEN

A nice change from traditional spaghetti.

4 chicken breast halves, boned
2 T. oil or no-stick cooking spray
1 large onion, sliced
1 red bell pepper, sliced
1 green pepper, sliced
1 (6 oz.) can tomato paste
1 (14½ oz.) can chicken broth
  (low- salt, if desired)

Oregano or other Italian herbs to
  taste
Black olives, sliced (optional)
Mushrooms, sliced (optional)
Mozzarella slices or grated
  Parmesan cheese
Spaghetti or other pasta, cooked

Brown chicken in oil and remove from pan. Cook onion and peppers until onion is transparent and peppers are slightly soft, but still firm. Remove peppers and onion. Return chicken to pan. Mix tomato paste, chicken broth and herbs and pour over chicken. Cover and simmer on medium heat for 20 to 30 minutes until chicken is done. Return peppers and onion to pan and heat for 5 minutes. Place cheese slices on top and cover pan for 1 to 2 minutes until cheese melts. Serve over spaghetti. Serves 6.

ALLYN CROSBY

CHICKEN ITALIANO

4 chicken breast halves, skinned
  and boned
Seasoned bread crumbs
2 T. cooking oil
1 c. dry white wine or chicken
  broth (or mixture of both)

2 T. white wine vinegar
1 T. capers, drained
1¼ t. Italian seasoning
¼ t. pepper
Romano cheese, grated (optional)

Coat chicken with crumbs. Heat oil in skillet and brown breasts, turning only once. Mix wine or broth, vinegar, capers, Italian seasoning, and pepper. Pour over chicken and cook over medium heat for 20 to 30 minutes. Sprinkle with Romano cheese if desired. Serve with rice. Serves 4.

MARTHA SUSAN SANDERS

L　　　EASY JAMBALAYA

½-1 lb. chicken, cooked, and
  cubed
1 T. oil
1 c. onion, chopped
1 c. green pepper, chopped
1 c. tomato, chopped
2-3 cloves garlic, minced
2 bay leaves

½ t. thyme
4 t. parsley, minced
¼ t. pepper
2-3 dashes cayenne pepper
  (optional)
2 c. chicken broth
1 c. uncooked rice

148

Sauté onion and pepper in oil in a 4-quart Dutch oven until softened. Add tomatoes, garlic, bay leaves, thyme, parsley, and peppers. Add chicken broth and bring to a boil. Add rice and chicken, then cover and simmer for 20 minutes. Uncover and let some of liquid evaporate. Fluff rice with a fork before serving. (You may add Creole seasoning and thinly sliced low-fat smoked sausage if desired.) Serves 4.

MELANIE JONES

OVEN JAMBALAYA

2 lb. chicken, cooked and chopped
2 lbs. smoked sausage, sliced
1 (10½ oz) can beef bouillon
1 (10¾ oz) can onion soup
1 (8 oz.) can tomato sauce
½ c. margarine
½-1 c. green onion, chopped

½ c. parsley, chopped
2 c. uncooked rice
1 t. fresh garlic, crushed
½ c. white onion, chopped
½ c. celery, chopped (optional)
Pepper to taste
Tabasco to taste

Combine all ingredients in a large casserole dish. Cover and bake at 350° for 1 hour and 15 minutes. Serves 6 to 8.

MELINDA WAY

CHICKEN JERUSALEM I

4 chicken breast halves, skinned and boned
¼ c. butter or margarine
¼ lb. mushrooms, sliced
1 t. MSG (optional)
1 t. salt
⅛ t. pepper

1 (9 oz.) pkg. frozen artichoke hearts
⅓ c. sherry
⅓ c. water
1 T. flour
1 c. sour cream
¼ t. paprika

Sauté mushrooms in butter. Remove from pan and reserve butter. Sprinkle chicken with MSG, salt, and pepper. Brown in reserved butter. Add artichoke hearts, sherry, and water. Cover and simmer 20 to 30 minutes, or until chicken is done. Return mushrooms to pan for last 5 minutes of cooking. Transfer chicken and vegetables to serving platter and keep warm. Blend flour and sour cream. Stir into liquid in skillet and heat, but do not boil. Spoon over chicken and sprinkle with paprika. Serves 4.

BRENDA WILKINS

CHICKEN JERUSALEM II

4 chicken breast halves, boned
¼ lb. mushrooms, sliced
1 clove garlic, finely chopped
1 T. chives, chopped (fresh or frozen)
3 T. butter or margarine

1 (10½ oz) can chicken consommé
⅓ c. white wine
1 (9 oz) pkg. frozen artichoke hearts
2 T. cornstarch
¼ c. water

Cook chicken breasts in microwave and set aside. Sauté mushrooms with garlic and chives in butter for 2 minutes. Add consommé, wine and artichoke hearts to mushroom mixture. Simmer until artichokes are tender. Combine cornstarch and water and add sauce to thicken. Cook over low heat, stirring constantly. Season to taste, add chicken, and keep warm until serving time. Serves 4.

GIGI GUNNELS

L LEMON CHICKEN I

6 chicken breast halves, skinned and boned
⅓ c. fresh lemon juice
¼ c. onion, minced
1 T. lemon peel, grated
½ t. thyme

¼ t. pepper
2 T. unsalted margarine
1 T. cornstarch
2 T. cold water
Parsley sprigs

Combine lemon juice, onion, lemon peel, thyme and pepper. Pour over chicken, toss, cover, and refrigerate overnight. Drain chicken and reserve marinade. Brown chicken in margarine. Place in baking dish. Pour marinade and margarine in skillet over chicken and bake uncovered at 350° for 30 minutes. Baste several times. Remove chicken to serving platter. Blend cornstarch and water. Add to marinade and cook until it thickens. Spoon over chicken and garnish with parsley. Serves 6.

CAROL FLIPPEN

L LEMON CHICKEN II

1 whole chicken
2 whole lemons

Salt and pepper to taste

Salt and pepper inside the cavity of the chicken, using lots of pepper. Roll lemons with palm of hand, then pierce all over to enable juice to come out during cooking. Place the 2 lemons inside the chicken and sew up the cavity. Salt and pepper outside of the chicken. Place breast side down in roasting pan (not on a rack) and bake at 400° for 15 minutes. Turn chicken over and continue cooking at 350° for 1 hour. Serve on a bed of rice. Serves 4 to 6.

NANCY McCANDLISH

TWENTY-MINUTE LEMON GARLIC CHICKEN *Q L*

6 chicken breast halves, skinned and boned
¼ c. butter or margarine, or no-stick cooking spray
4 cloves garlic, crushed
½ c. chicken broth
½ c. white wine
3 T. lemon juice
1 (2.5 oz.) can mushroom pieces, drained
¼ t. salt
⅛ t. pepper
Hot cooked rice or noodles

Melt butter in large skillet over medium heat, or spray pan with no-stick cooking spray. Add chicken and garlic; cook until chicken is golden brown, about 3 to 4 minutes on each side. Add broth, wine, lemon juice, mushroom pieces, salt, and pepper; bring to a boil. Cover, reduce heat, and simmer about 20 minutes or until chicken is tender. Serve with hot noodles or rice. Serves 6.

BEBE LUCK

LEMON CHICKEN AND THYME *Q L*

4 chicken breast halves, skinned and boned
3 T. flour
½ t. salt
½ t. pepper
2 T. olive oil, divided
1 T. margarine
1 medium onion, chopped
1 clove garlic, minced (optional)
1 c. chicken broth
3 T. lemon juice
½ t. thyme

Combine flour, salt, and pepper, and lightly dredge chicken in flour mixture; reserve flour. In skillet heat 1 T. oil, add chicken and brown for 5 minutes on one side. Turn, add 1 T. oil, and brown other side for 5 minutes. Remove chicken and keep warm. Add margarine to skillet and cook onion and garlic until softened. Stir in reserved flour mixture and cook about 1 minute. Add broth, lemon juice, and thyme, and bring to a boil, stirring constantly. Return chicken to skillet, cover, and reduce heat. Cook until chicken is done, about 5 minutes. Pour sauce over chicken when serving. Serves 4.

ALYCE OUTLAW

CREAMED CHICKEN MACARONI CASSEROLE

Kids love this!

2 c. chicken, cooked and cubed
3 T. canola margarine, melted
1 heaping T. flour
1 (3 oz) pkg. light cream cheese
1 (4 oz) jar pimiento, chopped
  (optional)

1 t. salt
Dash of pepper
1 c. milk
1 c. chicken broth
1½ c. cooked macaroni

Combine margarine, flour, cream cheese, pimiento, and seasonings over low heat. Add milk and broth gradually, stirring constantly. Heat to boiling and cook for 3 minutes. (This may be done in the microwave.) Add chicken and macaroni and pour into a 1½-quart casserole. Bake at 350° for 25 to 30 minutes. Serves 8.

KATHY SPAHN

CHICKEN MANDALAY

8 chicken breast halves, boned
4-5 T. flour
1 T. curry (or less)
2 t. salt
2 T. oil
1 c. water
1 T. sugar

2 beef bouillon cubes
1 large onion, chopped
1 (4¾ oz) jar strained apricots with
  tapioca (baby food)
2 T. lemon juice
2 T. soy sauce

Combine flour, curry and salt and roll chicken in mixture. Brown in oil and place in 9" x 13" baking dish. Pour off excess grease, leaving chicken drippings in skillet. Stir water, sugar, bouillon, onions, apricots, lemon juice and soy sauce into drippings. Heat to boiling and pour over chicken. Cover with foil and bake at 350° for 1 to 1½ hours. Let brown, uncovered, last 10 minutes of cooking time. Serves 6 to 8.

BRENDA MATHEWS

Q L SAUTÉED CHICKEN WITH MANDARIN ORANGES

1½ lbs. chicken breasts, pounded
  and cut into strips
Whole wheat flour
1 T. olive or sesame oil
1 large sweet onion, cut into strips
Dash of onion powder
Dash of garlic powder

Dash each of white and black
  pepper
2 T. sesame seeds
6 T. soy sauce
6 T. cashew halves
36 mandarin orange sections

Coat chicken lightly with flour and brown in oil with onion and seasonings until chicken is cooked through. Sprinkle with sesame seeds and soy sauce. Serve topped with cashew halves and orange segments. Serves 6.

JEAN JONES

MARG LEE CHICKEN

4 chicken breast halves, skinned and boned, cut into ½" strips
½ c. soy sauce
½ c. Hoisin sauce
¼ c. sherry
1 T. cornstarch
4 T. oil (peanut, corn or canola), divided

1 clove garlic, finely minced
2 t. fresh ginger root, finely minced
¼ c. green onions, chopped
1 c. carrots, shredded
½ lb. pea pods
¼ lb. fresh bean sprouts
Hot cooked rice

Marinate chicken in mixture of soy sauce, Hoisin sauce, sherry, and cornstarch. Cover and refrigerate for at least 30 minutes. Drain chicken, reserving marinade. Heat 1 T. oil in wok or frying pan, until hot but not smoking. Add garlic, ginger, and green onions, stirring quickly for 15 seconds. Add carrots and pea pods; stir quickly for 1 minute. Remove vegetables to side dish. Add 1 T. oil and quickly stir in the bean sprouts; remove to a side dish. Add 1 T. oil to pan, turn heat to high, add half the chicken and cook 2 to 3 minutes. Repeat. Add vegetables to pan; add marinade and stir until all ingredients are mixed, about 2 minutes. Serve with hot rice. Serves 4.

KAY WILLIAMS

MONTEREY CHICKEN

1 lb. small chicken breasts or chicken tenders
2 eggs, beaten
1½ c. bread crumbs
3 T. butter

1 (10¾ oz) can cream of broccoli soup
1½ c. Monterey Jack cheese, grated

Dip chicken pieces in egg and then roll in bread crumbs. Repeat. Melt butter in skillet and brown chicken on both sides. Place chicken pieces in buttered 10" x 10" dish. Spread dollop of broccoli soup over each piece, then top with Monterey Jack cheese. Bake at 350° for 30 minutes. Serve with rice or fettuccini. Serves 4.

PEGGY CONWAY

L   PAULINE MORRIS'S CHICKEN

Good weeknight supper.

4 whole chicken breasts
3 zucchini, cut in ⅛" slices
1 medium onion, minced
2 T. butter

1 (28 oz.) can tomatoes
1 t. curry
Salt and pepper
Parmesan cheese

Boil chicken until tender, remove skin and bones, and cut into bite-sized pieces. Sauté zucchini and onion in butter for 2 to 3 minutes. Combine chicken, zucchini mixture, tomatoes, and curry in a 3-quart casserole, adding salt and pepper to taste. Sprinkle with Parmesan and bake at 375° for 45 minutes. Serves 8.

ALICE McGUIRE

Q L   SAUTÉED CHICKEN IN MUSHROOM SAUCE

10 oz. chicken breasts, skinned
    and boned
2 t. flour
¼ t. salt
⅛ t. pepper
Small amount of margarine

1 c. mushrooms, sliced
¼ c. scallions, chopped
½ t. tarragon leaves
¼ c. dry white wine
¼ c. water

Combine flour, salt, and pepper. Sprinkle chicken breasts with flour mixture. Heat margarine in skillet. Add chicken and cook until light brown on both sides. Add mushrooms, scallions, and tarragon; sauté until soft. Add wine and bring to a boil. Add water, reduce heat, and simmer about 15 minutes. Turn chicken once during cooking time. Serves 2.

KATIE BELK

L   ORANGE GLAZED CHICKEN

1 (2-2½ lb.) chicken, cut-up
1 (1 oz.) pkg. Lipton onion soup mix

1 (6 oz.) can frozen orange juice,
    thawed
Hot cooked rice

Arrange chicken pieces in a casserole dish. Combine onion soup mix and orange juice; brush chicken with half the glaze. Bake at 400° for 1 hour, basting frequently with remaining glaze. If chicken gets brown too early, lower oven temperature. Serve with rice. Serves 6.

PRISCILLA BURBANK

ORIENTAL SUNSHINE CHICKEN *L*

Our family favorite!

1 (1¼ lb.) whole chicken breast, boned and cut into ½" cubes
¼ c. orange juice
1 T. dry sherry
1 T. cornstarch
1 T. Chinese mustard
2 T. soy sauce
½ t. hot pepper sauce
3 T. peanut oil

½ c. onion, chopped
1 (8 oz.) can water chestnuts, drained and cubed
½ c. green pepper, cubed
¼ lb. snow peas (optional)
1 (11 oz.) can mandarin oranges, drained
Hot cooked rice
Chinese noodles (optional)

Combine orange juice, sherry, cornstarch, Chinese mustard, soy sauce, and hot pepper sauce. Marinate chicken in mixture for 10 to 15 minutes. Heat oil in large skillet or wok. Add onion and stir-fry 1 minute. Remove chicken from marinade with slotted spoon. Add to hot oil. Stir-fry for 2 to 3 minutes. Add water chestnuts, green pepper, and remaining marinade. Cook with chicken for 3 minutes. Add snow peas and cook 1 minute longer. Add orange segments and heat thoroughly. Serve over rice with Chinese noodles, Chinese mustard, and sweet and sour sauce. Serves 4.

NANCYE WINTER

PARMESAN BAKED CHICKEN

Italian without a sauce!

1 (2½-3 lb.) chicken fryer, cut-up and skinned
1 c. plain bread crumbs
¼ c. Parmesan cheese, grated
1 T. dried parsley

½ (2.8 oz.) can Durkee's fried onions
½ c. butter or margarine
1-2 cloves garlic, crushed

Combine bread crumbs, Parmesan cheese, parsley, and onions in shallow dish and mix thoroughly. Melt butter in saucepan, add garlic and sauté 1 minute. Remove from heat. Dip chicken pieces in butter, then rolll in crumb mixture until well-coated. Arrange on foil-lined cookie sheet and pour remaining butter mixture over top. Bake at 350° for 1 to 1¼ hours. Serves 6.

LORNA ROWLAND

Q CHICKEN PARMIGIANA

4 chicken breast halves, skinned
   and boned
Salt and pepper to taste
2 T. olive oil
1 small green pepper, coarsely
   chopped

4 oz. fresh mushrooms, sliced
1 clove garlic, minced
1 (14-16 oz.) jar spaghetti sauce or
   2 c. homemade sauce
4 oz. Mozzarella cheese, grated
1 T. Parmesan cheese, grated

Flatten chicken with palm of hand to an even thickness. Sprinkle lightly with salt and pepper. Heat oil in large skillet and sauté chicken 3 minutes per side. Remove chicken to 2-quart baking dish. Add green pepper and mushrooms to pan drippings, and cook over medium heat for 4 minutes. Add garlic and cook 1 minute longer. Add spaghetti sauce and bring to a simmer while stirring. Pour sauce over chicken, top with Mozzarella and Parmesan and bake at 350° uncovered until cheese is melted and slightly browned, about 15 minutes. Serves 4.

JO ANN CHARLESWORTH

L PARSLEY AND PARMESAN BAKED CHICKEN

Kids love this!

3 lbs. chicken pieces, skinned
¼ c. fat-free Italian dressing
½ c. Parmesan cheese, grated
½ c. bread crumbs

2 T. parsley, chopped
½ t. salt
½ t. pepper
½ t. paprika

Combine chicken pieces and salad dressing and place in a plastic bag; marinate in the refrigerator for 4 hours. Combine cheese, bread crumbs, parsley, salt, pepper, and paprika in another plastic bag. Remove chicken from marinade, reserving marinade. Coat chicken with dry mixture and place in a 9" x 13" baking dish. Spoon remaining marinade over chicken and bake at 350° for 45 to 50 minutes. Serves 4.

KATHIE MARKEL

Q L CHICKEN PICCATA

8 chicken breast halves, boned
   and skinned
½ c. flour
1 t. salt
¼ t. pepper
¼ t. paprika
1 T. olive oil

¼ c. butter or margarine
2-4 T. Madeira wine
3 T. fresh lemon juice
2-3 T. capers
¼ c. parsley, minced
1 lemon, thinly sliced

Place each chicken breast in plastic bag and pound with a cleaver until thin. Combine flour, salt, pepper, and paprika in a large bag. Add breasts and shake well. Heat oil and butter; sauté chicken breasts 2 to 3 minutes on each side. Drain on paper towels and keep warm. Drain all but 2 T. fat from the pan and stir in Madeira. Scrape bottom of the skillet. Add lemon juice and heat briefly. Return chicken to pan and reheat. Add capers and sprinkle with parsley. Arrange on serving platter with lemon slices as a garnish. Serves 8.

JANET DAUGHDRILLE

VARIATION: Chicken broth can be substituted for Madeira wine.

BETTY HOFFER

POPPY CHICKEN CASSEROLE

4 whole chicken breasts
2 cloves garlic, minced
2 (10¾ oz) cans cream of chicken soup
8 oz light sour cream
2 t. poppy seeds
1½ rolls Ritz crackers, crushed
¾ c. butter, melted

Combine chicken with garlic and bake at 350° for 30 minutes. Cut into bite-sized pieces. Add soup, sour cream, poppy seeds and place in casserole dish. Combine crackers and butter, spread on top of chicken. Bake at 350° until hot and bubbly, about 15 to 20 minutes. Serves 6.

SUSAN KNAYSI

CHICKEN POT PIE

3-4 lb. chicken, cooked
1 (15 oz) can peas, drained
1 (16 oz) can sliced carrots, drained
2 potatoes, sliced
1 (15 oz) jar whole onions, drained
Salt and pepper to taste
1 c. broth from chicken
1 (8.5 oz) can mushrooms, drained
1 (10¾ oz) can cream of mushroom soup
2 T. cornstarch
Dash of Tabasco (optional)
White wine (optional)
½ c. margarine or butter
1 c. self-rising flour
½ t. black pepper
1 c. buttermilk

Debone and chop chicken, reserving 1 c. chicken broth. In 9" x 13" pan layer chicken, peas, carrots, potatoes, and onions. Sprinkle salt and pepper between each layer. Combine broth, mushrooms, soup, cornstarch, Tabasco and a little white wine if desired. Cover the top layer with mushroom mixture. Cut margarine into flour, add pepper, and stir in buttermilk; pour over casserole. (Can be frozen at this point.) Bake at 425° for 30 minutes. Serves 10.

BRENDA WILKINS

157

CHICKEN BREASTS ROMANO

6 chicken breast halves, skinned
  and boned
½ c. flour
1 t. salt
1 t. pepper
2 T. butter or margarine
½ c. onion, minced
2 c. tomato juice
1 c. Romano cheese, grated and
  divided

1 T. sugar
½ t. garlic salt
1 t. whole oregano
1 t. basil leaves
1 t. vinegar
1 (4 oz.) can sliced mushrooms,
  drained
1 T. fresh parsley, chopped
Hot cooked spaghetti
Parsley for garnish

Combine flour, salt, and pepper; dredge chicken in mixture, then brown in margarine. Drain chicken on paper towels. Pour off all but 1 T. of pan drippings; sauté onion in reserved drippings until tender. Add tomato juice, ¼ c. Romano cheese, sugar, garlic salt, oregano, basil, vinegar, mushrooms and parsley; stir well. Return chicken to skillet, cover and simmer for 45 minutes, spooning sauce over chicken several times while cooking. Place on a warm platter and sprinkle with remaining Romano cheese. Serve over pasta with parsley for garnish. Serves 6.

ANN CRENSHAW

GOURMET HOT CHICKEN SALAD

Great for luncheons.

5 c. chicken, cooked and diced
4 hard-boiled eggs, sliced
¾ c. light mayonnaise
2 T. lemon juice
1 t. onion, minced
1 t. salt
¾ c. cream of chicken soup

2 c. celery, chopped
2 pimientos, finely chopped
  (optional)
1½ c. potato chips, crushed
1 c. sharp Cheddar cheese,
  shredded
⅔ c. slivered almonds, toasted

Layer chicken and egg slices in large flat casserole. Combine next 7 ingredients and pour over chicken and eggs. Sprinkle top with potato chips, cheese and almonds. Cover and refrigerate overnight. Bake at 400° for 20 to 25 minutes. Serves 10.

BERENICE CRAIGIE

VARIATION: Omit pimiento in mayonnaise mixture; add 2 c. sliced water chestnuts and 1 (8 oz.) can sliced mushrooms (both drained). Omit hard-boiled eggs. Top dish with 2 (2.8 oz.) cans Durkee onion rings instead of potato chips.

DEB POVLISHOCK

CHICKEN SCALLOPINI   Q

4 chicken breast halves
Salt and pepper
½ c. flour
3 T. margarine

1 c. vermouth
¼ t. lemon peel
Chopped parsley for garnish
Lemon slices for garnish

Sprinkle chicken with salt and pepper. Dredge in flour, coating all sides. Melt margarine in saucepan and add chicken, cooking until browned. Remove pan from heat and add vermouth and lemon peel. Return to heat and boil rapidly until thickened, stirring constantly. Reduce heat and simmer 5 to 10 minutes. Serve garnished with parsley and lemon slices. Delicious with rice. Serves 4.

TEMPLE SHANKLIN

SLOW-COOK CHICKEN

Good and simple family supper.

10 pieces of chicken
Margarine
Salt or seasoned salt

Pepper
1 (10¾ oz.) can chicken broth
1 (8 oz.) can mushrooms, drained

Rub a little margarine, salt, and pepper on both sides of chicken. Bake for 1 hour at 350°. Remove from oven and pour broth over chicken. Cover tightly with foil and continue to bake at 200° for 2 hours. After about 1½ hours, pour mushrooms over chicken. The broth can be used for gravy, if desired. Serves 6 to 8.

BRENDA WILKINS

SPICY CHICKEN WITH RED AND GREEN PEPPERS   Q

1 lb. chicken breasts, skinned,
   boned, and cut into ¼" strips
4 T. rice wine vinegar (no substitute)
3 T. soy sauce
1 T. sugar
1 T. cornstarch
2 t. Oriental sesame oil
1 t. crushed red pepper
3 T. peanut oil

1 T. fresh ginger, minced
1 large onion, cut into ¼" strips
1 large red bell pepper, cut into
   ¼" strips
1 large green bell pepper, cut
   into ¼" strips
½ c. low sodium chicken broth
½ t. salt
½ t. pepper

Whisk together rice vinegar, soy sauce, sugar, cornstarch, sesame oil, and crushed red pepper. Add chicken, tossing to coat. Marinate for 5 minutes at room temperature. Heat wok to high. Add peanut oil, ginger, onion, red and green peppers. Stir-fry 2 minutes, until onion is a bit soft. Add chicken, marinade, and chicken broth. Stir until chicken is done, about 5 minutes. Season with salt and pepper. Serves 4.

ANN CRENSHAW

CURRIED CHICKEN SPAGHETTI CASSEROLE

4 chicken breast halves, skinned
 and boned
3 T. flour
2 T. curry
2½ t. salt
⅓ c. olive oil

1 large onion, thickly sliced
2 cloves garlic, crushed
2½ c. water
8 oz. uncooked spaghetti, broken
 into thirds
Chopped parsley for garnish

Mix flour, curry, and salt in a paper bag. Add chicken and shake to coat, reserving leftover flour mixture. Heat oil over medium heat. Brown chicken in oil, remove from pan, and keep warm. Sauté onion in drippings until tender. Stir in garlic and reserved flour mixture. Add water and pasta and place chicken on top. Reduce heat, cover and simmer for 20 minutes, until spaghetti is tender. Sprinkle with parsley. Serves 4.

ELIZABETH STOYKO

CHICKEN AND SQUASH CASSEROLE

3 c. chicken, cooked and cubed
1 (7 oz.) pkg. Pepperidge Farm
 Herb Dressing mix
½ c. butter or margarine, melted
2 c. squash, cooked and
 seasoned with salt, pepper, and
 onion

2 (10¾ oz.) cans cream of chicken
 soup
1 c. sour cream or plain yogurt

Combine dressing and butter. Sprinkle ¾ c. of dressing mixture in the bottom of a 9" x 13" pan. Place squash on top of dressing. Mix chicken, soup, and sour cream, and spread on top of squash layer. Place remainder of dressing on top of chicken mixture. Bake at 350° for 30 to 40 minutes, until hot and bubbly. Serves 6 to 8.

NANCY LIPSCOMB

CHICKEN TARRAGON (OR PAPRIKA)

6-8 chicken breasts, boned
½ c. margarine
3 onions, chopped
1 c. chicken broth, divided
1-2 T. tarragon (or paprika)

½-1 t. salt
2 T. flour
1 c. light sour cream
1 T. parsley

Melt margarine in large skillet and brown chicken. Add onions and cook until golden. Add ½ cup chicken broth, tarragon (or paprika), and salt. Cook slowly 15 minutes, turning once. Mix flour with remaining broth in small jar and shake vigorously to eliminate lumps. Add mixture to skillet; stir and cook another 15 minutes. Place chicken on platter and add sour cream to pan mixture. Heat slowly until bubbly and pour over chicken. Sprinkle with parsley and serve with rice. Serves 6 to 8.

JOANNE RAMSEY

CHICKEN IN A BASKET   *L*

Great for days when carpooling afternoon activities!

1 chicken breast half
2 T. uncooked long grain rice
1 small onion, sliced
1 small carrot, sliced
1 small bell pepper, sliced
1 small tomato, halved
1 stalk celery, chopped

Mushrooms
1 T. butter
1 T. Worcestershire
1 T. soy sauce
1 T. water
Salt, pepper to taste
Oregano to taste

Place rice on a sheet of aluminum foil. Top with chicken, then slices of vegetables and remaining ingredients. Season with salt, pepper, and oregano. Seal foil tightly and place in 9" x 13" baking dish. Bake at 350° for 1½ hours. Prepare as many chicken baskets as needed. Serves 1.

DIANNE GIBSON

CHICKEN YUM YUM

8 chicken breast halves, cooked
  and chopped
1 (10¾ oz.) can cream of
  mushroom soup
1 (10¾ oz.) can cream of chicken
  soup
1 (10¾ oz.) can cream of celery
  soup

3 c. Pepperidge Farm cornbread
  dressing
1½ c. mayonnaise
1 (8 oz.) can water chestnuts,
  sliced and drained
Salt and pepper

Combine all ingredients and place in 9" x 13" baking dish. Cover and let stand in refrigerator for 8 hours. (Dish may be frozen at this point.) Bake uncovered at 325° for 1 hour. Serves 8.

NANCY CHEELY

WINE BAKED CHICKEN BREASTS

An easy dish that can be made a day ahead.

6 chicken breast halves
1 c. red wine
½ c. soy sauce
¼ c. oil
2 T. water
1 clove garlic, sliced

1 t. confectioners' sugar
¼ t. oregano
¼ t. lemon pepper
1 T. brown sugar
Cooked wild rice

Combine wine, soy sauce, oil, water, garlic, confectioners' sugar, oregano, lemon pepper, and brown sugar, mixing well. Place chicken in large casserole, pour sauce over chicken, and cover. The chicken can be marinated overnight in the refrigerator at this point. Bake at 350° for 1½ hours. Uncover for the last 15 minutes, unless juice has cooked away. Serve with wild rice. Serves 6.

MELANIE GORSLINE

CHICKEN LIVERS DELICIOUS

1 lb. chicken livers
Flour
2 T. margarine
1 medium onion, chopped
Salt and pepper to taste
2 envelopes chicken gravy mix

1 bouillon cube, dissolved in ¾ c. water
1 c. fresh mushrooms, sliced and sautéed
½ c. red wine
Kitchen Bouquet
Cooked rice or noodles

Wash livers, dry with paper towels, and cut into quarters with scissors. Sprinkle flour on top of livers. Melt margarine and sauté livers and onions until done; add pepper and salt. While livers are cooking, prepare gravy mix according to package directions, using bouillon and wine for water; add mushrooms. Combine gravy, liver mixture, and enough Kitchen Bouquet for a rich brown color. Serve over rice or noodles. Serves 4.

MIMI BIGELOW

BAKED CORNISH HENS

8 Cornish hens
Salt and pepper
8 whole medium onions

¾ c. margarine
¼ c. Kitchen Bouquet
1 (8 oz.) jar orange marmalade

Salt and pepper hens. Place onion in cavity of each hen and place in baking dish. Combine margarine, Kitchen Bouquet, and marmalade in a saucepan. Heat until well blended and spoon over hens. Bake at 350° until tender, about 1 to 1½ hours. Baste about every 20 minutes, adding water if sauce cooks down. Sauce is delicious over rice. Serves 8 generously.

SALLIE THALHIMER

TACO PIE   Q

1 (8 oz.) can biscuits
1 lb. ground turkey
1 t. beef bouillon
2 t. onion, chopped
2 t. green pepper, chopped
Salt and pepper to taste

¾ c. tomato paste
¾ c. water
1 (1.25 oz.) pkg. taco seasoning
  mix
8 oz. Mozzarella cheese, grated

Press biscuits into 9" pie pan, forming a continuous crust. Brown turkey, drain, and sprinkle with bouillon. Add onions, green pepper, salt, pepper, tomato paste, water and seasoning mix. Heat thoroughly. Place half of meat mixture into crust and sprinkle with half of cheese; repeat. Bake at 400° for 15 minutes. Serves 8.

KIM BAIN

MICROWAVE TURKEY VEGETABLE LASAGNA   L

2 oz. turkey breast, cooked and
  shredded
2 c. low sodium tomato sauce,
  divided
2 T. fresh basil, chopped
¼ t. oregano
¼ t. salt
1½ c. fresh mushrooms, sliced
1 c. zucchini, chopped
½ c. onion, chopped

2 T. light soft margarine
1 c. part-skim Ricotta or non-fat
  cottage cheese
2 t. Parmesan cheese, grated
Pinch of nutmeg
6 lasagna noodles, cooked
18 whole basil leaves
2¼ oz. part-skim Mozzarella
  cheese, shredded

Combine tomato sauce, basil, oregano, and salt in 1-quart bowl. Microwave for 2 minutes, stirring after 1 minute. In 2-quart bowl combine mushrooms, zucchini, onion, and margarine. Microwave 3 to 4 minutes, stirring after 2 minutes. (Vegetables will be crisp.) Combine Ricotta, Parmesan, nutmeg, and turkey. Add to vegetables and mix well. Spread ¾ c. tomato sauce in 9" x 13" baking dish. On each lasagna noodle, spread 1 T. tomato sauce, ½ c. Ricotta mixture, and 3 basil leaves. Roll up noodles and place seam side down in baking dish. Top with remaining tomato sauce and Mozzarella cheese. Microwave on high for 5 to 7 minutes, turning dish once during cooking time. (Sauce should be bubbly.) Serves 6.

BARBARA LINGO

TURKEY TETRAZZINI

½ c. olive oil
½ c. unbleached white flour
1-2 t. salt
1 t. nutmeg
5 c. 2% milk
2 c. turkey stock or 1 (10½ oz.) can
   condensed chicken broth,
   undiluted
1-2 t. sugar

½ c. dry sherry
1 lb. fettuccini
1 lb. fresh mushrooms or 2 (6 oz.)
   cans mushrooms, drained
6 c. turkey, cooked and cut into
   1½" strips
8 oz. Muenster cheese, grated
¼-½ c. Parmesan cheese, grated

Heat 3-quart heavy pot and add oil. Slowly stir in flour, salt and nutmeg. Remove from heat and gradually add milk and turkey stock. Bring to boil, stirring constantly, until slightly thickened. Remove from heat and add sugar and sherry. Cook fettuccini according to package directions, until al dente and drain. Remove 2 cups of sauce and set aside. Add noodles to remaining sauce, along with mushrooms and turkey and mix well. Spoon entire mixture into large baking dish. Top with Muenster and Parmesan cheeses, cover with foil and refrigerate 1 hour or overnight. Bake, covered, at 350° for 45 minutes. Remove cover and continue baking until topping is brown. Reheat reserved cups of sauce and drizzle over each serving or allow guests to pour extra sauce on their servings. Serves 8 to 10.

PEGGY ROMER

SEA FOOD

Seafood

I beg my mother to wash the dishes and sometimes she lets me.
Laurel Thompson, '05

Crab:

Crab Cakes **Q** 168
New Orleans Crab Claws 168
Sautéed Crab Crêpes 168
Crab in Crumb Crust 169
Aunt Ellie's Deviled
   Crab **Q** 169
Crab Imperial I 170
Crab Imperial II **Q L** 170
Crab Remick **Q** 170
Seafood Casserole 178

Fish:

Dijon Fish Fillet **Q L** 171
Fillet of Flounder
   Ambassador **L** 171
Poached Flounder Fillet
   with Mushrooms **Q L** 172
Flounder Provençal in
   Parchment **L** 172
Zucchini Fish **Q** 172
Doc's Rockfish **Q** 173
Rappahannock Stuffed
   Rockfish 173
Poached Salmon with
   Horseradish Sauce **L** 174
Poached Salmon Steaks
   with Zucchini
   Noodles **Q L** 174
Roasted Salmon
   Steaks **Q L** 174
Grecian Snapper with Feta
   Cheese **L** 175
Swordfish with Tarragon
   Mustard Sauce **Q L** 175

Trout Meunière or
   Amandine 176

Shellfish:

Baked Stuffed Clams **Q** 176
Scalloped Oysters 177
Scallops Au Gratin **Q** 177
Oriental Scallop Stir-Fry **L** ... 177
Sautéed Scallops **Q** 178

Shrimp:

Seafood Casserole 178
Shrimp Alla Milanese 178
Shrimp Casserole
   Altamont 179
Jambalaya 179
Barbecued Shrimp 180
Broiled Butterfly Shrimp **Q** ... 180
Charleston Shrimp and
   Rice 180
Shrimp Curry Even Kids
   Eat **L** 181
Greek Shrimp 181
Shrimp Guadalajara **Q** 182
Wild Rice Shrimp
   Casserole 182
Shrimp and Chicken
   Casserole 182
Curried Shrimp and
   Chicken 183
Shrimp (or Chicken)
   Scampi **Q L** 183

Sauces:

Seafood Sauce **Q** 184
Mother Leone's Shrimp
   Sauce 184

SEAFOOD

Q CRAB CAKES

1 lb. fresh crabmeat
1 T. lemon juice
2 T. flour
½ c. mayonnaise

2 eggs
Dash of Worcestershire
Margarine for frying

Sprinkle lemon juice and flour over crabmeat. Mix eggs, Worcestershire, and mayonnaise; add crabmeat. Melt margarine in frying pan over medium heat. Drop crabmeat mixture into pan by heaping tablespoons and sauté until golden brown. Serves 4.

ADELAIDE MONTAGUE

NEW ORLEANS CRAB CLAWS

1 lb. can of crab claws
1 (.6 oz.) pkg. Italian salad dressing
   mix
¼ c. champagne vinegar
¾ c. olive oil
1 T. lemon juice
1 T. garlic, minced

1 T. Worcestershire
2 T. white wine
½ t. oregano
¼ c. dried parsley flakes
¼ c. Parmesan cheese, grated
½ t. pepper
Pinch of salt

Rinse crab claws in water and drain. To make marinade, combine remaining ingredients and mix well. Place marinade and crab claws in plastic bag. Lay the bag flat in shallow dish and refrigerate overnight, turning bag occasionally. Before serving, spray claws lightly with water so they will not be too greasy. Serves 8.

NANCY GEORGE

SAUTÉED CRAB CRÊPES

FILLING

1 lb. fresh crabmeat, flaked
¼ c. green pepper, chopped
¼ c. green onion, chopped
2 T. celery, minced
1 clove garlic, minced
¼ c. butter
2 T. dry white wine

1 T. fresh parsley, minced
1 t. seafood seasoning
¼ t. salt
¼ t. dry mustard
1 egg, beaten
3 T. mayonnaise
8 (8-inch) crêpes

Sauté first 5 ingredients in ¼ c. butter until vegetables are tender. Remove from heat and stir in next 5 ingredients. Combine egg and mayonnaise and add to crabmeat mixture. Fill each crêpe with ¼ cup crabmeat mixture. Roll up and place seam side down in lightly greased 9" x 13" baking dish.

MUSHROOM WINE SAUCE

½ lb. mushrooms, sliced
2 T. green onion, finely chopped
¼ c. plus 1 T. butter
1½ c. milk

3 T. flour
¼ c. dry white wine
1 T. parsley, minced
½ t. salt
¼ t. pepper

Sauté mushrooms and onions in 2 T. butter until tender. Remove from skillet and set aside. Melt 3 T. butter in skillet over low heat. Add flour and stir until smooth. Cook 1 minute, stirring constantly. Gradually add milk and wine. Cook over medium heat, stirring constantly, until thickened and bubbly. Stir in sautéed vegetables, parsley, salt, and pepper. Spoon sauce over crêpes and bake at 350° for 15 to 20 minutes. (Crêpes can be made and filled ahead of time and refrigerated. Do not add Mushroom Wine Sauce until just before crêpes go into oven.) Serves 4.

ANN BEAUCHAMP

CRAB IN CRUMB CRUST

4 slices firm bread
5 T. butter
½ lb. claw crabmeat
2 eggs
½ c. whipping cream

Salt and pepper to taste
Whites of 3 scallions, minced
1 t. chives, chopped
Additional butter

Make bread crumbs in blender. Melt butter over low heat and stir in bread crumbs until toasty brown in color. Spread crumbs in 9" pie plate and smooth over bottom and sides. Place crabmeat in pie shell. Beat eggs and add cream, seasonings, scallions, and chives. Pour over crab. Place six small shavings of butter on top. Bake at 350° for 35 minutes. Serves 6.

KATHY HERSHEY

AUNT ELLIE'S DEVILED CRAB   Q

SAUCE

¾ c. mayonnaise
1 T. lemon juice
¼ t. horseradish

¼ t. prepared mustard
¼ t. Worcestershire

Combine all sauce ingredients and mix well.

2 T. onion, chopped
3 T. fresh parsley, chopped
1 clove garlic, minced
2 T. vegetable oil

1½ lbs. backfin crabmeat
¼ t. salt
Buttered breadcrumbs

In skillet sauté onion, parsley and garlic in oil until tender. Stir in crabmeat and salt. Pour sauce over all and toss. Mound loosely in casserole dish or individual baking shells, top with breadcrumbs, and bake at 400° for 25 minutes. Serves 6.

KATE LEWIS

CRAB IMPERIAL I

1 lb. fresh backfin crabmeat   6 T. sherry
1 T. lemon juice

Pour lemon juice and sherry over crabmeat and chill 2 hours.

SAUCE

2 T. butter or margarine   1 t. dry mustard
2 T. flour   1 T. onion, minced
1 c. milk   1 T. parsley, chopped
1 t. salt   3 drops Tabasco
¼ t. pepper   Bread Crumbs
1 t. Worcestershire   Additional butter
1 t. horseradish

Melt butter or margarine over low heat and add flour. Slowly stir in milk. When the sauce is smooth and thickened, add seasoned crabmeat and remaining ingredients, except bread crumbs and additional butter. Pour into 6 baking shells or 1-quart casserole. Sprinkle with bread crumbs, and dot with butter. Bake at 350° until bubbly, about 20 minutes in shells and 30 minutes in casserole. Serves 6 generously.

ISABEL FINE

Q L

CRAB IMPERIAL II

Great low-calorie lunch!

3 c. crabmeat (imitation is fine)   2 T. plain yogurt
2 c. apple, finely chopped   ¼ c. Cheddar cheese, shredded
¼ c. green pepper, finely
  chopped

Combine crab, apple, green pepper, and yogurt. Sprinkle with cheese and broil to melt, about 1 minute. Serves 2 to 4.

KIM BAIN

Q

CRAB REMICK

1 lb. lump crabmeat   1 scant t. dry mustard
6 strips crisp bacon   ½ t. paprika
½ c. chili sauce   ½ t. celery salt
1½ c. mayonnaise   ½ t. Tabasco
1 t. tarragon vinegar

Place crabmeat in baking dish and crumble 3 slices bacon over top. Combine remaining ingredients (except 3 strips bacon) thoroughly and pour over crabmeat. Bake at 400° until hot and bubbly, about 15 to 20 minutes. Serve over toast points and garnish with crumbled bacon. Serves 4.

VARIATION: Can be served in chafing dish with small toast points or pita chips as appetizer.

KATHY HERSHEY

DIJON FISH FILLET   *Q L*

8 oz. fresh fish fillet such as
    flounder or cod
2 T. fresh lemon juice
2 T. Dijon mustard

2 T. Worcestershire
½ c. sour cream or substitute
Cracked pepper

Rinse fish and pat dry. Coat baking dish with no-stick cooking spray. Put fish in pan. Mix lemon juice, mustard, and Worcestershire and spread on fish. Cover with sour cream. Sprinkle with cracked pepper. Bake for 20 minutes at 350°. Serve immediately. Serves 2.

LAURA LEE CHANDLER

FILLET OF FLOUNDER AMBASSADOR   *L*

Great company fare!

4 pieces fresh flounder
⅛ t. salt
⅛ t. cracked pepper
½ c. fresh parsley, chopped
3 T. margarine
Juice of ½ lemon
¼ lb. fresh mushrooms, sliced

3 T. flour
1½ c. lowfat milk
1 T. Dijon mustard
2 T. Parmesan cheese
¼ c. bread crumbs
Paprika

Preheat oven to 475°. Rinse fish and pat dry. Arrange fish in 9″ x 13″ glass baking dish and sprinkle with salt, pepper, and parsley. Melt margarine in saucepan, add lemon juice and mushrooms, and sauté over low heat. Stir in flour. Allow to bubble for 2 to 3 minutes. Add milk and stir until slightly thickened. Add mustard and mix well. Pour sauce over fish. Sprinkle with cheese, bread crumbs, and paprika. Bake for 15 to 20 minutes or until top is golden brown and fish flakes easily with a fork. Serves 4.

VARIATION: Spread uncooked flounder with chipped beef or ham and white Monterey Jack cheese and roll. Cook 25 to 30 minutes.

LAURA LEE CHANDLER

Q L POACHED FLOUNDER FILLET WITH MUSHROOMS

1½ lb. flounder or sole fillets
½ c. dry white wine or dry
  vermouth
1 t. arrowroot for thickening
  (optional)

8 mushrooms, sliced
2 T. fresh lemon juice
Lemon slices for garnish
1 T. fresh parsley, chopped for
  garnish

Place fillets in large skillet and cover with water. Simmer over medium heat for 5 minutes. For a slightly thickened sauce combine arrowroot with ½ cup water and add to the skillet, simmering for three more minutes. Add mushrooms and lemon juice and simmer until the fish is done (about three more minutes). Carefully lift the fish and mushrooms out with a slotted spoon onto a platter. Garnish with lemon slices and parsley. Serves 4.

JEAN JONES

L FLOUNDER PROVENÇAL IN PARCHMENT

This is great! Don't be intimidated by the parchment.

4 (15" x 14") pieces of parchment
  paper
4 (4 oz) flounder fillets or other
  lean white fish fillets
2 T. Parmesan cheese, grated
¾ t. dried basil
¼ t. garlic powder

¼ t. coarsely ground black
  pepper
¼ t. salt (optional)
8 (¼-inch) slices tomato
4 (⅛-inch) slices green pepper
4 (⅛-inch) slices red pepper
4 (⅛-inch) slices onion

Fold pieces of parchment paper in half crosswise and crease firmly. Trim each piece into a heart shape and place on baking sheet. Place one fillet on each parchment heart near the crease. Combine Parmesan cheese, basil, garlic powder, and pepper; sprinkle evenly over fish. Arrange tomato, pepper and onion slices over cheese mixture. Fold over remaining half of each parchment heart. Starting with rounded edge, pleat and crimp edges together to make a seal. Twist ends tightly to secure. Coat top of parchment hearts with no-stick cooking spray. Bake at 400° for 12 minutes or until puffed and lightly browned. Place on individual serving plates and cut open. Serve immediately. Serves 4.

L. DOUGLAS WILDER, GOVERNOR OF VIRGINIA

Q ZUCCHINI FISH

8 oz. fresh fish fillet such as
  haddock, flounder, sole or cod
2-4 T. margarine, melted
1 can (about 12 oz) Italian
  zucchini and tomato sauce

¼ c. sherry (optional)
1 c. cooked rice
2 T. Parmesan cheese

Broil fish with melted margarine for 5 to 7 minutes until fish flakes easily with fork. Meanwhile, heat Italian zucchini and tomato sauce in pan with sherry until warm. Pour this over cooked fish. Sprinkle with Parmesan cheese. Serve over rice. Serves 2.

LAURA LEE CHANDLER

DOC'S ROCKFISH   **Q**

Any mild fish can be used.

6 (3-4 lb.) rockfish fillets, skinned
1 (15 oz.) can New England Clam
   Chowder or Cream of Shrimp
   Soup

¼ t. Cayenne pepper
2 T. butter, cut in pieces
2 hard-boiled eggs, grated

Preheat oven to 400°. Spray baking dish with no-stick cooking spray. Spread fish in single layer and cover with soup. Sprinkle with red pepper and butter. Bake 10 to 12 minutes. Remove from oven and sprinkle with eggs. Serves 6.

PAT AND BUDDY LIEBERT

RAPPAHANOCK STUFFED ROCKFISH

A pretty and tasty company dish.

5 lbs. of cleaned whole Rockfish,
   split to make cavity for stuffing
1 green pepper, sliced into rings
1 large white onion, sliced into
   rings
2 medium tomatoes, sliced
¼ fresh lemon

2 T. parsley, chopped
Salt and pepper to taste
6 slices bacon (can use turkey
   bacon)
2 c. water
4 beef bouillon cubes

Wash rockfish and pat dry. Layer alternate slices of onions, green pepper and tomatoes inside the cavity of the fish. Squeeze some of the lemon juice and sprinkle ½ of the parsley over the vegetables. Salt and pepper to taste. Close cavity of the fish. Lay bacon slices across top of fish and sprinkle with remaining lemon juice and parsley. Place fish in large roasting pan with water and bouillon cubes. Cover tightly with foil and bake at 375° for 35 minutes. Serves 4.

ANNE DINGLEDINE

L   POACHED SALMON WITH HORSERADISH SAUCE

HORSERADISH SAUCE

¼ c. non-fat mayonnaise
¼ c. non-fat plain yogurt

2 t. horseradish
1½ t. lemon juice
1½ t. chopped chives

Combine all ingredients for sauce and chill.

4 c. water
1 lemon or lime, sliced
1 carrot, sliced
1 stalk celery, sliced

1 t. peppercorns
4 (4 oz) salmon steaks (other fish
  may be used)

Combine water, lemon or lime, carrot, celery, and peppercorns in a large skillet. Bring to a boil and simmer for 10 minutes. Add salmon, cover, and simmer for 10 additional minutes. Remove skillet from heat and let stand 8 minutes. Transfer salmon steaks to serving platter and serve with horseradish sauce. Serves 4.

JOAN WILKINS

Q L POACHED SALMON STEAKS WITH ZUCCHINI NOODLES

4 (4 oz) salmon steaks, ½ inch
  thick
½ c. skim milk
2 T. water
¼ t. chicken-flavored bouillon
  granules

3 medium zucchini
¼ t. salt
¾ fresh basil, minced
1 t. poppy seeds
Additional basil sprigs for garnish

Place salmon in a large non-stick skillet that has been coated with cooking spray. Combine milk, water, and bouillon granules. Pour over fish, cover, and bring to a boil. Reduce heat, and simmer for 8 minutes or until fish flakes easily when tested with a fork. Using a vegetable peeler, cut the zucchini lengthwise into strips. Coat a large non-stick skillet with cooking spray. Place over medium high heat until hot, add zucchini, salt and basil, and sauté until tender. Add poppy seeds, tossing gently. Transfer zucchini to a serving platter. Top with salmon steaks. Garnish with basil sprigs, if desired. Serves 4.

KATHIE MARKEL

Q L   ROASTED SALMON STEAKS

2 T. Dijon mustard
1 T. fresh dill, chopped
2 t. honey
2 t. white wine vinegar

1 t. celery flakes
¼ t. black pepper
4 (4 oz) salmon steaks

Preheat oven to 500°. Spray large oven-proof skillet with no-stick cooking spray. Set aside. In small bowl, combine mustard, dill, honey, vinegar, celery flakes and pepper. Place the skillet in oven to heat. Meanwhile, spread half the mustard mixture evenly on the top of each salmon steak. With oven mitt, remove the skillet from the oven. Place salmon, mustard-side down, in skillet and return to oven for 5 minutes. Spread remaining mustard mixture over salmon and gently turn. Roast 3 minutes longer or until salmon is cooked through. Delicious with fettuccini and asparagus. Serves 4.

BARBARA LINGO

GRECIAN SNAPPER WITH FETA CHEESE *L*

1 T. olive oil
⅔ c. onion, chopped
½ t. garlic, minced
2 large tomatoes, chopped
1 t. oregano
1 T. lemon juice
3 T. white wine

1 t. salt
¼ t. pepper
4 (4 oz) snapper fillets (any firm white fish works well)
1½ oz. feta cheese, crumbled
2 T. black olives, chopped
2 T. fresh parsley, chopped

Preheat over to 350°. Coat a skillet with cooking spray. Add olive oil and heat. Add onion and garlic and sauté until tender. Stir in tomatoes, oregano, lemon juice, wine, salt and pepper. Bring to a boil. Reduce heat and simmer uncovered for 20 minutes. Meanwhile, rinse fish in cold water and pat dry. Place fish in a flat baking dish coated with cooking spray. Spoon simmered sauce over fillets. Bake uncovered for 15 minutes or until fish flakes easily. Sprinkle cheese, olives, and parsley over fish. Serves 4.

CAROLYN MEACHAM

SWORDFISH WITH TARRAGON MUSTARD SAUCE *Q L*

MUSTARD TARRAGON SAUCE

2 T. mayonnaise
4 T. plain yogurt
1 T. plus 1 t. stone ground or Dijon mustard

1 t. lemon juice
1 T. fresh tarragon, snipped, or 1 t. dried tarragon

Mix all sauce ingredients and set aside.

1¼ swordfish steaks (other steak-type fish may be used)

½ t. capers (optional)
½ fresh lemon

Heat broiler or grill. Cook fish on one side for 4 minutes. Squeeze fresh lemon juice over the fish. Carefully turn the fish with a spatula. If grilling, cover the cooked side of the fish with the sauce. If broiling, allow fish to cook for 1 minute before covering with the sauce. Continue to cook about 4 minutes with either method. Sprinkle the capers over the fish during last two minutes of cooking. Serves 4.

TRUE LUCK

TROUT MEUNIÈRE OR AMANDINE

8-12 trout fillets
Milk to cover
2 t. salt, divided
4 drops Tabasco

1½ c. flour
1 t. white pepper
½ c. butter
2 T. oil

SAUCE

1 c. butter
½ c. almonds, sliced
2 T. lemon juice

2 t. Worcestershire
1 t. salt
¼ c. parsley, chopped

Soak fillets in a mixture of milk, 1 t. salt, and Tabasco for at least 30 minutes. Season flour with 1 t. salt and white pepper. Remove fillets from milk and pat dry. Coat lightly with seasoned flour shaking off excess. In a saucepan, melt ½ c. butter and add oil. Pour butter mixture into a large skillet to a depth of ⅛ inch. When butter is very hot, fry fillets a few at a time, turning once. Cooking time will depend on the size of the fillets. Keep the butter very hot and at the proper depth by adding more from the saucepan as necessary. Place cooked fillets on a warm platter and keep hot. When all are cooked, empty skillet and wipe to remove flour. Prepare sauce in the same skillet by melting 1 c. butter and lightly browning almonds. Add lemon juice, Worcestershire, 1 t. salt and parsley. Mix and heat well. Just before serving, pour some sauce over the fillets and serve remaining portion in a sauceboat. Serves 8 to 12.

MIM SCHUTE

Q   BAKED STUFFED CLAMS

1½ c. butter or margarine
½ c. celery, chopped
½ c. onion, chopped
½ c. parsley, chopped
1 c. boiled ham, chopped
1 (10½ oz) can minced clams, undrained
1 (8 oz.) pkg. herb-seasoned stuffing mix

½ t. seasoned salt
¼ t. thyme leaves
¼ t. black pepper
Dash of celery seed
½ c. Parmesan cheese, grated
1 (10¾ oz.) can cream of mushroom soup

In a large skillet melt butter. Stir in celery, onion, and parsley. Sauté for 5 minutes. In a large bowl combine celery mixture and remaining ingredients. Spoon into 24 scrubbed clam shells (or shape 24 pieces of heavy-duty foil into 2½" x 2½" shell shapes and fill). Bake at 350° for 15 minutes. Yield: 24 stuffed clams.

DONNA JACOBS

SCALLOPED OYSTERS

6 slices bread
1 qt. oysters, drained
Salt to taste

Cayenne pepper to taste
Butter or margarine
Paprika to taste

Place bread on cookie sheet in 250° oven until thoroughly dried out. In round baking dish place a layer of oysters. Sprinkle lightly with salt and cayenne pepper. Crumble 1 to 1½ slices bread on top of oysters, and dot with pats of butter. Repeat layers two more times. On top layer use buttered bread crumbs instead of dry bread and pats of butter. Sprinkle with paprika and bake for 1 hour at 350°. Serves 4.

ADELAIDE MONTAGUE

SCALLOPS AU GRATIN   Q

3 T. butter or margarine
½ green pepper, minced
½ onion, chopped
3 T. flour
2 c. milk
1 lb. scallops

1 (8 oz.) can sliced water chestnuts
½ t. salt
Dash of nutmeg
1 c. Cheddar cheese, shredded
Buttered bread crumbs

Melt butter or margarine, add green pepper and onion, and cook for 5 minutes. Add flour, milk, scallops, water chestnuts, salt, and nutmeg. Sauté 15 minutes longer. Pour into 9" x 13" baking dish and sprinkle with cheese and buttered bread crumbs. Bake at 350° until cheese is well-browned. Serves 4.

JUDI NEWCOMB

ORIENTAL SCALLOP STIR-FRY   L

2 T. margarine
1 medium onion, chopped
1 lb. fresh mushrooms, sliced
1 lb. fresh sea scallops
1 t. pepper
2 T. fresh parsley, chopped
2 T. oregano

1 t. ginger
1 c. water
1 c. dry white wine
1 t. Worcestershire
½ lb. snow peas
2 c. broccoli florets
Chinese rice (optional)

In skillet or wok sauté onion in margarine until golden. Add mushrooms and continue to sauté until tender. Add scallops and cook 3 minutes on each side. Stir in pepper, parsley, oregano and ginger. Add water, wine and Worcestershire and cook for 3 minutes. Stir in snow peas and broccoli and cook over medium heat for 10 minutes. Serve over rice. Serves 4.

GINGER LEVIT

177

Q SAUTÉED SCALLOPS

2 T. butter
6 green onions, sliced
2 c. mushrooms, sliced

1 c. white wine
1 lb. scallops

Melt butter over medium heat. Sauté onions and mushrooms for 2 minutes. Add wine and bring to a boil. Add scallops and cook until done, about 1 minute longer. Serves 2.

KATIE BELK

SEAFOOD CASSEROLE

1 green pepper, chopped
1 medium onion, finely chopped
4 T. butter, melted
1 lb. crabmeat
1 lb. shrimp, cooked and
    deveined
1 (5 oz) jar Durkees sauce

1 c. mayonnaise
Dash of Worcestershire
Dash of Tabasco
Dash of salt
Bread crumbs
Additional butter

Sauté green pepper and onion slowly in butter until tender, but not browned. Combine with remaining ingredients and place in a buttered 2-quart casserole. Top with bread crumbs and dot with butter. Bake for 20 to 30 minutes in 400° oven. Serves 6 to 8.

MELANIE GORSLINE

SHRIMP ALLA MILANESE

4 T. butter, divided
1 T. vegetable oil
1 T. garlic, thinly sliced
1 T. mushrooms, (optional)
Salt, white pepper, cayenne
    pepper and paprika to taste
1½ lbs. shrimp, cooked and
    peeled

½ (16 oz) can whole tomatoes,
    chopped
¾ c. onions, chopped and
    divided
2 T. olive oil
1 c. saffron rice
2 c. chicken broth
2 t. salt
1 t. saffron

Combine 2 T. butter and vegetable oil in skillet and stir over low heat. Add garlic and sauté 2 minutes. Add mushrooms and season with salt, peppers and paprika. Add shrimp, shake skillet over medium heat for 5 minutes and set aside. In separate saucepan combine 1 T. butter, tomatoes and ¼ cup onions and sauté 5 minutes. Pour into shrimp mixture. In large skillet sauté ½ c. onion in 1 T. butter and olive oil until transparent and add rice. Slowly add chicken broth, stirring until absorbed. Stir in salt and saffron. Combine with shrimp mixture. Serves 4 to 6.

JOY HEINER

SHRIMP CASSEROLE ALTAMONT

2½ lbs. large raw shrimp, shelled
and deveined
1 T. lemon juice
3 T. salad oil
¾ c. uncooked rice
¼ c. green pepper, minced
¼ c. onion, minced
2 T. butter or margarine
1 t. salt

⅛ t. pepper
⅛ t. mace
Dash cayenne pepper
1 (10¾ oz.) can condensed
tomato soup
1 c. heavy cream
½ c. sherry
¾ c. almonds, slivered and
blanched, divided

Several hours before serving, cook shrimp in boiling salted water for 5 minutes and drain. Place in 2-quart casserole, sprinkle with lemon juice and salad oil, and refrigerate. Cook rice according to package directions and refrigerate also. At least 70 minutes before serving, assemble casserole. Set aside about 8 shrimp for garnish. Sauté green pepper and onion for 5 minutes in butter. Combine with rice, salt, pepper, mace, cayenne pepper, soup, cream, sherry, ½ c. almonds, and refrigerated shrimp. Place in casserole and bake at 350° for 35 minutes. Top with 8 reserved shrimp and ¼ c. almonds. Bake 20 minutes longer, or until mixture is bubbly and shrimp are lightly browned. Serves 6 to 8.

DONNA JACOBS

JAMBALAYA

1 c. scallions, chopped
1 c. celery, chopped
½ c. green pepper, chopped
2 cloves garlic, finely minced
½ c. butter
½ lb. country or Smithfield ham,
cut in small pieces
1 (28 oz.) can tomatoes and liquid,
chopped

1 (6 oz.) can tomato paste
2 (10¾ oz.) cans chicken broth
½ t. each pepper, oregano,
Tabasco
2 bay leaves
1 t. seafood seasoning
1½ lb. medium raw shrimp, shelled
1½ c. cooked rice

Sauté scallions, celery, green pepper, and garlic in butter in large saucepan for about 10 minutes. Stir in ham, tomatoes, tomato paste, chicken broth, and seasonings. Simmer over low heat for an hour or more. When ready to serve, reheat mixture to almost boiling and add shrimp. Cover the saucepan. Shrimp will cook in less than 5 minutes. Remove bay leaves and serve in bowls with cooked rice. If you have leftovers, remove shrimp while reheating broth and return them when ready to serve. Serves 6.

TYLER KILPATRICK

BARBECUED SHRIMP

MARINADE

3 c. Italian salad dressing
4-6 T. Worcestershire
1-2 cloves garlic
1 lemon, thinly sliced

1 t. salt
2-3 t. cayenne pepper
Tabasco to taste

Combine all ingredients.

3 to 4 lbs. raw shrimp, peeled and
    deveined

¾ c. butter, melted
½-1 c. dry white wine

Marinate shrimp for 4 to 6 hours or overnight. Place shrimp and one half of the marinade in an oven-proof dish. Add the butter and wine. Stir and bake at 400° for 15 minutes. Serves 6 to 8.

PATSY ARNETT

Q   BROILED BUTTERFLY SHRIMP

1 lb. fresh shrimp, peeled and
    deveined
Lemon pepper to taste
Paprika to taste

½ c. butter, melted
½ c. lemon juice
Salt to taste (optional)

Butterfly shrimp by cutting along the outside curve until almost through. In shallow pan place shrimp cut side down and sprinkle with lemon pepper and paprika. Pour butter over shrimp. Bake at 350° for 8 minutes. Pour lemon juice over shrimp and broil for 5 minutes longer. Serves 2.

SANDY KING

CHARLESTON SHRIMP AND RICE

½ c. butter or margarine
1-2 bunches green onions,
    chopped
8 oz. fresh mushrooms, sliced

1½ lbs. shrimp, peeled and
    deveined
1 (10 oz.) pkg. frozen green peas
1 c. rice, cooked
Soy sauce to taste

Melt butter or margarine in skillet and sauté onions until transparent. Add mushrooms and sauté until soft. Stir in shrimp and cook until pink. Cook peas according to package directions and add to shrimp mixture. Stir in rice and season with soy sauce. Serves 6.

BRENDA JOHNSON

SHRIMP CURRY EVEN KIDS EAT *L*

2 t. vegetable oil
1 large onion, sliced
2 cloves garlic, minced
1 T. curry powder
¼ t. cinnamon
½ t. salt
1¼ c. water
2 large carrots, sliced ¼-inch thick

2 large potatoes, peeled and cut
  into ½-inch cubes
1 (16 oz.) can tomatoes undrained,
  cut into chunks
1 zucchini, diced, or 1 c. broccoli
  florets
¼ c. raisins
½ lb. shrimp, peeled and
  deveined

Sauté onion and garlic in oil until soft. Stir in curry powder, cinnamon, salt, and water. Bring to a boil. Add the carrots and potatoes, cover and simmer for 10 minutes. Add zucchini or broccoli, tomatoes, raisins, and shrimp. Cover the pan and simmer 10 minutes longer, being careful not to overcook shrimp. Serve immediately with rice. (If you prepare this dish ahead of time, add the shrimp right before serving.) Serves 4.

ALEX THOMPSON

GREEK SHRIMP

1 c. fresh tomatoes, peeled and
  cut into chunks or 1 (16 oz.) can
  whole tomatoes, drained
3 T. onion, chopped
1 clove garlic, minced
¼ c. olive oil
½ c. celery, chopped
¼ c. red wine

1 bay leaf
½ t. basil
Salt to taste
½ t. pepper
1 lb. green shrimp, peeled with
  tails removed
½ c. feta cheese

Combine first 10 ingredients and simmer for 20 minutes. Pour over shrimp in 1-quart baking dish, top with cheese and bake at 350° for 25 minutes. Serve hot. (May be prepared ahead of time and refrigerated.) Serves 4 to 6.

JUDY GILMAN

Q SHRIMP GUADALAJARA

½ c. butter or margarine
2 green onions, chopped
2 cloves garlic, crushed
1½ T. steak sauce
1 T. lemon juice

¼ t. salt
8 green jumbo shrimp, peeled,
    leaving on tails
Angel hair pasta, cooked

In skillet melt butter or margarine. Combine onions, garlic, steak sauce, lemon juice and salt. Pour into skillet and sauté over low heat, stirring occasionally, until warm. Slice shrimp lengthwise, and place flat in greased baking dish. Broil shrimp for 4 minutes. Pour sauce over shrimp evenly and broil additional 1 to 2 minutes. Serve over pasta. Serves 2.

SUZANNE COWLEY

WILD RICE SHRIMP CASSEROLE

½ c. onion, chopped
⅓ c. green pepper, chopped
¼ c. butter or margarine
1-2 (8 oz.) cans tomatoes,
    undrained and chopped
1¾ c. water
½ t. salt
¼ t. pepper

¼ t. garlic salt
¼ t. rosemary (optional)
Paprika to taste
1 (6 oz) pkg. long grain wild rice
    mix
1 lb. fresh shrimp, peeled and
    deveined or 1 lb. fresh scallops

In 3-quart saucepan sauté onion and pepper in butter or margarine for 5 minutes. Add tomatoes, water and seasonings. Stir in both packets from rice mix, cover and simmer for 20 minutes. Add shrimp or scallops, cover and simmer for additional 10 minutes. Serves 4 to 6.

PATSY ARNETT

SHRIMP AND CHICKEN CASSEROLE

1 c. rice.
3 T. olive oil
4 whole chicken breasts, boned
    and sliced
½-¾ c. onion, chopped
1 (16 oz.) can sliced mushrooms,
    drained
1½ lbs. shrimp, cooked

1 (15 oz) can tomato sauce
2 c. whipping cream
½-¾ c. dry sherry
1 t. salt
¼ t. pepper
¼ t. thyme
1 T. Worcestershire

Cook rice, spoon into 9" x 13" baking dish and set aside. In skillet heat oil and sauté chicken until browned on both sides. Remove chicken and place on rice. In same skillet sauté onions until transparent, add mushrooms, and stir. Spoon shrimp over chicken. Combine all sauce ingredients, mix well and add to onion and mushroom mixture. Pour sauce over shrimp and bake uncovered at 350° for 60 minutes. Serves 8.

NANCY GEORGE

CURRIED SHRIMP AND CHICKEN

1 lb. shrimp, cooked and peeled
2 chicken breasts, cooked and
   cubed
4 T. butter or margarine, divided
½ c. onion, chopped
¼ t. garlic, chopped

½ c. celery, chopped
2 T. curry powder
1 T. tomato paste
½ banana, cut into ½" cubes
2 c. chicken broth
Salt and pepper to taste

Sauté onion and garlic in 2 T. butter in large skillet; add celery and cook 1 minute. Stirring after each addition, add curry, tomato paste, banana, and broth. Add salt and pepper to taste and simmer slowly. In another skillet, sauté chicken 2 to 3 minutes in 2 T. butter, add shrimp, and cook 2 minutes. Blend curry mixture in blender or food processor until smooth. Pour curry sauce over shrimp-chicken mixture. Simmer and stir for 2 minutes. Serve with rice. Serves 4.

PRISCILLA BURBANK

SHRIMP (OR CHICKEN) SCAMPI   Q L

1¼ lb. peeled shrimp or boneless
   chicken breasts, cut in chunks
2½ T. olive oil
3 T. fresh Parmesan cheese,
   grated
¼ t. garlic powder
1 t. oregano

2 T. Worcestershire
¼ t. pepper
1 T. dried parsley or 2 T. fresh
   parsley, chopped
3 T. lemon juice
½ t. salt
¼ c. white wine

Arrange shrimp or chicken in shallow pan or baking dish coated with no-stick cooking spray. Mix all other ingredients and pour over meat. Meat can marinate a while or be cooked immediately. Broil 8" from heat, turning once. Cook until shrimp is pink or chicken is done (about 15 minutes). Serve over rice and pour pan juices over all. Serves 4.

CAROLYN MEACHAM

Q   SEAFOOD SAUCE

¼ lb. butter
1 c. mild Cheddar cheese
1 (10¾ oz.) can tomato soup
1 c. half and half

1 (2 oz.) jar diced pimiento,
   drained
1 egg, beaten

In top of double boiler melt butter and cheese, stirring to mix well. Add soup, half and half and egg. Stirring constantly, cook until thickened. Add pimiento and seafood in quantity desired. Shrimp, lobster or crab may be used or combined. Serve on either rice or toast points.

SANDY LACY

MOTHER LEONE'S SHRIMP SAUCE

Serve at cocktail party or as a main course.

2 green onions, finely chopped, or
   1 T. sweet onion, grated
6 T. green or red pepper, finely
   chopped
2 T. capers, chopped
2 T. prepared horseradish

1 c. mayonnaise, regular or
   reduced calorie
½ c. chili sauce
½ crushed red pepper
½ t. black pepper, freshly ground
½ t. salt
1 clove garlic, crushed

Place onion, green or red pepper, capers and horseradish in strainer for 15 minutes. Combine mayonnaise, chili sauce, red and black peppers, salt and garlic salt in a bowl and mix with a whisk. Add drained ingredients and beat well. Refrigerate. Can also be used with crabmeat, lobster or cold chicken. Yield: 2 cups.

JULIA KIMBRELL

EGGS & CHEESE

Eggs and Cheese

*It was awesome when
my little sister started the blender
without the top on it.*
Alexandra Povlishock, '03

Blintzes **L** 188
Cheese Blintz Casserole 188
Mother's Chilequiles 189
Presnac 189
Company Quiche
    Lorraine 190
Newlyweds' Quiche 190

Crab Quiche 190
Smoked Salmon and
    Chèvre Quiche 191
Basil and Sausage Strata 191
Egg and Sausage
    Casserole **L** 192
Welsh Rarebit **Q** 192

EGGS AND CHEESE

L   BLINTZES

Nourishing and healthful.

CHEESE FILLING

1 (16 oz) carton cottage cheese   Cinnamon to taste

Place cottage cheese in blender and blend until smooth. Sprinkle with cinnamon to taste. Set aside.

BATTER

2 eggs	Vegetable oil
½ c. flour	Unsweetened strawberry jelly
1 T. cornstarch	Honey (optional)
1 c. milk	Berries (optional)

Place eggs, flour, cornstarch and milk in blender and blend until smooth. Brush oil into small hot frying pan or crêpe maker. Spoon 2 to 3 T. batter into pan and spread evenly. Cook until almost dry and flip to cook other side. Remove blintz from pan and spoon in heaping tablespoon of cheese filling. Roll up and top with unsweetened strawberry jelly, honey or other berries. Can be made day ahead and refrigerated. Place in 9" x 13" pyrex pan and microwave on high for 30 seconds or until warm. Yield: 8 to 10 crêpes.

ANNA DURHAM

CHEESE BLINTZ CASSEROLE

A nice change from overnight egg casseroles.

CHEESE FILLING

8 oz. cream cheese, softened	2 eggs
2 lbs. Ricotta cheese	¼ c. sugar
¼ c. lemon juice or juice of 1 lemon	Pinch of salt

Combine all filling ingredients and mix until smooth by hand mixer or food processor. Set aside.

BATTER

1 c. margarine, melted	3 t. baking powder
2 eggs	Pinch of salt
½ c. sugar	¼ c. milk
1 c. flour, sifted	1 t. vanilla

Combine all batter ingredients and mix well by hand. Set aside. Combine all cheese filling ingredients and mix until smooth with hand mixer or food processor. Spread half of batter in greased 9" x 13" baking dish. Pour filling on top and spread evenly. Do not mix. Spread other half of batter over filling. (This does not have to be perfect. Drop dollops of batter at regular intervals and spread as best you can.) Bake in preheated oven at 300° for 1½ hours. Serve with heated fruit preserves or puréed fruit, if desired. Reheats well. Serves 12.

ALLYN CROSBY

MOTHER'S CHILEQUILES

Tex-Mex meatless entree.

1 dozen corn tortillas
½ c. plus 2 T. vegetable oil
1 clove garlic, minced
2 medium onions, chopped
4 c. tomatoes, chopped
½ c. jalapeño peppers, chopped

Salt to taste
1 lb. white Monterey Jack or
    Cheddar cheese, shredded
1 pt. sour cream
Paprika to taste

Cut tortillas in strips. Heat ½ c. oil until very hot, and sauté strips. When crisp, drain. Sauté garlic and onions in 2 T. oil until tender, add tomatoes, peppers and salt and continue cooking 5 minutes. In 2-quart casserole alternate tortilla strips with tomato mixture and cheese, ending with cheese. Bake at 350° for 15 to 20 minutes. Top with sour cream and sprinkle with paprika. Serves 6.

ALEX THOMPSON

PRESNAC

A tasty cheese pudding—delicious for brunch or light dinner.

1 lb. Monterey Jack cheese,
    cubed
1 lb. cottage cheese
4 oz. cream cheese, softened
6 T. margarine, softened
6 eggs, beaten

1 c. milk
2 t. sugar
1 t. salt
1 t. baking powder
½ c. flour

Combine cheeses and mix with margarine. Add eggs, milk, sugar and salt to cheese mixture and beat well. Add baking powder and flour and stir until well blended. Pour into greased 11" x 14" baking dish and bake at 350° for 40 minutes. Serves 6.

VICKI WILSON

COMPANY QUICHE LORRAINE

4 frozen 9" pie shells
1 lb. bacon, cooked and
  crumbled
4 medium onions, sliced thin
¼ lb. Gruyère or Swiss cheese,
  grated
1 c. Parmesan cheese, grated

10 eggs
2½ c. heavy cream
1⅓ c. milk
1 t. salt
½ t. white pepper
1 t. nutmeg

Bake pie shells as directed for 8 to 10 minutes. Cook bacon until crisp and drain. In bacon grease cook onion until transparent. Sprinkle bacon, onion and cheeses over pie shells. Combine eggs, cream, milk and seasonings and pour over onion cheese mixture. Bake at 450° for 15 minutes, reduce oven to 350° and continue baking for 10 minutes. Serve hot. (May be cooled after baking, covered with plastic wrap and refrigerated. To reheat, bake at 350° for 20 minutes.) Yield: 4 pies.

MARGARET BARGATZE

NEWLYWEDS' QUICHE

1 9" deep dish pie shell
½ c. spring onions, sliced
½ c. mushrooms, sliced
1 T. butter
6 slices bacon, cooked and
  crumbled

1 c. Gruyère cheese, grated
¼ c. Cheddar cheese, grated
2 eggs
1½ c. half and half
¼ t. salt

Preheat oven to 450°. Bake pie shell for 5 minutes; set aside. Sauté onions and mushrooms in butter until soft. Layer bacon, onions and mushrooms in pie shell and sprinkle with Gruyère. Top with Cheddar cheese. With wire whisk beat eggs, half and half and salt until well blended. Pour over cheeses. Bake at 450° for 10 to 15 minutes, reduce heat to 350°, and continue cooking for 20 minutes. Serves 6.

KATIE BELK

CRAB QUICHE

1 deep dish frozen pie shell
2 eggs, beaten
½ c. mayonnaise
2 T. flour
½ c. milk

Dash nutmeg
¼ t. salt
⅛ t. pepper
½ lb. fresh crabmeat
6 oz. Swiss cheese, grated

Thaw pie shell slightly, prick with fork, and bake at 400° for 10 minutes. Remove from oven and set aside. Beat eggs with fork. Add mayonnaise,

EGGS AND CHEESE

flour, milk and spices. Mix well. Stir in crabmeat and cheese and pour in pie shell. Bake at 350° for 40 to 45 minutes. Yield: 1 deep dish pie.

GAY JEWETT

SMOKED SALMON AND CHÈVRE QUICHE

1 9" pie shell
4 oz. chèvre with garlic and herbs (goat's milk cheese)
½ c. heavy cream

4 eggs
3-4 oz. smoked salmon, shredded
¼-½ c. fresh basil

Bake pie shell as directed for 5 minutes. Beat chèvre and cream with electric mixer until smooth. Beat in eggs, one at a time. Fold in salmon and basil. Pour into pie shell and bake at 375° for 30 to 35 minutes. Serves 6.

NOTE: Rondelé cheese spread may be substituted for chèvre.

JANA THOMAS

BASIL AND SAUSAGE STRATA

1 baguette
4 T. butter
2 lbs. bulk sausage
1 lb. Vermont Cheddar cheese
10 eggs

4 c. milk
2 T. Dijon mustard
½ t. salt
2 shakes Tabasco
Fresh basil

Slice baguette into 1" slices. Butter one side of each slice and place, buttered side down, in 4-quart casserole. Cook sausage, drain and crumble. Sprinkle sausage over bread and sprinkle cheese over sausage. Beat eggs; stir in milk and seasonings. Pour over cheese, cover and refrigerate overnight. Remove from refrigerator 1 hour before baking. Snip basil leaves with scissors and sprinkle over top of casserole before baking. Bake 1 hour, uncovered, at 350°. Serves 12.

JANA THOMAS

191

EGG AND SAUSAGE CASSEROLE

6 eggs
2 c. milk
1 t. salt
1 t. dry mustard

4-6 slices bread, cubed
1 lb. sausage (hot or regular),
    cooked, drained and crumbled
1 c. sharp cheese

Beat eggs; add milk, salt and dry mustard. Grease a 9" x 13" baking dish and layer bread, sausage and cheese. Pour egg mixture over top and bake at 350° for 45 minutes. (May be frozen after cooking and reheated in oven when ready to serve.) Best when refrigerated overnight before baking. Serves 6.

KATIE BELK

L VARIATION: Use egg substitutes, skim milk, only 2 slices bread, turkey sausage (or low-fat regular sausage) and low-fat cheese for a light version.

JOAN WILKINS

Q WELSH RAREBIT

2 c. Cheddar cheese, grated
2 T. milk
2 T. beer
1 t. prepared mustard
Salt to taste

Pepper to taste
4 slices bread, toasted
Parsley (optional)
Paprika (optional)

Place cheese, milk and beer in medium saucepan and cook over medium heat until melted and thickened. Stir in mustard, salt and pepper. Cook for 30 seconds longer. Spread mixture over bread and brown under broiler. Garnish with parsley.

If using microwave: heat cheese, milk and beer on high for 1 minute. Stir in mustard, salt and pepper and return to microwave for 30 seconds. Spread mixture over toast and garnish with paprika. Serves 4.

EFFIE YOUNG

PASTA & RICE

Pasta and Rice

Like my hero Garfield the cat, lasagna is my life.

Reid Whitten, '98

Pasta:
Capellini Marco Polo **Q** 196
Angel Hair Pasta with
  Broccoli and Chipped
  Beef **Q**..................... 196
Fettuccini with Goat
  Cheese and
  Peppers **Q L**............... 196
Shrimp Fettuccini **Q** 197
Stir-Fry Shrimp with
  Fettuccini................... 197
Fresh from the Garden
  Lasagna **L**................. 198
Spinach Lasagna **L** 198
Shrimp Linguine **Q** 199
Linguine with Tomatoes
  and Basil 199
Macaroni and Cheese....... 200
Manicotti di Verdura.......... 200
Chicken and Pasta
  Primavera **Q L**............. 200
Greek Pasta **Q L**............. 201
Pasta for Your Pace **Q** 201
Pasta with Spicy Ham and
  Tomato Sauce **Q** 202
Pasta with Tomato-
  Artichoke Sauce **Q**....... 202
Penna con Salsiccia.......... 202
Stuffed Shells 203

Spaghetti Carbonara **Q** 203
Baked Spaghetti Casserole .. 204
Spaghetti with White Clam
  Sauce **Q L**................. 204
Crab Spaghetti............... 204
Broccoli-Cauliflower
  Tetrazzini..................... 205
Tortellini with Grilled
  Chicken Breast **Q** 205
Pasta Sauces:
Low-Fat Cheese
  Sauce **Q L**................. 206
Marinara Sauce **L**........... 206
Pesto Sauce **Q**.............. 206
Pasta Sauce Raphael........ 207
Homemade Spaghetti
  Sauce 207
Meatballs for Spaghetti
  Sauce 208
Special Spaghetti Sauce 208
Rice and Grains:
"I Can't Believe It's Barley".... 208
Baked Rice with
  Consommé 209
Brown Rice and Lentils **L**.... 209
Curried Rice.................. 209
Steve Wong's New York
  Fried Rice **Q**.............. 210
Riso con Salsa Cruda **Q** 210

Q   CAPELLINI MARCO POLO

1 carrot
1 zucchini
1 yellow squash
1 heart of celery
4 T. butter
1 qt. tomato sauce

2 T. salt
1 lb. angel hair pasta
Few leaves of fresh basil,
   chopped
¼ c. Parmesan cheese, grated

Slice vegetables into thin strips and sauté in butter. Add tomato sauce, bring to boil and set aside. Bring 4 quarts water and salt to boil, add angel hair pasta and cook 2½ to 3 minutes. Drain well. Toss pasta with sauce and garnish with basil and Parmesan cheese. Serves 4.

AMICI RISTORANTE

Q ANGEL HAIR PASTA WITH BROCCOLI AND CHIPPED BEEF

4 cloves garlic, minced
1 (4 oz.) pkg. chipped beef,
   shredded
1 bunch broccoli
1 T. olive oil
1 (9 oz.) pkg. angel hair pasta

¼ c. butter
1½ c. milk
1 c. Parmesan cheese, grated
Cheddar cheese, grated
   (optional)

Roughly chop broccoli, discarding tough stems. Sauté garlic, beef and broccoli in olive oil for 10 minutes. Cook pasta according to package directions, and drain. Fold garlic, beef and broccoli into pasta. Stir in butter, milk and Parmesan cheese, combine well and heat on medium heat. Serve immediately or cover and keep warm in oven. Top with Cheddar cheese before serving, if desired. Serves 6.

CINDY BROOKS

Q L   FETTUCCINI WITH GOAT CHEESE AND PEPPERS

8 sun-dried tomato halves
1 T. olive oil
1 c. scallions, sliced
2 cloves garlic, minced
1 medium red pepper, cut in thin
   strips
1 medium yellow pepper, cut in
   thin strips
¼ c. chicken broth or dry vermouth

½ c. fresh basil, chopped
10 pitted small black olives,
   chopped
1 T. capers, rinsed and drained
2 t. dried oregano
6 oz. fettuccini
4½ oz. herbed or plain goat
   cheese, crumbled

Soak tomatoes in 1 c. boiling water for 2 minutes. Drain, reserving ¼ c. liquid. Thinly slice tomatoes. Heat olive oil in no-stick skillet, add scallions and garlic, and sauté for 2 minutes. Add peppers and sauté 3 minutes. Stir in chicken broth and cook until liquid is almost evaporated. Reduce heat to low and add tomatoes, reserved liquid, basil, olives, capers and oregano. Simmer 5 minutes. Cook fettuccini in large pot of boiling water for 8 to 10 minutes, drain and place in large bowl. Add cheese and toss until melted. Add sauce and serve immediately. Serves 3 to 4.

BARBARA LINGO

SHRIMP FETTUCCINI   Q

3 cloves garlic, crushed
½ c. green, red, yellow peppers, cut in strips
¾ c. broccoli florets
½ c. olive oil
2 c. whipping cream
8 oz. fettuccini, uncooked
3 T. vegetable oil
1½ lbs. large shrimp, uncooked
3 T. Romano cheese, grated

Sauté garlic, peppers, and broccoli in olive oil in large non-stick skillet. When mixture is softened, add whipping cream and bring to boil. Remove from heat and set aside. Cook fettuccini for 10 minutes in boiling water and oil, and drain. Boil shrimp for 4 to 5 minutes, peel, devein, and cut each shrimp into 3 equal pieces. Add fettuccini and shrimp to skillet of vegetables and cook for 3 minutes. Serve immediately with Romano cheese sprinkled on top. Serves 6.

JAY HOFFMAN

STIR-FRY SHRIMP WITH FETTUCCINI

1 (12 oz.) pkg. fettuccini
⅓ c. canola oil
2 c. shelled raw shrimp (1-1½ lbs.)
1 clove garlic, minced
1 medium green pepper, sliced in strips
1 medium onion, sliced in thin rings
1 c. fresh mushrooms, sliced
½ t. dill weed (more if fresh)
½ t. salt
¼ t. pepper

Cook fettuccini according to package directions and drain. Pour oil into wok or skillet and sauté shrimp and vegetables with seasonings until shrimp is pink and vegetables are crisp-tender. Add pasta to shrimp and vegetables. Toss and serve. Serves 6.

BEVERLY BATES

PASTA AND RICE

L FRESH FROM THE GARDEN LASAGNA

½ c. onion, chopped
½ c. green pepper, chopped
2 cloves garlic, minced
2 c. zucchini, chopped
1½ c. tomatoes, peeled and
  chopped
½ c. fresh mushrooms, sliced
½ c. carrot, shredded
½ c. celery, chopped
1¼ c. tomato sauce
1 (6 oz.) can tomato paste

1 T. wine or herb vinegar
½ t. dried oregano
1 t. dried basil
½ t. salt
½ t. pepper
6 lasagna noodles
1½ c. part-skim Ricotta cheese
1 c. part-skim Mozzarella cheese,
  shredded
1 T. Parmesan cheese, grated

Spray large heavy saucepan with no-stick cooking spray. Sauté onions, green pepper and garlic until tender. Add next 12 ingredients, cover and bring to boil. Reduce heat and simmer 20 to 30 minutes, stirring occasionally. Cook noodles according to package directions. Drain well. Combine Ricotta and Mozzarella cheeses. In a greased 9" x 13" baking dish (or smaller), layer ⅓ vegetable sauce, ⅓ noodles and ⅓ cheeses. Repeat twice. Cover and bake at 350° for 25 minutes. Uncover, sprinkle with Parmesan cheese, and bake an additional 10 minutes. Let lasagna stand 10 minutes before serving. Serves 6.

WEEZIE WILTSHIRE

L SPINACH LASAGNA

1 medium onion, chopped
2 cloves garlic, minced or ½ t.
  powdered garlic
1 T. oil
1 lb. part-skim Ricotta cheese
¼ c. Parmesan cheese
2 (10 oz.) pkg. frozen chopped
  spinach, thawed and drained

¼ t. black pepper
2-3 T. fresh parsley, chopped
12 lasagna noodles
6 oz. part-skim Mozzarella cheese,
  grated
6 c. tomato sauce

Heat onion, garlic and oil in microware oven at 100% power until tender, or sauté in pan until limp. Combine with Ricotta, Parmesan, spinach, pepper and parsley. Mix well. Cook lasagna noodles according to package directions. Arrange 4 noodles on bottom of greased 9" x 13" baking pan. Layer with ⅓ of cheese and spinach mixture, ⅓ Mozzarella, and ⅓ tomato sauce. Repeat twice. Cover tightly and bake at 350° for 40 minutes. Uncover and bake 10 to 15 minutes. Serves 12.

JANIS CARRELL
DEANE MOUNTCASTLE

SHRIMP LINGUINE Q

1 lb. medium shrimp, shelled and deveined
½ c. dry white wine
1 T. lemon juice
1 T. lime juice
¼ lb. fresh snow peas, strings removed
6 green onions, thinly sliced
1 T. fresh parsley, chopped
¾ t. dried basil leaves
½ t. lemon pepper
2 cloves garlic, minced
1 bay leaf
½ lb. linguine

In large skillet, combine shrimp, wine and juices. Bring to boil, reduce heat and simmer covered about 3 minutes. Add all remaining ingredients, except pasta. Stirring constantly, cook until snow peas are tender but crisp and shrimp is opaque, about 5 minutes. Prepare linguine as package directs. Drain. Remove bay leaf from sauce. Combine shrimp mixture and linguine, tossing to mix thoroughly. Serves 6 to 8.

DEB POVLISHOCK

LINGUINE WITH TOMATOES AND BASIL

4 large ripe tomatoes
1 lb. Brie cheese
1 c. fresh basil leaves, cut into strips
3 cloves garlic, minced
1 c. plus 1 T. good quality olive oil, divided
2 t. plus ½ t. salt, divided
½ freshly ground pepper
1½ lbs. linguine
Parmesan cheese, grated

Cut tomatoes into ½ inch cubes. Remove rind from Brie and chop. In large serving bowl combine tomatoes, Brie, basil and garlic. Stir in 1 c. olive oil, ½ t. salt and pepper. Cover and let rest for 2 hours at room temperature. Bring 6 quarts water to boil, add 1 T. olive oil and 2 t. salt. Add linguine and boil until tender but firm, about 8 to 10 minutes. Drain pasta and add to sauce in bowl. Serve immediately, passing Parmesan cheese for topping. Serves 8 to 10.

KAKI NELSON

MACARONI AND CHEESE

½ lb. macaroni
1 t. butter
1 egg, beaten
3 c. sharp Cheddar cheese,
   grated and divided

1 t. salt
1 t. dry mustard
1 c. milk

Cook macaroni according to package directions, and drain. Stir in butter and egg. Fold in 2½ cups cheese. Mix salt and mustard with 1 T. hot water, then add to milk. Pour macaroni into 8" square buttered casserole, pour milk mixture over top, sprinkle with ½ c. cheese, and bake in 350° oven for 25 minutes or until custard is set and top is crusty. Serves 6.

JEAN ASCARI

MANICOTTI DI VERDURA

1 lb. manicotti noodles, cooked
   and drained
2 cloves garlic, minced
2 carrots, finely chopped
1 medium onion, minced
2-3 T. olive oil
1 (10 oz.) pkg. frozen spinach,
   cooked and drained
1 (12 oz.) container Ricotta cheese

1 (12 oz.) container low-fat cottage
   cheese
⅓ c. Parmesan cheese, grated
1 c. chicken, cooked and
   chopped (optional)
½ t. nutmeg
1 T. dried basil
1 (30 oz.) jar spaghetti sauce
1 c. Mozzarella cheese, grated

Sauté garlic, carrots and onion in olive oil about 5 minutes. Stir in spinach and remove from heat. In large bowl mix vegetables, Ricotta, cottage and Parmesan cheeses, nutmeg, and basil (chicken, if desired). With small spoon stuff noodles and place in greased 9" x 13" casserole. Cover each with spaghetti sauce and bake at 350° for 30 minutes. Sprinkle with Mozzarella cheese and bake an additional 15 minutes. (Freezes well.) Serves 6 to 8.

MARGARET LAMPE

Q L   CHICKEN AND PASTA PRIMAVERA

1 c. broccoli, chopped
⅓ c. onion, chopped
2 cloves garlic, minced
1 carrot, cut into thin strips
3 T. vegetable oil
2 c. chicken, cooked and cubed

2 medium tomatoes, chopped
Salt and pepper to taste
4 c. cooked macaroni shells or
   wheels
⅓ c. Parmesan cheese, grated
2 T. parsley, chopped

Sauté broccoli, onion, garlic, and carrot in oil in 10-inch skillet over medium heat until broccoli is crisp-tender (about 10 minutes). Stir in chicken and tomatoes and heat 3 minutes. Add salt and pepper, if desired. Spoon mixture over hot macaroni and sprinkle with cheese and parsley. Serves 6.

JANE ABBOTT

GREEK PASTA   *Q L*

1 c. onion, finely chopped
3 T. olive oil
2 (28 oz.) cans of plum tomatoes
½ c. dry white wine

4-6 T. carrots, finely grated
Pepper to taste
6-8 oz. feta cheese, crumbled
1 lb. linguine pasta

In heavy saucepan sauté onion in oil until softened. Drain tomatoes, reserving juice. Add tomatoes to pan, chopping with back of spoon. Stir in wine and carrots, and add pepper to taste. Bring to boil and simmer for 15 minutes, adding reserved juice as necessary. Stir in feta and keep warm over low heat. Cook linguine according to package directions. Drain and serve with sauce. Serves 4 to 6.

TRICIA GREGORY

PASTA FOR YOUR PACE   **Q**

¼ c. vegetable oil
2 c. onions, chopped
2 cloves garlic, minced
1 large green pepper, cut into strips
8 oz. vermicelli, uncooked and broken into pieces
2 c. chicken or turkey, cooked and diced

1 (16 oz.) can peeled whole tomatoes
1 (14 oz.) can chicken broth
1 (8 oz.) bottle Pace picante sauce
1 t. ground cumin
¾ c. cheese, shredded
½ c. cilantro, chopped (optional)

Sauté onion, garlic and green pepper in oil in large skillet for about 3 minutes. Add vermicelli and cook another 2 minutes, stirring constantly. Stir in chicken, tomatoes, broth, picante sauce and cumin. Break up tomatoes with back of spoon and cook 10 to 12 minutes, until most of liquid has been absorbed. Sprinkle with cheese and cilantro and serve, or place in greased casserole to heat later (freezes well). Serves 6.

PEGGY TALMAN

Q   PASTA WITH SPICY HAM AND TOMATO SAUCE

½ c. olive oil
8-10 oz. baked boneless ham, sliced thin and cut into small pieces
1 red onion, chopped
¼ t. red pepper flakes (or more, to taste)
½ c. dry white wine

1 (28 oz.) can Italian plum tomatoes, undrained
1 t. salt
1 lb. pasta (bucatini or spaghetti)
¾ c. Pecorino Romano cheese (or Parmesan)
½ c. feta cheese (optional)

Heat olive oil over medium heat. Add ham, onion and red pepper flakes. Sauté until onions are softened, about 5 minutes. Add wine, raise heat until mixture simmers, and cook about 2 minutes. Add tomatoes with their juice. Add salt and cook about 15 minutes. Cook pasta until al dente, drain and add to sauce (tomatoes will be somewhat pulpy and sauce juicy). Sprinkle with Romano cheese and add feta, if desired. Serves 4 to 6.

VARIATION: Polska kielbasa or good Canadian bacon (not the presliced packaged variety) can be substituted for the ham.

MOLLY JOHNSON

Q   PASTA WITH TOMATO-ARTICHOKE SAUCE

⅓ c. olive oil
1 small red onion, chopped
2 (6 oz.) jars marinated artichoke hearts, drained
1 (28 oz.) can Italian plum tomatoes
1 T. capers, chopped

1 t. salt
¼ t. pepper
12 oz. (or more) angel hair pasta, cooked
½ c. Parmesan, freshly grated
¾ c. feta cheese, crumbled (optional)

Heat olive oil in large pan over medium heat. Add onion and sauté 5 minutes or until softened. Add artichokes to onions and cook 3 minutes. Add tomatoes and crush in pan so that they are coarse. Add capers and season with salt and pepper. Cook briskly over medium heat about 10 minutes. Toss with pasta and add cheeses to taste. Serves 4 to 6.

MOLLY JOHNSON

PENNA CON SALSICCIA

1 lb. mild Italian sausage
¼ c. olive oil
1 clove garlic, minced
1 qt. tomato sauce

1 lb. Ricotta cheese
1 bunch fresh basil, chopped
2 T. salt
1 lb. Penna pasta

Skin and grind sausage. Pour olive oil in skillet, add garlic and sausage and sauté until slightly browned. Add tomato sauce, cheese, and basil. Bring to boil and set aside. Bring 4 quarts water and salt to boil, add pasta and cook 8 minutes. Drain. Toss pasta with sauce and serve immediately. Serves 4.

AMICI RISTORANTE

STUFFED SHELLS

1 lb. ground beef
½ c. onion, chopped
1 T. oil
8 oz. Mozzarella cheese, shredded

½ pkg. jumbo pasta shells
1 (30 oz.) jar spaghetti sauce with
    mushrooms

Brown beef and onions in oil. Drain. Fold in ½ of cheese. Cook shells according to package directions and drain, handling carefully to prevent splitting. In greased casserole, pour ¼ of the sauce. Stuff shells with meat and cheese mixture and place on top of sauce. Pour remaining sauce over shells. Cover with rest of cheese and bake at 350° for 30 minutes. Serves 4.

BRENDA BURGESS

SPAGHETTI CARBONARA   Q

¾ lb. bacon
1 small onion, chopped
1 lb. spaghetti or linguine
3-4 T. butter
1 pt. whipping cream

6 oz. Parmesan cheese, freshly
    grated
1 egg, beaten
Salt and pepper to taste

Cook bacon to desired doneness (brown, but still soft) and drain. Sauté onion in small amount of bacon grease. Add cooked, chopped bacon. Cook spaghetti according to package directions. Drain, return to pot, and toss with butter. Add bacon mixture, cream, cheese and egg. Mix well. Add salt and pepper to taste. Heat through and serve. Serves 4 to 6.

BETH JOOSTEN
LINDSAY WORTHAM

BAKED SPAGHETTI CASSEROLE

1 lb. ground beef
1 (30 oz.) jar spaghetti sauce with
   mushrooms
1 (8 oz.) pkg. cream cheese,
   softened

1 c. cottage cheese
½ c. sour cream
2 T. green pepper, finely chopped
1 (12 oz.) pkg. spaghetti
¼ c. butter, melted (optional)

Brown beef and drain off fat. Add spaghetti sauce and simmer briefly. In separate bowl combine cream cheese, cottage cheese, sour cream and green pepper. Cook spaghetti according to package directions and drain. In greased 3 or 4-quart casserole place half of spaghetti and cover with cheese mixture. Drizzle on butter, if desired. Add remaining spaghetti and cover with meat and spaghetti sauce. Cover and bake at 350° for 1 hour. Serves 6 to 8.

NANCY CHEELY

Q L   SPAGHETTI WITH WHITE CLAM SAUCE

3 cloves garlic, minced
1 T. olive oil
1 T. flour
1 (10 oz.) can baby clams, drained,
   reserving juice
1 (8 oz.) bottle clam juice
¼ c. dry white wine

½ bay leaf
⅛ t. dried thyme
¼ c. parsley, minced
Pinch of cayenne pepper
1 T. salt
1 (12 oz.) pkg. spaghetti
Parmesan cheese, grated

Over medium heat sauté garlic briefly in oil. Reduce heat to low and add flour, stirring constantly, for 2 minutes. Remove from heat and whisk in drained and bottled clam juice and wine all at once. Return to medium-high heat and bring to boil. Immediately reduce heat to simmer, add seasonings and parsley. Simmer 20 minutes or until reduced to light sauce. Boil large pot of water with 1 T. salt and cook spaghetti until done, but still firm. Drain and add warm sauce and reserved clams. (To keep clams tender, do not over-cook sauce once clams have been added.) Serve at once with grated Parmesan cheese. Serves 4.

JENNIFER WHITMAN

CRAB SPAGHETTI

1 (9 oz.) pkg. angel hair pasta
1 (10¾ oz.) can cream of
   mushroom soup
3 T. butter or margarine
1 c. milk

8 oz. Cheddar cheese, grated
   and divided
12 oz. fresh crab meat
Dash of pepper

Cook spaghetti according to package directions and drain. Heat soup stirring until smooth. Add butter, milk and ¾ of cheese. Combine cheese sauce with spaghetti, crab meat and dash of pepper. Place in greased casserole, sprinkle with remaining cheese, and bake at 350° for 30 minutes. Serves 8.

LEE BOTTOMS

BROCCOLI-CAULIFLOWER TETRAZZINI

1 (8 oz.) pkg. spaghetti
1 (16 oz.) pkg. frozen broccoli, cauliflower and carrots
2 T. margarine
3 T. flour
2 c. milk
1 t. instant bouillon

¼ t. thyme
½ c. plus 2 T. Parmesan cheese, divided
Pepper to taste
1 (4½ oz.) can sliced mushrooms, drained

Break spaghetti into thirds and cook according to package directions. Drain, rinse and keep warm. Cook vegetables until slightly tender, drain and set aside. Preheat oven to 400° and grease 9" x 13" baking dish. Melt margarine in medium saucepan and stir in flour, mixing until smooth. Gradually add milk, stirring constantly. Cook over medium heat, stirring constantly, until mixture boils and thickens (approximately 6 to 10 minutes). Stir in bouillon, thyme, ½ c. Parmesan cheese and pepper. Set aside. Place spaghetti in baking dish. Top with vegetables and mushrooms and pour sauce over all. Sprinkle with 2 T. Parmesan cheese and bake until heated and bubbly around edges, approximately 20 minutes. Serves 6.

## TORTELLINI WITH GRILLED CHICKEN BREAST 	Q

1 (4 oz.) chicken breast
½ c. carrots, sliced
½ c. zucchini, sliced
Butter for sautéing
3 slices bacon
1 T. onion, diced

1 c. whipping cream
Salt and pepper to taste
5 oz. tortellini
Romano cheese, grated, for garnish

Skin and grill chicken breast. Slice on diagonal. Sauté carrots and zucchini briefly in small amount of butter and set aside. Sauté bacon and onion until brown and pour off excess grease. Add cream and cook to reduce to half. Season with salt and pepper. Cook tortellini according to package directions, drain and place in warm bowl. Pour cream sauce over pasta. Arrange sliced chicken over pasta, top with vegetables and sprinkle with Romano cheese. Serves 1.

PATSY ARNETT

Q L LOW-FAT CHEESE SAUCE

1 (12 oz) container low-fat cottage
  cheese
1 (5 oz) can evaporated skim milk

½ c. Cheddar cheese, shredded
Freshly ground pepper

In blender or food processor, combine cottage cheese and milk and process until smooth. In small saucepan, heat mixture over medium-low heat, stirring constantly. Add cheese and pepper, stirring until cheese melts. Yield: 2 cups.

DEB POVLISHOCK

L MARINARA SAUCE

4-5 cloves garlic, chopped
Olive oil - to cover bottom of pan
2 (28 oz) cans whole tomatoes
1½ t. dried basil

½ t. crushed red pepper (more if
  desired)
½ t. oregano
1 t. sugar
Salt and pepper to taste

Sauté garlic in olive oil. Add tomatoes, crushing with back of spoon. Add rest of ingredients, stirring well. Simmer about 45 minutes. (Meatballs, shrimp, sausage or sliced chicken can be added to sauce or serve plain over pasta.) Serves 4 to 6.

LINDA STEPANIAN

Q PESTO SAUCE

2 c. firmly packed fresh basil
  leaves (no stems)
¼ c. pine nuts (substitute walnuts
  or almonds)

2 cloves garlic, peeled
½ c. Parmesan cheese, grated
2 T. Pecorino Romano cheese
½ c. olive oil

Process basil, nuts and garlic in food processor or blender until finely chopped. Add cheese and blend. Slowly pour in oil and process until mixture is fine paste. This keeps 3-4 days in refrigerator or may be frozen. Yield: 2 cups.

MARGARET BARGATZE

PASTA SAUCE RAPHAEL

2 (6 oz.) jars artichokes, marinated
  in oil
¼ c. olive oil
2 c. onion, chopped
4 cloves garlic, minced
½ t. oregano
½ t. basil
1 t. coarsley ground pepper

½ t. salt
Pinch of dried red pepper flakes
1 (28 oz.) can plum tomatoes with
  juice
¼ c. Parmesan cheese, grated
¼ c. Italian parsley (flat leaf),
  chopped

Drain artichokes, reserving oil. Heat olive oil in large saucepan and sauté onions, garlic, oregano, basil, black pepper, salt, red pepper flakes and reserved marinade about 10 minutes. Add tomatoes and simmer 30 minutes. Fold in artichoke hearts, cheese and parsley, stir gently and simmer 5 minutes. Serve over one pound tortellini or curly pasta. Serves 6.

HOLLY PHILLIPS

HOMEMADE SPAGHETTI SAUCE

4 T. olive oil
6-8 cloves garlic, chopped
1 medium onion, chopped
1 lb. fresh mushrooms, sliced
  (optional)
1½ lbs. extra lean ground beef
2 (18¾ oz.) cans whole tomatoes,
  cut in pieces

2 (12 oz.) cans tomato paste
3 c. water
¼ c. red wine
1 t. oregano
1 t. dried basil
1 t. crushed red pepper
1 t. sugar
Salt and pepper to taste

Sauté garlic and onions in olive oil until transparent. Add mushrooms and ground beef. Brown. Stir in tomatoes, tomato paste, water and wine. Add remaining ingredients. Mix thoroughly. Simmer at least 1 hour, partially covered. (This sauce is better the day after it is cooked.)

NOTE: Veal, pork or chicken can be added for more flavor. Add uncooked meat to last simmer stage, until meat cooks off bone. Serves 6 to 8 small portions or 4 to 6 large portions.

LINDA STEPANIAN

MEATBALLS FOR SPAGHETTI SAUCE

2 lbs. ground beef
½ lb. ground pork or veal
2 c. Italian bread crumbs
3-4 eggs
1 c. milk
1 c. fresh parsley, chopped

1 T. olive oil
½ c. Parmesan cheese, grated
2 cloves garlic, finely chopped
1 onion, minced
¼ c. red wine
Olive oil for frying

Place all ingredients in large bowl and mix well. Let stand ½ hour. Shape into meatballs. Fry gently in pan that has been glazed with olive oil. Remove when brown. Drain and add to spaghetti sauce or serve separately. (To freeze after cooking, place on cookie sheet, freeze slightly and place in freezer bags.) Serves 10.

LINDA STEPANIAN

SPECIAL SPAGHETTI SAUCE

¾ lb. lean ground beef
Garlic powder to taste
Worcestershire
1 (24 oz) can tomato pieces or purée
1 (6 oz) can tomato paste
1 (14 oz) jar Ragu spaghetti sauce, original flavor

1 (8 oz) jar mushroom pieces
1 (1½ oz) pkg. French's spaghetti sauce mix
1 green pepper, chopped
1 red pepper, chopped
2 onions, chopped
Italian seasoning to taste
Oregano to taste

Brown ground beef with garlic powder, drain off fat, and sprinkle with Worcestershire. Set aside. Combine all remaining ingredients in large pot and bring to boil. Add meat mixture, cover loosely and maintain slow simmer for 3 hours, stirring frequently. Serves 6 to 8.

RICHARD TRUSCOTT

"I CAN'T BELIEVE IT'S BARLEY"

2 onions, coarsely chopped
¾ lb. mushrooms, sliced
¼ c. butter, melted
1½ c. barley

3 pimientos, chopped
2 c. chicken stock
Salt and pepper to taste
Chopped parsley (for garnish)

Sauté onions and mushrooms in butter; add barley and cook until brown. Add pimientos and stock; season to taste and bake at 350° in covered 1½-quart casserole for 50 to 60 minutes. Garnish with parsley before serving. Serves 8.

TYLER KILPATRICK

BAKED RICE WITH CONSOMMÉ

½ c. rice, uncooked
1 (10¾ oz.) can beef consommé
¼ c. butter, chopped

1 (4 oz.) can mushroom pieces
1 small onion, chopped
1 T. parsley, chopped

In greased 1½-quart casserole combine all ingredients. Bake at 375° for 40 minutes, stirring several times, and adding water, if necessary. Serves 4.

MARGARET TRAYNHAM

BROWN RICE AND LENTILS   *L*

½ c. long grain brown rice
½ c. dry lentils
2 c. water
3 T. butter, divided

½ t. salt
1 medium onion, sliced
Plain yogurt (optional)

Combine rice, lentils and water in medium size saucepan, and bring to boil. Add 2 T. butter and salt, turn heat to low and cook 1 hour. Sauté onion in 1 T. butter and add to mixture before serving. (Can substitute plain yogurt as topping instead of onions.) Serves 6.

JEAN ASCARI

CURRIED RICE

3 T. butter, divided
1½ t. curry powder
1½ c. rice
3 c. chicken broth
1 c. seedless raisins
½ c. green onion, chopped
½ c. green pepper, chopped

½ c. celery, chopped
½ t. seasoned salt
1½ T. chutney
3 T. pimiento, chopped
3 T. pine nuts (optional)
1½ T. vinegar
1½ T. brown sugar

Melt 1½ T. butter in heavy saucepan. Add curry and rice. Cook, stirring over low heat for 5 minutes. Stir in broth and bring to boil. Cover tightly and simmer over low heat until liquid has been absorbed. In a separate pan, melt 1½ T. butter. Sauté raisins, onion, pepper and celery until soft. Add remaining ingredients. Toss slightly. Mound hot rice on platter and spoon raisin mixture over rice. Serves 6 to 8.

LIVY RANDOLPH

ℚ STEVE WONG'S NEW YORK FRIED RICE

1½ c. long grain rice
3 c. water
Peanut oil for frying
1 lb. boneless pork chops, diced
2 cloves garlic, minced
2 eggs

⅓ c. oyster sauce
⅓ c. soy sauce
1 bunch green onions, chopped
1 medium onion, chopped
1 green pepper, chopped

Cook rice in water until water has been absorbed. Set aside. Heat wok and add film of peanut oil. Brown pork and garlic, toss until meat is done, and remove from wok. Scramble eggs in wok and set aside. Film wok with oil, add rice and brown. Stir in oyster and soy sauces. Toss in meat, garlic, onions, pepper and eggs. Mix thoroughly and serve. Serves 4.

BARBARA VRANIAN

ℚ RISO CON SALSA CRUDA

2 c. rice (long grain or Basmati)
2 tomatoes, peeled and seeded
½ c. green, red or yellow peppers, chopped
½ c. carrots, chopped
½ c. cucumber, chopped
¼ c. sweet onion, chopped

¼ c. parsley, chopped
¼ c. fresh basil, chopped
¼ c. black olives, chopped
½ c. feta cheese
Salt and pepper to taste
½ c. oil
½ c. herb vinegar

Cook rice according to package directions and place in serving bowl. Add remaining ingredients except oil and vinegar and toss. (May slightly steam carrots and onion if desired.) Combine oil and vinegar and fold into vegetable-rice mixture. Serves 4.

CINDY CHEWNING
VIRGINIA CHEWNING

VEGETABLES
& SIDE DISHES

Vegetables and Side Dishes

I hate tomatoes, even from that nice vegetable man.

George Haw, '04

Vegetables:

Artichoke Hearts and
Scalloped Tomatoes **Q L** ... 214
Baked Asparagus **Q L** 214
Pan-Fried Asparagus **Q** 214
Black Beans and Rice **L** 214
Green Bean Bundles 215
Creole Green Beans 215
Italian Green Beans **Q** 215
Lemon Green Beans **Q** 216
Green Beans with Red
Peppers **Q** 216
Green Bean and Swiss
Casserole 216
Pinto Bean Creole **L** 217
Sweet and Sour Beans 217
Three Bean Bake 218
Broccoli Elizabeth............. 218
Broccoli with Horseradish
Sauce **Q L** 218
Broccoli and Tomatoes **Q** 219
Broccoli Stem Sauté **Q** 219
Cabbage Chop Suey **Q L**.... 219
Swedish Cabbage Dish **L**..... 220
Baked Carrots **L** 220
Carrot Casserole 220
Carrots with Dill **L** 220
Carrots Supreme 221
Low-Fat Corn Pudding **L**...... 221
Escalloped Eggplant à la
Parmesan 222
Mushrooms Florentine **L** 222
Okra and Tomatoes **Q**........ 222
Vidalia Onion Casserole 223
Peppers Stuffed with
Cheese...................... 223
Garlic Potatoes **L** 223
Potatoes and Onions........... 224
Potato and Onion Bake **L** 224
Roasted Red Potatoes **Q** 224
Rosemary Potatoes............. 225
Nip It in the Bud Spuds **L** 225
Best Scalloped Potatoes 225
Lightly Scalloped Potatoes 226
New Potatoes in Sour
Cream 226
Twice-Baked Potatoes.......... 226

Light Twice-Baked
Potatoes **L** 227
Hash Brown Casserole.......... 227
Spicy "French Fries" **L** 227
Sweet Potato Delight........... 228
Baked Sweet Potatoes with
Marshmallows................. 228
Sweet Potato Pudding.......... 228
Kahlua Candied Yams 229
Spinach Casserole I 229
Spinach Casserole II........... 229
Spinach Gratin 230
Baked Acorn Squash **L** 230
Squash Alfredo **Q L**.......... 230
Squash Casserole 231
Riverton Squash Casserole 231
Broiled Zucchini **Q L** 231
Green Tomato Casserole 232
Tomato Pie 232
Scoffield Tomatoes **L** 232
Skillet Tomatoes **Q L** 232
Stuffed Baked Tomatoes 233
Tomatoes Stuffed With
Spinach Soufflé **Q** 233
Turnip Greens Casserole 233
California Vegetables **L** 234
Colorful Vegetables over
Rice **L**.................... 234
Mu Shu Vegetables **Q L** 234
Vegetable Frittata.............. 235
Vegetable Casserole........... 236
Vegetable Medley 236
Vegetarian Pizza............... 236

Side Dishes:

Angel Hair Flans 237
Charlie Bread 237
Nana's Kugel (Noodle
Pudding) 238
Apple-Cranberry Casserole 238
Apple Delight................. 238
Healthy Fried Apples **L** 239
Hot Fruit Compote............. 239
Quick and Easy Spiced
Peaches..................... 239
Spiced Pineapple 240
Pineapple Casserole 240

VEGETABLES AND SIDE DISHES

Q L ARTICHOKE HEARTS AND SCALLOPED TOMATOES

1 (14 oz.) can artichoke hearts
½ c. onions, chopped
½ c. butter or margarine
1 (2 lbs. 3 oz.) can whole tomatoes, drained

½ t. dried basil
2 T. sugar
Salt and pepper to taste

Rinse artichokes in water and quarter, set aside. Sauté onions in butter until soft. Add drained tomatoes, artichokes and basil and cook 2 to 3 minutes. Add sugar, salt, and pepper. Pour into shallow greased casserole. Bake uncovered at 325° for 15 minutes. Serves 6.

ANNE NELSON MORCK

Q L BAKED ASPARAGUS

Asparagus (5 per person)
Olive oil

Salt and pepper to taste

Break off tough ends of asparagus, wash and pat dry. Brush with olive oil, place on cookie sheet and sprinkle lightly with salt and pepper. Bake at 500° for approximately 5 minutes, or until tender.

ANN CUTCHINS
LINDA MAY

Q PAN-FRIED ASPARAGUS

2 lbs. asparagus
2 T. butter

Salt and pepper

When buying asparagus, make sure tips are tightly closed. Select stalks similar in size. Snap off tough ends of asparagus and discard. Rinse well and store, if necessary, upright in refrigerator in a glass of water. Before cooking, cut asparagus diagonally into 2" pieces. Keep tips separate. Rinse all pieces well in cold water. Melt butter in skillet and add asparagus ends. Cover and cook for 5 minutes, tossing occasionally. Add tips and cook 3 minutes more, tossing occasionally. Season with salt and pepper. Serves 5.

JANA THOMAS

L BLACK BEANS AND RICE

1 (16 oz.) pkg. dried black beans
8 cloves garlic, minced
2 large onions, chopped
2 green peppers, chopped
⅓ c. olive oil
1 ham bone

4 t. salt
1 t. pepper
3 T. vinegar
Cooked rice (4-6 cups)
½ c. green onion, chopped
Sour cream (optional)

214

Cover beans with water and soak overnight. Drain. Combine beans with 7 c. water and next 7 ingredients in a large soup pot. Simmer for 3 to 4 hours, or until beans are tender and liquid is thick. Add vinegar just before serving. Serve over rice and garnish with green onion; or if you prefer, this can be served in a bowl with sour cream and scallions. Serves 8.

MARY-GILL LAWSON

GREEN BEAN BUNDLES

2 lbs. fresh green beans
6 strips bacon, partially cooked
Garlic salt to taste

4 T. butter, melted
3 T. light brown sugar

Clean green beans and steam until crisp-tender. Gather 6 to 10 beans in bundles and wrap one-half piece of bacon around the center of each bundle. Place bundles in baking dish and sprinkle with garlic salt. Pour butter over bundles and sprinkle with brown sugar. Bake at 350° for 15 to 20 minutes, until bacon is done. Serves 12.

JILL HUNTER

CREOLE GREEN BEANS

Quick and easy!

4 slices bacon
2 (2 lb.) cans cut green beans,
    drained

1 c. ketchup
1 c. brown sugar
1 medium onion, chopped

Fry bacon and pour drippings into 2-quart casserole. Add crumbled bacon and green beans. Combine ketchup, brown sugar, and onion and pour over bean mixture. Mix thoroughly and bake uncovered at 350° for 30 minutes. Serves 6.

MISSY BUCKINGHAM

ITALIAN GREEN BEANS   Q

2 lbs. fresh green beans
¾ c. Marie's Italian Garlic Dressing

½ can American-Style Salad
    Crispins (blue label)
Cracked pepper to taste

Steam beans for 7 minutes; drain. Mix with dressing, crispins, and pepper. Serves 6 to 8.

MIMI RHOADS

Q LEMON GREEN BEANS

½ lb. fresh green beans
2 T. onion, minced
2 T. margarine, melted

1 T. lemon juice
¼ t. salt
⅛ t. pepper

Cover and cook beans in small amount of boiling water for 12 to 15 minutes, or until crisp-tender. Drain. Sauté onions in margarine until tender. Stir in lemon juice, salt and pepper. Add beans and cook 1 minute until hot. Serves 2.

SHIRLEY WALKER

VARIATION: Add oregano to taste.

JOANNE RAMSEY

Q GREEN BEANS WITH RED PEPPERS

Chicken broth
1 small red bell pepper, cut into
  strips
Butter Buds

1 t. Mrs. Dash (lemon and herb
  flavor)
1 lb. fresh green beans
Salt and pepper to taste

Spray small skillet with no-stick cooking spray and pour in 2 to 3 T. chicken broth. Heat to boiling and add red pepper. Sprinkle with Butter Buds and Mrs. Dash. Cook over medium high heat until peppers are tender, stirring frequently. Add additional chicken broth to keep peppers moist and to create a sauce to pour over beans. Steam or boil beans until crisp-tender. Pour off liquid and sear beans in pan until almost dry. (Shake beans around in pan.) Place beans in serving dish, pour red pepper sauce over all and toss to coat, adding salt and pepper to taste. Serves 4.

VARIATION: Mushrooms can be used instead of red pepper.

CAROLYN MEACHAM

GREEN BEAN AND SWISS CASSEROLE

This is a great alternative to the standard green bean recipe.

2 T. butter
2 t. sugar
1 t. salt
2 T. flour
2 (16 oz) cans French-style green
  beans

8 oz sour cream
3 T. onion, chopped
4 oz Swiss cheese, chopped
1 (2.8 oz) can Durkees onion rings

Cream butter, sugar, salt, and flour; add remaining four ingredients. Pour into greased 2-quart casserole and top with onion rings. Bake uncovered at 350° for 30 to 40 minutes. Serves 6 to 8.

LINDA PHILLIPS

PINTO BEAN CREOLE   *L*

A hearty meal for a cold winter day.

1 (28 oz.) can pinto beans
1 (15 oz.) can pinto beans
1 (28 oz.) can tomatoes, drained
   and chopped
1 large onion, chopped
1 large green pepper, chopped

1 bay leaf
½ t. salt
½ t. thyme
Hot cooked rice
1 clove garlic, crushed
¼ t. pepper

Combine all ingredients and simmer uncovered over very low heat for 1½ hours. Serve over hot rice. (Remove bay leaf if refrigerated.) Serves 5.

SUSAN OSBORNE

SWEET AND SOUR BEANS

10 slices bacon, cut in pieces
4 large onions, cut in rings
1 green pepper, cut in strips
1½ c. brown sugar
1 T. dry mustard
½ t. garlic powder
1 t. salt
½ c. vinegar

2 (15 oz.) cans butter beans,
   drained
1 (16 oz.) can green lima beans,
   drained
1 (16 oz.) can kidney beans,
   drained
1 (1½ lb.) can B & M baked beans,
   undrained

In a very large skillet, fry bacon. Remove bacon from skillet, leaving 2 T. grease. Sauté onions and green peppers in grease until onions are transparent. Add brown sugar, mustard, garlic powder, salt, and vinegar. Mix well. In a 5-quart casserole, combine all beans with bacon and onion mixture. Cover and bake at 350° for 30 minutes. Uncover and bake 30 minutes longer. (It will be runny.) Serves 12.

HARRIET SCHNELL

THREE BEAN BAKE

A nice change from plain baked beans!

2 (16 oz.) cans baked beans
1 (15 oz.) can red kidney beans, drained
1 (16 oz.) can green beans, drained
½ c. vinegar
1 c. brown sugar

½ t. salt
½ t. pepper
¼ c. Worcestershire
½ c. onion, chopped
½ t. garlic powder
6 slices bacon, cooked and crumbled .

Combine beans, vinegar, brown sugar, salt, pepper, Worcestershire, onion, and garlic powder in large saucepan. Simmer for 10 minutes. Pour into casserole dish and top with bacon. Bake at 350° for 30 minutes, or until bubbly and thickened. Serves 8 to 10.

CINDY BROOKS

BROCCOLI ELIZABETH

A delicious company or holiday vegetable.

2 (10 oz.) pkgs. frozen broccoli spears
¼ c. almonds, slivered
2 T. butter
2 T. flour
2 c. milk

1 c. sharp Cheddar cheese, grated
1 t. salt
¼ t. white pepper
½ c. bread crumbs
4 slices bacon, cooked and crumbled

Cook broccoli slightly and drain. Place in a buttered 10" x 10" glass baking dish. Sprinkle with almonds. Melt butter in a saucepan, add flour, and stir. Add milk gradually, stirring until thickened. Add cheese, salt, and pepper. Remove from heat. Pour sauce over broccoli and almonds. Sprinkle bread crumbs and bacon over top. Bake uncovered at 350° for 20 to 25 minutes. (May be prepared early in the day.) Serves 6.

ANNE FONVILLE

Q L BROCCOLI WITH HORSERADISH SAUCE

Easy, delicious, and low in calories!

1 bunch fresh broccoli
¼ c. plus 2 T. plain low-fat yogurt
¼ c. plus 2 T. reduced-calorie mayonnaise

1½ t. prepared mustard
½-1 t. prepared horseradish
Paprika

Steam broccoli spears until tender. Combine yogurt, mayonnaise, mustard, and horseradish in a saucepan. Heat through, stirring constantly, but do not boil. Spoon sauce over broccoli and sprinkle with paprika. Serves 6.

ALICIA ALFORD

BROCCOLI AND TOMATOES   Q

Pretty at Christmas!

2 lbs. broccoli, separated into
   florets
¾ pt. cherry tomatoes

¼ c. unsalted butter
½ t. sugar
Salt and pepper to taste

In large pot of salted boiling water, cook broccoli florets for 3 minutes, or until just tender. Drain, refresh in ice water, and drain again. Sauté tomatoes in butter over medium high heat until hot, about 3 minutes. Sprinkle with sugar, salt, and pepper. Add broccoli and toss until heated through; serve immediately. If preferred, place in buttered casserole and heat in 350° oven for 10 to 15 minutes. Serves 6.

MARTHA SUSAN SANDERS

BROCCOLI STEM SAUTÉ   Q

1½ c. broccoli stems (8-10)
1½ c. celery
1 (8 oz.) can mushrooms, sliced

1 (8 oz.) can water chestnuts,
   sliced (optional)
1 T. butter or margarine
Salt and pepper

Cut stems into ¼" pieces. Cut celery diagonally into ¼" slices. Drain mushrooms and pour reserved liquid into large skillet. Add broccoli and celery and cook until crisp-tender. Add water, if necessary. Drain, leaving a small amount of liquid. Add mushrooms, water chestnuts, and butter. Heat thoroughly, stirring constantly. Add salt and pepper to taste. Serves 4 to 5.

ANNABELLE HILBERT

CABBAGE CHOP SUEY   *Q L*

3 c. cabbage, shredded
1 large sweet onion, thinly sliced
1 large green pepper, thinly sliced
1 c. celery, sliced

½ t. salt
¼ c. water
2 T. butter, corn oil, or reduced-
   calorie margarine

Combine all ingredients in a large skillet. Cover and steam 10 to 12 minutes, stirring twice. Serves 6 to 8.

BRENDA JOHNSON

VEGETABLES AND SIDE DISHES

L   SWEDISH CABBAGE DISH

Great with ham, pork, and ribs!

1 medium red cabbage, cut into
    strips
1 large onion, sliced
2 apples, sliced with core and skin
    attached
2 T. olive oil

1 t. nutmeg
1 t. white pepper
1 t. salt
2 t. sugar
1 T. vinegar
1 t. allspice

Sauté cabbage, onions, and apples in olive oil. Add remaining ingredients. Cover and let simmer about 1 hour, stirring occasionally. Serves 4.

VIVI LAUGHON

L   BAKED CARROTS

1½ lbs. carrots, peeled
½-1 t. salt

3 T. brown sugar, firmly packed
3 T. butter or margarine

Carrots may be left whole or cut in half. Arrange carrots in a lightly greased 2-quart casserole with tight-fitting lid. Sprinkle with salt and sugar, and dot with butter. Bake at 325° for 1 hour if carrots are whole; reduce cooking time for halved or sliced carrots. Serves 8.

NANCY KENNON

CARROT CASSEROLE

2 T. flour
1 t. baking powder
1 c. sugar
¼ t. cinnamon

1 lb. carrots, cooked and mashed
½ c. butter, melted
3 eggs, lightly beaten

Mix together flour, baking powder, sugar and cinnamon. Add remaining ingredients. Pour into well-greased casserole and bake for 15 minutes at 400°; then for 30 minutes at 350°. Serves 8.

SANDY LACY

L   CARROTS WITH DILL

A simple recipe suitable for everyday or formal dining.

2 lbs. carrots, peeled, and cut in
    ½" slices
3-4 T. butter or margarine

Salt and pepper
Dried dill weed or fresh dill,
    snipped

220

Cover carrots with water and cook for 20 to 30 minutes, or until tender. Drain. Add butter, salt, pepper and dill. If using fresh dill, add just before serving. Serves 6 to 8.

BARBARA PARKER

CARROTS SUPREME

5 lbs. carrots, scraped and sliced
Salt to taste
4 c. white vinegar
4 c. sugar
20 cloves
2 oranges, sliced

Cook carrots in boiling water until just tender. Drain, salt lightly, and set aside. Combine sugar and vinegar in medium saucepan and heat just until boiling. Add cloves and oranges. Pour syrup mixture over carrots and place in covered container in refrigerator. Keeps well for weeks. May be served hot or cold. When serving hot, remove carrots from syrup before serving. Serves 10 to 12.

INGER RICE

LOW-FAT CORN PUDDING   *L*

3 c. milk or 2 (12 oz.) cans
    evaporated skim milk
4 eggs (or 8 egg whites)
1 (28 oz.) bag frozen corn, divided
⅓ c. green pepper, diced
⅓ c. onion, diced
1 t. salt
12 drops hot pepper sauce

Heat oven to 325° and spray 2-quart baking dish with no-stick cooking spray. In a saucepan heat milk just to boiling. Combine eggs and 2 c. corn thoroughly in a blender or food processor. Add remaining ingredients to the hot milk, then add the egg mixture, stirring constantly until well-blended. Take saucepan off heat and pour mixture into casserole and bake 45 minutes, or just until firm. Serves 12.

JEAN JONES

ESCALLOPED EGGPLANT À LA PARMESAN

A good meatless entree!

1 medium eggplant, cut into ½"
  slices
2 large tomatoes, peeled and
  sliced
1 large onion, sliced and
  separated into rings
¾ c. margarine, melted and
  divided

½ t. basil
½ t. garlic salt
8 oz. light Mozzarella cheese, cut
  into triangular slices
2-3 slices wheat bread, toasted
  and crumbed
2 T. Parmesan cheese

Preheat oven to 450° for metal baking dish, 425° for glass baking dish. Arrange eggplant slices in the bottom of a 9" x 13" pan. Top with tomatoes and onion rings. Drizzle ½ c. margarine over entire casserole. Sprinkle with basil and garlic salt. Cover and bake for 20 minutes. Remove from oven and top with Mozzarella triangles. Toss bread crumbs with ¼ c. margarine and sprinkle over casserole. Top with Parmesan cheese and bake uncovered for 10 minutes. Serves 6 to 8.

BRENDA LIPSCOMB

L   MUSHROOMS FLORENTINE

2 (10 oz.) pkgs. frozen chopped
  spinach, cooked and drained
1 t. salt
¼ c. onion, chopped
2 T. Promise margarine, melted

1 c. Alpine Lace cheese, divided
1 lb. fresh mushrooms, sautéed in
  Promise
Garlic salt
Pepper

Grease a 10" pie or quiche pan with Promise. Season cooked spinach with salt, onion, and Promise. Line pan with spinach; sprinkle with ½ c. cheese. Arrange mushrooms over cheese layer and season with garlic salt and pepper. Cover with remaining cheese. (May be refrigerated at this point.) Bake at 350° for 20 minutes. Serves 6.

MARY-GILL LAWSON

Q   OKRA AND TOMATOES

2 slices bacon
3 c. okra, sliced
¼ c. onion, chopped
4 medium tomatoes, peeled and
  chopped

½ t. salt
¼ t. pepper
1 T. vinegar
2 t. Worcestershire

Cook bacon in microwave and crumble. Add okra and onion to bacon drippings. Cover and microwave on high for 9 minutes, stirring after 4 minutes, until okra is crisp-tender. Add tomatoes and the next 4 ingredients. Cover and microwave on high for 3 minutes. Let stand, covered, for 5 minutes. Sprinkle bacon on top. Serves 6 to 8.

CATHY LEE

VIDALIA ONION CASSEROLE

5 large Vidalia onions, sliced into rings
½ c. butter or margarine, melted

1 c. Parmesan cheese, grated
20 buttery crackers, crushed

Sauté onions in butter until limp and transparent. Pour half of onions into casserole and cover with half of the cheese. Sprinkle with half of the cracker crumbs. Repeat. Bake uncovered at 325° for 30 minutes, or until golden brown. (Any mild onion can be used if Vidalia onions are not in season.) Serves 4.

BEBE LUCK

PEPPERS STUFFED WITH CHEESE

Decorative and delicious on any luncheon plate!

1 large pepper, red or green (or 2 small peppers)
1 (8 oz.) pkg. cream cheese, softened

2 T. butter, softened (no substitutes)
⅓-½ c. pecans, chopped

Cut top off pepper and remove seeds. Mix cheese, butter, and pecans. Pack pepper very tightly with cheese mixture and chill. Slice thin and serve. Good on cold salad plate. (Red peppers are usually milder than green.) Serves 2 to 4.

NANCY KENNON

GARLIC POTATOES   *L*

2½ lbs. small new potatoes
¼ c. olive oil
2 large cloves garlic

⅛ t. red pepper
¼-⅓ c. Parmesan cheese

Pour olive oil into a 9" x 13" glass baking dish. Press garlic into olive oil; sprinkle red pepper over oil. Quarter potatoes and coat with oil. Bake at 400° for 45 minutes. Turn potatoes with a spatula after 25 minutes. When potatoes are done, sprinkle with Parmesan cheese. Continue to bake until cheese melts. Serves 6 to 8.

BONNY GREENBAUM

POTATOES AND ONIONS

Great for a cook out!

3-4 unpeeled baking potatoes, sliced
3-4 medium onions, sliced

¼ c. corn oil margarine
Salt and pepper
Dollop of sour cream (optional)

Place a long piece of aluminum foil on a cookie sheet. Alternate slices of potatoes and onions on foil. Dot liberally with margarine. Add salt and pepper to taste. Seal foil in a long "loaf" shape. Bake at 400° for about 1½ hours. When done, turn into a serving dish and "hash" together, perhaps with a dollop of sour cream. Serves 6 to 8.

BETTY KOONCE

L POTATO AND ONION BAKE

1¼ lbs. new potatoes, unpeeled and sliced
1 medium onion, sliced
1 T. olive oil
1½ t. clove garlic, minced

1 T. lemon juice
½ t. oregano
2 T. fresh parsley, chopped
2 T. chicken broth
Salt and pepper to taste

Place potatoes and onions in a 9" x 13" baking dish coated with no-stick cooking spray. Combine remaining ingredients and mix well. Pour over potatoes and onions and toss to coat. Cover pan with aluminum foil and bake at 400° for 45 minutes. Uncover pan and bake a few minutes longer, or until slightly browned. Serves 4.

CAROLYN MEACHAM

Q ROASTED RED POTATOES

Small red potatoes, cut into quarters (2 per person)
Olive oil

Paprika
Salt
Pepper

Mix olive oil and paprika in a bowl. Coat potatoes with olive oil mixture. Place potatoes on cookie sheet. Sprinkle with salt and pepper. Place potatoes in 500° oven for about 10 minutes.

ANN CUTCHINS

VEGETABLES AND SIDE DISHES

ROSEMARY POTATOES

Great with a roast or fish!

Small new potatoes (2 per person)
Butter, melted
Salt and Pepper
Rosemary (fresh)

Boil potatoes in jackets for 10 minutes in salted water. Drain. This can be done early in the day, if necessary. About an hour before serving, put potatoes in roasting pan and toss with butter and seasonings, being sure potatoes are completely coated. Roast at 350° for 45 to 60 minutes, until skins are crispy. These will keep well in the oven if serving is delayed.

JANA THOMAS

NIP IT IN THE BUD SPUDS   *L*

¼ c. onion, finely chopped
3 lbs. potatoes, peeled, cooked and hot
1 (8 oz.) pkg. light cream cheese (Neufchatel), softened and cubed
¼ c. light margarine
½ c. plain yogurt (low or non-fat)
½ c. low-fat or skim milk
2 eggs, lightly beaten or ½ c. egg substitute
1 t. salt

Microwave onions until limp and set aside. In large bowl, mash potatoes until smooth. Add margarine and cream cheese and beat until well blended. Stir in yogurt. In a separate bowl, combine milk, eggs, and onion. Stir into potato mixture and add salt. Beat until light and fluffy. Place in a 9" x 13" casserole and refrigerate several hours or overnight. Allow casserole to reach room temperature before baking. Bake uncovered at 350° for 45 minutes, or until top is lightly browned. Serves 8 to 12.

SUSAN OTTENI

BEST SCALLOPED POTATOES

7 large potatoes, peeled and thinly sliced
2 large onions, thinly sliced
Salt and pepper
2 c. sharp Cheddar cheese, grated
1-1¼ c. heavy cream

Grease a large casserole dish. Layer potatoes, onions, salt, and pepper, ending with onions on top. Sprinkle with cheese. Add cream half way to top. Bake at 350° for 1 to 1½ hours. Serves 6.

JEAN ASCARI

VEGETABLES AND SIDE DISHES

LIGHTLY SCALLOPED POTATOES

3 T. flour
Freshly ground black pepper
Salt to taste
4 c. potatoes, thinly sliced

1½ c. skim milk
3 T. margarine
½ c. Cheddar cheese, grated
1 T. parsley, chopped

Combine flour, pepper, and salt. Layer potatoes and flour mixture alternately in lightly greased casserole. Heat milk and margarine together and pour over potatoes. Sprinkle top with cheese and parsley. Cover and bake at 350° for 1 hour. Remove cover and bake 30 minutes longer, until browned. Serves 6.

VARIATION: Curry powder and onions can be used for seasoning. Cheese can be omitted.

CATHY BUTTNER

NEW POTATOES IN SOUR CREAM

18 small new red potatoes
2 small onions, finely chopped
3 T. shortening
3 T. sugar
1 T. salt

2 T. flour
1 c. sour cream
1¼ c. milk
2 T. white vinegar

Cook potatoes in jackets in salted boiling water until tender. Sauté onion in shortening until limp. Combine sugar, salt, and flour and add to onion mixture, stirring until smooth. Gradually, add sour cream and milk. Cook and stir over low heat until sauce begins to bubble. Add vinegar and continue cooking and stirring until sauce bubbles again. Remove skins from potatoes and add them to sour cream mixture. Keep warm until ready to serve. Serves 8 to 10.

MIM SCHUTE

TWICE-BAKED POTATOES

3 large baking potatoes
Vegetable oil
¼ c. butter, melted
¼ c. milk
3 T. sour cream
2 T. onion, finely chopped
1½ t. parsley flakes, dried
¼ t. dry mustard

⅛ t. salt (optional)
⅛ t. pepper
Cheddar or American cheese, grated
Paprika
Bacon, cooked and crumbled (optional)

Scrub potatoes and rub skins with oil. Place on baking sheet and bake at 400° for 1 hour or until done. Let cool until comfortable to handle. Cut potatoes in half lengthwise; carefully scoop out pulp leaving shells intact. Spoon pulp into

VEGETABLES AND SIDE DISHES

large mixing bowl; mash to remove large lumps. Add remaining ingredients except for cheese and paprika. Beat with electric mixer until fluffy. Stuff shells with potato mixture and garnish with grated cheese. Sprinkle with paprika. Bake at 400° for 15 minutes. (If made ahead and refrigerated, baking time will be longer.) Can be garnished with crumbled bacon, if desired. Serves 6.

ANN BEAUCHAMP

LIGHT TWICE-BAKED POTATOES　　*L*

4 medium to large russet potatoes
1 T. parsley
3 T. Molly McButter
2 T. dried chives
2 T. Parmesan cheese, grated

¼ t. pepper
¼ c. onion, finely chopped
1 c. 2% cottage cheese
¼ c. skim milk
Paprika

Microwave potatoes until done, approximately 15 to 20 minutes. When cool, cut in half lengthwise and scoop out as much potato as possible, leaving skins intact. Mix potato with next 8 ingredients, blending with electric mixer until smooth. Spoon potato mixture back into potato shells. Sprinkle with paprika and bake on cookie sheet for 30 minutes at 350°. Serves 8.

STUART TROPE

HASH BROWN CASSEROLE

1 (32 oz.) bag frozen hash brown
　potatoes, thawed
1 pt. sour cream
1 (10¾ oz.) can cream of chicken
　soup

2 c. Cheddar cheese, grated
1 c. onion, chopped
2 t. salt
½ c. margarine, melted

Mix all ingredients and spread in a 9" x 13" casserole. Bake at 350° for 45 to 60 minutes, or until brown on top. Serves 8 to 10.

MIM SCHUTE

SPICY "FRENCH FRIES"　　*L*

4 potatoes, any type
Molly McButter

Garlic powder and chili powder
or cumin and red pepper

Spray large baking sheet with no-stick cooking spray. Cut potatoes into strips. Arrange strips in rows on baking sheet and sprinkle with Molly McButter and either combination of seasonings. Place baking sheet in middle of oven with broiler on 500°. Bake for 15 minutes, or until brown. Turn strips over and bake another 15 minutes, until brown. Serve plain, with ketchup, or with salsa. Serves 4.

STUART TROPE

227

SWEET POTATO DELIGHT

Great for Thanksgiving and Christmas dinners!

3 c. canned or fresh sweet
   potatoes, mashed (fresh
   potatoes must be cooked and
   peeled)
2 eggs, beaten

½ c. milk
½ c. margarine, melted
1 t. vanilla
½ c. coconut, flaked
1 c. sugar

Combine all ingredients and pour into greased 9" x 13" baking dish.

TOPPING

½ c. margarine, softened
1 c. brown sugar

½ c. flour
½ c. nuts, chopped

Combine all ingredients and spread on top of sweet potato mixture. Bake at 350° for 30 to 40 minutes. Serves 8.

CATHY LEE

BAKED SWEET POTATOES WITH MARSHMALLOWS

1 c. 1% milk
1 t. vanilla
1 ½ T. brown sugar
½ c. margarine, softened
3 (1 lb. 13 oz.) cans sweet potatoes

½ t. cinnamon
Few dashes nutmeg
1 T. orange juice
1 (10 oz.) pkg. mini-marshmallows

Scald milk and add vanilla, sugar, and margarine. Mash potatoes and beat with mixer. Add cinnamon, nutmeg, and orange juice to potatoes. Add milk mixture and combine thoroughly. Grease an 8-cup baking dish. Place half of potatoes in dish and layer with half of marshmallows. Repeat. Bake at 350° for about 30 minutes. Serves 8 to 10.

KAY WILLIAMS

SWEET POTATO PUDDING

¼ c. butter
1 t. baking powder
2 T. flour
¼ t. cinnamon
1 c. sugar (if recipe is doubled, use 1½ c. sugar)

3 eggs, beaten
1 c. milk
2 c. cooked sweet potatoes, mashed
Marshmallows (optional)

Melt butter in 2-quart casserole dish. In large bowl combine dry ingredients. Blend together eggs, milk, and potatoes; add to dry mixture. Pour into

228

prepared casserole and bake at 325° for 45 to 60 minutes, or until crusty on top. Marshmallows can be placed on top for last 10 minutes of baking, if desired. Serves 4 to 6.

NANCY GEORGE

KAHLUA CANDIED YAMS

4 medium yams
¼ c. butter

⅓ c. brown sugar
¼ c. kahlua

Boil yams until tender but firm. When cool, peel yams and slice in half lengthwise. In sauce pan, melt butter and brown sugar over low heat. Add kahlua and stir. Add yams. Cover and simmer for 10 minutes. Serves 6 to 8.

SUZANNE COWLEY

SPINACH CASSEROLE I

2 (10 oz.) pkgs. frozen chopped
    spinach
1 beef bouillon cube
1 (8 oz.) pkg. light cream cheese

½ c. margarine, divided
2 c. Pepperidge Farm bread
    crumbs

Cook spinach with bouillon dissolved in a small amount of water. Drain well. Stir in cream cheese and ⅓ of margarine. Melt remaining margarine and mix with bread crumbs. Place spinach mixture in casserole dish and top with bread crumb mixture. Bake at 350° for 20 minutes. Serves 6.

PALMER GARSON

SPINACH CASSEROLE II

6 (10 oz.) pkgs. frozen spinach,
    cooked and well-drained
1 medium onion, chopped
1 clove garlic, minced
Margarine for sautéing

3 (8 oz.) pkgs. light cream cheese,
    beaten
Salt and pepper, to taste
1½ stacks low-salt Ritz crackers,
    crushed
⅓-½ c. margarine, melted

Sauté onion and garlic in small amount of margarine. Mix warm spinach with cream cheese. Add onion mixture to spinach mixture. Salt and pepper to taste. Pour into a 9" x 13" casserole dish. Combine cracker crumbs and margarine and distribute over top. Bake at 350° until hot and bubbly, about 25 to 30 minutes. This freezes well, but must be thawed completely before baking. Serves 10 to 12.

MELANIE JONES

229

SPINACH GRATIN

3 (10 oz.) pkgs. frozen chopped
  spinach, thawed
1 pkg. dry Hidden Valley Ranch
  original buttermilk dressing mix
1 (8 oz.) pkg. light cream cheese,
  softened, or 8 oz. light sour
  cream

1-2 T. dry onion flakes
¼ t. salt
¼ t. ground white pepper
½ c. Progresso Italian bread
  crumbs
¼ c. Parmesan cheese, grated
¼ c. margarine, melted

Press most, but not all, of the water from the spinach with the back of a spoon in a colander. Blend the spinach, dressing mix, cream cheese, onion, salt, and pepper. Place in a greased 8" x 10" casserole. Combine crumbs, cheese, and margarine and sprinkle over top. Bake at 350° for 25 to 30 minutes. Serves 10 to 12.

MARTHA RIPLEY

L BAKED ACORN SQUASH

Amazingly simple, but very good and sweet.

2 acorn squash
2 T. maple syrup, divided
½ c. orange juice, divided

Cinnamon
Nutmeg
1½ c. water

Cut squash in half crosswise. Scrape out seeds and threads. Cut a small slice across the bottom of each half, so it can stand upright being careful not to cut through. Place squash halves in baking dish. Put 1½ t. maple syrup and 2 T. orange juice in each half. Sprinkle with cinnamon and nutmeg. Pour water into baking dish, cover loosely with foil, and bake at 375° for 45 to 60 minutes, or until tender. Mash squash in their skins. Serves 4.

ALEX THOMPSON

Q L SQUASH ALFREDO

Everyone loves this!

10 medium yellow squash, sliced
1 onion, chopped
⅓ c. water
1 c. light sour cream

¼ t. nutmeg
1 t. Cavender's Greek seasoning
½ t. pepper
½ c. Parmesan cheese, grated

Cook squash and onion in water until soft, about 10 minutes. Add remaining ingredients and heat through. Serves 6.

MIMI RHOADS

SQUASH CASSEROLE

Light, fluffy, and easy!

2 lbs. yellow squash, sliced
1 medium onion, chopped
1 medium green pepper,
  chopped

2 eggs
½ c. mayonnaise
1 c. Parmesan cheese, grated

Cook squash, onion, and pepper in salted water until tender. Beat eggs, then blend in mayonnaise and Parmesan. Add egg mixture to vegetables. Place in 1 ½-quart casserole which has been sprayed with no-stick cooking spray. Bake at 350° for 30 to 40 minutes. Serves 6.

ANN CRENSHAW

RIVERTON SQUASH CASSEROLE

4 c. yellow squash, sliced
1 c. onion, chopped
1 c. green pepper, chopped
¼ c. butter or lighter substitute,
  softened

½ c. soda crackers, crushed
2 eggs, lightly beaten
Salt and pepper to taste
½ c. Cheddar cheese, grated

Steam squash, onion, and green pepper for 10 minutes or until tender. Transfer to a mixing bowl and stir in butter, cracker crumbs, and eggs. Add salt and pepper. Place in a 1-quart baking dish and top with cheese. Bake at 375° for 45 minutes. Serves 4.

BRENDA JOHNSON

BROILED ZUCCHINI *Q L*

3 small zucchini, cut in half
  lengthwise
1½ T. margarine, melted

Salt and pepper to taste
3 T. Parmesan cheese, grated
Paprika

Place zucchini, cut side up, in baking dish. Brush tops with margarine. Sprinkle with salt, pepper, cheese and paprika. Broil 6 to 8 inches from heat for 12 minutes or until tender. Serves 3.

SHIRLEY WALKER

GREEN TOMATO CASSEROLE

Great recipe if you just can't wait for those first tomatoes to turn red!

4 green tomatoes, cut into ¼" slices
Salt and pepper to taste

1 c. Cheddar cheese, shredded
1 T. butter

Place half of tomatoes in bottom of greased 1½-quart baking dish. Sprinkle with salt, pepper, and ½ c. cheese. Repeat layers and dot with butter. Cover and bake at 400° for 1 hour. Serves 4 to 6.

BEBE LUCK

TOMATO PIE

6-8 large Hanover tomatoes
1 deep-dish pie crust, baked
Fresh basil, chopped
Fresh chives, chopped

Fresh oregano, chopped
1 c. mayonnaise
1 c. Cheddar cheese, shredded

Sear and skin tomatoes; slice and sprinkle with herbs. Layer in pie crust. Combine mayonnaise and cheese and spread on top of tomatoes. Bake at 400° for 25 to 30 minutes, or until browned. Serves 6.

CINDY BROOKS

L SCOFFIELD TOMATOES

A great winter tomato recipe!

1 (29 oz) can Del Monte tomato
wedges (no substitute)
¼ c. oil
½ c. vinegar

¼-⅓ c. sugar
½ small onion, minced
Salt and pepper to taste

Drain tomatoes. Make marinade by combining remaining ingredients. Pour marinade over tomatoes and chill for 12 to 24 hours. Serves 4 to 6.

JULIA KIMBRELL

Q L SKILLET TOMATOES

4 large firm tomatoes, cut in half
1 T. butter
1 t. sugar
1 t. salt

1 T. parsley, chopped
1 clove garlic, minced
1 T. vinegar
2 T. olive oil

Cook tomatoes in butter in a skillet, cut side down, about 5 minutes. Turn tomatoes over. Combine remaining ingredients in a bowl, stirring well and pour over tomatoes. Simmer 5 minutes longer. Serves 8.

NANCY GEORGE

STUFFED BAKED TOMATOES

A good luncheon side dish!

6 medium tomatoes, cored
1 c. stuffing, moistened slightly with
  water
1 c. mayonnaise
1 (10 oz.) pkg. frozen chopped
  broccoli, cooked

1 c. white cheese, shredded (such
  as Monterey Jack)
2 T. onion, minced
Salt and pepper to taste
Parmesan cheese to taste

Sprinkle inside of tomatoes with a little salt. Turn upside down on a paper towel and drain for 10 minutes. Mix remaining ingredients except Parmesan and stuff tomatoes. Sprinkle Parmesan on top and bake for 30 minutes at 350°. Serves 6.

MOLLY JOHNSON

TOMATOES STUFFED WITH SPINACH SOUFFLÉ **Q**

Easy to fix; good for luncheons!

6 small firm tomatoes
Dijon mustard

1 pkg. Stouffer's spinach soufflé,
  thawed
Parmesan cheese

Slice off tops of tomatoes and scoop out centers. Turn upside down and let drain. Rub a little mustard in each tomato and stuff with thawed soufflé. Sprinkle with cheese and bake at 350° for 15 to 20 minutes. Serves 6.

KATHY WATSON

TURNIP GREENS CASSEROLE

1 (15 oz.) can Bush's chopped
  turnip or mustard greens
1 t. sugar
Salt and pepper to taste
½ (10¾ oz.) can cream of
  mushroom soup

½ c. mayonnaise
1½-2 T. wine vinegar
1 t. horseradish
2 eggs, lightly beaten
Bread crumbs
Cheddar cheese, grated

Combine all ingredients except bread crumbs and cheese. Place in a medium casserole and sprinkle with bread crumbs and cheese. Bake at 350° for 1 hour. Serves 6 to 8.

NANCY GEORGE

VEGETABLES AND SIDE DISHES

L   CALIFORNIA VEGETABLES

2 zucchini, diagonally sliced
1 T. butter or margarine
1 T. olive oil
12-15 mushrooms, sliced
1 onion, chopped

2-3 fresh tomatoes, chopped or 1
    (14½ oz) can tomatoes, drained
Salt and pepper
1 t. dried dill
1 t. Italian seasoning
4 oz Monterey Jack cheese, sliced

Sauté zucchini in butter and olive oil in 9" skillet. Add mushrooms, onions and tomatoes. Sauté until onions are transparent. Add seasonings and blend well. Top with sliced cheese, cover, and simmer until cheese is melted. Serves 4.

GIGI GUNNELS

L   COLORFUL VEGETABLES OVER RICE

A light meal by itself and a wonderful way to use leftovers!

2 cloves garlic, minced
1 small onion, sliced
2 T. olive oil
3 c. red, yellow, and/or green
    peppers, chopped
2 zucchini, sliced
1 (28 oz) can Italian plum
    tomatoes, drained

1 bay leaf
1 t. Italian seasoning
Salt and pepper to taste
Bite-sized pieces of leftover
    chicken or turkey (optional)
Hot cooked rice

In a large skillet, sauté garlic and onion in olive oil until tender. Add remaining ingredients except for meat and bring to a boil. Cover and simmer gently for 20 minutes. Add chicken or turkey during last 5 minutes of cooking and heat only until meat is warm and moist. Serve over hot rice. Serves 5 to 6.

LEE MERRICK

Q L   MU SHU VEGETABLES

2 large eggs, slightly beaten with 1
    T. water
2 t. peanut oil
½ c. reconstituted dried Chinese
    mushrooms
2 T. dry sherry or chicken broth
1 T. fresh ginger root, chopped
1 clove garlic, minced
1 T. low-sodium soy sauce

1 medium green pepper, cut in
    thin strips
1 medium red pepper, cut in thin
    strips
½ c. celery, cut in 2" strips
½ c. scallions, cut in 2" strips
½ c. fresh bean sprouts (or
    drained canned)
4 (9") refrigerated prepared crêpes
4 t. Hoison sauce

234

Spray large non-stick skillet or wok with no-stick cooking spray. Place over medium heat. Add eggs and swirl to coat entire bottom of pan. Cook 2 to 3 minutes, until mixture is set and edges are lightly browned. Remove from pan. When cool, cut into 4" strips. Set aside. Heat peanut oil in same skillet. Add mushrooms and sherry and stir-fry 1 minute. Stir in ginger, garlic, and soy sauce and stir-fry 1 minute longer. Add egg strips and vegetables and stir-fry 5 minutes, until vegetables are tender. To serve, place ½ c. vegetable mixture on each crêpe; top with 1 t. Hoison sauce. Fold crêpe over vegetables to enclose. Serves 4.

BARBARA LINGO

VEGETABLE FRITTATA

This is a great brunch recipe!

3 T. olive oil
1 large onion, thinly sliced
1 cloves garlic, minced
3 medium summer squash, sliced
  ¼" thick
3 peppers (red, green, and
  yellow), seeded and cut in ¼"
  strips
8 oz. fresh mushrooms, sliced

6 large eggs
¼ c. whipping cream
2 c. stale or toasted bread cubes
  (French is preferred)
1 (8 oz.) pkg. cream cheese, cut
  up
2 c. Swiss cheese, grated
1-2 t. salt
1-2 t. pepper

Sauté vegetables in olive oil until crisp-tender, about 15 minutes. While vegetables are cooking, whisk eggs and cream together. Add bread cubes, Swiss cheese, and cream cheese. Add vegetables to egg mixture. Add salt and pepper and mix well. Pour into greased 10" springform pan. Place on cookie sheet to catch any leaks and bake at 350° for about 1 hour, or until firm to the touch, puffed, and golden brown. If top gets too brown, cover with foil for remainder of baking time. Serve unmolded hot, cold, or at room temperature. (Can be reheated at 350° for 15 minutes, if desired.) Serves 6 to 8.

ALEX THOMPSON

VEGETABLE CASSEROLE

½ c. celery, chopped
½ c. green pepper, chopped
½ c. onion, chopped
1 (16 oz.) can French-cut green
  beans, drained
1 (16 oz.) can shoe peg corn

½ c. Cheddar cheese, grated
1 (10 ¾ oz) can cream of
  mushroom soup
1 c. sour cream
1 stack Ritz crackers, crushed
½ c. butter, melted

Mix first 8 ingredients and place in 9" x 13" baking pan. Mix cracker crumbs and butter, and sprinkle over top of vegetable mixture. Bake at 350° for 45 minutes. Serves 6 to 8.

NANCY GEORGE

VARIATION: Substitute cream of celery soup for cream of mushroom soup. Sprinkle 1 cup cheese and half of the buttered cracker mixture over top of casserole before baking.

LILLIAN HAMILTON

VEGETABLE MEDLEY

1 (16 oz.) bag frozen broccoli,
  carrots and cauliflower
1 (10 oz.) pkg. frozen peas
1 (10¾ oz.) can cream of
  mushroom soup

1 c. Swiss Cheese, shredded
⅓ c. sour cream
¼ t. pepper
1 (2.8 oz) can onion rings

Thaw and drain vegetables. Add soup, half the cheese, sour cream, pepper and half the onion rings to vegetables. Pour into a 2-quart casserole. Bake covered at 350° for 30 minutes. Top with rest of cheese and onions. Bake uncovered for 5 minutes more. Serves 6.

SHERRILL SMITH

VEGETARIAN PIZZA

A meatless entree.

2 prepared pizza crusts
1 large onion, chopped
2 T. olive oil
1 (15 oz) can tomato sauce
1 (6 oz) can tomato paste
½ c. red wine
1 t. oregano
1 t. basil
½ t. salt
2 medium zucchini, thinly sliced

½ green pepper, cut in thin strips
½ red pepper, cut in thin strips
4 green onions, thinly sliced
1 (2¼ oz) can black olives, sliced
1 (14 oz) can artichoke hearts,
  drained and quartered
12 oz Monterrey Jack cheese,
  shredded
¼ c. Parmesan cheese, grated

236

Over medium heat sauté onion in olive oil until tender. Stir in tomato sauce, tomato paste, wine, oregano, basil and salt. Simmer, uncovered, for 10 to 15 minutes. Spread sauce over crusts. Arrange zucchini, peppers, onions, olives and artichoke hearts over sauce. Sprinkle cheeses over vegetables. Bake at 450° for 12 to 15 minutes or until hot and cheeses are melted. Yield: 2 pizzas.

CLARE NEWBRAND

ANGEL HAIR FLANS

Excellent with pork, chicken, or beef.

1 c. whipping cream	½ t. nutmeg
3 large eggs	Salt and pepper to taste
1 t. fresh thyme, minced, or 1 pinch dried thyme	1 c. Parmesan cheese, grated
	3 oz. angel hair pasta, cooked

Butter 8 (½-cup) soufflé dishes. Whisk first 4 ingredients in a medium bowl to blend. Season with salt and pepper and stir in ⅔ c. Parmesan. Divide freshly cooked pasta evenly among prepared cups. Pour egg mixture over pasta. Sprinkle flans with remaining Parmesan. Place soufflé dishes in pan filled with water halfway up their sides. Bake at 350° for about 20 minutes, until flans are set and golden brown. Run a small sharp knife around sides of souffle dishes to loosen. Unmold and serve. Serves 8.

TRICIA CUSHNIE

CHARLIE BREAD

A cross between cornbread and a corn soufflé.

1 (8½ oz.) pkg. Jiffy cornbread mix	8 oz. sour cream
1 (6 oz.) can creamed corn	¼ c. oil
2 eggs	

Mix all ingredients together. Pour into a 8" square baking pan which has been greased with margarine. Bake at 400° for about 30 minutes, until golden and set. Serve with lots of butter or margarine. Serves 6.

MIRIAM CROSBY

NANA'S KUGEL (NOODLE PUDDING)

A traditional Jewish favorite. Can be eaten as a side dish, a dessert, or for breakfast!

1 lb. wide egg noodles, cooked
1 c. butter or margarine, melted
2 c. plus 1 t. sugar, divided
1 t. salt
1 c. golden raisins
4 eggs plus 2 eggs, beaten, divided

2 t. cinnamon, divided
2 c. milk
2 lbs. cottage or pot cheese
5 small peeled and sliced apples
(Macintosh or any tart type)

Mix noodles, butter, 2 c. sugar, salt, raisins, 4 eggs, 1 t. cinnamon, and milk together in large bowl. In another bowl combine cheese, 2 eggs, 1 t. sugar, and 1 t. cinnamon. Combine both mixtures and place in greased 12" x 18" casserole or 2 smaller casseroles. Set several apple slices aside and grate these. Spread remaining slices evenly over the pudding mixture and bury. Sprinkle grated apples over top and bake at 350° for 1 hour. Freezes well. Serves 24.

PRISCILLA BURBANK

APPLE-CRANBERRY CASSEROLE

3 c. apples, peeled and chopped
3 c. fresh cranberries
2 T. plus ½ c. flour, divided
1 c. sugar
¾ c. oats

½ t. cinnamon
¾ c. pecans, chopped
½ c. brown sugar, firmly packed
½ c. margarine, melted

Combine apples, cranberries, and 2 T. flour. Add sugar and mix well. Place in a 2-quart casserole. Combine oats, cinnamon, pecans, ½ c. flour, brown sugar, and margarine and blend. Spoon over apple mixture and bake at 350° for 45 minutes. Serves 6 to 8.

SHIRLEY WALKER

APPLE DELIGHT

6 medium apples, peeled, cored and cut into wedges
1 t. cinnamon
1 c. brown sugar
2 T. butter
3-4 slices of lemon, quartered

4 T. butter, melted
4 slices of bread, cubed (crust removed)
Additional brown sugar for sprinkling

Mix apples, cinnamon and brown sugar. Arrange in 1½-quart baking dish. Add dots of butter and lemon. Dip bread cubes in melted butter. Place on top of apples. Sprinkle with additional brown sugar. Cook at 350° for 30 to 40 minutes, or until bread is toasted and apples are tender. Serves 4.

CARPIE COULBOURN

HEALTHY FRIED APPLES *L*

7 red Virginia cooking apples
1 T. cinnamon
2 t. nutmeg

6 T. sugar or 15 packets Equal
3 T. no-cholesterol margarine
1 c. seedless red and green grapes

Wash and peel apples, leaving a little line of peel on each apple for color. Core and slice each apple (approximately 16 wedges from each apple). Place apples in mixing bowl with cinnamon, nutmeg and equal or sugar. Mix well. (Store in refrigerator overnight, if desired.) Over medium heat, add margarine to 12" skillet. Let skillet get hot. Add apples and cook about 20 minutes, stirring occasionally. While apples are cooking, wash grapes. Add grapes and cook an additional 5 to 10 minutes. Serves 6 to 8.

L. DOUGLAS WILDER, GOVERNOR OF VIRGINIA

HOT FRUIT COMPOTE

Great for Brunch!

1 (20 oz. or 28 oz.) can applesauce
1 (20 oz.) can pineapple chunks, drained
1 (28 oz.) can blue plums, drained

2 bananas, sliced
2-3 T. brown sugar
½ c. pecans, chopped

Spread most of applesauce in the bottom of a 2-quart casserole. Layer pineapple, plums and bananas; do not stir! Put remaining applesauce on top. Sprinkle with brown sugar and nuts. Bake at 350° for 30 minutes. Cool for 30 minutes and serve. Serves 6 to 8.

CHERYL BOSWELL

QUICK AND EASY SPICED PEACHES

An excellent addition to holiday meals.

2 (28 oz.) can peach halves
1 T. whole cloves
3 sticks cinnamon

¾ c. brown sugar, firmly packed
½ c. cider vinegar

Drain peaches, reserving liquid. Combine liquid with spices, sugar, and vinegar in a saucepan. Bring to a boil and simmer covered for 10 minutes. Pour syrup over peaches and chill. This keeps well stored in a large jar with lid.

SARA BAIRD

239

VEGETABLES AND SIDE DISHES

SPICED PINEAPPLE

2 (20 oz.) cans pineapple chunks
¾ c. cider vinegar
1 c. sugar
6 allspice berries

3 whole cloves
1 (3") stick cinnamon
Dash of salt
Fresh mint leaves for garnish

Drain pineapple, reserving ¾ c. syrup. Place syrup and remaining ingredients, except pineapple, in a large saucepan. Cook uncovered 15 minutes. Add pineapple chunks and bring to a brisk boil; cook 5 minutes longer. Remove from heat, cool, and pour into jar with tight-fitting lid. Refrigerate 24 hours before serving. Serve cold garnished with fresh mint.

MARGARET OWNBY

PINEAPPLE CASSEROLE

The perfect compliment to a ham dinner!

1 c. sugar
½ c. butter
3 eggs
1 (15 oz.) can crushed pineapple, drained

3 slices light bread, broken into small pieces
Milk

Cream sugar and butter. Add eggs one at a time, mixing well after each addition. Sprinkle bread with enough milk to moisten slightly. Add bread and pineapple to creamed mixture and fold together well. Pour into greased 1-quart casserole and bake at 350° for 1 hour. Serves 5 to 7.

SHARON PHILLIPS
KATHY WHITE

Breads

My best thing to cook is homemade bread with my Grandmommie.

Heather Hallberg, '04

Biscuits:
No-Fail Buttermilk Biscuits 244
Sour Cream Biscuits **Q** 244
Quick Breads:
Glazed Apple Bread 244
Apricot Bread 245
Beer Bread 245
Best-Ever Clifton Inn
    Cornbread 245
Favorite Cornbread **L** 246
Lemon Bread 246
Poppy Seed Bread 246
Pumpkin Bread 247
Pumpkin Tea Bread 247
Welsh Bread 247
Breakfast Specialties:
French Toast Sticks **Q L** 248
Special Occasion French
    Toast 248
Best-Ever Buttermilk
    Pancakes **Q** 248
Old-Fashioned
    Pancakes **Q** 249
Raisin Oatmeal Pancakes 249
Yorkshire Pancake **Q** 249
Coffee Cakes and Sweets:
Athalie's Danish Puff 250
Blueberry Boy-Bait 250
Sour Cream Coffee Cake 251
Caramel Rolls **Q** 251

Stonewall Court Cinnamon
    Puffs 252
Gooey Cinnamon Rolls **Q** .. 252
Muffins:
Apple Muffins **Q L** 252
Blueberry Muffins 253
Bran Raisin Muffins **Q L** 253
Carrot Raisin Muffins **Q L** ... 253
Corn Muffins **Q L** 254
Cornbread Muffins **Q** 254
Cranberry Muffins 254
Peach and Poppy Seed
    Muffins **Q** 255
Moist Pineapple Bran
    Muffins **Q L** 255
Pumpkin Clove Muffins **Q** ... 255
Sweet Potato Muffins 256
Yeast Breads:
American Baguettes 256
Applesauce Whole Wheat
    Bread 256
Busy Mom's Sourdough
    Bread 257
English Muffin Loaves 258
Judy's Gourmet Rolls 258
Old-Fashioned Oatmeal
    Bread **L** 258
Processor Wheat Bread **L** ... 259
Ricotta Cheese Bread 260

243

NO-FAIL BUTTERMILK BISCUITS

2 c. Bisquick
4 T. butter, softened
⅔ c. buttermilk

¼ t. baking soda
4-8 T. butter, melted

Combine Bisquick with butter using back of fork or two knives. Combine buttermilk and soda. Add buttermilk to flour mixture and stir until batter follows fork in bowl. Knead mixture 10 to 15 times on floured pastry cloth. Pat or roll dough until about ¼-inch thick. Cut with biscuit cutter that has been dipped in flour. Spread melted butter on biscuits with pastry brush. Bake in preheated oven at 450° for 10 minutes or until golden brown. Yield: 24 medium biscuits.

KATHY WATSON

Q SOUR CREAM BISCUITS

2 c. self-rising flour
1 c. margarine, melted

1 (8 oz.) container sour cream

Combine all ingredients and drop into ungreased muffin tins. Bake at 400° for 12 to 15 minutes. Remove and serve without butter. Yield: 24.

CARPIE COULBOURN

GLAZED APPLE BREAD

1 c. sugar
½ c. margarine
2 eggs
2 T. milk
1 t. vanilla
1 t. cinnamon
¼ t. salt

2 apples, unpeeled and cut into 8
    pieces
¼ c. nuts
2 c. flour
¼ t. baking soda
2 t. baking powder

GLAZE

½ c. confectioners' sugar
½ t. cinnamon

2 T. margarine
1 T. water

Place metal blade in processor bowl. Add sugar, margarine, eggs, milk, vanilla, cinnamon and salt. Process until light and fluffy. Add apples. Turn on and off 4 times. Add nuts. Turn on and off twice. Stir together flour, soda and baking powder. Add to processor bowl. Turn on and off until just barely mixed. Bake in well greased 9" x 5" loaf pan at 350° for 50 to 55 minutes. Process glaze ingredients until well blended and pour over loaf while warm. Yield: 1 loaf.

JANET DAUGHDRILLE

APRICOT BREAD

¾ c. dried apricots
1 orange, juice and rind
½ c. raisins
⅔ c. sugar
2 T. margarine, melted
1 egg

2 c. flour
2 t. baking powder
1 t. salt
1 t. baking soda
½ c. nuts, chopped
1 t. vanilla

Cover apricots with lukewarm water. Soak for 30 minutes. Drain. Grate rind from half of orange. Juice both halves. In food processor using metal blade, chop apricots, raisins and orange peel. Add enough boiling water to orange juice to make 1 cup. Pour into processor bowl with fruit. Add sugar and margarine and turn on and off 2 times. Beat in egg. Turn on and off 4 times. In separate bowl stir together flour, baking powder, salt and soda. Stir dry ingredients into apricot mixture until blended. Fold in nuts and vanilla. Spoon into well-greased 9" x 5" loaf pan and bake at 350° for 50 minutes. Remove from pan to cool. Yield: 1 loaf.

JANET DAUGHDRILLE

BEER BREAD

2 c. self-rising flour
8 oz. beer

2 T. sugar

Grease 9" x 5" loaf pan. Combine all ingredients and mix well. Batter will be foamy and lumpy. Pour into pan and bake at 400° for 35 to 45 minutes until golden. Place on rack to cool. Yield: 1 loaf.

MELINDA WAY

VARIATION: Add any of the following: fresh or dried onion, garlic salt, cheddar cheese, yogurt for sourdough flavor, or egg for texture.

BEST-EVER CLIFTON INN CORNBREAD

Great with chili for parties.

1 c. butter, softened
1 c. sugar
4 eggs
1 (12 oz.) can cream-style corn
½ c. Monterey Jack cheese, grated

½ c. Cheddar cheese, grated
1 c. flour
1 c. yellow cornmeal
4 t. baking powder
½ t. salt

Grease or spray a 9" x 13" baking dish. Cream butter and sugar until light and fluffy. Add eggs, one at a time. Stir in corn and cheeses. Whisk or sift together dry ingredients. Fold into creamed mixture. Bake at 325° for 1 hour or until golden brown. Freezes well. Serves 12.

JANE FAIN

FAVORITE CORNBREAD

L

1 (12 oz.) box Flako corn muffin mix
2 egg substitutes
½ c. light corn oil margarine, softened
1 (8 oz.) carton plain non-fat yogurt
1 (8 oz.) can whole-kernel corn, drained
1 (8 oz.) can cream-style yellow corn, undrained

Grease a 9" x 13" baking dish. Combine all ingredients and mix well. Pour into baking dish and bake at 350° for 50 minutes. Serves 12.

JACKIE THOMAS

LEMON BREAD

6 T. butter
1 c. sugar
2 eggs
1½ c. flour
1 t. baking powder
½ c. milk

GLAZE

⅓ c. sugar
Juice of 1 lemon

Grease a 9" x 5" loaf pan. Cream butter, sugar and eggs until light and lemon-colored. Combine flour and baking powder. Fold creamed mixture and milk into dry ingredients. Pour into loaf pan and bake at 325° for 1 hour or until knife comes out clean and loaf shrinks from sides of pan. Combine sugar and lemon juice for glaze and pour over loaf while still warm in pan. Cool slightly before removing from pan. Yield: 1 loaf.

CELIE GEHRING

POPPY SEED BREAD

3 c. flour
2 c. sugar
3 eggs
1½ t. baking powder
1½ t. salt
1½ T. poppy seeds
1½ c. milk
¾ c. vegetable oil
1½ t. each vanilla, almond extract and butter flavoring

GLAZE

1 c. confectioners' sugar
2 T. orange juice
¼ t. each vanilla, almond extract and butter flavoring

In large bowl using electric mixer, combine all ingredients for bread and beat until smooth. Pour batter into 2 greased 9" x 5" loaf pans or greased and floured 9-inch tube pan. Bake in preheated oven at 350° for 55 to 60 minutes. Cool 10 minutes in pans. Combine glaze ingredients and beat until smooth. Remove bread from pans, cool on rack and drizzle with glaze. Yield: 2 loaves or 1 tube pan.

SHIRLEY WALKER

PUMPKIN BREAD

1 lb. canned pumpkin
½ c. water
3 eggs
¾ c. vegetable oil
2½ c. flour
2¼ c. sugar

1½ t. baking soda
1¼ t. salt
¾ t. each cinnamon, cloves and
  nutmeg
Raisins (optional)
Nuts (optional)

Grease and flour 2 9" x 5" loaf pans. Combine and beat pumpkin, water, eggs and oil. Combine with dry ingredients and bake at 350° for 1 hour and 15 minutes. Yield: 2 loaves.

DONNA JACOBS

PUMPKIN TEA BREAD

1 c. vegetable oil
3 c. sugar
2 c. canned pumpkin
3 eggs
3 c. flour

1 t. each nutmeg, ground cloves
  and cinnamon
1 t. baking soda
1 t. baking powder
½ t. salt
1 c. pecans, chopped (optional)

Set aside ungreased tube pan or 3 loaf pans. In small bowl combine oil, sugar, pumpkin and eggs and mix well. In separate bowl combine dry ingredients, stir and fold in pumpkin mixture. Mix well. Pour into tube pan or loaf pans and bake at 350° for 1 hour 15 minutes for tube pan or 1 hour for loaves. Bread is done when knife comes out clean. Remove from pans to cool. (Freezes beautifully.) Yield: 1 tube pan or 3 loaves.

NAN LAGOW
KATHY WATSON

VARIATION: Add 1 cup semi-sweet chocolate or white chocolate chips to batter before baking.

CHRISTIE McLEAN

WELSH BREAD

1 pkg. mixed dried fruit, chopped
1 c. brown sugar, firmly packed
1 c. cold black tea

2 eggs
2 c. self-rising flour
2-3 T. butter, melted

Soak fruit and sugar in tea overnight. Grease a 9" x 5" loaf pan and line with wax paper. Beat eggs until light and fold in flour, fruit mixture and butter. Bake at 350° for 1 hour or until loaf shrinks from sides and tests done. Turn out onto rack to cool. Yield: 1 loaf.

EFFIE YOUNG

Q L   FRENCH TOAST STICKS

1 c. egg substitute
½ c. orange juice
½ t. vanilla
¼ t. cinnamon

6 slices firm light bread
2 T. margarine
2 t. confectioners' sugar

In shallow bowl whisk together egg, orange juice, vanilla and cinnamon. Cut each slice of bread into 4 sticks and press each slice into egg mixture, coating all sides. Melt margarine in skillet over medium heat and sauté sticks until toasted. Add additional margarine if needed. Dust with confectioners' sugar and serve immediately. Serves 6.

KIM BAIN

SPECIAL OCCASION FRENCH TOAST

4 eggs
1 c. milk
2 T. orange juice
3 t. sugar
1 t. cinnamon

½ t. vanilla
1 loaf French bread, sliced
4 T. margarine
Syrup (optional)
Confectioners' sugar (optional)

Combine eggs, milk, orange juice, sugar, cinnamon and vanilla and beat until well mixed. Arrange bread in a 9" x 13" baking dish. Pour egg mixture over bread, turning to coat both sides. Cover and refrigerate overnight. Melt margarine in skillet and cook bread until lightly browned on both sides. Serve immediately with syrup or confectioners' sugar. Serves 6 to 8.

SANDY KING

Q   BEST-EVER BUTTERMILK PANCAKES

3 eggs
1 c. flour
½ t. salt
2 t. sugar
1 t. light brown sugar

¾ t. baking powder
½ t. baking soda
1 c. buttermilk
2 T. butter, melted

Beat eggs until very light. Sift dry ingredients and fold into eggs. Add buttermilk and butter (batter does not have to be smooth). Heat skillet or griddle and grease lightly. Pour 2 T. batter at a time to make 4-inch cakes. Turn when bubbles appear on surface. Serve with melted butter and warm maple syrup. Batter can be prepared and stored in refrigerator for several days. Cover tightly.

MIM SCHUTE

OLD-FASHIONED PANCAKES   **Q**

2 c. whole wheat flour
3 t. baking powder
½ t. baking soda

3 eggs
2 c. buttermilk or plain yogurt
½ c. vegetable oil

Combine dry ingredients and mix with a whisk. Using blender, mix eggs, buttermilk or yogurt, and oil. Pour egg mixture into flour mixture and stir well. Batter will be very thick. Cook pancakes on greased hot griddle, spreading batter with spatula. Serve with butter and maple syrup. Serves 4 to 6.

ALEX THOMPSON

RAISIN OATMEAL PANCAKES

2 c. old-fashioned oats
2 c. buttermilk
2 eggs
¼ c. margarine, melted
⅓ c. raisins
½ c. flour

2 T. sugar
1 t. baking powder
1 T. baking soda
½ t. cinnamon
½ t. salt

In large bowl combine oats and buttermilk, cover and refrigerate overnight. When ready to cook, beat eggs with margarine and stir in raisins. Combine dry ingredients and stir into egg mixture. Fold in oats and buttermilk. Let stand 20 minutes. Cook on preheated greased griddle and turn as undersides brown. (These pancakes take longer to cook than most.) Serves 4.

SHIRLEY WALKER

YORKSHIRE PANCAKE   **Q**

¼ c. butter or margarine
2 eggs
½ c. flour

½ c. milk
Confectioners' sugar

Melt butter in oven-proof medium large skillet until bubbly. Beat together eggs, flour and milk and pour into skillet. Place in 400° oven for about 15 minutes or until light and puffy. Sprinkle with confectioners' sugar and return to oven for 1 to 2 minutes. Edges of pancake will roll over. Cut into wedges and serve immediately. Serves 2.

SUSAN STANEWICK

ATHALIE'S DANISH PUFF

Well worth the effort!

PASTRY

1 c. flour
½ c. butter, softened

2 T. water

Cut butter into flour using pastry blender or food processor. Sprinkle with water to form pastry. Divide dough into two parts. Pat each into a 3" x 12" rectangle on an ungreased baking sheet. Build up sides slightly.

PUFF

½ c. butter
1 c. water
1 t. almond extract

1 c. flour
3 eggs

Bring butter and water to a boil. Remove from heat and add almond extract and flour. Return to low heat and stir until mixture forms a ball, about 1 minute. Remove from heat and beat in eggs, one at a time. Spread half of mixture on each pastry rectangle. Bake at 350° for 1 hour. Check after 45 minutes and remove from oven if browned. Frost when cooled.

FROSTING

¼ c. butter, softened
4 oz. cream cheese, softened
½ lb. confectioners' sugar

Nuts, chopped (optional)
Candied Cherries (optional)

Combine butter, cream cheese, and sugar thoroughly and frost puffs. Sprinkle with nuts and cherries, if desired. Serves 8.

BARBARA SAMUELS

ALMOND FROSTING VARIATION:

1½ c. confectioners' sugar
2 T. margarine, softened
1 t. almond extract

1-2 T. warm water
Slivered or sliced almonds

Mix all ingredients except almonds. Frost pastries and sprinkle with almonds.

LYNN FELTON

BLUEBERRY BOY-BAIT

2 c. flour
1½ c. sugar
⅔ c. butter or margarine, softened
2 t. baking powder
1 t. salt

2 eggs, separated
1 c. milk
1 c. blueberries, drained (fresh, frozen or canned)

Sift flour and sugar together. Cut in butter until resembles corn meal. Take out ¾ cup of mixture for topping. To remaining mixture add baking powder, salt, 2 egg yolks and milk. Beat at low speed for 3 minutes. In separate bowl beat egg whites until stiff. Fold gently into batter. Grease and flour a 9" x 13" pan. Spread batter into pan. Spoon blueberries over batter. Sprinkle with reserved crumb mixture. Bake at 350° for 40 to 50 minutes. Serve warm as coffee cake or topped with whipped cream or ice cream for dessert. Serves 12.

LORNA ROWLAND

SOUR CREAM COFFEE CAKE

1 c. butter
2 c. sugar
2 eggs
1 c. sour cream
1 t. vanilla
2 c. flour

¼-½ t. salt
1 t. baking powder
2 t. cinnamon
4-5 T. brown sugar
¾ c. pecans, chopped
Confectioners' sugar (optional)

Grease and flour large bundt pan. Cream butter and sugar with electric mixer and add eggs, one at a time. Combine sour cream and vanilla. Sift flour, salt and baking powder together and add to creamed mixture alternately with sour cream. Pour ⅓ to ½ of batter into prepared pan. Combine cinnamon, brown sugar and nuts and sprinkle over batter. Spoon remaining batter into cake pan. Bake at 350° for 60 to 65 minutes. (Cake will rise; then fall slightly.) Cool at least 10 minutes before removing from pan. Sift confectioners' sugar over top of warm cake.

SUSAN HAMILL

CARAMEL ROLLS   Q

1 c. brown sugar
½ c. half and half
1 c. pecans, chopped

2 (10 oz) cans refrigerated biscuits
¼-⅓ c. margarine, melted

Grease a 9" x 13" baking dish or line with foil and spray with no-stick cooking spray. Combine brown sugar with half and half and pour into prepared baking dish. Sprinkle with pecans. Cut biscuits into fourths and place on brown sugar mixture. Brush on melted margarine. Bake at 350° for 20 to 25 minutes. Turn pan upside down to release rolls. Serve warm. Serves 8 to 10.

MELANIE JONES

STONEWALL COURT CINNAMON PUFFS

Great to have on a hectic Christmas morning!

1 egg
½ c. milk
1 loaf Pepperidge Farm white
  bread

½-1 c. butter or margarine, melted
1 c. sugar
1 t. cinnamon

Beat together egg and milk. Remove crusts from bread. Dip 1 piece of bread in egg mixture and place between 2 pieces of dry bread. Repeat for remaining slices. Wrap each 3-slice stack in foil and refrigerate overnight. Cut into thirds (strips) or fourths (triangles). Roll in butter, then cinnamon and sugar mixture. Freeze if desired. Bake in oven at 375° for 10 minutes or, if frozen, for 15 minutes. Yield: 27 strips or 36 puffs.

VARIATION: Substitute 8 oz. grated Parmesan cheese for cinnamon and sugar mixture for cheese puffs.

ALLYN CROSBY

Q GOOEY CINNAMON ROLLS

1 (8 oz.) can crescent rolls
¼ c. sugar
1 t. cinnamon

8 large marshmallows
¼ c. butter, melted

Unroll can and divide rolls into 8 triangles. Combine sugar and cinnamon and sprinkle on rolls. Dip marshmallows in butter and place on sugar mixture. Roll up triangles and seal tightly. Place in muffin tin, pouring remaining butter over rolls. Bake at 375° for 10 to 12 minutes. Serves 8.

VARIATION: Combine ¼ c. confectioners' sugar with 1 t. milk and pour glaze over warm rolls.

GAIL SMITH

Q L APPLE MUFFINS

½ c. unbleached flour
½ c. whole wheat flour
½ t. baking soda
½ t. salt
1½ t. baking powder
½ t. cinnamon

1 T. brown sugar
1 egg
½ c. buttermilk
1 T. maple syrup
¾ c. apple, shredded
2 T. butter or margarine, melted

Grease muffins tins. Whisk together dry ingredients. Beat together egg, buttermilk and syrup. Gently fold in apple and butter. Bake at 375° for 15 minutes or until brown. Turn out of pan immediately. Yield: 6 muffins.

VIRGINIA CHEWNING

BLUEBERRY MUFFINS

2 c. fresh blueberries, dusted with
  ⅓ c. flour
2 c. flour
1 c. sugar
2 t. cream of tartar
1 t. baking soda

½ t. salt
6 T. butter, softened
¾ c. milk
1 egg
½ t. vanilla

Toss blueberries with flour in small bowl and set aside. Sift flour, sugar, cream of tartar, baking soda and salt. Add butter and cut in until mixture resembles corn meal. In separate bowl mix milk, egg and vanilla. Beat lightly. Fold in dry ingredients. Gently fold in blueberries. Spoon into greased muffin tins. Bake at 350° for 25 to 30 minutes. Yield: 18 muffins.

KATHY HERSHEY

BRAN RAISIN MUFFINS   Q L

⅓ c. margarine, softened
½ c. brown sugar, firmly packed
1 egg white
⅓ c. molasses
1 c. flour
1 t. baking powder

1 t. salt
½ t. baking soda
1 c. raisins
2 c. whole bran cereal
1 c. skim milk

Cream together margarine and brown sugar. Beat in egg white and molasses. Combine flour, baking powder, salt and soda. Fold in raisins and cereal. Stir flour mixture alternately with milk into creamed mixture. Bake in muffin tins lined with paper cups at 400° for 20 minutes. Yield: 12 muffins.

SHIRLEY WALKER

CARROT RAISIN MUFFINS   Q L

Healthy and delicious!

⅔ c. margarine, softened
1 c. sugar
2 eggs (or 4 egg whites)
1 c. bran cereal
2 T. orange rind, grated
1 c. orange juice
1 c. carrots, grated

½ c. raisins
½ c. skim milk
2½ c. flour
4 t. baking powder
½ t. baking soda
½ t. salt

Cream margarine and sugar. Add eggs and beat well. Stir in bran, orange rind, orange juice, carrots, raisins and milk. Whisk together flour, baking powder, soda and salt. Fold into first mixture until flour disappears. Fill well-greased miniature muffin tins half full. Bake at 350° for 20 minutes. Yield: 48 small muffins.

DERENDA REYNOLDS

BREADS

Q L   CORN MUFFINS

Freeze well and always a hit.

1 (7½ oz.) box corn muffin mix
¼ c. vegetable oil
1 (8 oz.) carton light sour cream
4 egg substitutes
1 (8 oz.) can cream-style corn

Grease or spray muffin tins. Pour corn muffin mix in bowl and press out lumps with back of spoon. Add vegetable oil, sour cream and egg substitutes and mix well. Fold in corn. Fill muffin tins with mixture and bake at 350° for 25 minutes. Serve immediately. Yield: 12 muffins.

CARTER FILER

Q   CORNBREAD MUFFINS

¾ c. butter, softened
½ c. sugar
4 eggs
4 slices bacon, crisply cooked and drained
1 (12 oz) can cream-style corn
4 oz Cheddar cheese, grated
4 oz Monterey Jack cheese, grated
1 c. flour
1 c. yellow cornmeal
4 T. baking powder
1 t. salt

Cream butter and sugar. Add eggs, one at a time. Add remaining ingredients and mix until well blended. Fill well-greased muffin tins half full. Bake at 350° for 20 minutes. Yield: 24 muffins.

DIANNE GIBSON

CRANBERRY MUFFINS

1 c. cranberries, halved
½ c. sugar
2 c. flour
2 T. sugar
3 t. baking powder
1 t. salt
1 egg
1 c. milk
2 T. vegetable oil
1 T. orange peel, grated

Combine cranberries and sugar in bowl. In second bowl sift or whisk together dry ingredients. In third bowl beat egg, milk, oil and orange peel. Fold wet ingredients into dry and add cranberries. Fill greased muffin tins two-thirds full. Bake at 400° for 20 to 25 minutes. Yield: 12 muffins.

LUCY EADS

PEACH AND POPPY SEED MUFFINS   **Q**

1 t. baking soda	2 eggs
⅔ c. puréed peaches (fresh or	1¼ c. flour
junior baby food)	¼ t. salt
10 T. butter, softened	½ t. vanilla
1 c. sugar	3 T. poppy seeds

Grease 12 muffin tins. Stir soda into peaches (mixture will foam). Cream butter and sugar until smooth. Add eggs, one at a time. Add flour and peaches alternately to butter mixture. Stir in salt, vanilla and poppy seeds. Fill muffin tins two-thirds full and bake at 350° for 20 to 25 minutes. Yield: 12 muffins.

ANN SPENCE

MOIST PINEAPPLE BRAN MUFFINS   **Q L**

1 c. oat bran	2 T. margarine, melted
1 c. flour	¼ c. brown sugar
2 t. baking powder	1 (8 oz.) can crushed pineapple,
½ t. salt	drained
1 c. skim milk	1 t. vanilla
2 egg whites	Dash of cinnamon
¼ c. honey	

Grease muffin tins. Combine all ingredients and stir well. Fill tins almost to top and bake at 400° for 15 minutes or until golden. Turn out to cool. Yield: 12 muffins.

CAROLE RAYNER

PUMPKIN CLOVE MUFFINS   **Q**

1 c. sugar	½ t. baking soda
¼ c. canola oil	¼ t. each ground cloves,
2 eggs	cinnamon and nutmeg
¾ c. canned pumpkin	½ t. salt
1½ c. flour	¾ c. raisins
1 t. baking powder	½ c. walnuts, chopped (optional)

Generously grease muffin tins. In small bowl combine sugar, oil, eggs and pumpkin and mix well. In large bowl sift together flour, baking powder, baking soda, spices and salt. Gently fold pumpkin mixture into dry ingredients until combined. Fold in raisins and walnuts. Fill tins two-thirds full and bake at 400° for 18 to 20 minutes until golden brown. Cool a few minutes in tins before removing. Yield: 12 muffins.

MARTHA BAUMGARTEN

BREADS

SWEET POTATO MUFFINS

⅓ c. margarine
1 c. sugar
2 eggs
1¼ c. sweet potatoes, cooked and mashed
1½ c. flour
2 t. baking powder

¼ t. salt
1 t. cinnamon
¼ t. nutmeg
1 c. skim milk
¼ c. pecans, chopped
¼ c. raisins

Grease muffin tins or use liners. Cream margarine with sugar. Add eggs and beat well. Blend in sweet potatoes. Sift together flour, baking powder, salt and spices. Alternately stir dry ingredients and milk into creamed mixture. Do not beat or over-mix. Fold in nuts and raisins. Fill muffin tins half full and bake at 400° for 18 minutes. (Batter can be stored in refrigerator for 2 to 3 days.) Yield: 24 muffins.

YVONNE FARMER

AMERICAN BAGUETTES

"Taste this and you'll never buy bread again!"

1 pkg. dry yeast
1 t. sugar
½ c. warm water
1½ c. plain yogurt
¼ c. light molasses
2 T. butter

1 t. salt
3½ c. unbleached bread flour
1 c. whole wheat flour
¾ c. cornmeal
Oatmeal for dusting pans

Proof yeast in sugar and water until frothy. Heat yogurt, molasses, butter and salt in microwave until warm. Combine flours, yogurt mixture, and yeast. Using dough hook on heavy-duty mixer or by hand, knead bread for 10 minutes. Let mixture rise until doubled. Punch down and form 4 baguettes (long, slender loaves), slashing tops. Using greased baguette pans dusted with oatmeal, let rise until doubled. Bake at 350° for 30 minutes. Cool on racks. Yield: 4 loaves.

VIRGINIA CHEWNING

APPLESAUCE WHOLE WHEAT BREAD

2 pkgs. dry yeast
½ c. warm water
3 c. applesauce
2½ c. hot water
1 c. firmly packed brown sugar

½ c. vegetable oil
2 T. salt
6 c. whole wheat flour
6-8 c. white flour
Butter, melted

256

Proof yeast in warm water until frothy. In very large bowl combine apple-sauce, hot water, sugar, oil and salt. Add whole wheat flour. Let dough rest for 10 minutes. Add yeast mixture. Stir in enough white flour to make stiff dough. With dough hook on heavy-duty mixer or by hand, knead dough for 10 minutes. Shape into 4 loaves and place in greased 9" x 5" loaf pans. Brush with butter. Let rise until doubled in bulk, about 1 hour. Bake in preheated 350° oven for 30 to 35 minutes. Brush with butter again when they come out of oven. Cool on racks. Yield: 4 loaves.

ERLYNN LANSING

BUSY MOM'S SOURDOUGH BREAD

STARTER

1 pkg. dry yeast
1½ c. warm water, divided

¾ c. sugar
3 T. instant potato flakes

Dissolve yeast in ½ c. warm water. Combine 1 c. warm water, sugar and potato flakes with yeast. Let stand all day. Refrigerate 3 to 5 days, loosely covered. Bring to room temperature.

FEEDER

1 c. warm water
½ c. sugar

3 T. instant potato flakes

Combine 3 ingredients and add to starter. Leave loosely covered on counter all day. Remove 1 cup for bread and refrigerate remaining starter in container with holes in top.

BREAD

¼ c. sugar
½ c. vegetable oil
1½ c. warm water
1 T. salt

1 c. starter
6-7 c. flour (half can be whole wheat or rye)

Combine bread ingredients, adding flour gradually until dough becomes stiff. Knead briefly with dough hook or by hand. Place dough in greased bowl and turn dough to grease all sides. Cover loosely and store in cold oven overnight. Remove and punch down. Knead 3 or 4 times. Place in greased 9" x 5" loaf pans and return to cold oven covered with wax paper for all-day rising. Remove from oven and preheat oven to 350°. Bake for 35 to 40 minutes. Cool on rack. Yield: 3 loaves.

NOTE: Starter must be fed every 5 days. Remove 1 cup and use for bread or discard. Add feeder.

JANIS CARRELL

ENGLISH MUFFIN LOAVES

Cornmeal
5½-6 c. flour, divided
2 pkgs. dry yeast
1 T. sugar

2 t. salt
¼ t. baking soda
2 c. milk
½ c. water

Grease 2 (9" x 5") loaf pans and sprinkle with cornmeal. Combine 3 c. flour, yeast, sugar, salt and baking soda. Heat milk and water until warm and add to flour mixture. Beat well. Add as much additional flour as needed to make a stiff batter. Spoon into loaf pans, cover with damp cloth and let rise in warm place for 45 minutes or until doubled in size. Bake at 400° for 25 minutes. Remove from pans and cool on rack. Yield: 2 loaves.

ALLYN CROSBY

JUDY'S GOURMET ROLLS

"Award winning"!

1 pkg. dry yeast
¼ c. warm water
1 c. scalded milk
¼ c. sugar
¼ c. solid shortening

1 t. salt
1 egg, lightly beaten
3½ c. bread flour, divided
½ c. unsalted sweet cream butter,
     melted

Proof yeast in water until frothy. In large bowl combine sugar, shortening and salt. Stir in hot milk until sugar and salt are dissolved and shortening is almost melted. Let cool to lukewarm and add yeast, egg and 2 c. flour. Beat well by hand, gradually adding remaining flour, or enough to make soft dough. Place dough on floured surface and knead for 1 to 2 minutes. Place dough in greased bowl, cover and let rise for about 1½ hours or until doubled. Punch down, turn onto lightly floured surface, and roll out to desired thickness. Cut into circles with biscuit cutter. Brush with butter, fold in half and place with sides barely touching in pan. Brush tops of rolls with butter. Cover and let rise until doubled, about 30 minutes. Bake in preheated 400° oven for 12 minutes, or until rolls are golden brown. Remove from oven and brush tops again with butter. Yield: 48 rolls.

JUDY JOHNSON

L   OLD-FASHIONED OATMEAL BREAD

So easy made in a food processor.

1 c. water
½ t. salt
½ c. old fashioned oats,
     uncooked
1 pkg. yeast

¼-½ c. warm water
3 T. light brown sugar, packed,
     divided
2½ c. flour

258

Bring 1 c. water and salt to boil. Stir in oats and let cool. Cook 5 minutes, uncovered, and cool to luke warm. Proof yeast with ¼ c. warm water and 1 T. brown sugar until bubbly. Combine flour and 2 T. brown sugar in work bowl and process 15 seconds. Add yeast mixture and oatmeal to bowl. Turn on processor and add 1 to 2 T. water from top until mixture forms ball that cleans sides, about 25 times. Let dough rest 2 minutes. Turn on processor and slowly add 1 to 2 T. water until dough is soft and satiny smooth. Process 15 turns around bowl. (Add more flour if dough is too sticky, more water if too dry.) Remove and shape into ball. Place in greased bowl, cover loosely with wax paper, and let stand in warm place until doubled (about 1 hour). Punch down and place in greased 9" x 5" loaf pan. (At this point may refrigerate overnight and continue the next day if desired.) Let dough stand in warm place until doubled (about 45 minutes). Bake in preheated 375° oven for 25 to 30 minutes. Remove immediately from pan and cool on rack. Yield: 1 loaf.

MARY MADELYN TUCKER

PROCESSOR WHEAT BREAD   L

2 pkgs. dry yeast	3 c. whole wheat flour
½ c. hot (not boiling) water	4 c. white flour
1 T. sugar	6 T. margarine, cut into chunks
2 c. cold water	2 t. salt

In medium bowl mix yeast, hot water and sugar and set aside for 10 minutes. Add cold water. In processor bowl using plastic blade, combine flours, margarine and salt. Process 20 seconds. With machine running, pour liquid through feed tube in slow, steady stream for about 35 seconds. Continue processing until ball forms and cleans sides of bowl. Run 60 more seconds. Remove dough and knead 1 minute on floured surface. Shape into ball, place in greased bowl and cover. Let rise in warm place until doubled (about 1 hour). Punch down, divide in half and roll on lightly floured surface until dough is 8" x 12". Roll tightly from short end, pinching ends and edges to seal. Place seam down in 2 greased 9" x 5" loaf pans. Cover and let rise for 30 to 40 minutes. Bake in preheated oven at 375° for 30 minutes. Remove from pans and continue to bake for 5 more minutes. Cool on racks. Yield: 2 loaves.

SHIRLEY WALKER

RICOTTA CHEESE BREAD

1 pkg. dry yeast
1 t. sugar
½ c. warm water
2 c. Ricotta cheese
2 T. butter
1 T. dill weed

¼ c. sugar
½ t. baking soda
1-2 t. salt
2 eggs
1½ lbs. bread flour (about 5 c.)

Proof yeast in sugar and water until foamy. Heat cheese, butter, dill weed, sugar, baking soda and salt in microwave until warm. Beat eggs and add to cheese mixture. Add yeast. Pour into large mixing bowl and add flour. Knead for 10 minutes, using dough hook. (Kneading by hand is difficult because dough is soft. More flour may be needed.) In greased bowl let dough rise until doubled, about 1 hour. Punch down and place in 2 greased and floured 9" x 5" loaf pans. Let rise until doubled. Bake at 350° for 30 minutes, or until loaves sound hollow when thumped. Turn out on rack to cool. Yield: 2 loaves.

VIRGINIA CHEWNING

CAKES

Cakes

I like it when we have a cake we can decorate however we want with sprinkles and colored icing and candles and we sing happy unbirthday like on the tape of Alice in Wonderland.

Amy Staples, '05

Cheesecakes:
Divine Cheesecake 265
Heavenly Cheesecake *L* ... 265
Hollywood Cheesecake 266
Ginny's Lime Cheesecake.... 266
New York-Style Cheesecake .. 267
Oreo Cheesecake 268
Chocolate Marble
   Cheesecake 268
Chocolate-Raspberry
   Cheesecake 269
Chocolate Cakes:
Best Chocolate Cake 269
Hershey Syrup Cake 270
No-Frosting Chocolate
   Chip Cake 270
Chocolate Cream Cake 271
Chocolate Lime Cake with
   Mint Glaze 271
Double Chocolate Mousse
   Cake 272

Hot Fudge Pudding
   Cake *L* 273
Milky Way Cake 273
Fruit and Other Cakes:
Grandmother Rosie's Raw
   Apple Cake 264
Carrot Apple Cake 264
1-2-3 Coconut Cake 274
Easy Coconut Cake 274
Christmas Cake 275
Mandarin Orange Cake 275
Frozen Meringue Cake 276
Plum Cake 276
Pound Cakes:
Grandmother's Pound
   Cake 277
Lemon Pound Cake 277
Mom's Pound Cake 278
Sauce for Cakes and Desserts:
Lemon Curd 278

263

GRANDMOTHER ROSIE'S RAW APPLE CAKE

3 c. flour
2 t. baking soda
1 t. cinnamon
1 t. ground cloves
1 t. nutmeg
2 c. sugar
½ t. salt

2 eggs, beaten
1 c. canola oil
½-1 c. white raisins
4 c. apples, minced
2 T. lemon juice
¼-½ c. nuts, chopped (optional)

Combine dry ingredients in a large (12-quart) mixing bowl. Add eggs and oil. Stir in raisins, apples, lemon juice, and nuts until well mixed. The batter will be very dry. Pour into a greased and floured tube or bundt pan and bake at 325° for 1 hour or until the tester comes out clean. Serves 12 to 20.

SHARON PHILLIPS

CARROT APPLE CAKE

Men love it!

1½ c. sugar
1½ c. vegetable oil
3 eggs
2 t. vanilla
2 c. sifted flour
2 t. cinnamon
1 t. salt

1 t. baking soda
1 t. baking powder
2 c. carrots, shredded
1 c. apples, coarsely chopped
1 c. golden raisins
1 c. pecans, chopped

Combine first 4 ingredients in a large bowl; blend thoroughly. Sift together the dry ingredients, add to first mixture, and blend well. Stir in carrots, apples, raisins and pecans. Pour into 2 greased and wax paper-lined 9" cake pans. Bake at 350° for 35 to 45 minutes until center of cake is firm to touch. Cool in pan 10 minutes. Remove from pan and finish cooling on racks.

ICING

2 (3 oz.) pkgs. cream cheese, softened
1 T. milk
2 t. vanilla

Dash salt
1 lb. confectioners' sugar
½ c. pecans, chopped

In medium bowl, blend first 4 ingredients thoroughly. Gradually beat in sugar until frosting is smooth and of spreading consistency. Fold in pecans. Frost cake when it is cool. Serves 12 to 16.

KATIE BELK

DIVINE CHEESECAKE

This is better made a few days ahead. Top with peaches or puréed strawberries if you wish, but it's great by itself.

1 lb. cream-style cottage cheese (or regular, processed until smooth in food processor or blender)
4 eggs
2 (8 oz.) pkgs. cream cheese, softened

1 c. butter, melted
1½ c. sugar
3 T. flour
3 T. cornstarch
1 T. vanilla
1 pt. sour cream

Beat cottage cheese with eggs (food processor works well). Set aside. Beat cream cheese in a bowl with hand mixer. Add remaining ingredients except sour cream. Add cottage cheese mixture. Return all to processor and process until smooth. Add sour cream and blend briefly. Pour batter in a 9" springform pan and bake in a preheated 325° oven for 1 hour. Turn oven off and leave cake in oven 2 more hours. If convenient, open oven door and leave cake in for an additional hour before you refrigerate. This slow process lessens the chance of the top's cracking. Serves 12 to 16.

ALLYN CROSBY

HEAVENLY CHEESECAKE   *L*

Rich-tasting with less fat and calories.

¾ c. graham crackers, crushed
2 T. reduced-calorie or regular margarine, melted
1 (15 oz.) container part-skim Ricotta cheese
1 (8 oz.) container non-fat plain yogurt
1 c. sugar

2 T. flour
2 T. lemon juice
1 (8 oz.) pkg. light cream cheese, softened
¾ c. egg substitute, thawed
2½ t. vanilla
Fresh fruit slices for garnish (blueberries, kiwi or strawberries)

Combine graham crackers and margarine; press onto bottom of 9" springform pan. Bake at 325° for 5 minutes. Cool. In blender, combine Ricotta, yogurt, sugar, flour and lemon juice. Blend until smooth. Set aside. In large mixer bowl, beat cream cheese on medium speed of an electric mixer until smooth. Add egg substitute and vanilla. Beat on low speed until combined; beat on high speed until smooth. Slowly add Ricotta cheese mixture to cream cheese mixture, beating on low speed until combined. Pour into crust. Place on shallow baking pan in the oven. Bake at 325° for 1 hour or until center is nearly set when gently shaken. Cool for 15 minutes. Loosen crust from sides of pan. Cool for 30 minutes more. Remove sides of pan. Cool completely. Chill 4 to 6 hours. Top with fresh fruit. Serves 12.

SANDY ROBINS

HOLLYWOOD CHEESECAKE

Very rich!

CRUST

1¼ c. graham cracker crumbs   ¼ c. butter or margarine, melted
¼ c. sugar

Combine all ingredients and place in a greased 9" springform pan. Chill in freezer 30 minutes.

FIRST LAYER

2 (8 oz.) pkgs. cream cheese   3 medium eggs (½ c. total)
½ c. sugar   ¾ t. vanilla

Combine cream cheese and sugar and beat 2 to 3 minutes. Add eggs and vanilla and beat 3 more minutes. Pour into chilled crust and spread evenly. Bake 15 to 20 minutes at 375°. Remove from oven and let cool on rack at room temperature 15 minutes. While cake is cooling, increase oven temperature to 475° and prepare next layer.

SECOND LAYER

1 pt. sour cream   1 t. vanilla
¼ c. sugar

Mix these ingredients together. After cake has cooled 15 minutes, spoon this onto cake starting at outer edge and working to center in circles; spread evenly. Bake 10 minutes at 475°. Remove from oven and let cool on rack. Sprinkle some graham cracker crumbs around top edge as a border. Score slices with knife or cut with thread. Serves 12 to 16 thin slices.

BOB SEDIVY

GINNY'S LIME CHEESECAKE

Don't count on any leftovers!

1½ c. graham cracker crumbs   1 c. light or regular sour cream
1 c. sugar, divided   3 large eggs
¼ c. butter or margarine, softened   1 T. lime peel, grated
2 (8 oz.) pkgs. Neufchatel or   ¼ c. lime juice
     cream cheese, softened   2 T. flour

Mix crumbs, 2 T. sugar and butter. Press over bottom and ½" up sides of a 9" springform pan. Bake in a 350° oven until lightly browned, about 10 minutes. Beat cheese, sour cream, eggs, remaining sugar, peel, juice and flour until smooth. Pour into crust. Bake at 350° for 35 to 45 minutes, or until center jiggles slightly when pan is gently shaken. Cool.

TOPPING

1 c. light or regular sour cream
2 t. sugar

2 t. lime juice
Thin lime slices for garnish

Combine above ingredients and spread on cake. Cover and chill until cold, at least 4 hours. Top with lime slices. Serves 12 to 16.

VIRGINIA HENDERSON

NEW YORK-STYLE CHEESECAKE

CRUST

1 sealed pkg. graham crackers
1 T. sugar

2-3 T. butter, melted

Crush grahams into crumbs and combine with sugar and butter, and press into 9" springform pan.

FILLING

2 (8 oz.) pkgs. cream cheese, softened
1 (14 oz.) can sweetened condensed milk

3 eggs
¼ c. fresh lemon juice (1 lemon)

In large bowl, beat cream cheese with mixer until fluffy. Add sweetened milk and eggs. Beat until smooth. Stir in lemon juice. Pour batter into prepared pan, and bake for 325° for 50 to 55 minutes, or until toothpick comes out clean.

TOPPING

1 c. sour cream
3 T. sugar

1 t. vanilla

Combine above ingredients and spread on hot cheesecake. Return to oven for 5 minutes. Remove from oven and cool. Serves 10.

NANCY McCANDLISH

OREO CHEESECAKE

1¼ c. graham cracker crumbs
⅓ c. margarine, melted
¼ c. light brown sugar, firmly
    packed
1 t. cinnamon
4 (8 oz.) pkgs. cream cheese,
    softened
1½ c. sugar, divided

2 T. flour
4 large eggs
2 large egg yolks
⅓ c. whipping cream
2 t. vanilla, divided
1½ c. Oreo cookies, coarsely
    chopped
2 c. sour cream

Mix the graham cracker crumbs, margarine, brown sugar and cinnamon. Press into bottom and sides of a 9" springform pan. Refrigerate for at least 30 minutes. Preheat oven to 425°. Beat the cream cheese in a large bowl with an electric mixer on low until smooth. Beat in 1¼ c. sugar and flour until well blended. Beat in the eggs and egg yolks until mixture is smooth. Stir in cream and 1 t. vanilla. Pour half of this batter into the crust. Sprinkle with chopped Oreos. Pour remaining batter into pan. Bake at 425° for 15 minutes. Reduce oven temperature to 225° for 50 minutes (covering top loosely with foil if it is browning too quickly). Remove cheesecake from oven. Increase oven temperature to 350°. Blend sour cream, ¼ c. sugar and 1 t. vanilla in a small bowl. Spread over cake. Bake 7 minutes. Refrigerate immediately and chill overnight.

SWISS FUDGE GLAZE

1 c. whipping cream
8 oz. semi-sweet chocolate,
    chopped

1 t. vanilla
Oreo halves and cherries for
    garnish (optional)

Scald the cream in a heavy saucepan over high heat. Add chocolate and vanilla and stir 1 minute. Remove from heat and stir until the chocolate is melted. Refrigerate 10 minutes. Pour glaze over cake and smooth on top and sides. Garnish with Oreo halves and cherries if desired. Serves 10 to 12.

WEEZIE WILTSHIRE

CHOCOLATE MARBLE CHEESECAKE

1 c. sugar
3 (8 oz.) pkgs. cream cheese,
    softened
5 eggs
1 T. vanilla

4 oz. German sweet chocolate,
    melted in a double boiler and
    cooled
1 T. lemon juice
Whipped cream and chocolate
    curls for garnish (optional)

Add sugar to cream cheese in a bowl, blending well with an electric mixer. Beat in eggs, one at a time, blending well. Add vanilla. Measure 2 cups of cheese mixture and fold chocolate well into it. Add lemon juice to remaining mixture and pour into a well buttered 10" pie plate. Top with the chocolate mixture. Swirl to marbleize. Bake at 350° for 40 to 45 minutes. Cool, then chill. Garnish if desired. Serves 8 to 10.

ALLYN CROSBY

CHOCOLATE-RASPBERRY CHEESECAKE

You can change the raspberry to Amaretto, mint or orange!

10 chocolate wafers (Nabisco Famous), finely crushed
2 (8 oz.) pkgs. light (Neufchatel) cream cheese
1⅓ c. sugar
12 oz. fat-free cottage cheese
½ c. cocoa
¼ c. plus 1 T. flour

1 t. vanilla
1/3 c. Chambord (raspberry liqueur), or to taste
¼ t. salt
1 egg or ¼ c. egg substitute
¼-½ c. semi-sweet chocolate mini-chips

Sprinkle chocolate wafer crumbs in bottom(s) of 2 (6") or 1 (9") springform pan(s). Set aside. In food processor, process cream cheese until smooth. Add next 7 ingredients and process until smooth. Add egg and process until just blended. Fold in chocolate chips. Slowly pour mixture over crumbs in pan(s). Bake at 300° for about 45 minutes for 6" pans or 65 to 70 minutes for 9" pan, or until cheesecake is set. Let cool in pan on wire rack. Cover and chill at least 8 hours. Serves 12 to 16.

VARIATION: Substitute Amaretto, Crème de Menthe, or Grande Marnier for Chambord, if desired.

SUSAN OTTENI

BEST CHOCOLATE CAKE

3 c. flour
3 c. sugar
½ t. salt
1½ c. water
6 T. cocoa

¾ c. butter
3 eggs, slightly beaten
¾ c. buttermilk
1½ t. baking soda

Combine the flour, sugar, and salt. Combine water, cocoa and butter in a saucepan and bring to a boil. Pour these liquids over the flour mixture and mix well. Cool. Stir in eggs. Combine buttermilk and baking soda. Add this to the cake mixture. Pour into 2 greased and floured 9" round cake pans or a greased and floured Bundt pan. Bake at 350° for 25 minutes if using the 2 pans, or 45 minutes if using the Bundt pan.

ICING

½ c. butter
¼ c. plus 2 T. milk

4 T. cocoa
1 lb. confectioners' sugar

Combine butter, milk and cocoa in a saucepan and bring to a boil. Remove from heat and add sugar. Spread icing quickly on cooled cake, as it will thicken as it cools. Serves 12.

KATHY ELLIS

HERSHEY SYRUP CAKE

Remember this frosting. You'll want to use it again!

CAKE

½ c. butter, softened
1 c. sugar
4 eggs
1 c. flour

1 t. baking powder
Pinch of salt
1 t. vanilla
1 (16 oz.) can Hershey syrup*

(*Note: 16 oz. can is a measurement by weight, not by liquid volume. If you measure out 2 cups of syrup from a larger container, the cake turns out fine, but will take a little longer to cook.)

Cream butter with sugar. Add eggs 1 at a time. Sift dry ingredients and add on low speed to other mixture. Add vanilla and syrup. Bake at 350° in a 9" x 13" greased and floured pan for 35 minutes.

FROSTING

½ c. butter
1½ c. sugar
⅓ c. evaporated milk
1 t. vanilla

Pinch of salt
6 oz semi-sweet chocolate chips
½ c. black walnuts (optional)

Bring first 5 ingredients to a boil for 2 minutes. Stir in chocolate chips. Add walnuts, if desired. Pour over warm cake. Serves 12.

JAYNE UKROP

NO-FROSTING CHOCOLATE CHIP CAKE

Too rich for words!

4 oz. unsweetened chocolate
2 c. sugar
1 c. margarine
4 eggs
1 c. milk

1 c. sour cream
2 t. vanilla
3¼ c. flour
1 t. baking soda
12 oz. chocolate chips

Grease and flour a tube or Bundt pan. Melt the unsweetened chocolate and let cool. Cream sugar and margarine. Add eggs. In another bowl, mix milk, sour cream and vanilla. Combine flour and baking soda. Add milk mixture alternately with flour to the creamed mixture, ending with flour. Add the melted chocolate and all of the chips. Pour into prepared pan and bake at least 60 minutes at 350°, or until a knife inserted all the way down comes out clean. Let cake cool completely before removing from pan. Serves 20.

CHOCOLATE CREAM CAKE

11 oz. cream cheese
1 c. butter or margarine
2 lb. cor...ectioners' sugar
4 oz. pkg. German chocolate
¼ c. boiling water
¼ c. margarine or shortening

3 eggs
2¼ c. flour
1 t. salt
1 t. baking soda
1 c. buttermilk
1 t. vanilla

Combine cream cheese and butter in a large mixing bowl. Add sugar gradually. Melt chocolate in boiling water. Stir into the sugar mixture. Divide the sugar mixture and save 3 cups for the icing. To the remainder, add margarine and eggs. Beat well. Combine flour, salt and baking soda. Add flour mixture to the batter alternately with the buttermilk, beginning and ending with the flour mixture. Stir in vanilla and mix well. Pour batter into 3 (9") round cake pans that have been lined with wax paper. Bake at 350° for 30 to 35 minutes. Allow to cool in pans for 5 to 10 minutes. Remove from pans and cool completely. Frost with the reserved icing. Serves 12.

SUE MINER

CHOCOLATE LIME CAKE WITH MINT GLAZE

A pretty and refreshing dessert for the summer.

1 pkg. devil's food cake mix (plus cake mix ingredients)

3 pts. lime sherbet

Prepare cake according to package directions for 2-layer cake, baking in 2 (8") round cake pans. When cool, cut each layer horizontally in half. This may be done day before serving or up until a month before serving. To assemble cake, place 1 layer on freezer proof plate. Quickly spread with 1 pint slightly softened sherbet. Repeat layering, ending with cake. Freeze cake until sherbet filling is firm (about 1 hour).

MINT GLAZE

½ c. mint-flavored semi-sweet
   chocolate chips
1 T. butter or margarine

1½ t. skim milk
1½ t. light corn syrup

In double boiler over hot, but not boiling, water, melt chocolate chips, butter, milk and corn syrup until smooth. Stir occasionally. Remove from heat and spread top of cake with glaze. Freeze until cake and glaze are firm. Wrap cake with foil or plastic wrap and return to freezer until ready to serve. Remove cake from freezer 15 minutes before serving. Serves 12.

BONNIE MOREAU

DOUBLE CHOCOLATE MOUSSE CAKE

Save all your calories for a week and then indulge. It's worth it!

CAKE

2 (8 oz.) pkgs. semi-sweet
   chocolate squares
2 c. butter or margarine (butter is
   better!)
1 c. sugar

1 c. half and half
½ t. salt
1 T. vanilla
8 large eggs

Make the cake early in the day or a day ahead. Grease a 9" or 10" springform pan. Heat first 6 ingredients over low heat, stirring constantly, until the chocolate melts and the mixture is smooth. Remove from heat. Beat eggs slightly in a large bowl. Whisk chocolate mixture into the eggs and pour into the greased pan. Bake at 350° for 45 minutes until you can put a toothpick 2 inches from the edge and have it come out clean. Place a cookie sheet on a rack below your pan to catch any drips. When cake is done, cool completely at room temperature before removing side of pan. Wrap cake in plastic wrap and refrigerate for a minimum of 6 hours or overnight.

GLAZE

6 oz. semi-sweet chocolate chips
2 T. butter or margarine

3 T. milk
2 T. white corn syrup

Cook chips over low heat with butter until chocolate melts and mixture is smooth. Remove from heat and beat in the milk and corn syrup. Spread over top and sides of cake.

TOPPING

1 c. whipping cream

1 T. sugar, or to taste

Whip cream with sugar. Cake looks nice with whipped cream piped in star or flower shapes around the edges, or can be served with a dollop of whipped cream on each slice. Refrigerate until serving time. Serves 16.

ALLYN CROSBY

HOT FUDGE PUDDING CAKE *L*
Low-fat with a rich flavor.

1 c. Bisquick
1 c. sugar
1/3 c. plus 3 T. unsweetened cocoa
  powder

1/2 c. milk
1 t. vanilla
1 2/3 c. hot water

Mix Bisquick, 1/2 c. sugar and 3 T. cocoa in a greased 8" square baking pan. Stir in milk plus vanilla until well blended. Sprinkle with remaining 1/3 c. of cocoa plus remaining 1/2 c. of sugar. Pour on hot water. Bake in a preheated 350° oven 40 minutes until top is firm. Dessert will consist of the cake with its own fudge sauce. It can be reheated in individual servings in the microwave. Serves 8.

VARIATION: Use skim milk and spray the baking dish with no-stick cooking spray to lower the fat content.

ALLISON WILLIAMS

MILKY WAY CAKE

CAKE

3 (2.24 oz). Milky Way bars, cut into
  pieces
1/2 c. margarine or butter
2 c. flour
1/2 t. baking soda
1/2 t. baking powder

1 c. sugar
1/2 c. shortening
3 eggs
1 t. vanilla
1 c. buttermilk

Preheat oven to 325° and grease and flour 10" tube or 12" fluted tube pan. In small saucepan, over low heat, melt candy bars with margarine. Stir until blended. In medium bowl, combine flour, baking soda, and baking powder; set aside. In a large bowl, beat sugar and shortening until light and fluffy. Add eggs one at a time, beating well. Add vanilla and candy bar mixture. Blend well. Alternately add dry ingredients and buttermilk, beating well after each addition. Pour into pan and bake for 55 to 65 minutes, or until done. Cool upright for 10 minutes, then invert onto serving plate and cool completely.

FROSTING

2 (2.24 oz) Milky Way bars
1/2 c. margarine or butter
1 1/2 c. confectioners' sugar

1 t. vanilla
1-3 t. cream or milk

In medium pan over low heat, melt candy bars and margarine. Stir until blended. Remove from heat, cool 5 minutes, then add sugar, vanilla and cream. Beat until smooth, and frost top and sides of cake.

TOPPING

½ oz. (½ square) unsweetened chocolate, in pieces
½ t. margarine or butter

¾ c. confectioners' sugar
4-5 t. hot water

Mix ingredients together, and drizzle over top of cake. Serves 16.

LEIGH CRENSHAW

1-2-3 COCONUT CAKE

Great do-ahead cake!

1 pkg. butter flavored yellow cake mix (plus cake mix ingredients)
1 pt. light sour cream
2 c. sugar

3 (6 oz) pkgs. frozen fresh coconut
1 (4 oz.) container whipped topping

Prepare the cake according to package directions, baking in 2 (9") round cake pans. After the layers have cooled completely, split the layers in half to make 4 thin layers. Combine sour cream, sugar and coconut. Spread generously between each layer. To the remaining mixture, add the whipped topping. Frost the top and sides of the cake. Place in a cake container and refrigerate 3 days. The cake will be deliciously moist. It will keep in the refrigerator at least 1 week after preparation. Serves 16.

VARIATION: Add 2 t. vanilla or coconut extract to the sour cream mixture.

SUE MINER
INGER RICE

EASY COCONUT CAKE

1 pkg. yellow cake mix (plus cake mix ingredients)
1 (14 oz) can sweetened condensed milk

8 oz. cream of coconut
1 (8 oz) container whipped topping
¾ c. coconut, shredded

Prepare cake as directed on the package, using a sheet cake pan. When cake is done, prick at once all over with a fork and cover with a mixture of the sweetened condensed milk and the cream of coconut. Let cool. Cover with whipped topping and shredded coconut. Let set in the refrigerator several hours or overnight. Serves 8 to 10.

JUDI NEWCOMB

CHRISTMAS CAKE

2 c. sugar
3 c. cake flour
1 t. cinnamon
1 t. baking powder
1 t. salt
1 c. nuts, chopped
2 c. bananas, sliced

1 (8 oz.) can crushed pineapple, undrained
1 (7 oz.) can coconut
3 eggs, slightly beaten
1½ t. vanilla
1½ c. oil

Sift dry ingredients together. Blend in remaining ingredients with an electric mixer. Do not overbeat. Pour into a greased 10" tube pan. Bake at 325° for 1 hour and 20 minutes. This cake freezes well. Serves 16.

SALLY MAYNARD

MANDARIN ORANGE CAKE

A great luncheon cake.

1 pkg. butter-flavored yellow cake mix
½ c. vegetable oil
4 eggs

1 (11 oz.) can mandarin oranges with juice (reserve 12 orange slices for garnishing cake)

Mix together the dry cake mix, oil, eggs and oranges (with juice). Blend on medium speed with an electric mixer. Pour into 3 greased and floured 9" round cake pans. Bake in a 325° oven for 15 to 25 minutes until lightly browned. Turn onto racks to cool.

ICING

1 (3 oz.) pkg. instant vanilla pudding mix
1 (9 oz.) container whipped topping

1 (1 lb. 4 oz.) can crushed pineapple, drained

Combine all icing ingredients. Spread between layers and over top and sides of cooled cake. Garnish with mandarin orange slices. Store in refrigerator and serve cold. Serves 16.

SANDY ROBINS

FROZEN MERINGUE CAKE

A do-ahead dessert that's perfect for a hot summer day!

8 egg whites
Dash of cream of tartar
2 c. sugar
Paper grocery bag
2 c. whipping cream

1 t. almond extract
Sugar to taste
Sliced fresh strawberries or
   chocolate curls (optional)

Beat egg whites until soft peaks form, adding the cream of tartar. Gradually add the sugar and beat until stiff peaks form. Open the paper bag flat and cut out 2 (9") circles (use a compass or a 9" cake pan as a guide). Place paper circles on 2 pizza pans or cookie sheets and spread half of the meringue on each circle. Place in the center of oven and bake for 1½ hours at 250° Test for firmness. Turn off the oven and leave the meringues in the oven to cool for several hours or overnight. Beat cream until stiff, adding the almond extract and a little sugar to sweeten. Peel the paper off the bottoms of meringue layers and frost with the whipped cream as you would any layer cake (for an added touch, pipe edges with whipped cream through a pastry bag). Place in refrigerator for a day, then freeze. Remove from freezer about 15 minutes before serving. Garnish with sliced strawberries or chocolate curls. It's best to not make the meringues on a damp day, as the moisture in the air can make them chewy. Leftover cake can be re-frozen. Serves 8.

MIMSIE STEADMAN

PLUM CAKE

2 c. self-rising flour
2 c. sugar
1½ t. cinnamon
1½ t. cloves

1 c. oil
3 eggs
1 (6 oz.) jar junior baby food plums
1 c. pecans, chopped

Combine all ingredients and beat 3 minutes on medium speed. Pour into a greased and floured tube pan. Bake 50 minutes to 1 hour at 350°. Cool in the pan for 10 minutes.

GLAZE

1 c. confectioners' sugar   Juice of 1 lemon

Stir together sugar and lemon juice. Spread on the cake while it is still hot. Serves 12 to 15.

GAY JEWETT

GRANDMOTHER'S POUND CAKE

1½ c. butter, softened
2 c. sugar
6 eggs

2 c. plus 2 T. flour
1 t. almond or lemon extract
2 t. vanilla

Cream butter and sugar in mixing bowl. Add eggs, 1 at a time, beating constantly with mixer. Add flour slowly. Stir in extracts. Pour into large greased and floured tube pan and bake at 325° for 1 hour. Serves 12 to 16.

MARTY EAGLE

LEMON POUND CAKE

1 c. butter, softened
3 c. sugar
6 large eggs
8 oz. sour cream

3 c. sifted flour
¼ t. baking soda
¼ t. salt
2 t. lemon extract

Cream butter and sugar. Add the eggs, 1 at a time. Add the sour cream and mix. Combine flour, soda and salt. Add flour mixture to creamed mixture ½ cup at a time. Mix thoroughly. Add lemon extract. Pour into a greased and floured 10" tube pan. Bake at 350° for 1 hour.

GLAZE

¼ c. butter
⅔ c. sugar

⅓ c. fresh lemon juice

Combine glaze ingredients in a saucepan and boil for 2 minutes, stirring gently. Pour over the warm cake. For best flavor age this cake for at least 3 days. Serves 10 to 12.

KATHY ELLIS

MOM'S POUND CAKE

1 c. butter
2 c. sugar
4 eggs, separated
3½ c. sifted cake flour (sift before measuring)

3 t. baking powder
1 c. milk or cream
1 t. vanilla
⅛ t. almond extract
⅛ t. salt

Grease tube pan. Combine butter and sugar slowly, and beat until fluffy. Add egg yolks to the batter. In another bowl, combine flour and baking powder and stir lightly. Add dry ingredients to egg mixture alternating with milk or cream, beginning and ending with the flour mixture. Beat until just smooth—do not overbeat. Add flavorings. Beat egg whites and salt until firm, then fold whites into batter until they disappear. Pour batter into pan and bake at 350° for 55 to 60 minutes, or until cake is golden brown on top and slightly pulled away from pan. Let cool on rack for 20 minutes. Carefully remove from pan. Delicious with your favorite icing or ice cream. Serves 10.

BARBARA SAMUELS

LEMON CURD

Great over pound cake or as a filling for tarts.

½ c. butter, softened
1½ c. sugar

4 eggs
Grated rind and juice of 4 lemons

Cream butter and sugar. Add eggs, mixing well after each one. Add lemon rind and juice. Cook over low heat until shiny and thickened. Keep stirring or your egg whites might cook. If they do, strain them out. This will keep well in the refrigerator for 2 weeks. It does not freeze. Yield: 1 pint.

ALLYN CROSBY

Pies

I like big chunks of apple
in apple pie.

Gus Thompson, '03

Fruit Pies:

Apple Cranberry Pie.......... 282
Dutch Apple Pie............... 282
French Apple Pie.............. 282
Fresh Berry Pie................. 283
Blender Lemon Pie............ 287
Lemon Chess Pie.............. 287
Rosemary Key Lime Pie....... 287
Peach Pie..................... 288
Easy Summertime Peach
Pie 289
Peach Crumble Pie........... 289
Healthy Pineapple
Cheesecake Pie   **L**........ 290
Raspberry and Cream Pie ... 291
Fresh Strawberry Pie 291
Yogurt Fruit Pie 292

Chocolate Pies:

Chocolate Chess Pie 284

Roberta's Chocolate Chess
Pie 284
Chocolate Cream Cheese
Pie 285
Bourbon Chocolate Pecan
Pie 285
Moody's Chocolate Morsel
Pie 286
Frozen Chocolate Pecan
Pie 286

Other Pies:

Coconut Cream Pie 283
Cream Cheese Pie 284
One Hundred Year Old
Chess Pie.................... 284
Ice Cream Pie................. 286
Grasshopper Pie   **L** 288
Peanut Butter Pie.............. 290

APPLE CRANBERRY PIE

Nice combination of flavors. Great for the holidays!

¾ c. brown sugar
¼ c. sugar
⅓ c. flour
1 t. cinnamon
4 c. apples, pared and sliced

2 c. cranberries, washed and
   drained
2 T. butter or margarine
1 9″ double pie crust

In a large bowl, stir together both sugars, flour and cinnamon. Add apples and cranberries, mixing to coat well. Turn into pastry-lined pie pan. Dot with butter and cover with top crust. Cut slits in crust, seal and flute edges. Bake at 425° for 40 to 50 minutes. Cool before serving. Serves 6 to 8.

MELANIE JONES

DUTCH APPLE PIE

5 large tart firm apples (2½ lbs.)
⅓ c. plus 2 T. sugar
¼ c. flour
½ t. cinnamon
½ t. allspice

¼ t. cloves
½ t. nutmeg
¼ t. salt
Lemon juice
1 unbaked deep-dish pie shell

Pare, core, and slice apples. In saucepan on very low heat cook slightly, about 5 to 10 minutes, and pour off juice. Sprinkle with 2 T. sugar. Mix remaining sugar, flour, spices, and salt. Add to apples and toss lightly. Spoon into pie shell and sprinkle with lemon juice.

TOPPING

½ c. sugar
½ c. flour

½ c. butter
½ c. pecans, chopped

Combine sugar and flour. Cut in the butter and add the pecans. Sprinkle topping over apples and bake at 375° for 40 minutes. Serves 6 to 8.

KATHY ELLIS

FRENCH APPLE PIE

8 medium apples, peeled and
   sliced
¼ c. flour
1 c. sugar
⅓ c. butter, melted

¼ t. nutmeg
½ t. allspice
¼ t. cinnamon
1 unbaked 9″ pie shell

Slice half the apples into the pie shell. Mix flour, sugar, butter, and spices together until crumbly. Sprinkle half the crumbs over the apples. Repeat layers. Cover and bake 30 minutes at 350°C. Remove cover and bake 30 minutes longer. Serve hot or cold. Serves 6 to 8.

SUZANNE COWLEY

FRESH BERRY PIE

Really brings out the fresh taste of the berries.

1 qt. fresh blueberries or strawberries
½ c. sugar
1 fresh peach, peeled and sliced

Vanilla ice cream, whipped cream, or Cool Whip
1 baked pie shell

Wash and sort blueberries or wash, hull and slice strawberries. Place one-third of the berries in a saucepan with the sugar. Cook down, stirring often, until the fruit is thick and syrupy. Pile remainder of berries in pie shell. Pour cooked fruit over berries and arrange fresh peach slices on top. Refrigerate until serving time. Serve with vanilla ice cream, whipped cream, or Cool Whip. Serves 6 to 8.

MIMSIE STEADMAN

COCONUT CREAM PIE

½ c. sugar
5 T. flour
¼ t. salt
1 c. evaporated milk
1 c. whole milk

3 eggs, separated
1 t. butter
3½ oz. can coconut
1 t. vanilla
1 baked deep dish pie shell

Mix sugar, flour, and salt in top of double boiler. Add small amount of milk slowly to form a smooth paste, then add remaining milk. Cook over boiling water until thickened, stirring constantly. Beat egg yolks. Add small amount of thickened mixture to egg yolks, then return to double boiler and add butter. Continue cooking until very thick. Remove from heat. Add coconut and vanilla. Pour into pie shell. Top with stiffly beaten egg whites and coconut flakes. Bake at 350° for 12 to 15 minutes, or until top is lightly browned. Serves 6 to 8.

ADAM AND BECKI LOTTS

PIES

CREAM CHEESE PIE

1 (8 oz.) pkg. cream cheese,
  softened
1 c. confectioners' sugar
1 t. vanilla
1 c. whipping cream, whipped

½ c. pecans or walnuts, crushed
1 baked pie shell or crumb crust
Fresh fruit (peaches, strawberries,
  blueberries)

Mix cream cheese and sugar, then add vanilla. Fold whipped cream into cream cheese mixture. Spread nuts over bottom of pie shell, then pour filling over top. Refrigerate for 4 hours. Serve with your choice of fresh fruit. Serves 6 to 8.

GAIL SMITH

ONE HUNDRED YEAR OLD CHESS PIE

3 eggs
1½ c. sugar
½ c. butter, melted
1 t. vanilla

1 T. vinegar
½ c. nuts, chopped
½ c. coconut
1 unbaked 9" pie shell

Beat eggs well. Add sugar and butter and beat again. Stir in remaining ingredients. Pour into pie shell and bake at 350° for about 40 minutes, or until pie is solid in the middle. Serves 6 to 8.

LINDA STEPANIAN

CHOCOLATE CHESS PIE

1 c. butter
3 (1 oz.) squares semi-sweet
  chocolate
2 c. sugar

4 eggs
2 t. vanilla
Dash of salt
2 unbaked pie shells

Melt butter and chocolate together. Blend remaining ingredients, then add chocolate mixture. Pour evenly into the two pie crusts. Bake at 350° for 25 to 30 minutes. Serves 12 to 16.

SANDY LACY

ROBERTA'S CHOCOLATE CHESS PIE

CRUST

¾ c. flour
¼ t. salt

¼ c. margarine
Cold water (about 2½ T.)

Combine flour and salt. Cut margarine into flour mixture until it resembles small peas. Add cold water, 1 T. at a time until dough sticks together. Yield: 1 pie crust.

FILLING

2 (1 oz.) squares unsweetened
   baking chocolate
½ c. butter
1¼ c. sugar

2 eggs
¼ c. milk
1 T. yellow cornmeal

Melt chocolate and butter in saucepan. Remove from heat and add sugar, eggs, milk, and cornmeal. Mix well and set aside. Pour mixture into pie shell and bake at 350° for 30 minutes, or until set. Serves 6 to 8.

KATE LEWIS

CHOCOLATE CREAM CHEESE PIE

2 (4 oz.) pkgs. Baker's German
   sweet chocolate
½ c. milk, divided
1 (8 oz.) pkg. cream cheese,
   softened

2 T. sugar (optional)
1 (8 oz.) pkg. Cool Whip, thawed
1 9" chocolate wafer crumb crust

Heat all but three squares chocolate with ¼ c. milk until chocolate is melted, stirring constantly. Remove from heat and beat in cream cheese, sugar, and remaining ¼ c. milk. Gently stir in whipped topping until smooth. Spoon into crust and freeze until firm. Pie may be served frozen directly from the freezer or allowed to stand at room temperature 30 minutes first. Before serving, melt remaining 3 squares of chocolate and drizzle over pie. Serves 6 to 8.

CATHY BUTTNER

BOURBON CHOCOLATE PECAN PIE

4 eggs, beaten
6 T. butter, melted
1 c. light corn syrup
½ c. sugar
¼ c. firmly packed brown sugar
3 T. bourbon

1 T. flour
1 T. vanilla
1 c. semi-sweet chocolate morsels
1 c. pecans, coarsely chopped
1 unbaked deep dish pie shell or
   2 unbaked 8" pie shells

Combine all ingredients except nuts and chocolate in large mixing bowl and beat well. Stir in nuts and chocolate. Pour into pie shell(s) and bake at 350° until set, 35 to 40 minutes. Serves 12 to 16.

DEBBIE CUNNINHAM
ALICE GOODWIN

MOODY'S CHOCOLATE MORSEL PIE

1 c. sugar
½ c. flour
2 eggs, beaten
½ c. butter or margarine, melted
1 c. pecans, chopped

1 (6 oz.) pkg. semi-sweet
   chocolate morsels
1 t. vanilla
1 unbaked 9" pie shell

Combine sugar and flour. Stir in eggs and butter. Add pecans, chocolate morsels, and vanilla. Mix well. Pour into pie shell and bake at 350° for 40 to 45 minutes, until golden in color. (This pie is very gooey and needs to stand at room temperature 1 to 2 hours before serving.) Serves 6 to 8.

ANNE NELSON MORCK

FROZEN CHOCOLATE PECAN PIE

CRUST

2 c. toasted pecans, finely
   chopped

5½ T. brown sugar, firmly packed
5 T. butter, softened

Blend ingredients thoroughly and press into bottom and sides of 10-inch pie plate. Freeze 1 hour.

FILLING

6 oz. semi-sweet chocolate
½ t. instant coffee crystals
4 eggs, at room temperature

1 t. vanilla
1½ c. whipping cream, divided

Melt chocolate with coffee crystals on top of double boiler. Remove from heat and add eggs and vanilla, mixing quickly until smooth. Let filling cool about 10 minutes. Whip 1 cup of the whipping cream until stiff and gently fold into chocolate mixture. Pour into prepared crust and freeze. About 1 hour before serving, transfer pie to refrigerator. Whip remaining ½ c. whipping cream and garnish pie. (Can be frozen up to 3 months.) Serves 8 to 10.

LORNA ROWLAND

ICE CREAM PIE

1½ c. flour
¾ c. pecans, chopped
¾ c. margarine (not butter),
   melted

⅜ c. brown sugar
½ gal. ice cream (butterscotch
   marble or praline type is best),
   softened

Mix flour and pecans. Add margarine and mix well. Press mixture into 2 9-inch pie plates, reserving some crumb mixture for topping. Bake all (even topping) at 350° until brown, about 10 minutes. Cool slightly. Spread softened ice cream into pie shells. Crumble reserved topping over ice cream. Freeze. Serves 12 to 16.

ADELAIDE MONTAGUE

VARIATION: Use vanilla ice cream and serve with Hot Fudge Sauce.

SANDY LACY

BLENDER LEMON PIE

4 eggs
1 lemon, cut into 8 pieces
½ c. margarine, softened

2 c. sugar
2 unbaked 8" pie shells

Beat eggs well in blender. Add lemon pieces and blend until liquefied. Add margarine and blend again. Add sugar, slowly blending thoroughly. Pour into pie shells and bake at 350° for 30 to 35 minutes. Cool on wire racks. Serves 12 to 16.

KATIE BELK

LEMON CHESS PIE

4 T. butter, melted
3 eggs
1½ c. sugar

Juice of 1½ lemons
1 t. lemon rind, grated
1 unbaked 9" pie shell

Combine butter and eggs and beat well. Stir in remaining ingredients and pour into pie shell. Bake at 350° for about 40 to 45 minutes. Serves 6 to 8.

LINDA STEPANIAN

ROSEMARY KEY LIME PIE

2 c. sugar
4 T. cornstarch
Pinch of salt
½ c. fresh lime juice
Grated rind of 1 lime

2 eggs, lightly beaten
2 t. rosemary infusion (or vanilla)
2 c. heavy cream, whipped
1 or 2 graham cracker crusts

Combine sugar, cornstarch, and salt in a saucepan. Add lime juice and lime rind and stir until smooth. Add eggs and cook over low heat for about 4 minutes. Allow to cool. Stir in rosemary infusion (p. 288) and fold in whipped cream. Spoon into pie shell(s) and chill 2 hours. When serving, garnish with grated lime. (If using only 1 pie shell, use the remaining mousse to serve in individual dessert bowls and serve with cookies.) Serves 12 to 16.

ROSEMARY INFUSION

1 t. dry rosemary or 1 T. fresh   1 oz. vodka
   rosemary

Combine rosemary and vodka and simmer. After 30 minutes, strain out rosemary and use liquid remaining.

JANE FAIN

L GRASSHOPPER PIE

Luscious any season!

CRUST

15 grasshopper cookies   1 prepared graham cracker crust
3 T. hot water

Finely grind grasshopper cookies in food processor. Combine crumbs with hot water and stir until well mixed. Spoon into graham cracker crust and spread evenly over bottom.

FILLING

2 c. light Cool Whip   ½-1 t. green food coloring
3-4 oz light cream cheese,   2 (1 oz) squares semi-sweet
   softened   chocolate, melted (optional)
6 pkg. Sweet 'n Low   Strawberry slices (optional)
3 T. skim milk   Mints, crushed (optional)
2 t. peppermint extract

In a medium bowl, combine Cool Whip, cream cheese, Sweet 'n Low, skim milk, peppermint extract, and food coloring. Mix until smooth. Pour on top of cookie layer in pie shell. Freeze overnight or until firm. Remove from freezer 30 minutes before serving. Garnish with chocolate drizzle, strawberries, or mints on top. Serves 6 to 8.

KIM BAIN

PEACH PIE

6 large ripe peaches, peeled and   ⅓ c. lemon juice
   sliced   1 t. vanilla
1 (8 oz) pkg. light cream cheese   1 graham cracker pie crust
1 (14 oz) can sweetened
   condensed milk

Line pie crust with half the sliced peaches. Combine cheese, milk, lemon juice, and vanilla. Mix well. Pour over peaches, then top with remaining peaches. Cover with plastic wrap and chill 3 hours. Serves 6 to 8.

SUE NASCHOLD

EASY SUMMERTIME PEACH PIE

This one is quick to disappear!

4 large fresh ripe peaches,
   peeled and thinly sliced
1 c. sugar
⅓ c. butter or margarine
1 egg

⅓ c. flour
½ t. almond extract
1 t. vanilla
1 unbaked deep-dish pie shell

Arrange peaches in pie shell. Cream butter and sugar in food processor or mixer. Add egg, flour, flavorings and mix well. Spread mixture over peaches and bake at 300° for about 1 hour. Serves 6 to 8.

LYNN FELTON

PEACH CRUMBLE PIE

8 large ripe freestone peaches
¼ c. sugar
1 T. flour
¼ t. nutmeg

1 t. lemon zest, finely grated
1 unbaked deep-dish pie shell,
   chilled

Cut shallow cross in blossom end of each peach and plunge them a few at a time into a pan of boiling water, about 30 seconds. Remove to bowl of cold water and slip off skins. If peaches are ripe, skins will slip off easily. If not, use paring knife. Halve and pit peaches, then cut each half into 5 or 6 wedges. Place in bowl and sprinkle with sugar, flour, nutmeg, and lemon zest. Toss well to coat. Spoon into pie shell.

CRUMB TOPPING

½ c. butter
½ c. light brown sugar, firmly
   packed

1¼ c. flour

Melt butter and stir in brown sugar. Stir in flour and let stand 5 minutes, then break up into large crumbs using fingertips. Sprinkle crumb topping over peaches and bake at 350° for 50 to 55 minutes, until filling is bubbling and crumbs appear well-colored. Serve lukewarm. Serves 6 to 8.

VARIATION: This can also be made with a combination of peaches and raspberries.

CAROL SMITH

PEANUT BUTTER PIE

CRUST

1 c. graham cracker crumbs
¼ c. light brown sugar, firmly
   packed

¼ c. butter, melted

Combine ingredients. Press into bottom and halfway up sides of 9"
springform pan.

FILLING

2 c. creamy peanut butter
2 c. sugar
2 (8 oz.) pkgs. cream cheese,
   softened
2 T. butter, melted

2 t. vanilla
1½ c. whipping cream
4 oz. semi-sweet chocolate
3 T. plus 2 t. hot coffee

Beat peanut butter, sugar, cream cheese, butter and vanilla in large bowl
with electric mixer until smooth and creamy. Beat whipping cream until soft
peaks form. Fold whipped cream into peanut butter mixture. Spoon into
crust and refrigerate at least 6 hours. Melt chocolate with coffee in double
boiler. Spread on top of pie and refrigerate overnight. Serves 10 to 12.

DONNA JACOBS

L   HEALTHY PINEAPPLE CHEESECAKE PIE

Light and delicious!

1 (3 oz.) pkg. lemon or pineapple
   Nutrasweet gelatin
¾ c. boiling water
¼ c. pineapple juice (from
   canned pineapple)

2 (12 oz.) containers low-fat (1%)
   cottage cheese
¼ c. sugar or 6 pkgs. Equal
½ t. salt
2 graham cracker pie crusts

Dissolve gelatin in boiling water. Add pineapple juice. Cool to lukewarm. In
a blender, mix cottage cheese, sugar and salt until smooth. Slowly add
cooled gelatin and blend well. Pour mixture into the 2 pie crusts. Chill until firm.

TOPPING

1 (16 oz.) can crushed pineapple,
   undrained

2 T. water
2 T. cornstarch

Bring undrained pineapple, water and cornstarch to a boil, stirring constantly. Let cool to room temperature. Pour over the cheesecake so it covers
completely. This is best if chilled overnight. Serves 16.

LAURA LEE CHANDLER

RASPBERRY AND CREAM PIE

CRUST

4 egg whites	1 c. graham cracker crumbs
1 t. vanilla	½ c. coconut, shredded
¼ t. salt	½ c. hazelnuts, chopped
1 c. sugar	1 t. baking powder

In a large mixing bowl, beat together egg whites, vanilla, and salt until soft peaks form. Gradually add sugar and beat until stiff. In a small bowl stir together graham cracker crumbs, coconut, hazelnuts, and baking powder. Fold into egg white mixture. Spread mixture into a buttered and floured pie pan, building up the sides to form a shell. Bake at 350° for 20 to 25 minutes, until set and lightly browned. (Shell will puff somewhat, but will settle more when filling is added.) Cool on a wire rack.

FILLING

1 c. sugar	1 T. lemon juice
3 T. flour	3 egg yolks, lightly beaten
¼ t. salt	3 c. raspberries, fresh or frozen
4 T. Crème de Cassis or Chambord, divided	1-2 c. whipping cream
	Confectioners' sugar

In a 2-quart saucepan stir together sugar, flour, and salt. Stir in 2 T. cassis, lemon juice, and egg yolks. Cook and stir over medium heat until thickened and bubbly. Cook and stir 1 minute more. Spoon into cooled pie shell. Cool 30 minutes, then cover and chill. Whip cream with 2 T. cassis and confectioners' sugar to taste. Dollop on top pie. If you wish to pipe a decorative border, you will need 2 cups of whipping cream; otherwise 1 to 1½ cups are sufficient. Garnish with raspberries. Serves 6 to 8.

JENNIFER WHITMAN

FRESH STRAWBERRY PIE

A great springtime dessert!

1 c. sugar	1 qt. fresh strawberries, sliced
Dash of salt	1 baked 9" pie shell
2 T. cornstarch	Whipped cream or Cool Whip
1 c. water	(optional)
4 T. strawberry jello	

Combine sugar, salt, cornstarch and water. Cook over moderate heat until mixture is clear, stirring constantly. Add jello and stir until it is dissolved. Add strawberries and pour into cooled pie shell. Refrigerate until firm. Can be served with whipped cream or Cool Whip. Serves 6 to 8.

MARGARET BARGATZE

YOGURT FRUIT PIE

2 (8 oz.) containers Dannon yogurt (boysenberry, raspberry, strawberry preferred)

1 (8 oz.) pkg. Cool Whip
1 graham cracker crust

Mix yogurt and Cool Whip together thoroughly. Spoon into graham cracker crust, cover and freeze. Remove from freezer about 15 to 20 minutes before serving. Serves 6 to 8.

RICHIE HILBERT

DESSERTS

Desserts

My dinner section is full, but there's room in my dessert section.
Carolyn McCandlish, '03

Specialties:
Baklava 296
Buttery Shortcake **Q** 296
Fruit Desserts:
Apple Bavarian Torte 297
Easy Baked Apples **L** 297
Rum'd Apples 298
Spiked Apple Crisp 298
Grandma's Apple Pudding
  with Sauce 298
Grandma's Banana
  Pudding 299
Russian Cherries.............. 299
Fruit or Berry Crisp **L** 300
Fruit Clouds.................... 300
Fruit Pizza 300
Kiwi Sorbet with Raspberry
  Sauce **L** 301
Danish Plum Pudding 302
Raspberry Brûlée 302
Raspberry-Topped
  Soufflé **L** 302
Blanc Mange.................. 303
Nut Crust Strawberry Tart 303
Angel Food Trifle **L** 304
Strawberry Punch Bowl
  Cake 304

Tropical Punch Bowl Cake ... 305
Chocolate Dip for
  Strawberries................. 311
Frozen and Chilled Desserts:
Brownie Ice Cream Pie....... 305
Chocolate Chip Ice
  Cream Sandwiches 306
Heath Bar Pie.................. 306
Ribbon Cake **L** 306
Rum Coffee Macaroon....... 307
Viennese Torte 307
**Custards, Puddings and
  Soufflés:**
"Angel of Mercy" Baked
  Custard...................... 308
Perfect Baked Custards....... 308
Crème Caramel 309
Colombian Flan.............. 309
Dirt Pudding 310
Baked Chocolate Whiskey
  Pudding 310
Soufflé Vanille 311
Sauces:
Chocolate Dip for
  Strawberries................. 311
Hot Chocolate Sauce **Q** 312
Hot Fudge Sauce **Q** 312

BAKLAVA

Make a day ahead—will also freeze.

1 lb. walnuts, chopped
½ c. sugar
1 t. cinnamon

½ t. allspice
½ lb. phyllo dough
1 c. butter, melted

Preheat oven to 325°. Combine walnuts, sugar, cinnamon and allspice. Trim phyllo to 10½" x 15½". Keep phyllo covered with plastic wrap while you work. Brush a 15½" x 10½" x 1" jelly roll pan with melted butter. Place 1 sheet of phyllo in pan. Brush with butter. Layer and butter 5 more sheets of phyllo. Sprinkle with 1½ cups of nut and spice mixture. Layer and butter 2 more sheets and sprinkle with 1 cup of nut mixture. Repeat 2 more times. Top final nut layer with 6 sheets of buttered phyllo. Brush remaining butter over all. Trim edges. With a very sharp knife, cut baklava in 1½" strips, then cut strips diagonally at 2" intervals to form diamonds. Bake 50 to 60 minutes until lightly browned. Cool on rack for 30 minutes.

SYRUP

1½ c. sugar
1 c. water
5 whole cloves
1 cinnamon stick

½ c. honey
1 T. lemon juice
1 t. vanilla

Prepare syrup while baklava cooks and cools. In saucepan combine sugar, water, cloves and cinnamon stick. Simmer 2 minutes. Add honey and lemon juice and simmer 5 more minutes. Remove from heat; discard cloves and cinnamon stick. Stir in vanilla. Spoon over warm (not hot) baklava and allow to cool completely before serving. Yield: 45.

Q   BUTTERY SHORTCAKE

Great for strawberries, other fruit, ice cream or whipped cream.

2 c. flour
3 t. baking powder
½ t. salt
3½ T. sugar

½ c. butter (not margarine)
1 egg, slightly beaten
⅔ c. milk

Preheat oven to 450°. Stir together flour, baking powder, salt and sugar. Cut butter into flour mixture with 2 knives until this resembles coarse meal. Combine egg and milk. Make a well in center of the flour mixture and add egg mixture. Stir quickly until dough leaves the sides of bowl. Dough will be thick. Place in a greased 9" round cake pan or drop by spoonfuls onto a greased cookie sheet for individual shortcakes. Bake 15 to 20 minutes or until lightly browned. Split and fill with fruit, ice cream or whipped cream. Serves 4 to 6.

MELINDA WAY

APPLE BAVARIAN TORTE

CRUST

½ c. butter
⅓ c. sugar

¼ t. vanilla
1 c. flour

Cream butter, sugar and vanilla. Blend in flour. Press into bottom and slightly up sides of a 9" springform pan.

FILLING

1 (8 oz.) pkg. cream cheese, softened
¼ plus ⅓ c. sugar, divided
1 egg

½ t. vanilla
½ t. cinnamon
4 c. apple slices, peeled
¼ c. almonds, sliced (optional)

Combine cream cheese and ¼ c. sugar. Mix well. Add egg and vanilla. Pour into the pastry lined pan. Combine ⅓ c. sugar with cinnamon. Toss with apples and spoon over cream cheese layer. Top with almonds if desired. Bake at 450° for 10 minutes. Reduce to 400° for 25 minutes. Cool before removing sides. Serves 8.

JEAN BERKELEY
CHERYL BOSWELL

L   EASY BAKED APPLES

8 Rome apples
8 t. butter or margarine, divided
8 t. cinnamon-sugar mix, divided

Nutmeg to taste
Dash of cinnamon
2 c. apple juice (approximately)

Preheat oven to 325°. For each serving: Core apple, being careful not to go through to the bottom. Slice small section off the top. Place 1 t. margarine into the apple's cavity, then sprinkle inside with cinnamon-sugar mixture. Top with nutmeg and a dash of cinnamon. Place the apples in a deep casserole or baking dish. Pour apple juice into pan so that ¼ of each apple is submerged. Cover and bake approximately 40 minutes or until a knife inserted into the apple goes in easily. Do not allow apples to cook too long or they will burst. Serve with milk, cream or ice cream. Serves 8.

ELIZABETH POPE

RUM'D APPLES

4 large, firm, tart apples	½ c. sugar
Butter for greasing baking dish	½ c. water
4 T. peach or apricot preserves	2 T. rum (not rum flavoring)
Juice and grated rind of 1 orange	Whipped cream

Peel, core and cut apples in half horizontally. Place cut side up in buttered 7" x 10" baking dish. Cook preserves, orange juice, orange rind, sugar, and water over low heat until thickened. Remove from heat, stir in rum, and pour over apples. Cover loosely with foil and bake at 350° for 45 minutes to 1 hour or until apples are tender, basting occasionally. Serve at room temperature or chilled, with whipped cream. Serves 4.

NANCY KENNON

SPIKED APPLE CRISP

5 c. apples, peeled and sliced (Jonathan, Winesap or Granny Smith)	1 jigger Amaretto
	¾ c. sugar
	¼ c. light brown sugar, packed
½ t. cinnamon	¾ c. flour, sifted
1 t. lemon rind, grated	¼ t. salt
1 t. orange rind, grated	½ c. butter or margarine
1 jigger Grand Marnier	

Arrange apple slices in greased 2-quart casserole. Sprinkle cinnamon, lemon rind, orange rind, and both liqueurs on top of apples. In a separate bowl, mix sugars, flour, salt and butter with a pastry blender until crumbly. Spread mixture over apples. Bake uncovered at 350°C until apples are tender and top is lightly browned, approximately 1 hour. Serve warm with whipped cream or vanilla ice cream. Serves 8.

KAKI NELSON

GRANDMA'S APPLE PUDDING WITH SAUCE

PUDDING

¼ c. shortening	1 t. baking powder
1 c. sugar	1 t. cinnamon
1 egg	1 t. nutmeg
1 t. vanilla	2 T. water
1 c. flour	2½ c. apples, sliced
1 t. baking soda	½ c. pecans, chopped
½ t. salt	

Cream together shortening, sugar, egg and vanilla. Sift together flour, baking soda, salt, baking powder and spices. Add to the creamed mixture. Mix in water. Fold in apples and pecans. Bake at 350° for 30 minutes.

SAUCE

1 c. sugar
2 T. flour
1 c. milk

2 t. butter
1 t. vanilla

In small saucepan mix sugar and flour well. Add milk and butter. Bring slowly to a boil, stirring to prevent burning. When sauce begins to boil and thicken, add vanilla. Serve hot over pudding. Serves 6 to 8.

VARIATION: Substitute vanilla ice cream for sauce.

LINDA HUNLEY

GRANDMA'S BANANA PUDDING

3 (3¼ oz.) pkgs. instant banana
    pudding mix
5 c. cold milk
1 (8 oz.) container whipped
    topping

1 (8 oz.) container sour cream
1 (12 oz.) box vanilla wafers
5 ripe bananas

In large mixing bowl combine pudding mix and milk. Beat until well-mixed and thickened. Fold in half of whipped topping and all of sour cream. Line bottom of a 2-quart baking dish with vanilla wafers and layer bananas and pudding. Spread remaining whipped topping on top. Line edges of baking dish with additional vanilla wafers. Chill at least 1 hour. Serves 12.

MARIA COGHILL

RUSSIAN CHERRIES

½ c. currant jelly
1 T. lemon juice
1½ T. light rum

1 (16 oz.) can pitted dark sweet
    cherries, drained and chilled
¼ c. sour cream
Candied violets (optional)

Blend jelly, lemon juice and rum. Add cherries. Refrigerate for 30 minutes. Serve in champagne glasses. Top with sour cream and a violet. Serves 4.

DOROTHY MEYER

L

FRUIT OR BERRY CRISP

2 lbs. cut up fruit or berries
   (apples, blackberries,
   blueberries, or peaches)
3 T. flour
2 T. sugar

2 t. lemon juice
½ c. quick cooking oats
⅓ c. flour
⅓ c. brown sugar, firmly packed
3 T. butter

Sprinkle flour over fruit in bowl and toss to coat. Stir in sugar and lemon juice. Spoon mixture into an 8" square baking dish sprayed with no-stick spray. Combine oats, flour and brown sugar in a small bowl. Cut in butter until mixture resembles coarse meal. Sprinkle topping over fruit mixture. Bake at 350° for 30 minutes or until lightly browned. Serve warm. Serves 8.

CAROLYN MEACHAM

FRUIT CLOUDS

A study group favorite!

1 (8 oz) pkg. light cream cheese
½ c. sugar
1 T. lemon juice

2 t. lemon rind, grated
1 c. whipping cream, whipped
4 c. assorted fresh fruit, cut up

Combine cream cheese, sugar, juice, and rind, mixing well. Fold in whipped cream. Place waxed paper on a cookie sheet. Make 8 even piles of the cream cheese mixture, spaced evenly on the waxed paper. Use the smooth back of a spoon to form cups out of the cream cheese piles. Place the cookie sheet in the freezer until the cups are frozen. When ready to serve, fill cups with fruit as desired. These can be made ahead and stacked once they are frozen for a last minute dessert. Serves 8 to 10.

BRYAN "BO BO" NOONAN

FRUIT PIZZA

1 box yellow cake mix
2 eggs
¼ c. water
¼ c. butter, melted
½ c. brown sugar, firmly packed
½ c. nuts, chopped
1 (12 oz.) container whipped
   topping

2 pt. strawberries
1 c. pineapple chunks, well
   drained
1 lb. seedless grapes
1 (11 oz) can mandarin oranges
1 pt. blueberries
1 jar apricot preserves

Preheat oven to 350°. Line a 15½" x 10½" x 1" jelly roll pan with foil and coat with butter. Combine half of cake mix with water, eggs, butter, and brown sugar. Mix thoroughly. Fold in nuts and remaining mix. Bake 10 to 15 minutes. Cool and remove from foil. Spread whipped topping to cover entire top. Decorate with fruit. Heat preserves with 2 to 3 T. water until dissolved and drizzle over pizza. Serves 8 to 10.

ELLEN LeCOMPTE

KIWI SORBET WITH RASPBERRY SAUCE   *L*

Served at the Clifton Country Inn in Charlottesville.

SORBET

8 kiwis, peeled
1½ c. sugar

½ c. water
¼ c. lime juice

Stir sugar and water in a 2-quart saucepan. Bring to a boil. Boil 5 minutes to make syrup. Set aside. Purée kiwi in a blender. This will make about 2 cups of kiwi purée. Stir together with syrup and lime juice. Freeze in an 8" square pan until it resembles a semi-hard slush. Remove and whip with hand mixer and refreeze until hard. (This will also work in any electric or manual ice cream maker. Follow instructions for freezing ice cream or sorbet.) Pack like ice cream in an airtight container.

SAUCE

10 oz. frozen raspberries
1. T. lime juice

Sugar to taste

Combine raspberries, lime juice, and sugar in a blender. Purée until the sugar is dissolved and mixture is smooth. Strain mixture through cheesecloth to remove the seeds. Spoon over sorbet to serve. Serves 6 to 8.

VARIATION: Substitute raspberries or pineapple for kiwi.

NANCY McCANDLISH

DANISH PLUM PUDDING

A holiday favorite!

2 c. self-rising flour
1⅓ c. sugar
1¼ t. baking soda
1 t. each allspice, cinnamon, and nutmeg
¾ c. vegetable oil
3 eggs

1 c. buttermilk (low-fat buttermilk works fine)
1 (12 oz. box) prunes, chopped and cooked according to pkg. directions
1 c. pecans, chopped

Sift dry ingredients. Beat in oil, eggs and buttermilk. Fold in nuts and prunes. Grease and flour a 9" x 13" baking dish or 2 (8" square) baking dishes. Bake 40 minutes at 325°.

TOPPING

1 c. sugar
½ c. buttermilk
1 t. vanilla

1 T. corn syrup
½ c. margarine

Combine all ingredients in a medium saucepan. Bring to a boil and continue boiling for 2 minutes. Pour over the cake just as you take it from oven. Prick holes in top of cake so topping can soak in. This freezes beautifully. Serve warm with whipped topping or ice cream. Serves 10 to 12.

ANN CULLEN

RASPBERRY BRÛLÉE

1 lb. raspberries (fresh or frozen; drain if frozen)
Grand Marnier (to taste)

½ pt. whipping cream
8 oz. dark brown sugar

Place raspberries in flameproof soufflé dish and add Grand Marnier. Whip cream until very stiff. Spread over raspberries and seal to the edge of the dish. Cover with plastic wrap and refrigerate at least 1 hour or until ready to serve. Remove from refrigerator and spread brown sugar over cream, covering cream completely. Place under broiler until sugar is caramelized. Serve immediately. Serves 6.

BARBARA JONES

L RASPBERRY-TOPPED SOUFFLÉ

2 eggs, separated
2 T. plus ¼ c. sugar, divided
1½ t. unflavored gelatin

1½ c. skim milk, scalded
½ t. vanilla

302

TOPPING

Fresh or frozen raspberries or fruit
  preserves

Combine egg yolks, 2 T. sugar and gelatin in the top of a double boiler. Gradually add scalded milk, stirring until smooth. Reduce heat until water is just simmering. Cook, stirring constantly, 10 to 12 minutes until custard coats spoon. Remove from heat and stir in vanilla. Chill until slightly thickened. Beat egg whites until foamy. Add remaining sugar, gradually beating until stiff peaks form. Fold into custard. Spoon into 6 (6 oz.) dishes. Chill. Serve with raspberry topping. Serves 6.

MARTHA SUSAN SANDERS

BLANC MANGE

Bavarian mousse.

1 pkg. unflavored gelatin
1 pt. whipping cream
⅔ c. sugar

1 pt. sour cream (or imitation sour
  cream)
2 t. vanilla (or almond extract)
Fresh strawberries for garnish

Dissolve gelatin in cream. Warm over medium heat, stirring gently but constantly, until gelatin is dissolved. Remove from heat. Add sugar, sour cream, and vanilla and stir until smooth. Beat briefly with a hand rotary beater until no lumps remain. Place in a greased 1-quart mold and chill in the refrigerator for 1 or more days. Serve with strawberries on top. Serves 8 to 10.

NANCY CHEELY

NUT CRUST STRAWBERRY TART

NUT CRUST

10 oz. slivered almonds
1 c. unsalted butter
⅓ c. sugar
3 c. flour

1 egg, lightly beaten
1 t. vanilla or almond extract
Butter for greasing pan

Place nuts into a food processor with steel blade. Process until finely chopped. Add remaining ingredients. Pulse until mixture resembles coarse meal. Add ice water T. by T. if too dry. Divide dough into 2 balls. Wrap each in plastic bag. Refrigerate 30 minutes. Press into two 9" buttered springform tart pans. Bake at 350° for 15 to 20 minutes.

FILLING

Place 2-3 qts. strawberries on top of cooked nut crust, pointed up.

DESSERTS

GLAZE

2 (6 oz) jars red currant jelly
2 T. unflavored gelatin

½ c. Grand Marnier or Cognac
1 pt. whipping cream, whipped

Heat jelly in saucepan. Dissolve gelatin in Grand Marnier and add to the jelly. Heat on low until mixture is clear. Brush over berries. Refrigerate 4 hours to enhance the flavor. Decorate with fresh flowers. Spoon whipped cream onto each plate when serving. Yield: 2 9" tarts.

VARIATION: Substitute or add blueberries, grapes, kiwi, peaches or raspberries to or instead of strawberries. If fruit substitutions are made, add apricot jelly for peaches, etc.

MARY MADELYN TUCKER

L ANGEL FOOD TRIFLE

1 (16 oz.) pkg. angel food cake
  mix (plus cake mix ingredients)
⅓ c. sugar
¼ c. cornstarch
¼ t. salt
2 c. skim milk
¼ c. egg substitute

1 t. lemon rind, grated
¼ c. lemon juice
2 (8 oz) containers vanilla low-fat
  yogurt
2 c. strawberries, sliced
3 kiwis, sliced
3 strawberry fans to garnish

Prepare cake mix according to package directions. Cut into bite-sized cubes; set aside. Combine sugar, cornstarch, and salt in a saucepan. Gradually add milk, blending well. Cook over medium heat until mixture begins to thicken, stirring constantly. Remove from heat. Gradually add egg substitute, stirring constantly with a wire whisk. Cook over medium-low heat for 2 minutes, stirring constantly. Remove from heat and cool slightly. Stir in lemon rind and lemon juice. Chill. Fold yogurt into custard mixture and set aside. Place ⅓ of cake in bottom of a 16-cup trifle bowl. Spoon ⅓ of custard over the cake. Arrange half each of strawberry slices and kiwi slices around the lower edge of the bowl and over the custard. Repeat procedure with remaining ingredients, ending with the strawberry fans on top. Cover and chill 3 to 4 hours. This will not keep. (If short on time, use a store-bought angel food cake.) Serves 15.

JO ANN CHARLESWORTH

STRAWBERRY PUNCH BOWL CAKE

1 prepared angel food cake
1 (16 oz) box confectioners' sugar
1 (5 oz) can evaporated milk
2 c. sour cream

1 (12 oz) container whipped
  topping
1 (14 oz) jar strawberry glaze
2 (16 oz) pkgs. frozen strawberries,
  thawed

Tear cake into bite-sized pieces and place in large glass bowl. Combine sugar with milk and add sour cream and whipped topping. Mix well and pour over cake. Toss lightly. In mixing bowl combine glaze with strawberries and stir well. Pour over cake mixture and refrigerate. Serves 12.

DIANNE GIBSON

TROPICAL PUNCH BOWL CAKE

1 box yellow cake mix (plus cake mix ingredients)
1 (6 oz.) box vanilla instant pudding (plus milk as directed on pkg.)
1 (20 oz.) can crushed pineapple, drained

2 (10 oz.) pkgs. frozen strawberries, undrained, or 1 qt. fresh fruit (blueberries, kiwi, peaches or strawberries)
2 bananas
1 (16 oz.) container whipped topping
Chopped nuts (optional)

Bake the cake layers according to package directions and let cool. Make pudding and refrigerate. When cake is cool, cut one layer into chunks and put in bottom of a large punch bowl. Pour half of pudding on the cake. Spread half the pineapple on the pudding. Slice 1 banana onto the pineapple and add half the frozen strawberries or fresh fruit. Spread half the whipped topping over the fruit and sprinkle with nuts if desired. Cut the other cake layer and repeat layering as above, ending with whipped topping and nuts. Serves 12 to 15.

JUSTIN FRACKELTON

BROWNIE ICE CREAM PIE

A terrific, make-ahead, festive party dessert!

1 (21½ oz.) pkg. fudge brownie mix
½ gal. ice cream, (vanilla, peppermint, coffee, or chocolate mint)
1 c. pecans, chopped

2 c. confectioners' sugar
⅔ c. chocolate chips
1 c. evaporated milk
½ c. margarine
1 t. vanilla

Bake brownie mix as directed in 9" x 13" pan or round springform pan. Cool completely. Spread brownies with ice cream. Top ice cream with ½ cup pecans. Freeze. Combine remaining ingredients except vanilla and boil for 8 minutes, stirring constantly. Cool 1 hour and stir in vanilla. Spread over frozen ice cream layer and top with ½ cup chopped pecans. Store in freezer. Serves 24.

MARGARET BARGATZE
NANCY KENNON

CHOCOLATE CHIP ICE CREAM SANDWICHES

Popular with children and adults.

½ gal. vanilla ice cream (or ice milk)

1 pkg. refrigerated chocolate chip cookie dough (slice and bake type)

Freeze cookie dough slightly so it will slice easily. Slice cookie dough into ½" sections and bake as directed. Cool. Put 1 scoop of ice cream on a cookie and press another cookie on top until the ice cream spreads to the edges. Trim edges with a knife. Wrap ice cream cookie in plastic wrap and place in the freezer. Let freeze for 2 to 3 hours. Yield: 8 to 10.

JOANNE RAMSEY

HEATH BAR PIE

½ c. margarine
2 c. Ritz crackers, crushed
2 T. sugar
2 c. milk
1 qt. vanilla ice cream, softened

2 (3 oz.) pkgs. instant vanilla pudding
1 (12 oz.) container Cool Whip
2 Heath bars, crushed

Mix together margarine, cracker crumbs and sugar. Press into bottom of 9" x 13" pan. Mix milk, ice cream, and instant pudding together in mixing bowl. Pour over crust. Refrigerate until mixture sets. Spread Cool Whip over top. Sprinkle with crushed Heath bar pieces. Refrigerate until ready to serve. Serves 12.

DIANNE GIBSON

L   RIBBON CAKE

A sweet dessert for a sugar-restricted diet.

1 (3 oz.) pkg. sugar-free lime jello
1 (3 oz.) pkg. sugar-free raspberry jello
1 (15 oz.) jar applesauce (with no sugar added)

18 double graham crackers
1 envelope Dream Whip topping (plus ingredients per pkg. directions)
¼ t. almond extract

In separate bowls mix each jello dry mix with ¾ c. applesauce and stir until thoroughly blended. Place 2 double grahams end-to-end or side-to-side on a platter. Spread with ¼ c. lime mixture. Top with 2 more grahams and spread with ¼ c. raspberry mixture. Repeat layers, alternating flavors, ending with graham crackers. Prepare Dream Whip according to package directions, omitting vanilla and adding almond extract before whipping. Spread topping over top and sides of cake. Chill 30 minutes. Serves 6.

ELLEN LeCOMPTE

RUM COFFEE MACAROON

¼ lb. almond macaroons
¼ c. white rum
1 qt. coffee ice cream

1 (8 oz.) container light whipped
topping
2 oz. slivered almonds, toasted

Line bottom of a 1½-quart dish with macaroons. Pour white rum over macaroons. Spread softened coffee ice cream over macaroons and top with whipped topping. Sprinkle almonds on top. Cover with foil and freeze. Remove from the freezer at least 10 minutes before serving. Serves 8 to 10.

VARIATION: Substitute kahlua for rum.

MARION CHENAULT
BETTY KOONCE

VIENNESE TORTE

Easy, rich, and impressive.

1 (6 oz.) pkg. semi-sweet
chocolate chips
½ c. butter or margarine
¼ c. water

4 egg yolks, slightly beaten
2 T. confectioners' sugar, sifted
1 t. vanilla
1 (12 oz.) loaf pound cake

In a heavy saucepan heat chocolate, butter, water, and egg yolks over medium heat, stirring until blended. Cool slightly. Add sugar and vanilla. Stir until smooth. Chill until mixture is of a spreading consistency, about 45 minutes. Meanwhile, slice the cake horizontally into 6 layers (there is a tool sold in gourmet shops that makes this easy but a sharp serrated knife will do). Spread the chocolate between the layers, then frost the top and the sides. Chill again at least 45 minutes before serving. To serve, cut into ¼" slices. Serves 8 to 10.

GORDON KELLETT

"ANGEL OF MERCY" BAKED CUSTARD

"My mother-in-law's cure for anything that ails you!"

5 eggs, beaten
¾ c. sugar
¼ t. salt
3 c. milk (or 1 large can
  evaporated milk plus whole or
  skim milk to make 3 c.)

2 t. vanilla
Nutmeg, freshly ground, for garnish

Preheat oven to 300°. Butter a 1½-quart soufflé or baking dish. Beat eggs, sugar, and salt until mixture is lemon yellow. Gradually beat in milk, vanilla and a little nutmeg. Pour mixture into buttered dish and sprinkle top with nutmeg. Place dish into larger pan of hot water in oven. Bake 1 hour or until knife inserted into center of custard comes out clean. Serve warm or cool. Serves 4 to 6.

LYNN FELTON

PERFECT BAKED CUSTARDS

3 c. whole milk
3 eggs
½ c. sugar

1 t. vanilla
¼ t. salt
Nutmeg for garnish

Preheat oven to 350°. Spray 6 custard cups with no-stick cooking spray. Place 2 paper towels in the bottom of a rectangular roasting pan. Arrange custard cups on the paper towels. Scald milk over medium high heat. In a 4-cup measuring cup whisk together eggs, sugar, vanilla, and salt. Add half the scalded milk and blend well. Add remaining milk and blend carefully. Pour into the custard cups. Sprinkle tops with nutmeg. Fill the roasting pan with water, stopping about ¼" from the top of the custard cups. Bake 45 minutes or until a knife comes out clean. Cool 20 minutes on a rack. Refrigerate. Serves 6.

ELLEN LeCOMPTE

CRÈME CARAMEL

"My very favorite dessert!"

CARAMEL

1 c. sugar
½ c. water

Pinch cream of tartar

To line a 1-quart mold or 6 individual molds with caramel, it is necessary to work quickly and cautiously (the melted sugar is extremely hot). In a stainless steel frying pan, bring sugar and water to a boil over medium-high heat, stirring until sugar dissolves. Stir in cream of tartar and, holding the handle of the pan, gently shake skillet back and forth across burner, almost constantly, until the caramel turns golden brown. Carefully pour caramel into mold and tip mold to swirl caramel around the sides.

CUSTARD

2 c. milk
1 t. vanilla

¼ c. sugar
3 eggs plus 2 extra egg yolks

Preheat oven to 325°. In a medium saucepan, bring milk almost to boil over medium heat. Remove pan from stove and stir in vanilla. Beat sugar, eggs, and egg yolks until they are well-blended and thickened. Add milk and pour into caramel-lined bowl. Place mold in large pan in middle of oven and pour enough boiling water to come halfway up sides of pan. Bake for 1 hour until custard is set. Chill for 3 hours. Serves 6.

SANDY KING

COLOMBIAN FLAN

Delicious dessert from South America.

2⅔ c. sweetened condensed milk
2⅔ c. milk
6 eggs, separated (yolks beaten slightly, whites beaten into soft peaks)

1 t. vanilla
¼ c. sugar
3 T. water

Mix the two types of milk and beat well. Add vanilla to the beaten egg yolks. Fold in egg whites. Mix sugar and water over low heat, stirring until the sugar is dark brown. Line a baking mold or individual baking cups with the burnt sugar mixture. Fill the mold(s) with the milk mixture and place in a large pan filled with water. Bake in a 400° oven about 1½ hours, or until an inserted knife comes out clean. When cool, unmold onto serving platter or plates. Serves 8 to 12.

SYLVIA BEARER

DIRT PUDDING

A big hit with the kids!

2 c. cold milk
1 (4 oz.) box chocolate instant
  pudding
1 (8 oz) container of whipped
  topping, thawed

1 (16 oz.) pkg. Oreos, crushed and
  divided
8-10 (7 oz) clear plastic cups or a
  large glass bowl
Gummy worms, gummy spiders,
  candy flowers (optional)

Pour milk into a large bowl. Add the pudding mix. Beat with a whisk or hand mixer until well-blended. Let stand for 5 minutes. Stir in the whipped topping and half of the crushed cookies. Place 1 T. of the crushed cookies in the bottom of each cup or make a layer in the bowl. Fill the cups (or bowl) ¾ full with the pudding mixture. Top with the remaining crushed cookies. Refrigerate for 1 hour and then add the worms, spiders or flowers if desired. Children will enjoy pulling the worms out of the dirt. Serves 8 to 10.

ROBIN SLATER

BAKED CHOCOLATE WHISKEY PUDDING

1 c. flour, sifted
1¼ c. sugar, divided
5 T. unsweetened cocoa powder,
  divided
2 t. baking powder
Pinch of salt
2 T. unsalted butter, melted

½ c. milk
1 t. vanilla
½ c. light brown sugar, firmly
  packed
¼ c. whiskey
Whipped cream or vanilla ice
  cream (optional)

Preheat oven to 350°. In a large mixing bowl, combine flour, ⅔ c. sugar, 2 T. cocoa, baking powder, and salt. Mix thoroughly. Stir in the melted butter, milk, and vanilla. Mix until smooth. The batter will be very thick. Spray a 1½-quart soufflé dish or an ovenproof bowl with a no-stick cooking spray. Spread batter in the dish. In a bowl, combine remaining sugar, remaining 3 T. of cocoa and brown sugar. Sprinkle the mixture evenly over the batter. In a small bowl, combine whiskey with ¾ c. water and pour over the pudding. Bake the pudding for 35 minutes or until a thin crust forms on the top. Remove from oven and invert the pudding onto a serving platter or spoon into bowls directly from the baking dish. Serve warm with whipped cream or vanilla ice cream. Serves 6 to 8.

LYNN HAW

SOUFFLÉ VANILLE

1 c. milk
½ c. sugar
½ t. vanilla or to taste
½ c. flour

½ c. butter
8 eggs, separated (yolks lightly
    beaten, whites stiffly beaten)

Place the milk, sugar and vanilla into a saucepan and bring to a boil. Mix flour and butter into a paste and add this to the boiling milk. Mix well with a whisk until it resembles a smooth paste. Remove from heat. Cool slightly and add the egg yolks, mixing until smooth. Add the beaten egg whites, mixing well. Pour into a 4-cup buttered and sugared mold, filling ¾ full. Place in an aluminum pan filled with ½" water. Place in a 400° oven and bake until it rises ⅓ over the height of the mold (about 20 minutes). Do not allow it to rise higher; serve immediately.

VARIATIONS: Substitute various flavors of liqueurs for the vanilla.

For a chocolate soufflé, use 1-2 squares semi-sweet or unsweetened chocolate, melted. Use 1 extra egg, separated and 1 T. water.

SUZANNE RACKLEY

CHOCOLATE DIP FOR STRAWBERRIES

6 T. cocoa
6 T. vegetable shortening
¾ c. confectioners' sugar
1 oz. paraffin

2 doz. strawberries, washed
    (leaves may be left on for easy
    handling)

Melt cocoa and shortening in double boiler. Mix well. Add sugar and stir until smooth. Melt wax in a saucepan over low heat. Add wax to chocolate mixture. With a toothpick dip strawberries in chocolate. Set on a cookie sheet covered with wax paper or foil to set. Yield: 2 dozen.

NANCY KENNON

Q HOT CHOCOLATE SAUCE

This is the kind that hardens when poured over ice cream.

2 (1 oz.) squares unsweetened chocolate
½ c. (scant) sugar
½ c. water

1 T. butter
½ t. vanilla
¼ t. salt

Melt chocolate, sugar and water in the top of a double boiler. Remove pot from boiler and cook over low heat for 30 minutes. Add butter, vanilla and salt. Continue cooking over low heat for 10 minutes. Serves 4.

CANDY MATERNE

Q HOT FUDGE SAUCE

4 (1 oz.) squares unsweetened chocolate
6 T. butter

2 c. sugar
1 (12 oz.) can evaporated milk

In a heavy saucepan over medium heat, melt chocolate and butter. Alternately add sugar and evaporated milk. Stir well. Cook until creamy over low heat—do not boil. Cool. Serve warm over ice cream. Store in refrigerator and reheat as needed. Yield: 2 cups.

EILEEN SMITH

COOKIES & CANDIES

Cookies and Candies

My best thing to cook is chocolate chip cookies for my Dad.
Lee Hallberg, '01

Bar Cookies:
Charleston Wafers 316
Cheesecake Dreams 316
Chess Bars 316
Brownies 317
Drop Dead Brownies 317
Dreamy Iced Brownies 317
Chocolate Iced Cake
   Squares 318
Gee Gee's Hawaiian
   Brownies 318
Lemon Crumb Squares 319
Pecan Bars 319
Strawberry-Almond Bars 319
Sunshine Krisps **Q** 320
Theresa's Tennis Bars 320
English Toffee Bars 320
Drop and Formed Cookies:
Birds' Nests 321
Mini Cheesecakes 321
Miniature Chocolate Chip
   Cheesecakes 322
Giant Chocolate Chip
   Cookies 322
White Chocolate Chunk
   Macadamia Nut Cookies ... 322
Chocolate Mixed Fruit
   Cookies 323
Ginger Snaps 323
Holly Wreaths 323
Lace Cookies 324
Scotch Oat Crispy Cookies ... 324

Oatmeal Cookies 324
Low-Fat Cholesterol-Free
   Oatmeal Cookies **L** 325
Chocolate Peanut Butter
   Cookies 325
Peanut Butter Cookies 325
Pecan Butter Fingers 325
Mr. George's Famous
   Raisin Cookies 326
Nana's Rocks 326
Russian Tea Balls 326
Refrigerated and Roll Cookies:
Hickory Chips 327
Kacey's Harlequin
   Pinwheels 327
Nut Cookies 328
Painted Cookies 328
Peanut Butter Cup Tarts 328
Swiss Cinnamon Stars **L** 329
Sugar Cookies 329
Ornamental Frosting for
   Cookies **Q** 330
Candies:
Butter Creams 330
Apricot Coconut Balls 330
Coconut Balls 331
Easy $5,000 Fudge 331
Cholesterol-Free
   Microwave Fudge 331
Peanut Butter Balls 332
Dog Treats:
Toby Treats 332

315

COOKIES AND CANDIES

CHARLESTON WAFERS

1 c. butter or margarine
1 c. sugar
1 egg, divided
2 t. vanilla

Pinch of salt
2 c. flour
1½ c. pecans, chopped

Mix butter or margarine, sugar, egg yolk, vanilla, salt, and flour and spread in a 17" x 11" greased pan. Beat the egg white until foamy and spread over batter. Sprinkle with nuts and pat them gently. Bake at 325° for 20 minutes. Cut in small squares while hot and let cool in pan. Yield: 6 to 7 dozen.

MARY LOU FERGUSSON

CHEESECAKE DREAMS

⅓ c. light brown sugar, firmly
   packed
1 c. flour, sifted
½ c. walnuts, chopped
⅓ c. butter, melted
1 (8 oz) pkg. cream cheese,
   softened

¼ c. sugar
1 egg
2 T. milk
1 T. lemon juice
1 t. vanilla

Grease an 8" square baking pan. Mix first three ingredients in a small bowl. Stir in butter until well combined. Reserve one-third cup of crumbs. Pat remaining mixture gently into prepared pan. Bake at 350° for 12 to 15 minutes. Mix cream cheese and sugar at medium speed until smooth. Beat in remaining ingredients and pour over crust. Sprinkle reserved crumb mixture over top. Return to oven and bake 25 minutes more, or until set. Cool and cut into 2-inch squares. Cut each square diagonally. Yield: 32.

NANCYE WINTER

CHESS BARS

1 box Pillsbury Plus Yellow Cake
   mix or lemon flavored cake mix

½ c. margarine, melted
1 egg

Mix ingredients with a fork. Pat into greased 9" x 13" pan.

TOPPING

1 (8 oz) pkg. cream cheese
2 eggs

1 lb. confectioners' sugar

Combine all ingredients thoroughly with mixer. Pour over first layer and bake for 40 to 45 minutes at 350°. Let cool and cut into squares. Store in refrigerator. Yield: 24.

DIANNE GIBSON

BROWNIES

Wonderfully rich and chewy brownies

4 (1 oz.) squares unsweetened
   chocolate
1 c. butter or margarine
2 c. sugar
4 eggs, beaten

1 c. self-rising flour
1 t. vanilla
½-1 c. pecans, chopped (optional)
Confectioners' sugar (optional)

Melt chocolate and butter in top of double boiler. Remove from heat. Add sugar, mixing well. Add eggs and mix well. Add flour and vanilla. Stir in pecans. Pour in greased and floured 9" x 13" pan. Bake at 350° for 30 minutes. Turn out of pan. Slice into squares when cool. Dust with confectioners' sugar, if desired. Yield: 24.

PEGGY LARUS

DROP DEAD BROWNIES

⅓ c. brewed coffee
1 (16 oz.) pkg. semi-sweet
   chocolate pieces
1 c. butter, cut into 1 T. pieces

4 eggs
1½ c. sugar
½ c. flour
1½ c. pecans, chopped (optional)

Line 9" x 13" baking pan with foil. Grease with margarine. Heat coffee, chocolate and butter over low heat in heavy saucepan until melted and smooth. Cool 10 minutes. Beat eggs with mixer until frothy. Gradually add sugar and continue beating 2 minutes more until light and fluffy. Blend in chocolate mixture. Fold in flour, then nuts. Bake at 375° for about 28 minutes. Cool, cover with foil, and chill at least overnight. Uncover and cut into squares. Store in refrigerator in an air-tight container. Delicious served with raspberry sauce or fresh raspberries. Yield: 24 to 48.

ANDY BENNETT

DREAMY ICED BROWNIES

Well worth the calories!

1 c. butter
4 (1 oz.) squares unsweetened
   baking chocolate
4 eggs, slightly beaten
2 c. sugar

1 t. vanilla
1½ c. plus 2 T. flour
½ t. baking powder
½ t. salt
1 c. pecans, chopped

Melt butter and chocolate and cool. Beat eggs and sugar; add chocolate mixture and vanilla. Blend well with mixer. Stir in dry ingredients and nuts. Pour into 9" x 13" pan sprayed with no-stick cooking spray. Bake at 375° for 25 to 30 minutes. Frost when cool. Yield: 24.

FROSTING

2 (1 oz.) squares unsweetened
 baking chocolate
3 T. butter
5 T. milk

Pinch of salt
1 t. vanilla
2-3 c. confectioners' sugar

Combine chocolate, butter, and milk in double boiler. Stir until smooth. Remove from heat and add salt and vanilla. Beat in confectioners' sugar until of spreading consistency.

BETTY KOONCE

CHOCOLATE ICED CAKE SQUARES

½ c. butter or margarine
1 c. sugar
1 c. flour, sifted
1 t. vanilla

1 t. baking powder
4 eggs
Pinch of salt
1 (16 oz.) can chocolate syrup

Beat all ingredients for 2 minutes. Pour into greased and floured 9" x 13" baking pan and bake at 350° for 20 minutes.

ICING

1 c. sugar
½ c. butter or margarine

⅓ c. evaporated milk
½ c. semi-sweet chocolate chips

Combine sugar, milk, and butter and let come to a boil for 2 minutes. Remove from heat and add chocolate chips, stir until smooth. Ice brownies while still warm. Yield: 24.

BRENDA WILKINS

GEE GEE'S HAWAIIAN BROWNIES

¾ c. margarine
1 lb. light brown sugar
3 eggs
2 c. flour, measured after sifting

2½ t. baking powder
1 T. vanilla
1 c. pecans, chopped

Cream margarine and sugar. Add eggs and mix well. Combine sifted flour, baking powder and sift into the creamed mixture. Add vanilla and pecans. Divide into 2 (8") square pans and bake at 350° for 15 to 20 minutes, until set. It is important that you flatten brownies with a spatula 2 or 3 times while they cook. If desired, ice with your favorite fudge frosting when cool. Yield: 24.

ALLYN CROSBY

LEMON CRUMB SQUARES

1 (14 oz) can sweetened
   condensed milk
½ c. lemon juice
1 t. grated lemon peel
1 c. dark brown sugar

⅔ c. margarine
1½ c. flour
1 t. baking powder
½ t. salt
1 c. regular oats, uncooked

Mix milk, lemon juice and lemon peel. Set aside. Cream brown sugar and margarine. Mix flour, baking powder, salt and oatmeal. Add this to creamed mixture and mix until crumbly. Spread half this mixture in a greased 9" x 13" pan. Pat down. Spread milk mixture over top. Cover with remaining crumb mixture, crumbling over top. Bake at 350° for 25 minutes. Cool and cut into squares. Yield: 24.

PECAN BARS

1 c. brown sugar
¼ c. butter, softened
1 egg, beaten
1 c. flour

½ t. baking powder
1 c. chopped pecans
1 t. vanilla

Cream sugar and butter. Beat in egg. Mix flour and baking powder and add to creamed mixture. Mix well. Mix in pecans and vanilla. Pour into a greased and floured 8" square pan. Bake at 325° for 25 minutes. Cool, then cut into squares. Yield: 16 to 20.

SHARON PHILLIPS

STRAWBERRY-ALMOND BARS

1¼ c. flour
⅓ c. light brown sugar, firmly packed

½ c. butter, softened

Grease and flour a 9" square baking pan. In a large bowl combine all ingredients. Beat at low speed, scraping sides of bowl often, until mixture is crumbly (about 1 to 2 minutes). Press into prepared pan and bake at 350° for 15 to 20 minutes, or until edges are lightly browned.

FILLING

¾ c. flour
½ c. light brown sugar, firmly packed
¼ c. butter, softened

⅛ t. salt
½ t. almond extract
¾ c. strawberry preserves

Combine all filling ingredients except preserves. Beat at low speed, scraping sides of bowl often, until well mixed (about 1 to 2 minutes). Set aside. Spread preserves to within ½ inch of hot crust. Sprinkle filling over preserves. Return to oven and continue baking at 350° for 20 to 25 additional minutes, or until edges are lightly browned. Let cool.

GLAZE

¾ c. confectioners' sugar   1 T. milk

Combine sugar and milk and mix until smooth. Drizzle glaze over bars when they have completely cooled. Cut into bars and serve. Yield: 36 small bars.

CELIE GEHRING

Q   SUNSHINE KRISPS

Fabulous and easy—everybody wants the recipe!

1½ to 2 pkgs. plain or cinnamon
   graham crackers
1 c. butter or margarine
1 c. brown sugar

1 c. chopped nuts; any
   combination of pecans,
   walnuts, almonds

Cover bottom of foil-lined jelly roll pan with graham crackers. Melt butter in saucepan and add brown sugar. Add nuts and boil for 2 minutes, stirring constantly. Pour hot mixture evenly over graham crackers. Bake at 350° for 10 minutes. Cut into squares while warm.

MARGARET BARGATZE

THERESA'S TENNIS BARS

Great to serve your tennis buddies after a match!

½ c. butter
½ c. brown sugar
1 c. flour
1 c. brown sugar
2 t. vanilla
½ t. baking powder

½ c. coconut
2 eggs
2 T. flour
¼ t. salt
1 c. nuts (optional)

Mix first 3 ingredients until crumbly and pat into a 9" x 9" or 9" x 13" pan. Bake at 350° for about 10 minutes or until slightly brown. Mix together remaining ingredients and pour over crust. Bake at 350° for 20 to 25 minutes longer, until slightly brown. Cool and cut into squares. Yield: 25.

ENGLISH TOFFEE BARS

1 c. butter
1 c. brown sugar, packed
1 t. vanilla
½ t. salt

2 c. flour
10 (1.55 oz) Hershey milk
   chocolate bars
1 c. chopped nuts

Cream butter, sugar, vanilla and salt. Add flour slowly, while mixing well. Press dough into ungreased jelly roll pan. Bake at 300° for 45 to 55 minutes until golden brown. Remove from oven and arrange chocolate bars on top. As soon as melted, spread chocolate to completely cover, then sprinkle with nuts. Press nuts lightly with hand to make them adhere. Cut in bars while warm, remove from pan, and refrigerate. (If you attempt to cut after cool, the bars and chocolate will break.) Shorter cooking time results in a softer, chewy cookie bar; longer cooking time produces a harder, crisper, and toffee-like bar. Yield: 50.

JULIA KIMBRELL

BIRDS' NESTS

Perfect for Easter jellybeans.

2½ c. crisped rice cereal
1 c. coconut, shredded
⅓ c. light corn syrup

½ c. brown sugar
¾ c. peanut butter
1 t. vanilla

Combine cereal and coconut in bowl and set aside. Bring remaining ingredients just to a boil, stirring constantly. Remove from heat and stir in the cereal mixture. Let cool until you can handle and then, using buttered hands, shape into nests. Fill with jellybeans. Yield: 12.

ROBIN SLATER

MINI CHEESECAKES

They melt in your mouth!

5 T. margarine, melted
1 c. graham cracker crumbs, finely
  crushed

2 (8 oz.) pkgs. cream cheese
¾ c. sugar
3 eggs, separated

Put ¼ t. melted margarine in each of 48 mini tart sections. Add 1 t. graham cracker crumbs to each. Shake pans until crumbs mix with margarine, then turn over once to remove excess crumbs. Beat cream cheese and sugar. Add egg yolks and mix well. Beat egg whites until stiff and fold into creamed mixture. Put 1 T. of cream cheese mixture into each tart section. Bake at 325° for 15 minutes.

TOPPING

1 pt. sour cream
5 T. sugar

2 t. vanilla

Blend sour cream, sugar and vanilla. Fill hollow of tarts with 1 t. of sour cream mixture. Bake an additional 5 minutes at 350°. Cool completely. After removing from pans, store in refrigerator. Freeze well. Yield: 48.

GAY JEWETT

321

MINIATURE CHOCOLATE CHIP CHEESECAKES

1 (8 oz.) pkg. cream cheese
⅓ c. sugar
1 egg

Pinch of salt
½-1 c. chocolate chips
8 to 12 paper cupcake liners

Mix all ingredients except chocolate chips with a hand mixer. Stir in chocolate chips by hand. Place cupcake liners in muffin tin. Fill liners with cream cheese mixture close to top of liner. These do not rise much. If you fill them to the top, you'll get about 8; smaller amounts yield about 12. Bake at 350° 20 to 25 minutes for larger ones, 15 to 20 minutes for smaller ones. Cool to room temperature, then store in refrigerator, if desired. Yield 8 to 12.

GIANT CHOCOLATE CHIP COOKIES

2½ c. flour
1 t. baking soda
1 c. butter or margarine, softened
½ c. sugar
1 c. light brown sugar, packed

2 t. vanilla
3 eggs, beaten
1 (12 oz) pkg. mini chocolate chips
1 c. chopped nuts (optional)

Grease cookie trays. Mix flour and soda together, set aside. Combine butter, sugars and vanilla until creamy. Stir in eggs and gently add flour mixture. Add chips and nuts. Bake 5 to 6 large cookies per pan for 11 minutes at 375° or until center section is just barely done. Allow to set on pan several minutes before removing. Yield: 12 to 15 cookies.

WHITE CHOCOLATE CHUNK MACADAMIA NUT COOKIES

⅔ c. butter
½ c. sugar
½ c. dark brown sugar, packed
1 egg
1 t. vanilla

1½ c. flour
1 jar (3½ oz.) macadamia nuts,
   chopped coarsely
2 bars (3 oz.) white chocolate,
   chopped in ½ inch pieces

Lightly grease cookie sheet. In a large bowl, mix butter, sugars, egg and vanilla until fluffy. Reduce speed and add flour. Stir in nuts and chocolate. Drop by tablespoons onto prepared cookie sheet and bake at 325° for 17 minutes or until edges are slightly brown and tops look dry. Cool on rack.

DIANNE GIBSON

CHOCOLATE MIXED FRUIT COOKIES

2 T. milk
½ c. butter
½ c. sugar
5 T. powdered milk
1-2 T. cocoa

½ t. vanilla
Dash of sherry (optional)
1 c. mixed dried fruit bits
1 c. flaked coconut
2 c. cornflakes, crushed

Put milk, butter, and sugar in a saucepan and stir until sugar is dissolved. Pour contents into bowl. Add powdered milk and beat until well-mixed. Stir in cocoa, vanilla, and sherry. Add fruit, coconut, and cornflakes and mix thoroughly. Form into small balls. The balls are difficult to form, but they stay together once refrigerated. Place on a tray covered with wax paper. Chill balls uncovered until firm to touch. Yield: 36.

EFFIE YOUNG

GINGER SNAPS

¾ c. shortening
1 c. sugar
1 egg
¼ c. molasses
2 c. flour

1 T. ground ginger
2 t. ground cinnamon
½ t. salt
2 t. baking soda
Additional granulated sugar

Cream shortening and sugar until light and fluffy. Add egg and molasses and mix well. Combine remaining dry ingredients except sugar and add to creamed mixture one-fourth at a time. Roll dough into 1" balls and drop in bag of granulated sugar. Bake 2 inches apart on ungreased cookie sheets at 350° for 10 minutes. Yield: 4 dozen.

JUDY BRANHAM

HOLLY WREATHS

Fun for children and a must for Christmas caroling parties!

½ c. margarine
30 large marshmallows
½ t. vanilla
3½ c. cornflakes

1-2 t. red cinnamon candies
1½ t. green food coloring (or
     more, for greener wreaths)

Melt margarine. Add marshmallows and stir over low heat. Add vanilla and coloring. Stir until well blended. Remove from heat and fold in cornflakes. Line cookie sheets with wax paper and grease a tablespoon. Drop by spoonfuls onto paper. By hand, shape into 2-inch wreaths. Decorate with cinnamon candies for berries. To harden quickly, place in freezer until firm. Yield: 24.

ALLYN CROSBY

COOKIES AND CANDIES

LACE COOKIES

Great Christmas cookies. Very thin and light.

1 c. sifted flour
1 c. pecans, finely chopped
½ c. light corn syrup

¼ c. butter
¼ c. shortening
⅔ c. brown sugar, firmly packed

Blend flour and chopped pecans. Bring next 4 ingredients to a boil. Add to flour mixture. Drop by spoonful on greased cookie sheet (use new or good condition cookie sheets for best results). Bake at 325° for 8 to 10 minutes.

ANDY BENNETT

SCOTCH OAT CRISPY COOKIES

1 (6 oz.) pkg. butterscotch chips
1 c. sugar
½ c. oleo
1 egg
1 t. vanilla
1 t. almond extract
1 c. sifted flour

½ t. salt
1 c. rolled oats
1 c. flaked coconut
Raisins (optional)
Nutmeg
Sliced almonds

Melt chips over hot water and let cool. Cream oleo and sugar until light and fluffy. Add egg and beat. Blend in melted chips and extracts. Sift flour and salt and add to creamed mixture. Mix well. Stir in oats, then coconut. Add raisins, if desired. Drop by teaspoonfuls onto greased cookie sheets. Sprinkle with nutmeg and press almond on top of each. Bake at 350° for 8 to 12 minutes, or until very lightly browned. Let set a minute before trying to remove them carefully from cookie sheets. Yield: 5 dozen.

LILLIAN HAMILTON

OATMEAL COOKIES

3 c. brown sugar
1½ c. butter
3 eggs
3 c. flour
1½ t. baking soda
Dash of salt

3 c. oatmeal
1 t. vanilla
1 c. raisins
1 c. coconut
1 c. nuts (pecans or walnuts)

Cream sugar and butter. Add eggs and beat well. Sift flour, soda and salt. Fold in egg mixture. Add oatmeal, then vanilla, raisins, coconut and nuts. Bake at 350° for 10 minutes or less. Do not overbake. Remove from oven when moisture is gone from top. Cookies bake more easily if dough is made the night before. Yield: 5 dozen.

GAIL SMITH

LOW-FAT CHOLESTEROL-FREE OATMEAL COOKIES *L*

¼ c. margarine
½ c. brown sugar
½ c. sugar
1 egg white
1 t. vanilla

1 c. flour
1 c. rolled oats, uncooked
½ t. baking powder
½ t. baking soda
½ c. raisins

Cream margarine and sugars together. Beat in egg white and vanilla. Combine remaining ingredients and add to creamed mixture. Drop onto greased cookie sheets and bake at 350° for 10 minutes. Yield: 30 (2-inch) cookies.

KATHARINE MAXWELL

CHOCOLATE PEANUT BUTTER COOKIES

A real hit with children!

½ c. peanut butter
40 round Ritz crackers

8 (1 oz.) squares chocolate
flavored candy coating

Spread about 1 teaspoon peanut butter on 20 crackers and top with remaining crackers. Melt chocolate candy coating in top of a double boiler and dip crackers in chocolate. Place on plastic wrap paper to cool. Yield: 20.

SANDY KING

PEANUT BUTTER COOKIES

These remind me of "the ones my mother used to make."

1 (16 oz.) jar natural peanut butter
1⅔ c. sugar

4 egg whites

Combine peanut butter and sugar. Beat egg whites until stiff. Fold in egg whites. Drop by teaspoons onto pans. Flatten with prongs of a fork. Bake at 325° for 20 minutes. Remove from pan quickly. Yield: 4 to 5 dozen.

SUE JETT

PECAN BUTTER FINGERS

1 c. butter, softened
½ c. confectioners' sugar
2 c. flour

½ t. salt
2 t. vanilla
1 c. chopped pecans

Beat butter and sugar until creamy and fluffy. Gradually mix in flour. Stir in salt, vanilla and pecans. Using level tablespoon of dough, shape into 2" long fingers. Place on ungreased cookie sheet. Bake at 350° for 15 to 20 minutes, until lightly browned. Remove from cookie sheet. Cool completely. Yield: 48.

CAROL FLIPPEN

MR. GEORGE'S FAMOUS RAISIN COOKIES

3 eggs, beaten
1¼ c. raisins
2 t. vanilla
1 c. margarine
1 c. brown sugar
1 c. sugar

2½ c. flour
1 t. salt
1 t. cinnamon
2 t. baking soda
½ t. almond extract
2 c. oatmeal

Combine the eggs, raisins and vanilla. Store covered in the refrigerator for at least 1 hour or as long as overnight. Cream together the margarine and sugars. Set aside. Mix together the flour, salt, cinnamon and baking soda. Add this dry mixture to the creamed. Stir the almond extract into the raisin and egg mixture. Add this to the dough. Stir in the oatmeal. The dough will be very stiff. Spoon onto greased cookie sheets and bake 18 to 20 minutes at 375°. Cool on wire racks and store in airtight containers or zip lock bags when cooled. Yield: 5 to 6 dozen.

LEIGH FARMER

NANA'S ROCKS

A family favorite at Christmas!

3 c. light brown sugar
2 c. butter
6 eggs
½ t. salt
5 c. flour

3 t. baking soda dissolved in ½ c. hot water
2½ t. ground cinnamon
1½ lbs. raisins
3 lbs. chopped nuts

Combine all ingredients. Drop by spoonfuls on greased pan. Bake at 350° until browned, about 10 to 15 minutes. Yield: 50.

CINDY BROOKS

RUSSIAN TEA BALLS

2 c. corn flakes, finely crushed
1 c. butter or margarine
⅓ c. sugar
2 t. vanilla

2 c. sifted cake flour
1 t. cinnamon
1 c. finely chopped nuts
1½ c. sifted confectioners' sugar

Cream butter, sugar, and vanilla. Sift together flour and cinnamon; add with corn flake crumbs and nuts to creamed mixture. Mix well. Shape into small 1½" balls and place on greased baking sheets. Bake at 350° about 20 minutes. Roll at once in powdered sugar. Yield: 48.

JANET DAUGHDRILLE

HICKORY CHIPS

Rich, delicious cookies!

1 c. butter
1 c. confectioners' sugar
1½ c. flour
½ t. baking soda

1 t. vanilla
1 c. oatmeal
½ t. salt
Chocolate sprinkles

Cream butter and sugar. Add remaining ingredients except sprinkles and mix well. Form into several (more than 3) rolls. Roll in chocolate sprinkles, wrap in wax paper, and chill until firm. (For instant baking, put in freezer for 30 minutes.) Slice into ¼-inch slices and bake at 325° for about 10 minutes. Yield: 5 dozen.

SUSAN STANEWICK

KACEY'S HARLEQUIN PINWHEELS

Worth the effort!

¾ c. margarine, very soft
1½ c. light brown sugar
3 egg yolks

1½ t. vanilla
3 c. flour
¾ t. baking powder

Mix margarine and sugar. Add egg yolks, vanilla, flour, and baking powder. Mix well. Divide dough in 3 parts and roll with rolling pin between 2 pieces of waxed paper. Shape into rectangles, using your fingers.

FILLING

3 T. butter
1½ (6 oz.) pkgs. chocolate chips
1 (14 oz.) can sweetened
   condensed milk

1 T. vanilla
1½ c. pecans, chopped and
   divided into thirds

Melt butter and chocolate chips together. Add condensed milk and vanilla. Divide into 3 parts. Spread ⅓ of filling on each of three dough rectangles. Sprinkle each rectangle with ⅓ of nuts. Roll up rectangles from longest edge, lifting up waxed paper to help. When completely rolled, place in freezer. Slice frozen and bake on cookie sheets covered with foil at 350° for approximately 15 minutes. Have oven rack up one notch from bottom. Do not try to remove from cookie sheets until completely cool.

KACEY CARNEAL

COOKIES AND CANDIES

NUT COOKIES

Great gift cookies!

1 lb. butter
1 lb. light brown sugar
2 eggs
2 t. vanilla

4 c. flour
1 t. baking powder
1 lb. chopped pecans, macadamia or cashews

Combine all ingredients. (If using Macadamias, add 1 t. grated orange and 1 t. orange extract.) Divide dough into 6 portions, shaping each into a roll approximately 1¾" in diameter. Wrap in wax paper and freeze or chill for at least 2 hours. Slice ¼" thick. Bake at 350° for about 10 minutes, being careful to not let them get too brown.

KACEY CARNEAL

PAINTED COOKIES

A nice alternative to dyeing boiled eggs for Easter.

1½ c. sifted confectioners' sugar
1 c. butter
1 egg
1 t. vanilla
½ t. almond extract

2½ c. flour
1 t. baking soda
1 t. cream of tartar
Additional sugar for sprinkling

Cream sugar and butter. Mix in egg and flavorings. Sift flour, baking soda, cream of tartar and add to creamed mixture. Refrigerate 2 to 3 hours. Divide dough in half and refrigerate unused portion. Roll out dough onto floured surface to ¼-inch thickness. Cut with cutters or homemade cardboard shapes. Paint designs on cookies, sprinkle with sugar, and bake at 375° for 7 to 8 minutes, until lightly browned. Yield: 5 dozen.

PAINT

For each color, use:

1 egg yolk
¼ t. water

Food coloring (amount depends on intensity desired)

For each paint color, combine ingredients in custard cup and mix well. Use a separate small paintbrush for each color.

PEANUT BUTTER CUP TARTS

Kids love to help with these!

36 Reese's miniature peanut butter cups, refrigerated ahead of time

1 (15 oz.) roll of refrigerated peanut butter cookie dough

328

Refrigerate candies so wrappers will peel off easily. Unwrap each. Spray mini-muffin tins with no-stick vegetable spray. Follow slicing instructions on cookie dough and quarter each slice. Place each piece in a mini-muffin pan. Bake at 350° for 8 to 10 minutes, or until cookies puff up. Remove from oven and immediately push a candy cup into each cookie filled muffin cup. The cookie will deflate and come around the candy. Let pan cool, then refrigerate until shine leaves the chocolate. Remove from refrigerator and lift each tart from the cup with the tip of a knife. Yield: 36.

CATHY LEE

SWISS CINNAMON STARS *L*

Traditional Swiss Christmas cookies

2 egg whites
1¼ c. sugar
1 T. cinnamon
9 oz. unblanched almonds, ground

1 T. lemon juice
1 T. lemon rind, grated
1½ c. confectioners' sugar

Beat egg whites until stiff. Add sugar and cinnamon slowly and beat another 10 minutes. Set aside 5 T. of this mixture for the glaze. Fold in almonds, lemon juice and rind and knead into a dough. Let stand for 15 minutes. On a flat surface heavily dusted with confectioners' sugar, roll out the dough to about ⅓-inch thickness. Cut out with a star cookie cutter. Place on cookie sheets lined with wax paper. Let stand for 30 minutes. Make a glaze from the reserved egg white mixture and enough confectioners' sugar to slightly thicken. Brush the glaze on the cookies and bake at 390° for 15 minutes.

MARGARET LAMPE

SUGAR COOKIES

⅔ c. shortening
¾ c. sugar
½ t. vanilla
1 egg

4 t. milk
2 c. sifted flour
1½ t. baking powder
¼ t. salt

Cream first 3 ingredients together. Add the egg, then the milk. Mix dry ingredients and add to creamed mixture. Chill for an hour. Roll out and cut with cookie cutters. Bake on greased cookie sheet at 375° for 6 to 8 minutes. (Can be iced with frosting of confectioners' sugar thinned with milk and colored with food coloring or can sprinkle with sugar.) Yield: 36.

ROBIN SLATER

Q   ORNAMENTAL FROSTING FOR COOKIES

3¾ c. sifted confectioners' sugar   3 egg whites
¼ t. cream of tartar

In a small bowl at low speed mix all until just combined. Increase speed to high and beat until stiff enough that a knife drawn through leaves a clean line. Food coloring may be added for color, if desired.

BUTTER CREAMS

½ c. butter, softened
1 lb. plus 2 c. sifted confectioners'
  sugar
½ t. salt (scant)

½ (14 oz) can sweetened
  condensed milk
1 T. vanilla

Mix all ingredients together with hands until well-blended and form into a large ball. Refrigerate, covered, for several hours. Roll into 3 to 4 dozen small bite-sized balls, cover and return to refrigerator for several additional hours.

CHOCOLATE COATING

2 T. butter
4 (1 oz) squares unsweetened
  chocolate

1" paraffin

Melt butter, chocolate and paraffin over hot water and stir until thoroughly mixed. Dip balls in chocolate mixture and cool on wax paper. Work quickly so that chocolate coating will not harden. Store in refrigerator. Yield: 3 to 4 dozen.

JANE NOTT

APRICOT COCONUT BALLS

1½ c. dried apricots, minced
1 c. coconut
½ c. sweetened condensed milk

Confectioners' sugar
Glacéed cherries (optional)

Mix together all ingredients. Refrigerate 1 to 2 hours, then shape mixture into balls. Roll balls in confectioners' sugar. Place ½ glacéed cherry on top of each ball, if desired. Yield: 30 to 40.

EFFIE YOUNG

COCONUT BALLS

Tastes like Mounds!

1 lb confectioners' sugar	1 (14 oz) bag coconut
1 (14 oz) can sweetened condensed milk	1 (12 oz) bag chocolate chips
	1 block paraffin wax

Mix first 3 ingredients by hand and chill for 20 minutes. After mixture has cooled, form into balls. Prepare chocolate mixture by melting chips and wax together in microwave on high in 45 second intervals, stirring in between, until melted. Dip each ball into chocolate, using either a dipping fork or toothpick. Cool on aluminum foil. Refrigerate until use. Yield: 3 to 4 dozen.

BARBARA VRANIAN

EASY $5,000 FUDGE

Easy to make and great for gifts!

3 (6 oz) pkgs. semi-sweet chocolate chips	¼ t. cream of tartar
1 lb. margarine	1 (12 oz) can evaporated milk
4½ c. sugar	1 t. vanilla
	1 c. pecans, chopped

Place chocolate chips and margarine in a large bowl. In a saucepan, mix sugar, cream of tartar and milk. Let come to a boil and boil for 6 minutes stirring constantly. Pour over chocolate chips and margarine. Stir until melted. Add vanilla and nuts. Pour into greased 9" x 11" pan and cool for 1 hour. Refrigerate. Yield: 99 (1") squares.

BANE WILLIAMS

CHOLESTEROL-FREE MICROWAVE FUDGE

1 lb. confectioners' sugar	¼ c. milk
½ c. cocoa	1 t. vanilla
½ c. margarine (not butter), melted	1 c. nuts, chopped (optional)

Mix sugar and cocoa in a microwave safe bowl. Make a hole in the center and pour in milk and margarine. Microwave on high for 2 minutes; stir. Add vanilla and nuts. Stir completely. Pour into buttered 8" square pan and refrigerate until set. Yield: Approximately 36 squares.

SALLY BAGLEY
PAGE MARCHETTI

VARIATION: Use skim milk, canola margarine and omit the vanilla.

SUE WHITTAKER

COOKIES AND CANDIES

PEANUT BUTTER BALLS

1 c. butter
1 (18 oz) jar crunchy peanut butter
1 T. vanilla
1 c. graham cracker crumbs
1 c. coconut

1 lb. confectioners' sugar
1 (12 oz.) pkg. semi-sweet
   chocolate chips
½ bar paraffin wax

Melt butter. Add peanut butter and vanilla. In a large bowl, mix next 3 ingredients. Blend peanut butter mixture into dry ingredients. Form into balls and refrigerate for ½ hour or more. Melt paraffin in small pan, and add chocolate chips. Dip peanut butter balls (on toothpicks) in warm chocolate coating. Place on wax paper, remove toothpicks and dot hole with chocolate. Keep in refrigerator or freezer for months. Yield: 90 to 100 balls.

GAIL SMITH

This recipe is dedicated with appreciation and affection to Sparky and Toby, who never failed to greet us cheerfully at our early morning meetings, who lay at our feet and warmed our toes on damp days, and who willingly shared their territory with five women bearing sometimes strange foods to be tasted. We thank you.

THE COOKBOOK COMMITTEE

TOBY TREATS

An unusual and thoughtful holiday gift for your favorite dog lover and his faithful companion.

¾ c. hot canned condensed
   chicken broth
⅓ c. margarine

½ c. non-fat dry milk
1 egg, beaten
3 c. whole wheat flour

In a large bowl, pour hot broth over margarine and stir until melted. Stir in dry milk and egg. Add flour, 1 c. at a time. (Dough becomes very stiff; it will have to be mixed by hand.) Knead for several minutes. Pat to ½" thickness and cut with a dog bone-shaped cookie cutter. Bake on a cookie sheet for 50 minutes at 325°. Allow to cool completely and dry out for at least 3 hours. These are not overly crunchy, but are enough so that pooches like them.

ANN BEAUCHAMP

Hints for Healthier Eating

Visit your nearest bookstore or library and you will be amazed by the growing numbers of health, nutrition, and diet books. With all of that variety available, it is possible to choose a few basic principles by which to formulate an eating plan for a healthy, active life. The American Heart Association (AHA) suggests the following:

- Meet your daily needs for protein, vitamins, minerals and other nutrients.
- Achieve and maintain your ideal body weight.
- Reduce your total fat intake to about 30% of your calories (1 gram of fat equals 9 calories; thus, for a daily calorie intake of 1500, grams of fat should not exceed 50).
- Limit your saturated fat intake to less than 10% of your total daily calories.
- Keep your cholesterol intake under 300 milligrams per day.
- Limit polyunsaturated fat to less than 10% of your total daily calories.
- Make changes in your diet gradually so that they become permanent eating habits.

Other recommendations include:

- Regular exercise (increase activity if cholesterol is high);
- High fiber (complex carbohydrates);
- Low sodium (average 2,000 to 3,000 mg. daily);
- Low caffeine;
- Low sugar;
- 6 to 8 cups of water daily.

HOW TO LOWER FATS AND CHOLESTEROL

According to Dr. Art Ulene of the American Medical Association's Campaign Against Cholesterol, fats are important in a well-balanced diet as a source of energy; as building blocks for vital substances made by the body; and as transportation for compounds, such as fat-soluble vitamins, throughout the body. The American Heart Association tells us that saturated fats are found in most animal products and hydrogenated vegetable products. These fats raise the blood cholesterol level, although sometimes appear in products advertised as "cholesterol-free". Examples are meat fats from beef, pork, ham and lamb; the fat in butter, cream, whole milk and whole milk cheeses; hydrogenated shortenings in coconut oil, cocoa butter, palm oil and palm kernel oil. These oils are found in many store-bought bakery goods, candies, fried foods , and in non-dairy milk and cream substitutes.

The AHA recommends substituting polyunsaturates and monosaturates for those fats that are saturated. Polyunsaturated oils are usually liquid oils of vegetable origin. These oils tend to lower the blood cholesterol level. Look for "liquid oil" as the first ingredient on the label. Examples are corn, cottonseed, soybean, safflower and sunflower oils. Monosaturated oils may also lower blood cholesterol, but not as effectively as the polyunsaturates. Examples are olive, canola and peanut oils.

Dr. Ulene suggests that if saturated fat consumption is limited, then the cholesterol will take care of itself. Usually cholesterol and saturated fat go hand in hand; that is, if one is low, then so is the other. Two foods which are exceptions, shrimp and egg yolks, are both high in cholesterol but low in saturated fats. Cholesterol is a fat-like substance found in all animal products, but in especially high levels in egg yolks and organ meats, and moderately high levels in shellfish. Saturated fat can cause your cholesterol blood level to rise more than a cholesterol-rich food itself. The liver uses saturated fats to make cholesterol. The excess forms "plaques" which block the flow of blood through the heart's arteries. The higher the cholesterol rises, the more rapidly the cardiovascular risk increases. Lowering your cholesterol level reverses that risk factor, and may even reverse the plaque build-up itself.

Consider the following substitutions suggested by the American Heart Association:

INSTEAD OF:	USE:
1 c. butter (498 mg. cholesterol)	⅞ c. polyunsaturated oil (0 mg. cholesterol) or 1 c. tub margarine (polyunsaturated oil partially hydrogenated—0 mg. cholesterol) or 1 c. margarine (partially hydrogenated, but lower in polyunsaturates than tub margarine— 0 mg. cholesterol)
1 c. heavy cream (832 calories, 286 mg. cholesterol)	1 c. evaporated skimmed milk (176 calories, 8 mg. cholesterol)
1 medium whole egg (274 mg. cholesterol)	¼ c. egg substitute (0 mg. cholesterol, but check labels, some brands do contain cholesterol)
1 c. high-fat (creamy) yogurt, plain (250 calories)	1 c. part-skim yogurt, plain (125 to 145 calories)
1 c. sour cream (416 calories)	1 c. Mock Sour Cream (See Dairy Products—160 calories)
1 oz. baking chocolate (8.4 grams saturated fat)	3 T. cocoa powder plus 1 T. polyunsaturated oil (1.7 grams saturated fat plus 1.1 grams saturated fat)

HINTS FOR HEALTHIER EATING

Try these other ideas to reduce the intake of food and cholesterol in your food plan:

FATS

Use the tub or liquid varieties of margarine. More air is whipped in, providing fewer fats and calories.

Use non-stick cookware and/or vegetable oil spray. One and a quarter seconds of spray is about 7 calories and 1 gram of fat. One tablespoon of oil is about 120 calories and 14 grams of fat. One tablespoon of margarine is 100 calories and 11 grams of fat.

Use shakeable dry butter substitute in place of butter or margarine as a vegetable topper.

Use sodium-free packets of chicken broth instead of cooking oil when sautéing. Broth can be made ahead and stored in the refrigerator.

When choosing margarine, select the one that lists liquid vegetable oil rather than partially hydrogenated vegetable oil as the first ingredient. Also, check that the amount of cholesterol-raising saturated fat is no more than 2 grams per tablespoon. The healthiest forms of margarine are "diet", squeeze bottle, and tub margarines; they are the lowest in saturated fat.

Instead of flour roux requiring fat, use cornstarch mixed with water as a thickener.

Skim excess fat from cooked foods prior to eating them. If refrigerated, hardened fat can be removed from the tops of soups and gravies. If hot, use a bulb baster to skim fat from the tops. Celery leaves can be used to skim the fat from the top of soup as it cooks.

For marinating and basting, use no-oil Italian dressings or 4 t. Dijon mustard + 2½ t. honey + 2½ t. rough-grain mustard.

Try substituting juice for some of the oil in a cake (such as apple juice in an apple cake).

Replace oil or fat with corn syrup in muffin recipes.

If a recipe calls for bacon fat, use only one-forth the suggested amount. Substitute canola or safflower oil for one-fourth and water, vinegar, or cooking stock for the remaining half.

HINTS FOR HEALTHIER EATING

DAIRY PRODUCTS

Mock Sour Cream Recipes:

- 2 T. skim milk + 1 T. lemon juice + 1 c. low-fat cottage cheese, processed in blender until smooth and creamy. (American Heart Association)
- 1 c. low-fat cottage cheese + 1 t. minced prepared horseradish. Purée cheese in blender, then add horseradish.
- ½ c. water or skim milk + 1 c. low-fat cottage cheese + 1 T. lemon juice + ⅛ t. salt. Cream all in blender. (Laura Lee Chandler)
- 1 T. white vinegar + 1 c. evaporated milk.
- In most dishes, you can substitute plain, non-fat yogurt for sour cream.

(If using sour cream or mock sour cream in a hot dish, add it at the last minute so that it does not separate.)

Try non-fat yogurt as an easy way to cut fat and calories in traditional recipes:

Mayonnaise = 1 c. yogurt + 1 t. prepared mustard + salt and pepper to taste.
Pudding = 1 c. yogurt + 1 pack sugar-free instant pudding mix.
Base for dips = 1 c. yogurt + 1 c. Ricotta cheese.
Ranch dressing = 1 c. yogurt + 1 envelope Ranch dressing mix.
Fresh fruit dressing = 1 c. yogurt + ½ c. chopped chutney.
Meat dressing = ½ c. yogurt + 1 t. prepared horseradish.
Raw vegetable dip = 1 c. yogurt + 1 T. salsa.
Mock Hollandaise = 1 c. yogurt + 1 t. Dijon mustard.
Hot pasta dressing = 1 c. yogurt + ⅓ c. Dijon mustard.

Cream Cheese Substitute:
Line a strainer with doubled cheesecloth or 2 coffee filters. Spoon in 2 cups plain or flavored yogurt without added gelatin or pectin. Place strainer over a bowl, but do not allow strainer to touch bottom of bowl. Bowl will catch draining whey. Cover and refrigerate until of desired consistency. (Wait 30 minutes for sour cream consistency and 14 to 24 hours for cream cheese consistency.) Note: yogurt cheese will separate or thin in cooking. This can be remedied by adding a little flour, yogurt, and egg or egg substitute. Add to hot foods at the end of cooking time. (Joan Wilkins)

Drink 1%, ½%, or skim milk instead of 2% milk. These percentages designate the amount of fat in the milk by weight. If computed on a volume basis, 2% milk actually contains 35% fat (5 grams of fat per cup). Whole milk contains 49% fat (8 grams of fat per cup). Non-fat or skim milk contains less than ½ gram of fat per cup.

Choose dairy products that are made from skim or low-fat milk such as: light sour cream, light cream cheese, part-skim ricotta cheese, and reduced-fat cheese.

Evaporated skim milk is a tasty substitute for cream in sauces and other recipes. It has fewer calories and almost no fat. Low-calorie, low-fat buttermilk is another good sauce base.

Substitute 1% low-fat or dry-curd cottage cheese for Ricotta cheese in recipes.

Replace one whole egg with two egg whites. This saves 3 grams of fat and 210 milligrams of cholesterol. Replace only half the yolks in a baked dish because the yolks act as tenderizers.

For "creamy" soups, use cooked, puréed vegetables instead of cream. (Dr. Art Ulene)

Use cheese with a strong flavor so you can cut down on the amount you use. Any cheese with more than 2 grams of total fat per ounce must be eaten sparingly. (Dr. Art Ulene)

MEATS

Try to think of meat as your side dish. Decreasing your meat portion and supplementing it with vegetables lowers your fat, cholesterol and calories.

Look for the leanest cuts of meat. For beef choose sirloin, round, and loin. For pork choose tenderloin, leg (fresh), and shoulder (arm or picnic). For lamb choose leg, arm or loin.

"Select" cuts are lower in fat than "choice" or "prime".

Limit processed meats such as hot dogs, bacon and sausage. Use deli products which substitute turkey for other higher-fat meats. Buy processed meats with no more than 1 gram of fat per serving. Also consider the many low-salt deli meats which are now readily available.

Ounce for ounce, Canadian bacon has 116 fewer calories than regular bacon. Try it in soups that call for bacon.

Substitute ground turkey for ground beef in recipes. Have your turkey ground to order. Commercially ground turkey may include the skin and consequently, more fat.

If you believe the skin is the best part of the chicken, try dipping skinless pieces in skim milk, then in crushed oat bran cereal. Bake.

Add flavor to foods by cooking them in wine. The alcohol evaporates, but the flavor remains. Use wine for sautéing mushrooms and onion. (Dr. Art Ulene)

Remove the skin from poultry before cooking. Otherwise, fat from the skin will be absorbed by the meat as it cooks.

Broil meats on a metal rack so that fat drips off and calories, fat and cholesterol are reduced.

Bake, broil, boil, grill, poach or steam foods instead of frying.

SEAFOOD

Sedentary shellfish (clams, scallops, and mussels) are low in saturated fat and moderately low in cholesterol. Shrimp are high in cholesterol, but low in saturated fat.

Fish low in saturated fat are halibut, cod, sea bass, rockfish, snapper, haddock and perch. The following are higher in saturated fat, but are rich in fatty acids that lower LDL cholesterol and triglycerides: swordfish, tuna, salmon and mackerel.

Sardines, anchovies and caviar are high in cholesterol.

A FEW WORDS ABOUT FIBER

Another means of lowering your blood cholesterol is to increase your intake of soluble fiber, found in complex carbohydrates. Fiber forms a gel which prevents the body's absorption of substances that the liver could potentially use to manufacture cholesterol. Fiber is low in calories and filling. It prevents constipation and helps in weight control by absorbing water to help create a "full feeling".

The amount of soluble fiber that is right for you depends on your sex, weight and activity level. There is the possibility of consuming too much. While Dr. Art Ulene recommends a maximum of 18 grams per day and warns against side effects, author Joseph Piscatella refers to studies suggesting that Americans could benefit from doubling or tripling their average intake of soluble fiber. Consult your family physician to help you determine what is right for you.

Fiber can be found in a wide range of food sources. Beans are rich in protein and can be mixed with rice or other grains, or with vegetables, to become a more complete source of protein. Particularly good are pinto beans, navy beans, kidney beans, black-eyed peas, lentils and soybeans.

Vegetables are high in water content and provide bulk. They are best for you eaten raw. If you choose to cook them, steam lightly, microwave or stir-fry. Remember, the crunchier the better. Among the best fruits are figs, raisins and apples. Apples contain pectin, a substance which helps lower blood cholesterol. The pulp in orange and grapefruit juice is also rich in fiber. Cantaloupe and strawberries help you to feel full without adding many calories and help to satisfy your sweet cravings as well.

Of the natural cereals, those served hot are best, particularly oatmeal and oat bran. Cold cereals tend to be over-processed to the point that they hardly contain any fiber. "Instant" hot cereals are often too rich in sugar and salt.

Breads highest in fiber are whole grain and made from stone-ground flour. The next best are 100% whole wheat, rye or pumpernickel. Do not judge a bread by its color. Ingredients such as raisin juice can be used to color bread. French or Italian breads are low in fat, but also low in fiber. White and French breads and bagels are low in fiber.

When choosing pasta, go for the high-quality brands. Try orzo and some of the unusual Oriental noodles for variety. Rice and other grains include proteins and nutrients as well as fiber. Although more pleasing to the average American eye, white rice has sacrificed nutrients to acquire its color. Try brown and wild rices, bulgur, barley and oatmeal.

WHAT ABOUT SALT?

Each cell of your body is bathed continually in a saline solution. The amount of salt that the body needs daily, however, is only 220 milligrams, or one-tenth of a teaspoon. The average American consumes 4,000 to 8,000 mg. of salt daily, or 15 pounds of salt per year. Nutrition guidelines on the average suggest a daily intake of 2,000 to 3,000 mg. of salt. Author Joseph Piscatella cites the National Research Council's recommendation of ½ to 1½ teaspoons daily, or 1100 to 3300 milligrams.

Excessive salt has been linked to hypertension (high blood pressure), stroke, and kidney and thyroid disease. Sodium causes the body to retain fluid. Too much sodium and fluid overwork the kidneys whose job it is to eliminate them. Blood volume also increases with too much fluid. The heart pumps harder and blood pressure increases. Sodium also causes the small blood vessels to constrict.

Most processed foods and "fast foods" are loaded with sodium. The taste for salt is not innate, but acquired only when we are introduced to it as children. Try to do without your salt shaker. Use spices instead of salt, keep processed foods to a minimum and read labels. At the very least, become aware of the quantity of sodium you are consuming. Try using some of the following substitutes for salt and sugar.

HINTS FOR HEALTHIER EATING

SALT AND SUGAR REPLACEMENTS

Using spices to replace salt and sugar in food can fool the palate and decrease the desire to add salt.

SPICE	USE
oregano, garlic powder	sprinkle directly on green salads or in dressings
fennel	add to low-sodium spaghetti sauce
nutmeg, allspice, cinnamon	sprinkle onto baked apples, cooked carrots, cooked winter squash
cinnamon, vinegar, pinch sugar	mix and pour on sliced tomatoes
Italian or pizza seasonings	rub on chicken before baking
Cajun seasoning	add to low-sodium prepared soups or lean hamburgers
celery seed	add to chicken or egg salad (using a mayo sub!)
caraway seed	add to coleslaw
toasted sesame seeds	sprinkle over steamed vegetables, baked, broiled fish and chicken
garlic cloves	grind over meats, red peppers, before broiling
cilantro, parsley	mince in low-sodium tomato based sauces

IF I DRINK A LOT OF WATER, WON'T I RETAIN THE FLUID?

When we eat foods high in salt, we introduce excess sodium into our bodies. If we then exercise and lose fluid as sweat, the sodium concentration increases. A mechanism triggers our thirst so that when we drink, a proper sodium-to-fluid balance will be restored. When water to the kidneys is insufficient, the liver picks up some of the kidney's functions. At this point the liver cannot do its routine job of metabolizing fat. Sufficient water actually relieves fluid retention. When the body lacks water, it tends to store emergency water supplies outside the cells to be available if needed. This water results in swollen feet, ankles, wrists, hands and legs.

It is recommended that you drink 6 to 8 (8 oz.) glasses of water daily. Water is filling. It helps the body feel satisfied without adding calories. It actually decreases hunger pains. Author Joseph Piscatella refers to research suggesting that snacking is often the result of our mistaking thirst for hunger.

So drink up! Water will help your body to use fat for fuel. Try having a glass before each meal.

WHAT'S SO BAD ABOUT CAFFEINE?

The average person drinks 450 cups of coffee a year. Americans drink 33 million gallons of coffee a day, the equivalent of 30 seconds of full flow at Niagara Falls!

Caffeine is a diuretic, causing the body to expel fluids. It overstimulates the heart and causes your blood sugar level to drop, which in turn causes feelings of hunger, jitters or weakness. Do not skip breakfast, relying on a cup of coffee to jump-start you in the morning. Wake up to a high-fiber cereal or other fiber-rich dish (muffins, pancakes, waffles, etc.) Add fresh fruit or have a glass of juice. Use low-fat or skim milk on your cereal. You will have plenty of energy without stressing your heart. Your teeth will appreciate it, too.

IF A TEASPOON OF SUGAR HAS ONLY 16 CALORIES, WHAT'S WRONG WITH THAT?

The average American adult consumes 128 pounds of sugar each year, and the average American adolescent, 274 pounds of sugar a year! That is roughly 24% of the individual's total calories. Thirty percent of that sugar comes from the sugar bowl, usually for cereal, coffee or tea. Sugar from the processed foods we eat contributes 70%.

There are two problems with overdoing the sugar. One is the obvious impact on our weight. While it is true that a teaspoon of sugar has only 16 calories, enormous amounts of sugar can be packed into very small quantities of food. It may take a lot of that particular food for you to feel full. It is just the opposite with high fiber, water-dense, low-calorie foods such as cantaloupe or strawberries. The second problem is that sugar elevates our triglycerides, a blood fat that can work like cholesterol to clog the arteries.

SO WHY NOT A "LIGHT" COOKBOOK?

Our initial goal was that THE STUFFED COUGAR, TOO would contain only light recipes. What we discovered is that although we are all beginning to give more thought to the food choices we make, we are slow to let go of the tried-and-true favorites that taste so good. For many of us, the word "light" still implies "bland". Low-fat, low-sodium recipes were often returned from our recipe testers marked "needs more cheese" or "would be better with real mayonnaise and sour cream". Consequently, we have included recipes to satisfy a wide range of tastes. For the present, enjoy some good food, have fun in the kitchen, and plan ahead for your indulgences!

Three resources we found most helpful and which we recommend to you are the American Heart Association (particularly the pamphlets "Recipes for Low-Fat, Low-Cholesterol Meals" and "The American Heart Association Diet, reprinted with permission of the American Heart Association; An Eating Plan for Healthy Americans"); the American Medical Association Campaign Against Cholesterol's *Count Out Cholesterol Cookbook* with an introduction by Dr. Art Ulene and recipes by Mary Ward, copyright © 1989 by Feeling Fine Programs, Inc. and Alfred A. Knopf, Inc.; *Controlling Your Fat Tooth* © 1991 by Joseph Piscatella, reprinted by permission of Workman Publishing.

TABLES

DRY MEASUREMENTS

3 t.	=	1 T.
2 T.	=	1 oz.
4 T.	=	¼ c.
16 T.	=	1 c.
2 c.	=	1 pt.
4 c.	=	1 qt.
16 oz.	=	1 lb.
1 lb.	=	454 grams

LIQUID MEASUREMENTS

1 c.	=	8 fluid oz.
2 c.	=	16 fluid oz.
4 c.	=	32 fluid oz.
2 c.	=	1 pt.
2 pt.	=	1 qt.
4 c.	=	1 qt.
4 qt.	=	1 gal.

METRIC MEASUREMENTS*

1 t.	=	5 ml.
1 T.	=	15 ml.
1 c.	=	2 ml.
1 fl. oz.	=	28.35 grams
1 lb.	=	454 grams
1 c.	=	226.8 grams
1 gram	=	.035 oz.
100 grams	=	7 T.
200 grams	=	14 T. or 7 oz.

*milliliter = ml.

TABLE OF EQUIVALENTS

DRY GOODS & BREADS

4 c. all-purpose flour	1 pound
2 c. granulated sugar	1 pound
4 to 4½ c. confectioners' sugar	1 pound
2¼ c. brown sugar	1 pound
3 to 4 c. cooked rice	1 c. uncooked rice
2 c. cooked rice	1 c. uncooked quick rice
2¼ c. cooked macaroni	1 c. (8 oz.) raw noodles
4 c. cooked spaghetti	8 oz. raw spaghetti
6 c. cooked beans	1 pound dry beans (2½ c.)
1 c. soft bread crumbs	2 slices bread
1 c. vanilla wafer crumbs	26 to 30 cookies
1 c. graham cracker crumbs	11 to 12 squares (¼ lb.)

DAIRY

1 c. egg whites	whites of 6 to 7 large eggs
1 c. egg yolks	yolks of 11 to 12 large eggs
2 c. whipped cream	½ pt. heavy cream (1 c.)
2 c. butter or margarine	1 pound
1 c. grated cheese	4 oz.
1 c. cream or cottage cheese	8 oz.
1 c. Parmesan cheese	3 oz.

FRUITS & VEGETABLES

1 c. sliced or chopped apple	1 medium apple
1 c. mashed banana	3 medium bananas
3 c. shredded carrots	1 pound (6 to 8 medium)
1½ c. sweet potatoes	1 pound fresh
1 c. mashed potatoes	2 medium potatoes
2 c. sliced mushrooms	½ pound
5 c. cubed eggplant (14 oz.)	1 medium eggplant
2¾ c. chopped cranberries	3 c. whole (12 oz.)
3 to 4 c. shredded cabbage	½ small head
1 c. chopped bell pepper	1 large pepper
1 c. diced celery	2 medium stalks
1½ c. cooked spinach	12 c. (1 lb.) fresh
3½ c. broccoli	1 medium (9 oz.) bunch
1 c. chopped onion	1 large (5 to 6 oz.) onion
1 c. shelled peas	8 oz. peas
2⅓ c. dry lentils, peas	1 lb. bag peas

TABLES

NUTS & DRIED FRUITS

4 c. chopped pecans, walnuts. . . . . 1 lb. shelled nuts
2 c. shelled pecans. . . . . 1 lb. in shell
3 c. shelled almonds, peanuts . . . . 1 lb. shelled nuts
¾ c. raisins . . . . ¼ lb.
1½ c. candied fruit, peel . . . . ½ lb.
1¼ c. chopped dates. . . . . ½ lb.
1⅓ c. flaked coconut . . . . 4 oz.

MEATS

3 c. cooked chicken, cubed. . . . . 3 lb. whole chicken
2 c. cooked chicken, cubed. . . . . 1½ lbs. chicken breasts
3 c. cooked meat. . . . . 1 lb. raw
2¾ c. cooked ground beef . . . . 1 lb. raw
3 c. crumbled bacon. 1 lb. raw

MISCELLANEOUS

2 to 4 T. lemon juice and 1 t. grated rind. . . . . . 1 lemon
6 to 8 T. orange juice and
   2 to 3 T. grated rind . . . . 1 orange
1 c. chocolate chips. . . . . 6 oz.
1 square unsweetened chocolate. . . . . 1 oz.
2 c. cocoa . . . . 8 oz.
2 T. fat . . . . 1 oz.
80 T. ground coffee . . . . 1 lb.
5 c. popped popcorn . . . . ¼ c. unpopped
40 large marshmallows . . . . 12 oz.

Index

Almond
Trout Meunière or Amandine 176
Athalie's Danish Puff 250
Nut Crust Strawberry Tart 303
Strawberry-Almond Bars 319
Swiss Cinnamon Stars 329
American Baguettes 256
Andy's Gourmet Chili 52
Angel Food Trifle 304
Angel Hair Flans 237
Angel Hair Pasta with Broccoli and
Chipped Beef 196
"Angel of Mercy" Baked Custard 308
Antipasto Sea Shell Salad 82
APPETIZERS AND SNACKS
(See Chapter Index, 9)
Cold Appetizers 10–13
Chocolate Dip for Strawberries 311
Cold Dips 13–15
Cold Spreads 16–20
Hot Appetizers 20–24
Baked Stuffed Clams 176
Hot Dips 24–26
Crab Remick 170
Hot Spreads 26
Snacks 27–30
Apple & Applesauce
Apple Bavarian Torte 297
Apple-Cranberry Casserole 238
Apple Cranberry Pie 282
Apple Delight 238
Apple Muffins 252
Applesauce Whole Wheat Bread 256
Delicious Apple Spread 16
Hot Spiced Cider 38
Wassail 38
Winter Squash and Apple Soup 48
Swedish Cabbage Dish 220
Nana's Kugel (Noodle Pudding) 238
Healthy Fried Apples 239
Glazed Apple Bread 244
Grandmother Rosie's Raw Apple Cake 264
Carrot Apple Cake 264
Dutch Apple Pie 282
French Apple Pie 282
Easy Baked Apples 297
Rum'd Apples 298
Spiked Apple Crisp 298
Grandma's Apple Pudding with Sauce 298
Fruit or Berry Crisp 300
Apricot
Apricot and Currant Chicken 138
Apricot Bread 245
Apricot Coconut Balls 330
Filled Fruit Halves 73
Chicken Breasts with Cheeses 141
Arabian Schwarma Bassett 138
Armenian Meatballs 122
Artichoke
Artichoke Hearts & Scalloped Tomatoes . . . 214
Artichoke Puffs 20
Artichoke Rice Salad 60
Spicy Artichoke Spread 26
Sunday-Best Aspic 67
Chicken Jerusalem I 149
Chicken Jerusalem II 150
Pasta with Tomato-Artichoke Sauce 202
Pasta Sauce Raphael 207
Vegetarian Pizza 236

Asparagus
Festive Vegetable Salad 68
Baked Asparagus 214
Pan-Fried Asparagus 214
Aspic
Sunday-Best Aspic 67
Tomato Aspic I 67
Tomato Aspic II 68
Miss Molly's Aspic Dressing 85
Athalie's Danish Puff 250
Augusta Bloody Mary Mix 35
Aunt Ellie's Deviled Crab 169
Aunt Ollie's Broccoli Cauliflower Salad 62
Avocado
Avocados Stuffed with Crabmeat
au Gratin 20
Tortilla Roll-Ups 13
Tostito Olé 15
Backpackers' Mix 28
Baked Acorn Squash 230
Baked Asparagus 214
Baked Carrots 220
Baked Chocolate Whiskey Pudding 310
Baked Cornish Hens 162
Baked Rice with Consommé 209
Baked Spaghetti Casserole 204
Baked Stuffed Clams 176
Baked Sweet Potatoes with Marshmallows 228
Baklava 296
Banana
Golden Banana Slush Punch 36
Hot Fruit Compote 239
Christmas Cake 275
Grandma's Banana Pudding 299
Barbara's Famous Chicken Salad 77
Barbecue (See also Grilled Foods)
Barbecue Chicken I 95
Barbecue Chicken II 95
Barbecue Sauce 107
Barbecued Shrimp 180
Barbecued Spareribs 102
Barbecued Swordfish 105
Carolina-Style Barbecue Sauce 107
Easy Barbecued Brisket 115
Rocky Mountain Brisket With Barbecue
Sauce 116
Lemon Barbecued Pork Chops 126
Cypress Banks Barbecued Duck 132
Barley
Hearty Beef and Barley Soup 51
"I Can't Believe It's Barley" 208
Bars (See Cookies Chapter Index, 315)
(See also recipes in Desserts Chapter)
Basil and Sausage Strata 191
Beach Weekend Fizzies 34
Bean Relish Salad 60
Beans
Hummus 14
Nacho Dip Supreme 26
New Year's Day Good Luck Bean Soup 42
Black Bean Soup 43
Gourmet's Black Bean Soup 43
Homemade Chili 51
White Chili Casserole 52
Dixie's Chicken Chili 53
Bean Relish Salad 60
Chick Pea Salad 60
Marinated Bean Salad 61
Green Bean and Celery Salad 61

347

INDEX

Taco Salad. 76
Pork Burritos or Chalupas 128
Black Beans and Rice 214
Green Bean Bundles 215
Creole Green Beans 215
Italian Green Beans 215
Lemon Green Beans 216
Green Beans with Red Peppers. 216
Green Bean and Swiss Casserole 216
Pinto Bean Creole 217
Sweet and Sour Beans. 217
Three Bean Bake 218
Vegetable Casserole. 236
Beef
Easy Beef Stew. 50
Hearty Beef and Barley Soup. 51
Harvey Garnage Salad 76
Beef Saté Indonesia. 94
Grilled Flank Steak 94
Marinated Shish Kabobs. 94
Beef Marinade. 107
Low-Calorie Marinade for Beef or
    Chicken 108
Boeuf Bourguignon 112
Lazy Beef Casserole. 112
Beef Broccoli Stir-Fry. 113
Beef Stroganoff Without Panic 113
Lean and Light Stroganoff. 114
Flank Steak Teriyaki. 114
Marinated Broiled Flank Steak 114
Boeuf Au Gingembre. 115
Rosy Eye of Round Roast 115
Easy Barbecued Brisket 115
Finland Brisket. 116
Rocky Mountain Brisket With Barbecue
    Sauce. 116
Chipped Beef
Pickle Delights 12
Angel Hair Pasta with Broccoli and
    Chipped Beef 196
Ground Beef
Taco Tartlets. 23
Nacho Dip Supreme 26
Easy Ground Beef Vegetable Soup 50
Homemade Chili 51
Andy's Gourmet Chili 52
Taco Salad. 76
Chuck Wagon Skillet 116
Five Spice Beef and Rice. 117
Meatloaf with Potato and Mozzarella 117
Moist and Easy Meatloaf 118
Gumbo Sloppy Joes. 118
Sloppy Joes 118
Spaghetti Pie 118
Taco Casserole 119
Upside Down Pizza 119
Quick and Easy Beef 'N Cheese Pie 120
Stuffed Shells 203
Baked Spaghetti Casserole 204
Homemade Spaghetti Sauce 207
Meatballs for Spaghetti Sauce. 208
Special Spaghetti Sauce 208
Veal
Veal Cutlets with Garlic Mint Sauce. 120
Veal à la Normande 120
Veal à L'Orange. 121
Zurich Geschnitzeltes 121
Beer Bread 245
Best Chocolate Cake. 269
Best-Ever Buttermilk Pancakes 248
Best-Ever Clifton Inn Cornbread. 245

Best Scalloped Potatoes. 225
BEVERAGES (See Chapter Index, 33)
Alcoholic Drinks 34–38
Non-Alcoholic 34, 36–38
Birds' Nests 321
Biscuits. 244
Black Bean Soup 43
Black Beans and Rice 214
Blackened Chicken Salad 77
Blanc Mange. 303
Blender French Dressing. 86
Blender Lemon Pie. 287
Bleu Cheese Walnut Dressing 86
Blintzes 188
Blueberry
Blueberry Boy-Bait. 250
Blueberry Muffins 253
Fresh Berry Pie 283
Fruit or Berry Crisp 300
Boeuf Au Gingembre. 115
Boeuf Bourguignon 112
Bok Choy Chicken. 139
Bourbon Chocolate Pecan Pie 285
Bourbon Pork Tenderloin with Mustard
    Sauce. 129
Bourbon Slush. 35
Braised Pork with Pickles. 124
Bran Raisin Muffins 253
Breaded Pork Tenderloin Royale 126
BREADS (See Chapter Index, 243)
Biscuits and Quick Breads 244–247
    Charlie Bread. 237
Breakfast Specialties 248–249
Coffee Cakes and Sweets 250–252
Muffins. 252–256
Yeast Breads 256–260
Brie en Croûte 26
Bristol Bacon Roll-Ups. 22
Broccoli
Broccoli and Tomatoes 219
Broccoli Cauliflower Salad. 62
Broccoli-Cauliflower Tetrazzini 205
Broccoli Cheese Dip 24
Broccoli Elizabeth. 218
Broccoli Salad 62
Broccoli Stem Sauté. 219
Broccoli with Horseradish Sauce 218
Sesame Broccoli Stems 10
Aunt Ollie's Broccoli Cauliflower Salad. . . . 62
Festive Vegetable Salad 68
Vegetable Marinade. 68
Mediterranean Pasta Salad 84
Beef Broccoli Stir-Fry. 113
Light Chicken Divan. 145
Angel Hair Pasta with Broccoli and
    Chipped Beef 196
Stuffed Baked Tomatoes 233
Vegetable Medley. 236
Broiled Butterfly Shrimp. 180
Broiled Zucchini 231
Brown Rice and Lentils. 209
Brownie Ice Cream Pie 305
Brownies 317–318
Busy Mom's Sourdough Bread 257
Butter Creams 330
Buttery Shortcake 296
Cabbage
Cabbage Chop Suey 219
Creamy Cabbage Soup 44
Fumi Salad 63
Fruited Cole Slaw. 64

348

Healthy Cole Slaw 64
Low-Cal Cole Slaw. 65
Marinated Slaw 65
Barbara's Famous Chicken Salad 77
Swedish Cabbage Dish 220
Cajun Dishes (See also Creole)
    Cajun Grilled Shrimp 104
    Cajun-Style Chicken. 96
CAKES (See Chapter Index, 263)
    Cheesecakes 265–269
    Chocolate Cakes 269–274
    Fruit & Other Cakes 264, 274–276
    Pound Cakes 277–278
California Vegetables 234
Candies
    Butter Creams 330
    Apricot Coconut Balls. 330
    Coconut Balls. 331
    Easy $5,000 Fudge 331
    Cholesterol-Free Microwave Fudge. 331
    Peanut Butter Balls 332
Cantaloupe
    Sweet and Sour Cantaloupe 71
Capellini Marco Polo. 196
Caramel
    Caramel Corn 27
    Caramel Rolls. 251
    Crème Caramel 309
    Colombian Flan. 309
    Gee Gee's Hawaiian Brownies. 318
Caribbean Chicken. 140
Carolina Plantation Salad 77
Carolina-Style Barbecue Sauce. 107
Carroll Cottrell's Romaine Salad 69
Carrots
    Carrot Apple Cake 264
    Carrot Casserole 220
    Carrot Raisin Muffins. 253
    Carrots with Dill 220
    Carrots Supreme 221
    Marinated Carrot Sticks 11
    Cream of Carrot Soup. 44
    Golden Carrot Soup 45
    Vegetable Marinade. 68
    Baked Carrots 220
Cashew Nuts
    Cashew Spread. 17
    Chicken and Cashew Stir-Fry. 140
    Nut Cookies 328
Casseroles (Main Dish)
    White Chili Casserole 52
    Lazy Beef Casserole. 112
    Chuck Wagon Skillet 116
    Five Spice Beef and Rice. 117
    Meatloaf with Potato and Mozzarella 117
    Spaghetti Pie 118
    Taco Casserole 119
    Upside Down Pizza. 119
    Quick and Easy Beef 'N Cheese Pie 120
    Chicken Curry Casserole 144
    Light Chicken Divan. 145
    Chicken and Dressing Casserole 145
    Chicken Enchiladas 145
    Chicken Fiesta 146
    Easy Jambalaya. 148
    Oven Jambalaya. 149
    Creamed Chicken Macaroni Casserole . . . 152
    Pauline Morris's Chicken. 154
    Poppy Chicken Casserole 157
    Chicken Pot Pie 157
    Gourmet Hot Chicken Salad 158

Curried Chicken Spaghetti Casserole 160
Chicken and Squash Casserole. 160
Chicken in a Basket. 161
Chicken Yum Yum 161
Taco Pie 163
Microwave Turkey Vegetable Lasagna 163
Turkey Tetrazzini 164
Sautéed Crab Crêpes 168
Crab Imperial I. 170
Crab Remick 170
Scalloped Oysters 177
Scallops Au Gratin 177
Seafood Casserole. 178
Shrimp Casserole Altamont 179
Jambalaya. 179
Charleston Shrimp and Rice 180
Shrimp Curry Even Kids Eat. 181
Wild Rice Shrimp Casserole 182
Shrimp and Chicken Casserole 182
Cheese Blintz Casserole. 188
Mother's Chilequiles. 189
Presnac 189
Basil and Sausage Strata 191
Egg and Sausage Casserole 192
Fresh from the Garden Lasagna 198
Spinach Lasagna. 198
Macaroni and Cheese 200
Manicotti di Verdura 200
Pasta for Your Pace 201
Stuffed Shells 203
Baked Spaghetti Casserole 204
Crab Spaghetti 204
Broccoli-Cauliflower Tetrazzini 205
Cauliflower
    Cauliflower Soup 45
    Aunt Ollie's Broccoli Cauliflower Salad. 62
    Broccoli Cauliflower Salad. 62
    Holiday Vegetable Salad. 63
    Vegetable Marinade. 68
    Shrimp Salad Supreme. 80
    Broccoli-Cauliflower Tetrazzini 205
Caviar Mold. 16
Caviar Pie. 16
Charleston Shrimp and Rice 180
Charleston Wafers. 316
Charlie Bread. 237
Cheddar Cheese Soup 45
CHEESE (See Eggs & Cheese Chapter Index, 187)
    Cheese and Bacon Puffs. 23
    Cheese Blintz Casserole. 188
    Cheese Dip 24
    Cheese Glazed Chicken 140
    Cheese Straws 11
    Cheese Wafers. 12
    Tostito Olé 15
    Chutney Cheese Appetizer 17
    Strawberry Preserves Cheese Ball. 17
    Liptauer Cheese Balls. 18
    Lulu Paste. 18
    Spinach Cheese Squares. 21
    Sarah's Hot Cheese Appetizers 21
    Stonewall Court Cheese Puffs 22
    Horse Point Crab Appetizers. 22
    Cheese and Bacon Puffs. 23
    Pepperoni Quiche 24
    Broccoli Cheese Dip 24
    Chili Con Queso. 24
    Nacho Dip Supreme 26
    Brie en Croûte 26
    Cheddar Cheese Soup 45

INDEX

Bleu Cheese Walnut Dressing 86
Creamy Bleu Cheese Dressing. 86
Quick and Easy Beef 'N Cheese Pie 120
Chicken Breasts with Cheeses 141
Grecian Snapper with Feta Cheese 175
Blintzes 188
Mother's Chilequiles. 189
Presnac 189
Company Quiche Lorraine 190
Newlyweds' Quiche 190
Crab Quiche 190
Smoked Salmon and Chèvre Quiche 191
Basil and Sausage Strata 191
Egg and Sausage Casserole 192
Welsh Rarebit. 192
Fettuccini with Goat Cheese and
   Peppers 196
Fresh from the Garden Lasagna 198
Spinach Lasagna 198
Linguine with Tomatoes and Basil 199
Macaroni and Cheese 200
Manicotti di Verdura 200
Penna con Salsiccia. 202
Low-Fat Cheese Sauce 206
Peppers Stuffed with Cheese. 223
Spinach Gratin. 230
Vegetable Frittata 235
Vegetarian Pizza 236
Cornbread Muffins. 254
Ricotta Cheese Bread 260
Cheesecake
   Divine Cheesecake 265
   Heavenly Cheesecake. 265
   Hollywood Cheesecake. 266
   Ginny's Lime Cheesecake 266
   New York-Style Cheesecake 267
   Oreo Cheesecake. 268
   Chocolate Marble Cheesecake 268
   Chocolate-Raspberry Cheesecake 269
   Healthy Pineapple Cheesecake Pie 290
   Apple Bavarian Torte 297
   Cheesecake Dreams. 316
   Mini Cheesecakes 321
   Miniature Chocolate Chip Cheesecakes. . . . 322
Chef Salad by Committee. 69
Chess Bars 316
Chex After-School Mix 28
Chick Pea Salad 60
Chicken (See Poultry Chapter Index, 137)
Main Dishes (includes Pasta, Grilled Foods)
   Apricot and Currant Chicken. 138
   Arabian Schwarma Bassett. 138
   Barbecue Chicken I. 95
   Barbecue Chicken II 95
   Bok Choy Chicken 139
   Cajun-Style Chicken. 96
   Caribbean Chicken. 140
   Cheese Glazed Chicken 140
   Chicken and Cashew Stir-Fry. 140
   Chicken and Dressing Casserole 145
   Chicken and Pasta Primavera 200
   Chicken and Squash Casserole. 160
   Chicken Antonio 138
   Chicken Breasts Romano. 158
   Chicken Breasts with Cheeses 141
   Chicken Breasts with Herbs and Wine 147
   Chicken Cacciatore 139
   Chicken Curry Casserole 144
   Chicken Dijon. 144
   Chicken Enchiladas 145
   Chicken Fiesta 146

Chicken in a Basket. 161
Chicken Italiano. 148
Chicken Jerusalem I. 149
Chicken Jerusalem II 150
Chicken Kossuth. 97
Chicken Livers Delicious. 162
Chicken Mandalay 152
Chicken Parmigiana 156
Chicken Piccata. 156
Chicken Pot Pie 157
Chicken Scallopini 159
Chicken Tarragon (or Paprika). 160
Chicken Teriyaki. 99
Chicken Yum Yum 161
Colorful Vegetables over Rice. 234
Company Chicken. 141
Creamed Chicken Macaroni Casserole . . . 152
Crispy Chicken. 142
Curried Chicken I. 142
Curried Chicken II 143
Curried Chicken III 143
Curried Chicken Spaghetti Casserole 160
Curried Shrimp and Chicken 183
Curry Glazed Chicken 144
Doves (or Chicken) Cacciatore 131
Easy Jambalaya. 148
Flat Chicken. 146
Francie's Marinade 108
Gourmet Hot Chicken Salad 158
Grilled Fruited Chicken. 96
Grilled Lemon Chicken 98
Harriet's Italian Chicken 148
Herb Baked Chicken Breasts 146
Herbed Roast Chicken. 147
Kenzie's Chicken 97
Lemon Chicken and Thyme. 151
Lemon Chicken I 150
Lemon Chicken II. 150
Lemon Mustard Chicken 98
Light Chicken Cordon Bleu 142
Light Chicken Divan. 145
Low-Calorie Marinade for Beef or
   Chicken 108
Manicotti di Verdura 200
Marg Lee Chicken. 153
Marinated Chicken Breasts 99
Monterey Chicken 153
No-Salt Fajitas. 101
Orange Glazed Chicken 154
Oriental Sunshine Chicken. 155
Oven Jambalaya. 149
Parmesan Baked Chicken 155
Parsley and Parmesan Baked Chicken 156
Pasta for Your Pace 201
Pauline Morris's Chicken. 154
Poppy Chicken Casserole 157
Sautéed Chicken in Mushroom Sauce. 154
Sautéed Chicken with Mandarin
   Oranges. 152
Shrimp (or Chicken) Scampi 183
Shrimp and Chicken Casserole 182
Slow-Cook Chicken 159
Southside Curried Marmalade Chicken. . . . 96
Spicy Chicken with Red and Green
   Peppers 159
Tortellini with Grilled Chicken Breast 205
Twenty-Minute Lemon Garlic Chicken. 151
Vegi-Chicken Grill 100
Wine Baked Chicken Breasts 162
Salads
   Barbara's Famous Chicken Salad 77

INDEX

Blackened Chicken Salad 77
Carolina Plantation Salad 77
Cuban Chicken Salad 78
Curried Chicken Salad. 78
Tarragon Chicken and Rice Salad 78
Cold Pasta New Orleans 83

Soups and Stews
Dixie's Chicken Chili 53
White Chili Casserole 52

Chili
Chili Con Queso 24
Homemade Chili 51
Andy's Gourmet Chili 52
White Chili Casserole 52
Dixie's Chicken Chili 53
Chilled Cucumber Soup 42
Chinese Cole Slaw 64

Chocolate
Cakes, Pies and Desserts
Oreo Cheesecake 268
Chocolate Marble Cheesecake 268
Chocolate-Raspberry Cheesecake 269
Best Chocolate Cake 269
Hershey Syrup Cake 270
No-Frosting Chocolate Chip Cake 270
Chocolate Cream Cake 271
Chocolate Lime Cake with Mint Glaze . . . 271
Double Chocolate Mousse Cake 272
Hot Fudge Pudding Cake 273
Milky Way Cake 273
Chocolate Chess Pie 284
Roberta's Chocolate Chess Pie 284
Chocolate Cream Cheese Pie 285
Bourbon Chocolate Pecan Pie 285
Moody's Chocolate Morsel Pie 286
Frozen Chocolate Pecan Pie 286
Brownie Ice Cream Pie 305
Chocolate Chip Ice Cream
    Sandwiches 306
Viennese Torte 307
Dirt Pudding 310
Baked Chocolate Whiskey Pudding 310
Soufflé Vanille (Variation) 311
Chocolate Dip for Strawberries 311
Hot Chocolate Sauce 312
Hot Fudge Sauce 312

Cookies, Candies and Snacks
Brownies 317
Drop Dead Brownies 317
Dreamy Iced Brownies 317
Chocolate Iced Cake Squares 318
English Toffee Bars 320
Miniature Chocolate Chip
    Cheesecakes 322
Giant Chocolate Chip Cookies 322
White Chocolate Chunk Macadamia
    Nut Cookies 322
Chocolate Mixed Fruit Cookies 323
Chocolate Peanut Butter Cookies 325
Kacey's Harlequin Pinwheels 327
Peanut Butter Cup Tarts 328
Butter Creams 330
Coconut Balls 331
Easy $5,000 Fudge 331
Cholesterol-Free Microwave Fudge 331
Peanut Butter Balls 332
Cholesterol-Free Microwave Fudge 331

Chowders (See Soups and Stews)
Christmas Cake 275
Chuck Wagon Skillet 116
Chutney Cheese Appetizer 17

Clams
Clam Chowder I 53
Clam Chowder II 54
Manhattan Clam Chowder 54
Sailing Stew 55
Baked Stuffed Clams 176
Spaghetti with White Clam Sauce 204

Coconut
Fruit Kabobs with Coconut Dressing 10
Homemade Granola 27
Backpackers' Mix 28
1–2–3 Coconut Cake 274
Easy Coconut Cake 274
Christmas Cake 275
Coconut Cream Pie 283
Birds' Nests 321
Apricot Coconut Balls 330
Coconut Balls 331

Coffee Cakes and Sweets 250–252
Cold Pasta New Orleans 83
Cold Salmon Mousse 19
Cole Slaw 63–65
Colombian Flan 309
Colorful Vegetables over Rice 234
Company Chicken 141
Company Quiche Lorraine 190
COOKIES AND CANDIES (See Chapter Index, 315)
Bar Cookies 316–321
Drop and Formed Cookies 321–326
Refrigerated and Roll Cookies 327–330
Candies 330–332

Corn
Caramel Corn 27
Frogmore Stew 55
Low-Fat Corn Pudding 221
Vegetable Casserole 236
Charlie Bread 237
Best-Ever Clifton Inn Cornbread 245
Favorite Cornbread 246
Corn Muffins 254
Cornbread Muffins 254

Cornish Hens
Raspberry Grilled Cornish Hens 100
Baked Cornish Hens 162
Country Herb Potato Salad 65
Country Spinach Soup 47

Crab
Crab Cakes 168
Crab Imperial I 170
Crab Imperial II 170
Crab in Crumb Crust 169
Crab Louis 79
Crab Quiche 190
Crab Remick 170
Crab Spaghetti 204
Crabmeat Dip 25
Thelma Phillips' Crab Spread 18
Avocados Stuffed with Crabmeat
    au Gratin 20
Horse Point Crab Appetizers 22
Hot Crab Dip 25
Creamy Crabmeat Dip 25
Yellow Peppers Stuffed with Crab and
    Dill 80
New Orleans Crab Claws 168
Sautéed Crab Crêpes 168
Aunt Ellie's Deviled Crab 169
Seafood Casserole 178

Cranberry
Cranberry Freeze 72
Cranberry Muffins 254

INDEX

Fresh Cranberry Relish Salad 72
Frozen Cranberry Salad 72
Thanksgiving Cranberry Salad 72
Apple-Cranberry Casserole 238
Apple Cranberry Pie 282
Cream Cheese Pie 284
Cream of Carrot Soup 44
Creamed Chicken Macaroni Casserole 152
Creamy Bleu Cheese Dressing 86
Creamy Cabbage Soup 44
Creamy Crabmeat Dip 25
Creamy Pepper Dressing 88
Crème Caramel 309
Creole Dishes (See also Cajun)
    Creole Green Beans 215
    Creole-Style Pork Chops 125
    Easy Jambalaya 148
    Jambalaya 179
    Pinto Bean Creole 217
Crêpes
    Sautéed Crab Crêpes 168
    Blintzes 188
    Mu Shu Vegetables 234
Crispy Chicken 142
Cuban Chicken Salad 78
Curried, Curry
    Curried Chicken I 142
    Curried Chicken II 143
    Curried Chicken III 143
    Curried Chicken Salad 78
    Curried Chicken Spaghetti Casserole 160
    Curried Rice 209
    Curried Rice and Shrimp Salad 81
    Curried Shrimp and Chicken 183
    Curried Shrimp Salad 81
    Curry Glazed Chicken 144
    Honey Curry Dip 15
    Southside Curried Marmalade Chicken . . . 96
    Company Chicken 141
    Chicken Curry Casserole 144
    Chicken Mandalay 152
    Shrimp Curry Even Kids Eat 181
Custard
    "Angel of Mercy" Baked Custard 308
    Perfect Baked Custards 308
    Crème Caramel 309
    Colombian Flan 309
Cypress Banks Barbecued Duck 132
Danish Plum Pudding 302
Delicious Apple Spread 16
Demi-Glacé 130
Dessert Sauces
    Hot Chocolate Sauce 312
    Hot Fudge Sauce 312
    Lemon Curd 278
DESSERTS (See Chapter Index, 295)
(See also Cakes, Pies, Cookies, Fruit Side Dishes)
    Fruit Desserts 297–305
    Frozen or Chilled Desserts 305–307
    Custards, Puddings, Soufflés 308–311
    Other Dessert Specialties 296–297, 311
    Sauces 278, 312
Dijon Fish Fillet 171
Dill Weed Dip 14
Dips (See Appetizers Chapter Index, 9)
Dirt Pudding 310
Divine Cheesecake 265
Dixie's Chicken Chili 53
Doc's Rockfish 173
Dog Treats 332
Double Chocolate Mousse Cake 272

Doves
    Doves Cacciatore 131
    Island Farm Doves 131
    Peter's Favorite Doves 132
Dreamy Iced Brownies 317
Dressings (See Salads Chapter Index, 59)
Drop Dead Brownies 317
Duck
    Cypress Banks Barbecued Duck 132
    Peter's Favorite Doves (or Ducks) 132
    Grilled Wood Ducks 133
Dutch Apple Pie 282
Easy Baked Apples 297
Easy Barbecued Brisket 115
Easy Beef Stew 50
Easy Coconut Cake 274
Easy $5,000 Fudge 331
Easy Grilled Shrimp 104
Easy Ground Beef Vegetable Soup 50
Easy Ham in the Crock Pot 124
Easy Jambalaya 148
Easy Pasta Salad 83
Easy Summertime Peach Pie 289
Egg and Sausage Casserole 192
Eggnog 37
Eggplant
    Escalloped Eggplant à la Parmesan 222
EGGS (See Eggs & Cheese Chapter Index, 187)
    Presnac 189
    Company Quiche Lorraine 190
    Newlyweds' Quiche 190
    Crab Quiche 190
    Smoked Salmon and Chèvre Quiche 191
    Basil and Sausage Strata 191
    Egg and Sausage Casserole 192
    Vegetable Frittata 235
    Angel Hair Flans 237
    "Angel of Mercy" Baked Custard 308
    Perfect Baked Custards 308
    Crème Caramel 309
    Colombian Flan 309
    Soufflé Vanille 311
Ellen's Seafood Kabobs 103
English Muffin Loaves 258
English Toffee Bars 320
Equivalents 345–346
Fajita Seasoning 101
Fat-Free Pasta Salad 83
Favorite Cornbread 246
Festive Vegetable Salad 68
Fettuccini with Goat Cheese and Peppers . . . 196
Filled Fruit Halves 73
Fillet of Flounder Ambassador 171
Finland Brisket 116
Fish (See Specific Types: Flounder, Haddock,
Salmon, Snapper, Swordfish, Trout, Tuna)
(See also Sauces, Marinades)
Fish Marinade 108
Five Spice Beef and Rice 117
Flank Steak Teriyaki 114
Flat Chicken 146
Flounder
    Flounder Provençal in Parchment 172
    Dijon Fish Fillet 171
    Fillet of Flounder Ambassador 171
    Poached Flounder Fillet with
        Mushrooms 172
    Zucchini Fish 172
Francie's Marinade 108
French Apple Pie 282

French-Style Potato Salad 66
French Toast Sticks 248
French Vinaigrette 90
Fresh Berry Pie 283
Fresh Cranberry Relish Salad 72
Fresh from the Garden Lasagna 198
Fresh Strawberry Pie 291
Frogmore Stew 55
Frostings and Icings
Pastry Frosting & Variation 250
Best Chocolate Cake 270
Hershey Syrup Cake 270
Milky Way Cake .273–274
Lemon Curd 278
Dreamy Iced Brownies 318
Chocolate Iced Cake Squares 318
Ornamental Frosting for Cookies 330
Frozen Chocolate Pecan Pie 286
Frozen Cranberry Salad 72
Frozen Meringue Cake 276
Fruit(s) (See Specific Types; See also Salads,
Fruit Side Dishes, Cakes and Desserts)
Fruit Clouds 300
Fruit Kabobs with Coconut Dressing 10
Fruit or Berry Crisp 300
Fruit Pizza 300
Fruit Salad 73
Fruit Side Dishes
Nana's Kugel (Noodle Pudding) 238
Apple-Cranberry Casserole 238
Apple Delight 238
Healthy Fried Apples 239
Hot Fruit Compote 239
Quick and Easy Spiced Peaches 239
Spiced Pineapple 240
Pineapple Casserole 240
Easy Baked Apples 297
Rum'd Apples 298
Fruited Cole Slaw 64
Fumi Salad 63
Game
Doves Cacciatore 131
Island Farm Doves 131
Peter's Favorite Doves 132
Cypress Banks Barbecued Duck 132
Grilled Wood Ducks 133
Grilled Quail 133
Tuckahoe Vermouth Venison 133
Schnucki's Spiedies 134
Garlic Grilled Pork Tenderloin 102
Garlic Potatoes 223
Gee Gee's Hawaiian Brownies 318
Giant Chocolate Chip Cookies 322
Ginger Snaps 323
Ginny's Lime Cheesecake 266
Glazed Apple Bread 244
Glazed Peanuts 29
Golden Banana Slush Punch 36
Golden Carrot Soup 45
Gooey Cinnamon Rolls 252
Gourmet Hot Chicken Salad 158
Gourmet's Black Bean Soup 43
Grandma's Apple Pudding with Sauce 298
Grandma's Banana Pudding 299
Grandmother Rosie's Raw Apple Cake 264
Grandmother's Pound Cake 277
Granola
Granola 27
Homemade Granola 27
Outrageous Granola 28
Grasshopper Pie 288

Great Gazpacho 42
Grecian Snapper with Feta Cheese 175
Greek Pasta 201
Greek Shrimp 181
Green Beans
Green Bean and Celery Salad 61
Green Bean and Swiss Casserole 216
Green Bean Bundles 215
Green Beans with Red Peppers 216
Bean Relish Salad 60
Chick Pea Salad 60
Marinated Bean Salad 61
Creole Green Beans 215
Italian Green Beans 215
Lemon Green Beans 216
Three Bean Bake 218
Vegetable Casserole 236
Green Tomato Casserole 232
GRILLED FOODS (See Chapter Index, 93)
Beef and Game .94–95
Marinated Broiled Flank Steak 114
Cypress Banks Barbecued Duck 132
Grilled Wood Ducks 133
Grilled Quail 133
Schnucki's Spiedies 134
Poultry 95–101
Caribbean Chicken 140
Curry Glazed Chicken 144
Tortellini with Grilled Chicken Breast 205
Pork 101–103
Seafood 103–106
Swordfish with Tarragon Mustard
Sauce 175
Sauces, Marinades 107–108
Grilled Flank Steak 94
Grilled Fruited Chicken 96
Grilled Lemon Chicken 98
Grilled Pork Tenderloin 101
Grilled Quail 133
Grilled Rockfish Coriander 105
Grilled Shrimp 103
Grilled Tuna Mediterranean 105
Grilled Wood Ducks 133
Ground Beef (See Beef)
Gumbo Sloppy Joes 118
Gypsy Soup 49
Haddock
Zucchini Fish 172
Halleluia Soup 47
Ham
Easy Ham in the Crock Pot 124
Light Chicken Cordon Bleu 142
Jambalaya 179
Pasta with Spicy Ham and Tomato
Sauce 202
Happy New Year Good Luck Salad 61
Harriet's Italian Chicken 148
Hartley's Eggnog 37
Harvey Gamage Salad 76
Hash Brown Casserole 227
Healthy Cole Slaw 64
Healthy Fried Apples 239
Healthy Pineapple Cheesecake Pie 290
Hearty Beef and Barley Soup 51
Heath Bar Pie 306
Heavenly Cheesecake 265
Herb Baked Chicken Breasts 146
Herbed Roast Chicken 147
Hershey Syrup Cake 270
Hickory Chips 327
Hidden Valley Ranch Pinwheels 11

INDEX

Hints for Healthier Eating. 333
Holiday Raspberry Salad Mold. 76
Holiday Vegetable Salad. 63
Holly Wreaths 323
Hollywood Cheesecake. 266
Homemade Chili 51
Homemade Granola. 27
Homemade Spaghetti Sauce 207
Honey Curry Dip. 15
Honey Mustard Dressing. 87
Hors D'Oeuvres (See Appetizers)
Horse Point Crab Appetizers. 22
Hot Chocolate Sauce 312
Hot Crab Dip 25
Hot Fruit Compote 239
Hot Fudge Pudding Cake 273
Hot Fudge Sauce 312
Hot Spiced Cider 38
Hummus. 14
"I Can't Believe It's Barley" 208
Ice Cream and Sorbet
Ice Cream Pie 286
Chocolate Lime Cake with Mint Glaze 271
Kiwi Sorbet with Raspberry Sauce 301
Brownie Ice Cream Pie 305
Chocolate Chip Ice Cream
  Sandwiches 306
Rum Coffee Macaroon 307
Icings (See Frostings)
Island Farm Dove 131
Island Fruit Salad 74
Italian Dressing. 87
Italian Green Beans 215
Italian-Style Pasta Salad 84
Italian-Style Potato Salad 66
Jambalaya. 179
Jebbie's Spinach Salad Dressing 88
Judy's Gourmet Rolls 258
Kacey's Harlequin Pinwheels 327
Kahlua 35
Kahlua Candied Yams. 229
Kahlua Coffee 38
Kenzie's Chicken 97
Kiwi Sorbet with Raspberry Sauce 301
Lace Cookies. 324
Lamb
Lamb Roast 123
Armenian Meatballs. 122
Rack of Lamb with Raspberry Mint
  Sauce. 122
Stuffed Leg of Lamb. 123
Lassi 34
Lasagna
Microwave Turkey Vegetable Lasagna 163
Fresh from the Garden Lasagna 198
Spinach Lasagna 198
Lazy Beef Casserole. 112
Lean and Light Stroganoff 114
Leisy's Favorite Salad 70
Lemon
Lemon Barbecued Pork Chops 126
Lemon Bread 246
Lemon Chess Pie 287
Lemon Chicken and Thyme. 151
Lemon Chicken I 150
Lemon Chicken II 150
Lemon Crumb Squares 319
Lemon Curd. 278
Lemon Green Beans 216
Lemon Mustard Chicken 98
Lemon Pound Cake. 277

Grilled Lemon Chicken 98
Twenty-Minute Lemon Garlic Chicken 151
Blender Lemon Pie. 287
Lentils
Brown Rice and Lentils 209
LIGHT (L) DISHES
L Light Appetizers:
Fruit Kabobs with Coconut Dressing. 10
Marinated Carrot Sticks 11
Dill Weed Dip 14
Low-Fat High-Taste Vegetable Dip. 14
Hummus. 14
Artichoke Puffs 20
Pita Chips. 30
L Light Beverages:
Beach Weekend Fizzies 34
Lassi 34
Shelley's Orange Julius. 34
Mint Tea 37
Wassail 38
L Light Soups, Stews:
Great Gazpacho 42
Dixie's Chicken Chili 53
L Light Salads, Salad Dressings:
Holiday Vegetable Salad. 63
Fruited Cole Slaw. 64
Healthy Cole Slaw 64
Low-Cal Cole Slaw. 65
Marinated Slaw 65
French-Style Potato Salad 66
Italian-Style Potato Salad 66
Marinated Summer Garden. 67
Island Fruit Salad 74
Minty Fruit Salad. 74
Cuban Chicken Salad 78
Yellow Peppers Stuffed with Crab and
  Dill 80
Fat-Free Pasta Salad 83
Miss Molly's Aspic Dressing 85
Creamy Pepper Dressing. 88
Ranch Dressing 88
Norwood Dressing 89
Tomato Marinade II 89
L Light Grilled Foods:
Barbecue Chicken I. 95
Cajun-Style Chicken. 96
Grilled Fruited Chicken. 96
Grilled Lemon Chicken 98
Lemon Mustard Chicken 98
Vegi-Chicken Grill 100
Raspberry Grilled Cornish Hens 100
Garlic Grilled Pork Tenderloin. 102
Cajun Grilled Shrimp 104
Grilled Tuna Mediterranean. 105
Carolina-Style Barbecue Sauce 107
Low-Calorie Marinade for Beef or
  Chicken 108
L Light Meats and Game:
Beef Broccoli Stir-Fry 113
Lean and Light Stroganoff 114
Marinated Broiled Flank Steak 114
Veal Cutlets with Garlic Mint Sauce. 120
Veal à L'Orange. 121
Creole-Style Pork Chops. 125
Mushroom Pork 127
Orange Pork Tenderloin 129
Pork Tenderloin with Rosemary and
  Thyme. 130
Grilled Wood Ducks 133
Grilled Quail. 133
Schnucki's Spiedies. 134

INDEX

L Light Poultry:
Light Chicken Cordon Bleu 142
Curried Chicken II 143
Curry Glazed Chicken 144
Light Chicken Divan. 145
Chicken Enchiladas 145
Chicken Breasts with Herbs and Wine 147
Easy Jambalaya. 148
Lemon Chicken I 150
Lemon Chicken II. 150
Twenty-Minute Lemon Garlic Chicken 151
Lemon Chicken and Thyme. 151
Sautéed Chicken with Mandarin
  Oranges. 152
Pauline Morris's Chicken. 154
Sautéed Chicken in Mushroom Sauce. 154
Orange Glazed Chicken 154
Oriental Sunshine Chicken. 155
Parsley and Parmesan Baked Chicken 156
Chicken Piccata. 156
Chicken in a Basket 161
Microwave Turkey Vegetable Lasagna 163
L Light Seafood:
Crab Imperial II 170
Dijon Fish Fillet 171
Fillet of Flounder Ambassador 171
Poached Flounder Fillet with
  Mushrooms. 172
Flounder Provençal in Parchment. 172
Poached Salmon with Horseradish
  Sauce. 174
Poached Salmon Steaks with Zucchini
  Noodles 174
Roasted Salmon Steaks 174
Grecian Snapper with Feta Cheese 175
Swordfish with Tarragon Mustard
  Sauce. 175
Oriental Scallop Stir-Fry. 177
Shrimp Curry Even Kids Eat. 181
Shrimp (or Chicken) Scampi 183
L Light Eggs, Cheese, Pasta:
Blintzes 188
Egg and Sausage Casserole 192
Fettuccini with Goat Cheese and
  Peppers. 196
Fresh from the Garden Lasagna 198
Spinach Lasagna. 198
Chicken and Pasta Primavera 200
Greek Pasta 201
Spaghetti with White Clam Sauce 204
Low-Fat Cheese Sauce 206
Marinara Sauce. 206
L Light Rice, Vegetables, Fruit:
Brown Rice and Lentils. 209
Artichoke Hearts and Scalloped
  Tomatoes 214
Baked Asparagus. 214
Black Beans and Rice 214
Pinto Bean Creole 217
Broccoli with Horseradish Sauce 218
Cabbage Chop Suey 219
Swedish Cabbage Dish 220
Baked Carrots 220
Carrots with Dill 220
Low-Fat Corn Pudding 221
Mushrooms Florentine 222
Garlic Potatoes 223
Potato and Onion Bake. 224
Nip It in the Bud Spuds. 225
Light Twice-Baked Potatoes 227
Spicy "French Fries". 227

Baked Acorn Squash 230
Squash Alfredo. 230
Broiled Zucchini 231
Scoffield Tomatoes. 232
Skillet Tomatoes 232
California Vegetables 234
Colorful Vegetables over Rice 234
Mu Shu Vegetables 234
Healthy Fried Apples 239
L Light Breads:
Favorite Cornbread 246
French Toast Sticks 248
Apple Muffins. 252
Bran Raisin Muffins 253
Carrot Raisin Muffins. 253
Corn Muffins. 254
Moist Pineapple Bran Muffins. 255
Old-Fashioned Oatmeal Bread 258
Processor Wheat Bread 259
L Light Cakes, Pies, Desserts, Cookies:
Heavenly Cheesecake. 265
Hot Fudge Pudding Cake 273
Grasshopper Pie 288
Healthy Pineapple Cheesecake Pie 290
Easy Baked Apples. 297
Fruit or Berry Crisp 300
Kiwi Sorbet with Raspberry Sauce 301
Raspberry-Topped Soufflé 302
Angel Food Trifle 304
Ribbon Cake 306
Low-Fat Cholesterol-Free Oatmeal
  Cookies 325
Swiss Cinnamon Stars. 329
Light Chicken Cordon Bleu 142
Light Chicken Divan. 145
Light Twice-Baked Potatoes 227
Lightly Scalloped Potatoes. 226
Lime
  Ginny's Lime Cheesecake 266
  Chocolate Lime Cake with Mint Glaze 271
  Rosemary Key Lime Pie 287
Linguine with Tomatoes and Basil 199
Liptauer Cheese Balls. 18
Low-Cal Cole Slaw. 65
Low-Calorie Marinade for Beef or
  Chicken 108
Low-Fat Cheese Sauce 206
Low-Fat Cholesterol-Free Oatmeal
  Cookies 325
Low-Fat Corn Pudding 221
Low-Fat High-Taste Vegetable Dip. 14
Lulu Paste. 18
Macadamia Nuts
  White Chocolate Chunk Macadamia
    Nut Cookies 322
  Nut Cookies 328
Macaroni and Cheese 200
Mandarin Orange Cake 275
Mandarin Orange Tossed Salad 70
Manhattan Clam Chowder 54
Manicotti di Verdura 200
Marg Lee Chicken. 153
Marinades, Marinated
  Marinated Bean Salad. 61
  Marinated Broiled Flank Steak 114
  Marinated Carrot Sticks 11
  Marinated Chicken Breasts 99
  Marinated Shish Kabobs. 94
  Marinated Slaw 65
  Marinated Summer Garden. 67
  Marinated Swordfish or Tuna 106

355

INDEX

Marinated Thai Shrimp 104
Marinated Tuna Steaks 106
Vegetable Marinade 68
Tomato Marinade I 89
Tomato Marinade II 89
Minty Fruit Salad 74
Beef Marinade 107
Francie's Marinade 108
Low-Calorie Marinade for Beef or
    Chicken 108
Fish Marinade 108
Beef Saté Indonesia 94
Grilled Flank Steak 94
Grilled Pork Tenderloin 101
Garlic Grilled Pork Tenderloin 102
Teriyaki Pork Chops 102
Barbecue Chicken I 95
Barbecue Chicken II 95
Cajun-Style Chicken 96
Southside Curried Marmalade Chicken 96
Grilled Fruited Chicken 96
Kenzie's Chicken 97
Chicken Kossuth 97
Grilled Lemon Chicken 98
Lemon Mustard Chicken 98
Chicken Teriyaki 99
Raspberry Grilled Cornish Hens 100
Ellen's Seafood Kabobs 103
Barbecued Shrimp 180
Grilled Shrimp 103
Easy Grilled Shrimp 104
Grilled Rockfish Coriander 105
Barbecued Swordfish 105
Grilled Tuna Mediterranean 106
Pork Tenderloin with Rosemary and
    Thyme 130
Marinara Sauce 206
Measures 344
MEATS AND GAME (See Chapter Index, 195)
(See Specific Types: Beef, Veal, Lamb,
    Pork, Game)
Meatballs for Spaghetti Sauce 208
Meatloaf
    Meatloaf with Potato and Mozzarella 117
    Moist and Easy Meatloaf 118
Mediterranean Pasta Salad 84
Meringue Cake, Frozen 276
Mexican Dishes
    Priscilla's Taco Dip 15
    Tostito Olé 15
    Taco Tartlets 23
    Chili Con Queso 24
    Nacho Dip Supreme 26
    Taco Salad 76
    No-Salt Fajitas 101
    Taco Casserole 119
    Pork Burritos or Chalupas 128
    Chicken Enchiladas 145
    Mother's Chilequiles 189
Microwave Turkey Vegetable Lasagna 163
Milky Way Cake 273
Mini Cheesecakes 321
Miniature Chocolate Chip Cheesecakes 322
Mint
    Mint Tea 37
    Minty Fruit Salad 74
    Veal Cutlets with Garlic Mint Sauce 120
    Chocolate Lime Cake with Mint Glaze 271
    Grasshopper Pie 288
Miss Molly's Aspic Dressing 85
Moist and Easy Meatloaf 118

Moist Pineapple Bran Muffins 255
Mom's Cole Slaw Dressing 86
Mom's French Dressing 87
Mom's Pound Cake 278
Monterey Chicken 153
Moody's Chocolate Morsel Pie 286
Mother Leone's Shrimp Sauce 184
Mother's Chilequiles 189
Mousse
    Cold Salmon Mousse 19
    Double Chocolate Mousse Cake 272
    Blanc Mange 303
Mr. George's Famous Raisin Cookies 326
Mu Shu Vegetables 234
Muffins 252–256
Mushroom
    Mushroom Pork 127
    Mushrooms Florentine 222
    Stuffed Mushroom Caps 21
    Sautéed Chicken in Mushroom Sauce 154
    Sautéed Crab Crêpes 168
    Poached Flounder Fillet with
        Mushrooms 172
    Vegetable Frittata 235
Nacho Dip Supreme 26
Nana's Kugel (Noodle Pudding) 238
Nana's Rocks 326
New Orleans Crab Claws 168
New Orleans Vinaigrette 90
New Potatoes in Sour Cream 226
New Year's Day Good Luck Bean Soup 42
New York-Style Cheesecake 267
Newlyweds' Quiche 190
Nip It in the Bud Spuds 225
No-Fail Buttermilk Biscuits 244
No-Frosting Chocolate Chip Cake 270
No-Salt Fajitas 101
No-Yolk Eggnog 37
Noodles (See also Pasta Chapter Index, 195)
    Fumi Salad 63
    Barbara's Famous Chicken Salad 77
    Chuck Wagon Skillet 116
    Poached Salmon Steaks with Zucchini
        Noodles 174
    Nana's Kugel (Noodle Pudding) 238
Norwood Dressing 89
Nuts (See Specific Types: Almond, Cashew,
    Macadamia, Peanut, Pecan, Walnut)
Nut Cookies 328
Nut Crust Strawberry Tart 303
Oatmeal
    Oatmeal Cookies 324
    Granola 27
    Homemade Granola 27
    Outrageous Granola 28
    Raisin Oatmeal Pancakes 249
    Old-Fashioned Oatmeal Bread 258
    Lemon Crumb Squares 319
    Scotch Oat Crispy Cookies 324
    Low-Fat Cholesterol-Free Oatmeal
        Cookies 325
    Mr. George's Famous Raisin Cookies 326
    Hickory Chips 327
Okra and Tomatoes 222
Old-Fashioned Oatmeal Bread 258
Old-Fashioned Pancakes 249
One Hundred Year Old Chess Pie 284
1–2–3 Coconut Cake 274
Onion
    Vidalia Onion Casserole 223
    Potatoes and Onions 224

Potato and Onion Bake 224
Best Scalloped Potatoes. 225
Orange
Orange Glazed Chicken 154
Orange Pecans 29
Orange Pork Tenderloin 129
Shelley's Orange Julius. 34
Mandarin Orange Tossed Salad 70
Spiced Orange Salad 74
Veal à L'Orange. 121
Sautéed Chicken with Mandarin
    Oranges. 152
Oriental Sunshine Chicken. 155
Mandarin Orange Cake 275
Oreo Cheesecake. 268
Oriental Scallop Stir-Fry. 177
Oriental Sunshine Chicken. 155
Ornamental Frosting for Cookies 330
Outrageous Granola 28
Oven Jambalaya 149
Oyster
Oyster and Spinach Bisque 56
Oyster Bisque 55
Oyster Stew—Chick's Beach Style 56
Scalloped Oysters 177
Pork Strips with Oyster Sauce 127
Painted Cookies. 328
Pam's Pork Tenderloin 13
Pancakes 248–249
Pan-Fried Asparagus 214
Parmesan Baked Chicken 155
Parsley and Parmesan Baked Chicken 156
Party Pasta Salad 84
Party Punch 36
PASTA AND RICE (See Chapter Index, 195)
(See also: Meats, Poultry, Seafood chapters)
Main Dishes 196–205
Salads 82–85
Sauces. 206–208
Side Dishes 237–238
Rice and Grains 208–210
Pasta for Your Pace 201
Pasta Sauce Raphael. 207
Pasta with Spicy Ham and Tomato Sauce 202
Pasta with Tomato-Artichoke Sauce. 202
Pauline Morris's Chicken. 154
Peach
Peach and Poppy Seed Muffins 255
Peach Crumble Pie 289
Peach Pie. 288
Easy Summertime Peach Pie 289
Fruit or Berry Crisp 300
Filled Fruit Halves 73
Quick and Easy Spiced Peaches 239
Peanut, Peanut Butter
Peanut Butter Balls 332
Peanut Butter Cookies 325
Peanut Butter Cup Tarts 328
Peanut Butter Pie 290
Backpackers' Mix 28
Glazed Peanuts 29
Chocolate Peanut Butter Cookies 325
Pear
Fruited Cole Slaw 64
Filled Fruit Halves 73
Peas
Hummus 14
Split Pea Soup 46
Bean Relish Salad. 60
Chick Pea Salad 60
Happy New Year Good Luck Salad 61

Vegetable Medley. 236
Pecan
Pecan Bars. 319
Pecan Butter Fingers 325
Orange Pecans 29
Toasted Pecans 29
Bourbon Chocolate Pecan Pie 285
Frozen Chocolate Pecan Pie 286
Charleston Wafers 316
Nut Cookies 328
Penna con Salsiccia. 202
Pepperoni Quiche 24
Peppers
Peppers Stuffed with Cheese. 223
Yellow Peppers Stuffed with Crab and
    Dill 80
Creamy Pepper Dressing. 88
Spicy Chicken with Red and Green
    Peppers 159
Fettuccini with Goat Cheese and
    Peppers 196
Green Beans with Red Peppers. 216
Colorful Vegetables over Rice 234
Mu Shu Vegetables 234
Vegetable Frittata 235
Perfect Baked Custards 308
Pesto Sauce 206
Peter's Favorite Doves 132
Pickle Delights 12
Pickled Shrimp 12
Pico de Gallo. 101
PIES (For main list, See Chapter Index, 281)
Caviar Pie. 16
Spaghetti Pie 118
Quick and Easy Beef 'N Cheese Pie 120
Chicken Pot Pie 157
Taco Pie 163
Tomato Pie 232
Brownie Ice Cream Pie 305
Heath Bar Pie 306
Pineapple
Pineapple Buttermilk Salad 75
Pineapple Casserole 240
Pineapple Strawberry Ring. 75
Hot Fruit Compote 239
Spiced Pineapple 240
Moist Pineapple Bran Muffins. 255
Christmas Cake 275
Mandarin Orange Cake 275
Healthy Pineapple Cheesecake Pie 290
Tropical Punch Bowl Cake. 305
Pinto Bean Creole 217
Pita Chips. 30
Pizza
Veggie Pizzas 10
Upside Down Pizza 119
Vegetarian Pizza 236
Fruit Pizza 300
Plum Cake 276
Poached Flounder Fillet with Mushrooms. . . . 172
Poached Salmon Steaks with Zucchini
    Noodles. 174
Poached Salmon with Horseradish Sauce 174
Poppy Chicken Casserole 157
Poppy Seed Bread. 246
Pork
Pork Burritos or Chalupas 128
Pork Chops with Black Currant
    Preserves 125
Pork Strips with Oyster Sauce 127
Pork Tenderloin with Raisin Sauce 128

INDEX

Pork Tenderloin with Rosemary and
Thyme. 130
Pam's Pork Tenderloin 13
Grilled Pork Tenderloin. 101
Garlic Grilled Pork Tenderloin. 102
Teriyaki Pork Chops 102
Barbecued Spareribs. 102
Easy Ham in the Crock Pot. 124
Zucchini Sausage Boats 124
Braised Pork with Pickles. 124
Creole-Style Pork Chops. 125
Lemon Barbecued Pork Chops 126
Roast Pork with Sweet and Sour Sauce 126
Breaded Pork Tenderloin Royale 126
Mushroom Pork 127
Bourbon Pork Tenderloin with Mustard
Sauce. 129
Orange Pork Tenderloin. 129
Pasta with Spicy Ham and Tomato
Sauce. 202
Penna con Salsiccia. 202
Spaghetti Carbonara. 203
Meatballs for Spaghetti Sauce. 208
Steve Wong's New York Fried Rice. 210

Potato
Potato and Onion Bake. 224
Potato Soup. 46
Potatoes and Onions. 224
Ruthie's Parsley Soup 46
Halleluia Soup 47
Clam Chowder I 53
Clam Chowder II 54
Country Herb Potato Salad 65
French-Style Potato Salad 66
Italian-Style Potato Salad 66
Refrigerator Potato Salad. 66
Meatloaf with Potato and Mozzarella 117
Garlic Potatoes 223
Roasted Red Potatoes 224
Rosemary Potatoes 225
Nip It in the Bud Spuds. 225
Best Scalloped Potatoes. 225
Lightly Scalloped Potatoes. 226
New Potatoes in Sour Cream. 226
Twice-Baked Potatoes 226
Light Twice-Baked Potatoes 227
Hash Brown Casserole 227
Spicy "French Fries". 227
Sweet Potato Delight 228
Baked Sweet Potatoes with
Marshmallows. 228
Sweet Potato Pudding 228
Kahlua Candied Yams. 229
Sweet Potato Muffins 256
POULTRY (See Chapter Index, 137)
**(See specific types: Chicken, Turkey,
Duck, Quail, Cornish Hens)**
Pound Cakes. 277–278
Presnac. 189
Priscilla's Taco Dip 15
Processor Wheat Bread 259
Pudding
Low-Fat Corn Pudding 221
Sweet Potato Pudding 228
Nana's Kugel (Noodle Pudding). 238
Hot Fudge Pudding Cake 273
Grandma's Apple Pudding with Sauce 298
Grandma's Banana Pudding 299
Danish Plum Pudding. 302
Dirt Pudding. 310
Baked Chocolate Whiskey Pudding. 310

Pumpkin Bread. 247
Pumpkin Clove Muffins. 255
Pumpkin Tea Bread 247
Punches 36
Quail
Grilled Quail. 133
Quick and Easy Beef 'N Cheese Pie 120
Quick and Easy Spiced Peaches. 239
QUICK (Q) THIRTY-MINUTE RECIPES
Q Quick Appetizers and Snacks:
Pickle Delights 12
Tortilla Roll-Ups. 13
Simply Scrumptious Fruit Dip. 13
Priscilla's Taco Dip 15
Tostito Olé 15
Delicious Apple Spread 16
Artichoke Puffs 20
Avocados Stuffed with Crabmeat au
Gratin. 20
Sarah's Hot Cheese Appetizers 21
Horse Point Crab Appetizers. 22
Cheese and Bacon Puffs 23
Broccoli Cheese Dip 24
Cheese Dip 24
Hot Crab Dip 25
Creamy Crabmeat Dip 25
Granola 27
Homemade Granola. 27
Outrageous Granola 28
Backpackers' Mix. 28
Chex After-School Mix 28
Glazed Peanuts 29
Orange Pecans 29
Toasted Pecans 29
Pita Chips. 30
Q Quick Soups, Stews:
Creamy Cabbage Soup 44
Ruthie's Parsley Soup 46
Potato Soup. 46
Country Spinach Soup. 47
Sailing Stew 55
Frogmore Stew. 55
Oyster Stew—Chick's Beach Style 56
Q Quick Salads and Salad Dressings:
Broccoli Cauliflower Salad. 62
Fumi Salad 63
Carroll Cottrell's Romaine Salad 69
Leisy's Favorite Salad 70
Walnut Salad 71
Sweet and Sour Cantaloupe 71
Filled Fruit Halves 73
Fruit Salad 73
Taco Salad 76
Blackened Chicken Salad 77
Carolina Plantation Salad 77
Crab Louis 79
Yellow Peppers Stuffed with Crab and
Dill 80
Shrimp Salad Supreme. 80
Creamy Bleu Cheese Dressing. 86
Mom's Cole Slaw Dressing. 86
Blender French Dressing. 86
Mom's French Dressing 87
Honey Mustard Dressing. 87
Italian Dressing. 87
Creamy Pepper Dressing. 88
Ranch Dressing 88
Spinach Salad Dressing 88
Norwood Dressing. 89
Tomato Dressing. 89
Tomato Marinade II 89

INDEX

Q Quick Grilled Foods:
Beef Saté Indonesia 94
Teriyaki Pork Chops 102
Ellen's Seafood Kabobs 103
Easy Grilled Shrimp. 104
Q Quick Meats, Game:
Beef Broccoli Stir-Fry 113
Gumbo Sloppy Joes. 118
Sloppy Joes 118
Taco Casserole 119
Veal Cutlets with Garlic Mint Sauce. 120
Veal à la Normande 120
Zurich Geschnitzeltes 121
Mushroom Pork 127
Pork Strips with Oyster Sauce 127
Pork Tenderloin with Raisin Sauce 128
Q Quick Poultry:
Chicken Antonio 138
Bok Choy Chicken 139
Chicken and Cashew Stir-Fry 140
Light Chicken Cordon Bleu 142
Flat Chicken 146
Chicken Breasts with Herbs and Wine 147
Twenty-Minute Lemon Garlic Chicken 151
Lemon Chicken and Thyme. 151
Sautéed Chicken with Mandarin
  Oranges. 152
Sautéed Chicken in Mushroom Sauce. 154
Chicken Parmagiana. 156
Chicken Piccata. 156
Chicken Scallopini 159
Spicy Chicken with Red and Green
  Peppers 159
Taco Pie 163
Q Quick Seafood:
Crab Cakes 168
Aunt Ellie's Deviled Crab 169
Crab Imperial II 170
Crab Remick 170
Dijon Fish Fillet 171
Poached Flounder Fillet with
  Mushrooms. 172
Zucchini Fish 172
Doc's Rockfish. 173
Poached Salmon Steaks with Zucchini
  Noodles 174
Roasted Salmon Steaks 174
Swordfish with Tarragon Mustard Sauce. . . . 175
Baked Stuffed Clams 176
Scallops Au Gratin 177
Sautéed Scallops 178
Broiled Butterfly Shrimp. 180
Shrimp Guadalajara 182
Shrimp (or Chicken) Scampi 183
Seafood Sauce 184
Q Quick Cheese, Pasta, Rice:
Welsh Rarebit 192
Capellini Marco Polo. 196
Angel Hair Pasta with Broccoli and
  Chipped Beef 196
Fettuccini with Goat Cheese and
  Peppers 196
Shrimp Fettuccini 197
Shrimp Linguine 199
Chicken and Pasta Primavera 200
Greek Pasta 201
Pasta for Your Peace 201
Pasta with Spicy Ham and Tomato
  Sauce. 202
Pasta with Tomato-Artichoke Sauce. 202
Spaghetti Carbonara. 203

Spaghetti with White Clam Sauce 204
Tortellini with Grilled Chicken Breast 205
Low-Fat Cheese Sauce 206
Pesto Sauce 206
Steve Wong's New York Fried Rice 210
Riso con Salsa Cruda 210
Q Quick Vegetables:
Artichoke Hearts and Scalloped
  Tomatoes 214
Baked Asparagus 214
Pan-Fried Asparagus 214
Italian Green Beans 215
Lemon Green Beans 216
Green Beans with Red Peppers. 216
Broccoli with Horseradish Sauce 218
Broccoli and Tomatoes 219
Broccoli Stem Sauté 219
Cabbage Chop Suey 219
Okra and Tomatoes 222
Roasted Red Potatoes 224
Squash Alfredo. 230
Broiled Zucchini 231
Skillet Tomatoes 232
Tomatoes Stuffed With Spinach Soufflé 233
Mu Shu Vegetables 234
Sour Cream Biscuits 244
Q Quick Breads, Sweets:
French Toast Sticks 248
Best-Ever Buttermilk Pancakes 248
Old-Fashioned Pancakes. 249
Yorkshire Pancake 249
Caramel Rolls. 251
Gooey Cinnamon Rolls 252
Apple Muffins 252
Bran Raisin Muffins 253
Carrot Raisin Muffins. 253
Corn Muffins 254
Cornbread Muffins. 254
Peach and Poppy Seed Muffins 255
Moist Pineapple Bran Muffins. 255
Pumpkin Clove Muffins. 255
Buttery Shortcake 296
Hot Chocolate Sauce 312
Hot Fudge Sauce 312
Sunshine Krisps 320
Ornamental Frosting for Cookies 330
Rack of Lamb with Raspberry Mint Sauce . . . 122
Raisin Oatmeal Pancakes 249
Ranch Dressing 88
Rappahannock Stuffed Rockfish 173
Raspberry
Raspberry and Cream Pie 291
Raspberry Brûlée 302
Raspberry Grilled Cornish Hens 100
Raspberry-Topped Soufflé 302
Holiday Raspberry Salad Mold. 76
Rack of Lamb with Raspberry Mint
  Sauce. 122
Chocolate-Raspberry Cheesecake 269
Kiwi Sorbet with Raspberry Sauce 301
Refrigerator Potato Salad. 66
Ribbon Cake 306
Rice
Artichoke Rice Salad 60
Tarragon Chicken and Rice Salad. 78
Shrimp Salad Supreme. 80
Curried Rice and Shrimp Salad 81
Five Spice Beef and Rice 117
Charleston Shrimp and Rice 180
Wild Rice Shrimp Casserole 182
Baked Rice with Consommé 209

359

INDEX

Brown Rice and Lentils. 209
Curried Rice. 209
Steve Wong's New York Fried Rice. 210
Riso con Salsa Cruda. 210
Black Beans and Rice. 214
Colorful Vegetables over Rice. 234
Ricotta Cheese Bread 260
Riso con Salsa Cruda. 210
Riverton Squash Casserole. 231
Roast Pork with Sweet and Sour Sauce 126
Roasted Red Potatoes 224
Roasted Salmon Steaks 174
Roberta's Chocolate Chess Pie 284
Rockfish
Grilled Rockfish Coriander. 105
Doc's Rockfish. 173
Rappahannock Stuffed Rockfish 173
Rocky Mountain Brisket With Barbecue
Sauce. 116
Rosemary Infusion 288
Rosemary Key Lime Pie 287
Rosemary Potatoes 225
Rosy Eye of Round Roast 115
Rum Coffee Macaroon 307
Rum'd Apples. 298
Russian Cherries. 299
Russian Tea Balls. 326
Ruthie's Parsley Soup 46
Sailing Stew 55
SALADS (See Chapter Index, 59)
Vegetable Salads 60–71
Fruit Salads. 71–76
Meat and Poultry Salads. 76–79
Seafood Salads. 79–82
Pasta Salads. 82–85
Salad Dressings 85–90
Salmon
Cold Salmon Mousse. 19
Poached Salmon with Horseradish
Sauce. 174
Poached Salmon Steaks with Zucchini
Noodles 174
Roasted Salmon Steaks 174
Smoked Salmon and Chèvre Quiche 191
Sarah's Hot Cheese Appetizers 21
Sauces
Chicken Kossuth. 98
No-Salt Fajitas. 101
Barbecued Spareribs 102
Barbecue Sauce 107
Carolina-Style Barbecue Sauce 107
Rocky Mountain Brisket With Barbecue
Sauce. 116
Veal Cutlets with Garlic Mint Sauce. 120
Rack of Lamb with Raspberry Mint
Sauce. 122
Roast Pork with Sweet and Sour Sauce 126
Pork Strips with Oyster Sauce 127
Pork Tenderloin with Raisin Sauce 128
Bourbon Pork Tenderloin with Mustard
Sauce. 129
Demi-Glacé 130
Chicken Breasts with Cheeses. 141
Sautéed Chicken in Mushroom Sauce. . . . 154
Sautéed Crab Crêpes 169
Poached Salmon with Horseradish
Sauce. 174
Swordfish with Tarragon Mustard Sauce. . . 175
Seafood Sauce 184
Mother Leone's Shrimp Sauce 184

Pasta with Spicy Ham and Tomato
Sauce. 202
Pasta with Tomato-Artichoke Sauce. 202
Spaghetti with White Clam Sauce. 204
Low-Fat Cheese Sauce 206
Marinara Sauce 206
Pesto Sauce 206
Pasta Sauce Raphael. 207
Homemade Spaghetti Sauce 207
Meatballs for Spaghetti Sauce. 208
Special Spaghetti Sauce 208
Broccoli with Horseradish Sauce 218
Lemon Curd. 278
Grandma's Apple Pudding with Sauce 298
Kiwi Sorbet with Raspberry Sauce 301
Hot Chocolate Sauce 312
Hot Fudge Sauce 312
Sausage
Frogmore Stew. 55
Zucchini Sausage Boats 124
Oven Jambalaya. 149
Basil and Sausage Strata 191
Egg and Sausage Casserole 192
Penna con Salsiccia. 202
Sautéed Chicken in Mushroom Sauce. 154
Sautéed Chicken with Mandarin Oranges. . . . 152
Sautéed Crab Crêpes 168
Sautéed Scallops 178
Scalloped Oysters 177
Scallops
Ellen's Seafood Kabobs 103
Scallops Au Gratin 177
Oriental Scallop Stir-Fry. 177
Sautéed Scallops 178
Wild Rice Shrimp Casserole 182
Schnucki's Spiedies. 134
Scoffield Tomatoes. 232
Scotch Oat Crispy Cookies 324
Scotch or Whiskey Sour Mix 35
SEAFOOD (See Chapter Index, 167)
(See Specific Types: Fish (by name),
Oysters, Clams, Scallops, Shrimp, Crab)
Seafood Casserole. 178
Seafood Sauce 184
Sesame Broccoli Stems 10
Shelley's Orange Julius. 34
Shellfish (See Specific Types by name)
Shrimp
Shrimp Alla Milanese 178
Shrimp and Chicken Casserole 182
Shrimp and Macaroni Salad 80
Shrimp and Shells. 81
Shrimp Butter 19
Shrimp Casserole Altamont 179
Shrimp Curry Even Kids Eat. 181
Shrimp Fettuccini 197
Shrimp Guadalajara 182
Shrimp Linguine 199
Shrimp Mold. 20
Shrimp (or Chicken) Scampi 183
Shrimp Salad Supreme. 80
Pickled Shrimp. 12
Sailing Stew 55
Frogmore Stew. 55
Carolina Plantation Salad 77
Curried Shrimp Salad. 81
Curried Rice and Shrimp Salad 81
Ellen's Seafood Kabobs 103
Grilled Shrimp. 103
Easy Grilled Shrimp. 104
Cajun Grilled Shrimp 104

INDEX

Marinated Thai Shrimp 104
Seafood Casserole. 178
Jambalaya. 179
Barbecued Shrimp. 180
Broiled Butterfly Shrimp. 180
Charleston Shrimp and Rice 180
Greek Shrimp. 181
Wild Rice Shrimp Casserole 182
Curried Shrimp and Chicken. 183
Mother Leone's Shrimp Sauce 184
Stir-Fry Shrimp with Fettuccini 197
Simply Scrumptious Fruit Dip. 13
Skillet Tomatoes 232
Sloppy Joes 118
Slow-Cook Chicken 159
Smoked Salmon and Chèvre Quiche 191
Snacks (See Appetizers)
Snapper
Grecian Snapper with Feta Cheese 175
Soufflés
Raspberry-Topped Soufflé 302
Soufflé Vanille. 311
SOUPS AND STEWS (See Chapter Index, 41)
Cold Soups 42, 46
Vegetable Soups 42–49
Meat and Poultry Soups, Stews 50–53
Seafood Soups, Stew 53–56
Sour Cream Biscuits 244
Sour Cream Coffee Cake 251
Southside Curried Marmalade Chicken. 96
Spaghetti (See also Pasta Chapter Index, 195)
Spaghetti Carbonara. 203
Spaghetti Pie 118
Spaghetti with White Clam Sauce 204
Baked Spaghetti Casserole 204
Curried Chicken Spaghetti Casserole 160
Crab Spaghetti 204
Homemade Spaghetti Sauce 207
Meatballs for Spaghetti Sauce. 208
Special Spaghetti Sauce 208
Special Occasion French Toast 248
Special Spaghetti Sauce 208
Spiced Orange Salad 74
Spiced Pineapple 240
Spicy "French Fries" 227
Spicy Artichoke Spread 26
Spicy Chicken with Red and Green
Peppers 159
Spiked Apple Crisp. 298
Spinach
Spinach Casserole I 229
Spinach Casserole II. 229
Spinach Cheese Squares. 21
Spinach Gratin. 230
Spinach Lasagna 198
Spinach Salad Dressing 88
Low-Fat High-Taste Vegetable Dip. 14
Country Spinach Soup 47
Tortellini and Spinach Soup 48
Oyster and Spinach Bisque 56
Jebbie's Spinach Salad Dressing 88
Manicotti di Verdura 200
Mushrooms Florentine 222
Tomatoes Stuffed With Spinach Soufflé 233
Split Pea Soup 46
Spreads (See Appetizers Chapter Index, 9)
Squash (See also Zucchini)
Squash Alfredo. 230
Squash Casserole. 231
Chicken and Squash Casserole. 160
Capellini Marco Polo 196

Baked Acorn Squash 230
Riverton Squash Casserole. 231
Broiled Zucchini 231
Vegetable Frittata 235
Winter Squash and Apple Soup. 48
Steve Wong's New York Fried Rice 210
Stews (See Soups and Stews Chapter Index, 41)
Stir-fry Dishes
Beef Broccoli Stir-Fry. 113
Pork Strips with Oyster Sauce 127
Bok Choy Chicken 139
Chicken and Cashew Stir-Fry 140
Marg Lee Chicken. 153
Oriental Sunshine Chicken. 155
Spicy Chicken with Red and Green
Peppers 159
Oriental Scallop Stir-Fry. 177
Stir-Fry Shrimp with Fettuccini 197
Steve Wong's New York Fried Rice 210
Mu Shu Vegetables 234
Stonewall Court Cheese Puffs 22
Stonewall Court Cinnamon Puffs 252
Strawberry
Strawberry Preserves Cheese Ball. 17
Pineapple Strawberry Ring. 75
Fresh Berry Pie 283
Fresh Strawberry Pie 291
Buttery Shortcake 296
Blanc Mange 303
Nut Crust Strawberry Tart 303
Angel Food Trifle 304
Strawberry Punch Bowl Cake. 304
Tropical Punch Bowl Cake 305
Chocolate Dip for Strawberries 311
Strawberry-Almond Bars 319
Stuffed Baked Tomatoes 233
Stuffed Leg of Lamb. 123
Stuffed Mushroom Caps. 21
Stuffed Shells 203
Sugar Cookies 329
Sunday-Best Aspic 67
Sunshine Krisps 320
Swamp Water 36
Swedish Cabbage Dish 220
Sweet and Sour Beans 217
Sweet and Sour Cantaloupe 71
Sweet Potatoes
Sweet Potato Delight 228
Sweet Potato Muffins 256
Sweet Potato Pudding 228
Baked Sweet Potatoes with
Marshmallows. 228
Kahlua Candied Yams 229
Swiss Cinnamon Stars. 329
Swordfish
Swordfish with Tarragon Mustard Sauce. . . . 175
Barbecued Swordfish 105
Marinated Swordfish or Tuna 106
Francie's Marinade 108
Fish Marinade. 108
Tables of Equivalents 345, 346
Tables of Measurements 344
Taco Casserole 119
Taco Pie 163
Taco Salad. 76
Taco Tartlets. 23
Tarragon Chicken and Rice Salad. 78
Teriyaki Pork Chops 102
Thanksgiving Cranberry Salad 72
Thelma Phillips' Crab Spread 18
Theresa's Tennis Bars 320

INDEX

Three Bean Bake 218
Toasted Pecans 29
Toby Treats 332
Tomato
  Tomato Aspic I 67
  Tomato Aspic II 68
  Tomato Dressing 89
  Tomato Marinade I 89
  Tomato Marinade II 89
  Tomato Pie 232
  Tomatoes Stuffed With Spinach
    Soufflé 233
  Marinated Summer Garden 67
  Sunday-Best Aspic 67
  Harvey Gamage Salad 76
  Norwood Dressing 89
  Linguine with Tomatoes and Basil 199
  Pasta with Spicy Ham and Tomato
    Sauce 202
  Pasta with Tomato-Artichoke Sauce 202
  Marinara Sauce 206
  Artichoke Hearts and Scalloped
    Tomatoes 214
  Broccoli and Tomatoes 219
  Okra and Tomatoes 222
  Green Tomato Casserole 232
  Scoffield Tomatoes 232
  Skillet Tomatoes 232
  Stuffed Baked Tomatoes 233
  California Vegetables 234
Tortellini and Spinach Soup 48
Tortellini Salad 85
Tortellini with Grilled Chicken Breast 205
Tortilla Roll-Ups 13
Tostito Olé 15
Tropical Punch Bowl Cake 305
Trout Meunière or Amandine 176
Tuckahoe Vermouth Venison 133
Tuna
  Waterfront Tuna Salad 82
  Mediterranean Pasta Salad 84
  Barbecued Swordfish 105
  Grilled Tuna Mediterranean 105
  Marinated Swordfish or Tuna 106
  Marinated Tuna Steaks 106
  Francie's Marinade 108
Turkey
  Turkey Salad 79
  Turkey Tetrazzini 164
  Tortilla Roll-Ups 13
  Curried Chicken Salad 78
  Taco Casserole 119
  Taco Pie 163
  Microwave Turkey Vegetable Lasagna 163
  Pasta for Your Pace 201
Turnip Greens Casserole 233
Twenty-Minute Lemon Garlic Chicken 151
Twice-Baked Potatoes 226
Upside Down Pizza 119

Veal
  Veal Cutlets with Garlic Mint Sauce 120
  Veal à la Normande 120
  Veal à L'Orange 121
  Zurich Geschnitzelttes 121
VEGETABLES AND SIDE DISHES (See Chapter Index, 213) (See Specific Types by Name)
Vegetable Casserole 236
Vegetable Frittata 235
Vegetable Marinade 68
Vegetable Medley 236
Vegetable Soup 49
Vegetarian Pizza 236
Veggie Pizzas 10
Vegi-Chicken Grill 100
Venison
  Tuckahoe Vermouth Venison 133
  Schnucki's Spiedies 134
Vidalia Onion Casserole 223
Viennese Torte 307
Virgin Mary Mix 34
Walnut
  Walnut Salad 71
  Bleu Cheese Walnut Dressing 86
  Baklava 296
Wassail 38
Waterfront Tuna Salad 82
Welsh Bread 247
Welsh Rarebit 192
White Chili Casserole 52
White Chocolate Chunk Macadamia Nut
  Cookies 322
White French Dressing 87
Whole Wheat
  American Baguettes 256
  Apple Muffins 252
  Applesauce Whole Wheat Bread 256
  Old-Fashioned Pancakes 249
  Processor Wheat Bread 259
  Toby Treats 332
Wild Rice Shrimp Casserole 182
Wine Baked Chicken Breasts 162
Winter Squash and Apple Soup 48
Yams (See Sweet Potatoes)
Yeast Breads 256–260
Yellow Peppers Stuffed with Crab and Dill 80
Yogurt Fruit Pie 292
Yorkshire Pancake 249
Zucchini
  Zucchini Sausage Boats 124
  Zucchini Fish 172
  Broiled Zucchini 231
  California Vegetables 234
  Colorful Vegetables over Rice 234
  Fresh from the Garden Lasagna 198
  Pauline Morris's Chicken 154
  Poached Salmon Steaks with Zucchini
    Noodles 174
  Vegetarian Pizza 236
Zurich Geschnitzelttes 121

RE-ORDER INFORMATION

We hope you have enjoyed our cookbook.

You may reorder <u>The Stuffed Cougar</u> or
<u>The Stuffed Cougar, Too</u>
by calling The Collegiate School at
(804) 741-7077 or **(800) 522-1915**
or by visiting our website at
http://www.collegiate.ind.k12.va.us